'This is the long-awaited story of one of the most remarkable and most modest of the heroes of the South African resistance. Ahmed Kathrada has been a key figure for over fifty years in both bringing down apartheid, and achieving reconciliation between old enemies. As one of Mandela's closest friends, he shared his sufferings through a quarter-century in prison, and his ordeals afterwards. With typical honesty, humour and insights he tells an intensely human story behind the great events he witnessed at first hand. It is both a moving personal record, and a document of crucial historical importance.'

– **Anthony Sampson, author and historian**

'Delightful and often amusing anecdotes of the life of a very self-effacing and yet deeply committed freedom fighter.'   – **Archbishop Desmond Tutu**

'The great significance of these memoirs lies in the window they open onto the personal experiences of those who fought so steadfastly for the freedom we now enjoy. Memoirs such as these enrich our understanding of the events that have shaped our present by offering us insight into the intimate dimensions of lives that have been lived on the public stage of political struggle.'

– **Njabulo Ndebele, vice-chancellor of the University of Cape Town**

'Great people, like great music, have the ability to inspire and uplift us. The life of Ahmed Kathrada is such a catalyst, drawing forth the compassion, humanism, tolerance and love in each of us. His experiences and South Africa's history symbolise the high and low notes of humanity's common struggle for a better world, proving what is possible if we have the ability to forgive.'

– **Quincy Jones, musician and producer**

'Kathy's power lies in his humility, intelligence and love for his fellow human beings. I have been deeply moved by the bonds and common experiences that define the relationship between the democratic people of South Africa and those of India. Kathy's story speaks of a fundamental aspect of our shared history, playing out, as it does, across epic events and key moments in the forging of our shared vision.'   – **Amitabh Bachchand, film actor**

'A book of questions and answers … When humanity leaves the room, what do you do if you're left inside it? The extraordinary strength and almost inconceivable grace in these pages are as mind-blowing as the justice and peace Ahmed Kathrada helped bring about.'

– Bono, musician and human rights activist

'Early one morning Ahmed Kathrada took my wife and me to Robben Island to see the cells in which he and his comrades lost years of their lives. I was struck then, and again in reading his letters from prison, at what a great spirit he is, so able to move on from those dark years into a future of hope for South Africa. His life is a lesson for his nation and the world, and I rejoice that he has given us his memoirs.'

– Roger Ebert, film critic

'What has Kathrada shown? Don't confuse being good with being naive, being brave with drama, being wise with a whole lot of high-sounding words. And – above all – don't dig the past for the leaden weight of its hated memories. Do so for the gold of a new awakening.'

– Gopal Gandhi, Indian leader

Ahmed Kathrada

MEMOIRS

ZEBRA

Published by Zebra Press
an imprint of Struik Publishers
(a division of New Holland Publishing (South Africa) (Pty) Ltd)
PO Box 1144, Cape Town, 8000
New Holland Publishing is a member of Johnnic Communications Ltd

First published 2004

3 5 7 9 10 8 6 4 2

Publication © Zebra Press 2004
Text © Ahmed Kathrada 2004
Cover photograph courtesy of Hillary Clinton

PUBLISHING MANAGER: Marlene Fryer
MANAGING EDITOR: Robert Plummer
RESEARCHER: Kimberley Worthington
EDITOR: Marléne Burger
PROOFREADER: Ronel Richter-Herbert
COVER AND TEXT DESIGNER: Natascha Adendorff
TYPESETTER: Monique van den Berg
INDEXER: Robert Plummer
PRODUCTION CONTROLLER: Valerie Kommer

Set in 11 pt on 13.4 pt Bembo

Reproduction by Hirt & Carter (Cape) (Pty) Ltd
Printed and bound by Paarl Print, Oosterland Street, Paarl, South Africa

ISBN 1 86872 918 4

www.zebrapress.co.za

This book is dedicated to the countless unsung heroes whose identities remain unknown. They were the tens of thousands of women, men and children in their workplaces, in their homes and in schools and universities whose contribution and sacrifices on the road to freedom were of immense significance. They will forever be remembered with gratitude and pride.

Contents

List of Illustrations

Additional photographs between pages 136 and 137 and pages 264 and 265

≈ (≈

Foreword
by Nelson Mandela

Ahmed Kathrada has been so much part of my life over such a long period that it is inconceivable that I could allow him to write his memoirs without me contributing something, even if only through a brief foreword. Our stories have become so interwoven that the telling of one without the voice of the other being heard somewhere would have led to an incomplete narrative.

Kathy's contribution to our liberation struggle and to our movement is well known and well documented. His courage and his commitment to his comrades are legendary. His mature wisdom was an important ingredient of our deliberations and discussions.

What further distinguished him was that he, together with a few other comrades, was an important depository of organisational memory. It is important that the history of our struggle and of our movement be recorded as fully and with all the different perspectives and nuances. Kathy was always analysing and trying to understand, even while he was an active participant.

After our release from prison he, characteristically, became involved in archival, historical and legacy projects about the liberation movement. Few others have spent as much time and energy on tracing and finding the masses of files and other material from the police and prison authorities, providing a rich base for future research and writing. He was instrumental in establishing and driving the Robben Island Museum project.

It is fitting that he now writes his own memoirs, giving us all the benefit of his remarkable memory about events and periods in which he was actively and centrally involved.

I, for one, look forward to reading his memoirs. He had been of so much assistance to me in the writing of my own. I am eager to read his independent version of the events and times that we shared.

Mandela

Foreword
by Arthur Chaskalson
Chief Justice of the Constitutional Court

At the Rivonia Trial, Ahmed Kathrada was being cross-examined about an entry in Nelson Mandela's diary, which referred to an occasion during the period when Mr Mandela was operating underground. The entry noted that he had enjoyed a delicious curry prepared for him by K. It was put to Kathrada that this had to be a reference to him. He denied it. The cross-examiner, raising his voice to a high pitch, declared: who else K could be? Overwhelmed by the possibilities, Kathrada paused for a moment, and then responded: Khrushchev. The matter ended there. In memory of that incident, I will refer to Kathy in this brief foreword as K.

These memoirs are both the story of a life and a chronicle of the struggle against apartheid. At one level, it is the story of K's life, told by himself, in which he describes incidents in his life as a child and as a young man that had led to his becoming deeply involved in the struggle against apartheid, and of his experiences in the course of that struggle. At another level, it is an account of the reality of living under apartheid, of the day-to-day humiliations suffered by black South Africans, and of the manner in which apartheid was enforced and resisted. It is a history of the times as witnessed and experienced by a participant in the struggle.

The first part of the book tells of K's early life and his participation in action from the mid-1940s until 1963, organising and mobilising resistance against apartheid, of the state's reaction to this activism, of the attempts to silence him, and of his trials, including the Rivonia Trial, at which he was ultimately convicted and sentenced to life imprisonment.

We met as a result of the Rivonia Trial, where I was a junior member of the defence team. As I got to know K during the period of almost a year that the trial lasted, my respect and admiration for him grew. He is a person of great courage and integrity, and although he makes no claims for these qualities himself, they shine through in his memoirs.

The second part of the book is the story of his life as a political prisoner for more than twenty-five years; of how, despite attempts by the authorities to crush it, the spirit of resistance was kept alive by political prisoners until they eventually emerged victorious to participate in the process of establishing and implementing democracy in South Africa. It is also the story of his relationship with some of the men and women who were his comrades in the struggle, of their experiences before and during their imprisonment, of what they endured at the hands of the security police and prison officers, and of what happened to them after their release from prison.

In the detail of what he recounts, we learn more about other legendary figures such as Nelson Mandela, Walter Sisulu, Govan Mbeki, Bram Fischer and other leaders of the struggle against apartheid. In a moving evocation of the Rivonia Trial and its aftermath, he describes the way in which the trialists required their trial to be conducted; the resolution, foresight and courage with which they faced the trial and the ever-real possibility of the death penalty; and the courage and dignity with which they subsequently confronted a quarter of a century in prison.

The second half of the twentieth century is the time of the rise and fall of apartheid. It is a crucial period in the history of our country, and it is important that the facts be captured accurately, for they raise profound questions concerning the use and abuse of political power, the adoption and use of draconian security measures to achieve political ends, the resistance to oppression and injustice, and the means by which such resistance is pursued. These are questions that recur again and again in our imperfect world.

Apartheid is a particularly egregious illustration of the abuse of power. Today there are few who seek to justify it or the methods by which it was implemented and enforced. Yet at the time apartheid was enforced, the functionaries charged with that task carried out their duties rigorously with the support of parliament and the great majority of white voters in whom political power was vested. Why were so many willing to do this? And why were they willing to accept the means by which apartheid was kept in place? Why did some white, as well as black people, resist oppression and injustice, whilst others colluded with or passively accepted it? We need to record our history, to ask these questions, and to answer them, lest in failing to heed the lessons of the past, we slip back into practices that contradict the ideals that underpinned the struggle for freedom and justice in our country. History is replete with examples of where this has happened at other times in other countries.

K's book is not only the story of his life. It is a history of events that shaped the struggle against apartheid and the form that it took. Although Kathy's account of the struggle is personalised, it is much wider than the personal. What he gives us in relating his memories and knowledge is a portrait of our land in the long turmoil of its rebirth. In so doing, he makes a valuable contribution to the history of South Africa in the second half of the last century. In this lies the double strength of his book, which adds to the important and growing body of literature that links our past to the present and to the aspirations we have for our future.

Preface

One scarcely ever repents of having waited.
  – **Alexander I of Russia, conqueror of Napoleon,
  renowned for his procrastination**[1]

These memoirs serve to fulfil a promise I made to myself while I was in prison. It was prompted by the dearth of information on important events in liberation history, and the realisation that much, if not most, of what had been published in books, newspapers and magazines was incomplete or riddled with error and distortion.

These inadequacies were brought home to me with renewed force when I wrote my honours dissertation, while at Pollsmoor Prison, on *The Radicalisation of Black Politics in South Africa*. Circumstances placed me in the unique position of having uninterrupted access to the memory of my comrade and mentor, Walter Sisulu, who was acknowledged as the living authority on the subject.

This book is by no means an effort to fill the void. Far from it. It would be presumptuous of me to even think so. My memoirs make no claim to being a documented history, nor is this my autobiography, both of which would demand serious research and qualified writers.

This volume is no more than what I remember, from my childhood, through the years of the struggle in which I was one of thousands of participants, my prison years, and the ushering in of democracy. Naturally, there has been some reference to books and libraries, largely in attempts to confirm some of my hazier recollections, but this is not an academic book, nor was it intended to be.

At the very most, I view it as a modest addition to the growing and most welcome body of work that is emerging about a particularly significant period in South Africa's recent history. My fervent hope is that it will influence historians and writers to embark on some serious research about the events and experiences that I have recounted, with a view to producing authoritative accounts of the struggle era and preserving it for posterity. In fact, I consider this a debt that they owe to present-day South Africa, and to the generations to come.

I came out of prison at the age of sixty, having spent almost half of my adult life behind bars. In compiling my memoirs, I tried to resist the (understandable) temptation to overplay my prison experience by placing it in context between my rural childhood and political events that preceded the Rivonia Trial, and those that happened twenty-six years later.

I felt uncomfortable about the liberal use of the pronoun 'my' for fear of sounding egoistic or conceited, but allowed myself to be guided by a couple of my writer friends who reminded me that, after all, this is *my* book, about *my* experiences. It therefore follows that I take full responsibility for the contents. In retracing my steps I have tried to be objective and dispassionate, relying chiefly on my personal recollections of events. Where information, documentation or verification was needed, my colleague and researcher, Kim Worthington, succeeded in jogging my memory by consulting libraries, archives, books, newspaper files, research papers, transcribed interviews, my prison documents and the Internet.

I'm very conscious of the fact that memories tend to differ, especially when they relate to events several decades old, but I have been as accurate as I could possibly be. Furthest from my mind has been any desire to rake up old grievances and disagreements. Some unfounded and even mischievous stories about dissent, internal debate and tensions have found their way into the public arena.

I will not deny that we had differences of opinion, or that some of these gave rise to heat and tension. It would be most surprising if an organisation as large as the ANC did not encompass a diversity of views, but some of the stories and anecdotes that have found their way into the public domain are simply not true.

I sincerely hope that by setting out my memories, I cause no embarrassment and give no offence to any of my comrades. If I do, the transgression is inadvertent and I apologise.

I fully expect, and welcome, corrections based on memories less fallible than my own, along with criticism, but the one incontrovertible fact on which I will not be challenged is that after twenty-six years of incarceration, the ANC's leaders and members were as united and committed to the cause as they had been at the beginning.

Any account of life behind bars must needs include stereotypical images of forbidding grey walls and barred windows, austere, cold cells, inedible food and inhumane punishment, manifold deprivation and man-made efforts to strip one of all dignity and self-respect.

My experience was no different, but the picture of political prisoners was one of 'great warmth, fellowship and friendship, humour and laughter; of strong convictions and a generosity of spirit and compassion, solidarity and care. It is a picture of continuous learning, of getting to know and live with your fellow beings, their strengths as well as their idiosyncrasies; but more important, where one comes to know one's self, one's weaknesses, inadequacies and potential. Unbelievably, it is a very positive, confident, determined – yes, even a happy community.'[2]

In 1993, I was invited to open the Robben Island Exhibition organised by the Mayibuye Centre. My concluding remarks were: 'While we will not forget the brutalities of apartheid, we will not want Robben Island to be a monument of our hardship and suffering. We would want it to be a triumph of the human spirit against the forces of evil; a triumph of the wisdom and largeness of spirit against small minds and pettiness; a triumph of courage and determination over human frailty and weakness; a triumph of the new South Africa over the old.'

This remains the message that the Robben Island Museum Council and its staff try to convey through all our activities, publications and personal interaction with the public.

In its short life as a Museum and World Heritage Site, Robben Island's story has been one of success. Of course some patches were rougher than others, and we are aware of the shortcomings and the work that still needs to be done. But thanks to the hard work and dedication of the management and staff, the facility has shown continuous growth, and we look forward to the future with confidence. Finally, I extend my appreciation, pride and congratulations to everyone connected with the island – the members of the council, the directorate, managers and staff.

AHMED KATHRADA
CAPE TOWN, 2004

~ 〔 ~

Acknowledgements

Getting a manuscript ready for publication may be the easy part. Far more challenging is remembering who to thank, not only for bringing the book to this point, but for featuring in my life and thus providing the material for the book.

At the top of the list are my parents, my brothers and sister, all my nephews and nieces, their spouses and children, and every member of our extended family. They have stood by me, unfailingly, at every stage of my life, through good times and bad.

The same must be said of my friends and comrades, all over South Africa and abroad. Their courage, loyalty and support proved indispensable during the dark apartheid years and, thankfully, continue to sustain and encourage me.

For their professional interest, guidance and support, I thank especially Nadine Gordimer, Verna Hunt and Anthony Sampson. More recently, Mark Gevisser perused the manuscript and made some valuable comments, as did my friends and comrades Haji Ismail Vadi, Laloo Chiba and Yunus Chamda.

My friend Anant Singh and Sudhir Pragjee of Video Vision, Durban, were most helpful. They took a personal interest in every stage of the book and were willing to render any assistance that I required.

Special mention must be made of Jose Colon, a visiting information technology executive from America, whom I met only twice. Over dinner in Cape Town, the question of my memoirs cropped up, and he spontaneously offered to help. A few months later, he sent me a state-of-the-art computer system and printer as a gift. It made preparation of the manuscript a pleasure.

On the subject of information technology, I owe special thanks to Afzal Moolla, who not only placed his expertise in this field at our disposal, but gave generously of his time to set up additional resources in Johannesburg.

I must also express my gratitude to Madiba and Chief Justice Arthur Chaskalson for writing the Foreword. My initial fears that they would think me presumptuous for requesting their contributions were totally dispelled by the warmth and willingness of their responses.

I have been privileged to know and work with Madiba for more than fifty years, and Arthur's contribution to our defence during the Rivonia Trial cannot be underestimated. After all, if not for him, Bram Fischer, Vernon Berrangé, George Bizos and Joel Joffe, my life story could have ended on the gallows.

Last, but definitely not least, I must single out certain individuals without whom this book would almost certainly never have been written. Chief among them is my partner, Barbara Hogan, who has been a source of constant encouragement, and whose interest in the project has been as consistent as that of two American friends: Sharon Gelman, chief executive officer of Artists for a New South Africa, and Hari Dillon of San Francisco.

And my boundless appreciation to my friend and colleague, Kimberley Worthington. Soon after we combined forces, she made the project her own, and put her everything into it. While I did much of the writing, it was Kim who spent endless hours scouring libraries, archives, old newspapers, books and my prison files for pertinent material. She also interviewed several individuals.

It was Kim who suggested the structure and framework of the book and pored over my secret prison notebooks to cull appropriate quotations from the hundreds I had collected over the years.

And, on those occasions when I lagged behind in the writing, or was a little slow in responding to her requests, she chastised me in no uncertain terms! In the end, it was Kim who produced coherent chapters out of my writing, speeches and interviews, and if not for her extremely hard work, understanding, intellect, commitment and enthusiasm, this book might not have got off the ground.

Abbreviations

ANC	African National Congress
ANCYL	African National Congress Youth League
AWB	Afrikaner Weerstandsbeweging
BBC	British Broadcasting Corporation
BOSS	Bureau of State Security
CIA	Central Intelligence Agency
CNN	Cable News Network
CODESA	Convention for a Democratic South Africa
COP	Congress of the People
COSATU	Congress of South African Trade Unions
FEDSAW	Federation of South African Women
FIFA	Fédération Internationale de Football Association
Frelimo	Liberation Front for Mozambique
IFP	Inkatha Freedom Party
MK	Umkhonto we Sizwe
MPLA	Popular Movement for the Liberation of Angola
NEUF	Non-European United Front
NP	National Party
NRC	Native Representative Council
NUSAS	National Union of South African Students
PAC	Pan Africanist Congress
PWV	Pretoria–Witwatersrand–Vereeniging
RC	Revolutionary Council
RITA	Robben Island Teachers' Association
SABC	South African Broadcasting Corporation
SACP	South African Communist Party
SACPO	South African Coloured People's Organisation
SACTU	South African Congress of Trade Unions
SAIC	South African Indian Congress
SAIO	South African Indian Organisation
SASO	South African Students' Organisation
SWAPO	South West African People's Organisation
TIC	Transvaal Indian Congress
TIYC	Transvaal Indian Youth Congress

TRC	Truth and Reconciliation Commission
UDF	United Democratic Front
UN	United Nations
Unisa	University of South Africa
UP	United Party
WFDY	World Federation of Democratic Youth
WFTU	World Federation of Trade Unions
Wits	University of the Witwatersrand
YCL	Young Communist League
ZAPU	Zimbabwe African People's Union

THE MAN WHO DECLINES THE PROFFERED HANDCUFFS IS MR. AHMED ('KATHY') KATHRADA.

Prologue

At the bottom of the heart of every human being, from earliest infancy until the tomb, there is something that goes on indomitably expecting – in the teeth of all the crimes committed, suffered and witnessed – that good and not evil will be done to him. It is that above all that is sacred in every human being.
— **Simone Weil**[1]

BACK TO RIVONIA

Johannesburg, 11 July 1963. We have moved from Rivonia. Walter Sisulu, Govan Mbeki, Raymond Mhlaba and Wilton Mkwayi are staying at Travallyn, the newly rented MK farm near Krugersdorp. Denis Goldberg is with them, posing as Charles Barnard. He has taken a lease on the farm and bought a couple of vehicles for MK. Denis has been asked by the High Command to perform these tasks before going into exile and continuing to work from outside the country.

I have moved to a garden cottage in Mountain View that the Communist Party is renting as a base. My relocation was not without complications, but we have satisfied the politically sympathetic owners of the property that I can pass for a Portuguese. This is to protect them in the event of possible problems from the police. They need to be able to convince the security forces that they have rented the cottage to a bona fide 'white tenant', so Arthur Goldreich has disguised me as one 'Pedro Perreira'.

We are applying the basic rules of the underground, namely not to stay in one place for long periods, to keep moving and remain anonymous, and have quit Rivonia on the understanding that we will not return for some time. This decision was reaffirmed at a meeting on Saturday, 6 July.

But life is unpredictable and we need to continue with our work. A far-fetched strategy for guerrilla warfare, Operation Mayibuye, has been drawn up, and is causing much debate and consternation among some of us. We do not know it yet, but we will argue this issue robustly for decades to come.

A suitable venue has to be found to discuss a critique of Operation Mayibuye by Rusty Bernstein, so we decide to meet at Rivonia one last time.

Alternatives have been considered, but there are various obstacles. Travallyn has been ruled out, and an unexpected development, in the form of Comrade Reggie September, has excluded my cottage in Mountain View.

The underground is in its infancy, with safe houses, trusted messengers, anonymous vehicles and secure communications all extremely scarce. The Johannesburg network is already stretched to the limit by having to service the half-dozen or so of us who have already gone underground, and accommodating even a single new arrival is simply beyond our resources.

But an urgent message from Cape Town has advised that Reggie will soon be in Johannesburg, and arrangements have to be made to smuggle him out of the country. We have sent an equally urgent response, telling Cape Town not to send him until the timing is more opportune.

The message has either not reached them or it has simply been ignored, because the next thing we hear is that Reggie is already on a train, travelling in disguise in a 'whites only' compartment.

This places us in a precarious situation. He can't be housed at Rivonia or Travallyn, since our departure from the former is imminent, and the latter is to be used for the accommodation of only the National High Command and those immediately involved in its functioning. There is no time to scout out other venues, so we are left with no choice but to house him in my cottage until he can leave the country. This, of course, puts paid to the idea of meeting in Mountain View to discuss Rusty's analysis.

I was brought to Liliesleaf Farm last night and the meeting is scheduled for this afternoon. It is bitterly cold, and I had an early night, my sleep deep and peaceful, with no sense of foreboding or any inkling that the events to follow will change not only my life, but also the country.

I will return to that night many times in the years to come, every detail of it etched into my mind: the last night of freedom.

The morning has passed peacefully, but just before 2 p.m., I notice a strange car arrive. I quickly run to the bathroom and peep through the window. A well-dressed white man in his early forties steps out of the car and casts a careful look at the buildings and surroundings before heading towards the main house. After a few minutes, he emerges and heads towards the small outbuilding where we will shortly meet.

I can't remain in the bathroom indefinitely, so I go outside and ask the visitor his business. It turns out he is a dentist who has been asked to construct a false plate for Walter's mouth, in order to enhance his disguise. I have no reason to distrust this man, but I am uncomfortable throughout the time we spend together waiting for Walter to arrive. He strikes me as unduly curious, and seems nervous. He keeps looking at his watch, saying he is going to be late for his golf appointment.

Eventually, he seems unable to contain his nervous excitement and, at 2.40 p.m., says he can wait no longer, and is going to leave. Just then, Walter arrives, with Govan and Raymond, in a minibus driven by Denis, and the dentist has no option but to do the job he came to do. It takes him about ten minutes, and as he works, he can't stop himself from asking me: 'Will there be much bloodshed in South Africa?'[2] I express my views at length.

Soon after this, Rusty arrives, then Bob Hepple. By 3 p.m., our meeting has just started. Denis is in the main house.

Although we notice a closed delivery vehicle bearing the name of a dry-cleaning firm drive up to the main house, we ignore it. It's not unusual for merchants to deliver meat, groceries and other items to the Goldreichs, who are living on the farm as a 'front' for the underground Communist Party, and our attention is focused on the merits and demerits of the grand plans we are contemplating.

Suddenly, the rear doors of the vehicle open, disgorging armed security police and trained attack dogs. We are electrified with shock.

One group of intruders races towards the main house, while another heads for the outbuildings, where we are meeting. Govan quickly stuffs the Operation Mayibuye documents into the unlit stove, hoping they will not be found. Walter and I jump through a window at the back of the room, facing the road, but are stopped in our tracks by police with dogs and guns.

They don't recognise me at first, and it's only when I speak that they realise who I am. Among our captors are Warrant Officer Dirker and Lieutenant van Wyk of the Special Branch, both of whom know me well.

After removing the mass of incriminating articles they find, the police detain everyone on the farm, including labourers, who are wholly ignorant of the clandestine role the property has played. We are taken to the Johannesburg prison, the notorious Old Fort, where we are locked up individually in the single cells reserved for prisoners who have been sentenced to death and are awaiting transfer to Pretoria, and the gallows.

The strategy is deliberate. From the word go, the police, prison officials and prosecutors have made up their minds that we are going – that we deserve – to hang.

In the morning, we are taken to be photographed. I think our removal from the cells before we have a chance to wash or get properly dressed is deliberate; they want to capitalise on our dishevelled and unkempt appearance, which will reinforce the stereotype that we are dangerous 'terrorists'.

I believe this is the first step of a campaign to mobilise public support for the death sentence. The police and prison authorities are confident, even at this early stage, that this will be the outcome of our detention, and make a point of reminding us of their expectations at every opportunity.

After spending two chilly nights at the Fort, we are transferred to the Pretoria Local Prison, under unusually heavy escort, on the morning of Saturday 13 July.

It is mid-winter, but at Pretoria Local, the routine procedure, no matter the season, is for incoming prisoners to shower before being formally registered. The shower is in an open courtyard, and the security police and prison warders line up to witness and enjoy our baptism of ice.

There are no towels, and one by one my colleagues step under the shower, then try to dry themselves as best they can with their handkerchiefs.

When my turn comes, I jump quickly in and out and start drying myself, but a security policeman immediately tells Colonel Aucamp, head of prison security, 'Kolonel, hy het nie gestort nie' ['Colonel, he hasn't showered'].

It is as if he knows that I am not used to taking cold showers – certainly not icy ones, outdoors in the middle of a Highveld winter. Much to the delight of the onlookers, Aucamp orders me back under the water.

My relationship with the police is one of mutual antagonism, and I have had constant quarrels with the Special Branch. Now my worst enemies are watching, along with the warders, waiting gleefully to witness my humiliation.

In that instant, I grasp a fundamental lesson on how to survive the personal privations and indignities of incarceration with my integrity, honour and self-respect unscathed. I will afford no one the pleasure of my discomfort.

I walk slowly back under that stream of icy water and stand, gazing up at the cold, clear, indifferent blue sky, determined to stay there as long as it takes to deprive them of their victory. It is my first triumph – but I know we will have to steel ourselves, every moment of every day, for the harsh and bumpy road ahead, when the spectre of the gallows will never be far from our thoughts.

It is probably on that Saturday morning that I resolve to become accustomed to the coldest showers on earth. This decision will stand me in good stead throughout the years of our imprisonment and become a habit that persists even after my release. The only difference is that when I resume my normal life, I will start and soap myself with warm water, but even in an American autumn or a Scandinavian December, from this day forward, every shower I take will end under a cascade of cold water.

NINETY DAYS

What is hell? Hell begins when the simple and necessary acts of life become monstrous, and this knowledge has been shared through all the ages by those who taste the hell men make on earth. Now it is frightful to walk, to breathe, to see, to think. — **Howard Fast, Spartacus**[3]

The formalities of admission over, we are taken to our individual cells on the second floor. Our ninety-day detention has begun.

The security police have initiated an amendment to the Sabotage Act that allows them to hold those suspected of involvement in political 'crimes' for three months at a stretch, in solitary confinement and without being charged. The ninety-day clause gives the Special Branch sweeping powers and unfettered access, since the detention period can be renewed indefinitely. For at least a quarter of a year, we will be held without access to lawyers, the press, priests, members of our family, friends or acquaintances.

The passage leading to the single cells where the four of us are detained is blocked off, and only certain warders are allowed entry or contact with us. We are not allowed to talk to one another, and warders patrol the area outside our cells day and night to ensure that there is no communication between us. No books, magazines or newspapers are permitted, and I will not even be given an English edition of the Holy Koran that my family bring to the prison. In fact, the authorities will never even tell me it is there. Mercifully, I will receive a Bible.

We are housed on the second floor, separated from one another by several empty cells in between. We are neither allowed to write nor receive letters, and our only human contact will be with our custodians and our interrogators, the security police. In addition to a sadistic desire to harass and torment us, the purpose of ninety-day detention in strict solitary confinement is to break down the morale of the individual, in order to extract information.

After the first weeks of being completely alone, one starts longing to speak to someone ... anyone, even the police. I am probably in that state of mind when

I have my first visit from Sergeant van Zyl. Not only does he know my family in Schweizer-Reneke, but he and I once dined together.

Before being transferred to the Special Branch, Van Zyl was an inspector under the Group Areas Act, and in the course of his work he visited various country towns that had established Indian communities. Though it was clearly not in the line of duty for him to accept invitations of hospitality from Indian families, or 'gifts' from their stores, the Indians clutched at any straw in the hope of gaining some relief, big or small, in the face of the hugely destructive onslaught of the Group Areas Act. Being in Inspector van Zyl's 'good books' was thus an expediency to be endured.

I had long since been banned and confined to the magisterial district of Johannesburg, but on one of many occasions when I broke my ban to go home to Schweizer-Reneke, I found preparations under way for a special dinner. It was certainly not in my honour, as I could never inform the family in advance of my visits. Our guest turned out to be Inspector van Zyl, and as we shared a meal that evening, he had no idea of my political involvement, let alone that I had contravened two laws to be there – first by leaving Johannesburg, and then by attending a 'gathering'.

The next time we meet, I am in detention. From what I have heard and read, the approach by the security police is standard: first the soft, friendly tack, and when that fails, the brutal one.

Van Zyl is warm and affable; he brings greetings from the family (I never checked whether this was true) and points out that, as decent, law-abiding people, they will be devastated if I am to hang. His purpose is to save me from the gallows. He cannot understand why I should protect 'Jews' and 'kaffirs' and hang for them. He is sure I have been misled by them. If I only knew how much they have been talking about me, I would cooperate with the police. All he needs from me are two bits of information – the location of my hideout, and that of the farm, Travallyn, to which Sisulu, Mbeki, Mhlaba, Mkwayi and Goldberg had moved.

'We would not require you to give evidence. And we will give you a substantial sum of money and take you across the border.'

He gives me coffee and sweets and urges me to think seriously about his offer. Then I am taken back to my cell, alone once more. After a couple of weeks, Van Zyl reappears, with the same friendly demeanour, disappointed that I still refuse to 'cooperate', and again advises me to supply the information that he wants. This time, there is just a hint that if my silence persists, less amiable interrogators will take his place, and things could get really bad.

The ground has been laid for Captain 'Rooi Rus' Swanepoel, a sadistic, racist brute and murderer.

Essentially, he tries to extract the same information as Van Zyl, but the difference is Swanepoel's crudeness, blatant racism and gruff voice, his threats, his impatience and intolerance. Swanepoel has a piggy face, with small, mean eyes. He wears a perpetual look of anger and has an unhealthy, ruddy complexion. He is habitually rude and derogatory, and as he speaks, spittle escapes from his mouth in little darts, lubricating the flow of his ugly words.

He flaunts a few sheets of paper before my eyes, claiming that they contain a wealth of incriminating information about me, provided by my 'Jewish friends'. Why, he demands, should I continue to protect them?

This, of course, is a universal interrogation tactic, and in the hands of a trained expert, armed with just enough information – not necessarily derived from fellow detainees at all – it can be used to great effect to break down an individual's resistance.

Let us consider the detainee's state of mind. He or she has been in solitary confinement for a considerable period, with virtually nothing to do but think. Those thoughts turn overwhelmingly to self, to the fate that awaits one. Even without the worst-case scenario of the gallows, the future is grim and daunting. At the very least, I am facing years of incarceration, and even if no charges are ever brought, due to lack of evidence, my problems will not be over. In some cases, release without indictment may be only the start of one's travails. Swanepoel and other interrogators routinely warn detainees: 'If you don't cooperate, we can use other methods. We will simply release you without charging you; and the word will quickly spread that you have sold out. You will be distrusted by your people and ostracised. You might even be killed.'

No such prospect is held out for me, but Swanepoel becomes increasingly impatient and aggressive. At times, he comes towards me in a threatening manner, but stops short of physical assault.

ISOLATION

The real struggle begins when you have to contend against a part of your own self. Up to that point, it's all plain sailing. Yet it's only from such inner conflicts that a real man emerges. Yes, we've always got to fear the world within ourselves, there's no escaping it. — **André Malraux**[4]

Never before have I been so utterly alone, cut off from my fellow beings, from books and newspapers, radios and films and photographs; from animals and birds and flowers and trees; from the entire world outside prison. I am in my early thirties, with about twenty years of 'political activism' behind me, including arrest and imprisonment, but for the very first time I am face to face with the harsh reality of solitary confinement.

My cell is 2.4 metres square, with a single naked light bulb in the centre of the roof that glares all day and night. The narrow window, covered with steel mesh and divided by thick, metal bars, is too high off the ground to see out of. I have two thin mats, one on top of the other and neither of them too clean, to sleep on, and a bucket in the corner. This is for my ablutions, and I have to empty it every morning. I have a single metal plate and a spoon to eat with, and I am given a jug of water every evening.

If not for the deprivation and threat of an untimely death, some people might welcome an opportunity to spend time alone, away from the hustle and bustle of everyday life, an environment conducive to contemplation. Solitary confinement certainly gives one time to think, and I spend a considerable amount of time in thought. But even reflection has its limits. There are just too many hours and too many minutes in each day, and it is simply not feasible to spend them all in thought. Other ways have to be found to get through each twenty-four-hour period and, more importantly, to remain sane.

With so much time at one's disposal, thoughts inevitably turn to mundane detail. A whole minute can pass while carefully following the movements of an ant, before being suddenly distracted by the sound of an unheeding procession of passing motor vehicles; and wondering for the next hour or more if perhaps this was a military convoy, speeding towards some emergency situation.

Apart from a primary concern about oneself, the greatest anxiety under detention is about the well-being of near and dear ones, comrades, and the movement. One spends hours and hours, every day and every night, thinking about the outside world. Thoughts rush through my mind: Who else has been detained? Have the police broken any detainees? Is Sylvia safe?

The thirst for news is great, and I am becoming increasingly worried and desperate. I am prepared to take any risk to keep myself informed, but what, exactly, can I do? Any attempt to bribe the warders would be futile. Common-law prisoners are not allowed anywhere near us. Our food is left outside our cell doors, or brought to us by warders. To approach the prison doctor or visiting magistrate is unthinkable and, in any event, I will see each of them only once throughout my detention. Neither encounter will bring any relief, but at least the visits break the monotony.

I have only my thoughts and memories to keep me company. Concern for the struggle and the safety of comrades is my sole companion. I also worry a great deal about my girlfriend, Sylvia, a political activist known to the police. Is she being harassed? Has she been detained? I long for just a few words with the comrades who were arrested with me. I dearly wish to know how they are faring. Years later, it will still be impossible for me to put into words the frustration of not being able to communicate with my comrades and fellow detainees, people whose cells are right next to my own. Have they been tortured? Has any one of them broken down? Has he talked? If so, has he talked about me, and how much?

Because, I must confess without shame or apology, uppermost in my mind, always, is *my* life, *my* safety.

I take a long look at my past, at a life that has known little other than politics. I think of the indignities, the humiliation and the insults that have been part and parcel of the lives of all of us who are not white. I examine and re-examine my relatively modest role in the freedom struggle, and the resulting situation in which I have landed. I ask myself, 'Has it been worth it?' And more than once, the thought crosses my mind: Should I grab the lifeline that my interrogators have been dangling before me in exchange for just two bits of information that they regard as vital?

After much agonising and many sleepless nights, I convince myself that I will not talk – I will not betray the struggle, my comrades and my people. In the loneliness of my cell, I manage to build up sufficient courage to say 'No' to my interrogators.

But will determination and noble intent give me enough strength to withstand physical torture? I wonder if Walter, Govan and Raymond are waging similar harrowing debates with themselves.

When the cells are unlocked in the mornings so that we can empty our toilet buckets and shower, and again at exercise time, I glance eagerly at my comrades for the slightest signal or some message of assurance that all is well. I even study their body language in the hope that it might convey something. Although I fervently wish and pray for good news, in my desperation it does not matter whether things are good or bad, just as long as there is some communication.

I begin to notice something, a change that becomes more glaring by the day. The black hair of one of my comrades has started turning white. This is the worst possible sign, I think. But I cannot speak to him, and the warders are diligent in making sure that during the short periods when we are together for exercise or to empty our buckets, we do not communicate with each other. My sleepless nights are filled with concern and frustration. I am deeply worried, having learnt that under conditions of extreme stress and worry, the hair of some people can turn white overnight. My speculation knows no bounds. 'Indeed,' I muse, 'since our youth we have been told that certain traumatic experiences can lead to hair turning white, or even to loss of hair.' The questions come back with renewed force and urgency. Have my comrades been tortured? Have they broken? Have they spoken about me? The spectre of the gallows looms larger in my mind's eye. Little more than a month after being arrested, I had my thirty-fourth birthday. My life will surely be cut short before I see another.

We four are taken out for exercise twice a day for half an hour, just to walk around the hall. Warders regard themselves essentially as members of the working class, although they don't do a great deal of actual work, their tasks consisting chiefly of locking and unlocking doors, and when it gets to 4 p.m. they want to go home, especially over weekends. Our custodians are no different. They are not interested in what the Special Branch has to say, and often, when the shifts change, instructions are not passed on, so it sometimes happens that they take us all from our cells together, either because they don't know that this is contrary to instructions, or because they are simply indifferent to the rules and it suits them better to deal with us as a group rather than singly.

Coupled with inefficiency and laziness is the fact that many warders are just not prepared to carry out all the orders they receive, particularly those issued by anyone outside the prison system, such as the Special Branch. The security police are the most hated of the law enforcers, disliked equally by the uniformed police, detectives and prison warders, mainly because of the way they habitually throw their weight around. Sometimes, this inter-service rivalry works in our favour, with certain warders turning a blind eye to our interaction and permitting us, however briefly, to talk to one another. Throughout our ninety-day detention period, we will be allowed to receive both food and fresh clothing from outside.

After several days of living in fear, my equilibrium is restored on one of the rare occasions when it is possible to exchange a few words with my fellow detainees. I confront my comrade and ask why his hair is turning white. Back comes a pithy answer from Comrade Govan: 'My black hair dye has begun to wear off, and I cannot replenish my supply while I am in detention.' What a relief! I can look forward to a couple of nights of restful sleep again. How I wish and pray that such good news will continue to come. But alas, such luck is not to be.

TRIBULATION

... when our songs we lose,
we have nothing left.
If our song perishes,
Everything we have perishes.
We too shall live no more ...
    – Maurice Hindus, *To Sing with the Angels*[5]

Though I have successfully managed to overcome the psychological torture meted out by Swanepoel – future murderer of a dear comrade and brother, and the sadist who will torture many of my closest friends and colleagues – my tribulations are not over.

To while away the time in solitary confinement, I try to recall and recite every bit of poetry and prose and song that I have learnt since childhood.

I spend hours and hours recalling and giving voice to a repertoire that ranges from 'Humpty Dumpy' to lines from *Macbeth*, *Hamlet* and *The Merchant of Venice*. I croon aloud the lyrics of 'Galway Bay' and 'Ole Man River', even the 'Banana Boat Song'. It is inspiring to recite Lincoln's 'Gettysburg Address' and Rabindranath Tagore's 'Bankruptcy of European Civilisation'. From my trip to Europe in 1951 I remember 'Freundschaft', 'Soviet Land' and 'Red Flag'. And, of course, I relish the singing of struggle songs, still fresh in my mind. What a boon it is to remember so much! 'Whoever would have imagined,' I ask myself, 'that in adult life, "Humpty Dumpty" would make such a positive contribution towards keeping one's mind occupied and sane?'

Some of the best material that comes to me, bubbling up from the deepest layers of my consciousness to help quench my thirst for stimulation, are the Afrikaans songs from my childhood in my mother's home, such as 'Stellenbosch', 'Suikerbossie', 'O Boereplaas', 'Sarie Marais', and this one:

Suid-Afrika o land van my geboorte
Suid-Afrika ek is so lief vir jou
Mees pragtig is jou skone ope velde
Mees dierbaar is jou liewe hemelsblou.
Suid-Afrika
Jy is daarom maar die beste land vir my.[6]

These 'musical interludes' allow me to escape, albeit briefly, from the harsh reality of the present to memories of Schweizer-Reneke – my place of birth, and home. My mind and spirit travel back to my early years there, arguably the most pleasant and carefree days of my life. Memories of my mother and father, my only sister and four brothers, their children and my friends fill me with joy and yearning. I often reminisce about the good folk of Schweizer who, for a variety of reasons, made a lasting impression on me – David Mtshali, Ouma Oosthuizen and others.

Afrikaans poetry, too, comes to mind. Among the numerous works I remember are those of the leading Afrikaans poet, Jan F Cilliers. During one of the interrogation sessions with Swanepoel, I try to shame him and penetrate his intense Afrikaner chauvinism by reciting one of these verses. I pluck up courage and recite:

Ek hou van 'n man wat sy man kan staan,
Ek hou van 'n arm wat 'n slag kan slaan,
'n Oog wat nie wyk, wat 'n bars kan kyk
En 'n wil wat so vas soos 'n klipsteen staan.[7]

'Captain,' I say to Swanepoel, 'a great Afrikaner poet wrote those words. How can you, as an Afrikaner, ask me to turn traitor?' I believe the words are most appropriate for the situation in which I find myself, but I am mistaken in hoping that, hidden somewhere deep in the psyche of the hard-hearted Swanepoel, is a grain of morality and understanding of our struggle.

Later, when Swanepoel is under cross-examination during the Rivonia Trial, Advocate Berrangé will cite the same verse to him, and from his reaction on both occasions, I think it did make some impact on him, however small.

As it turns out, this particular interrogation session will be my penultimate one with this compassionless man.

Prison regulations dictate that detainees have to be taken out of their cells for exercise daily. In our case, this consists of walking around the hall where church services are held in single file and in complete silence. One day, due to a staff shortage, we are taken out to exercise with other detainees, under the supervision of a single warder. In a brief moment, while his attention is distracted, one of the detainees manages to whisper that Comrade Looksmart Ngudle, an ANC activist from Cape Town, has been tortured to death under interrogation.

The news spreads fast. We return to our cells in a state of severe shock, anxiety and fear. Ngudle was the second ninety-day detainee, and the first to be killed by the police. Increased anxiety and sleepless nights plague us, and I need all the courage I can muster to sustain my non-cooperation with the police. The question now is: How long will it last?

I am sure our thoughts all centre on the same questions: What will happen to me at the next interrogation? Will I also be tortured? Will I survive?

The ubiquitous spectre of a death sentence assumes terrifying new proportions. I begin to imagine and picture my life expiring at the end of a rope, and the thought that keeps recurring is: What an undignified manner of death.

'If I have to die an unexpectedly early and unnatural death, please God, let me die with dignity,' I pray. I try to keep up my courage and self-esteem by reciting the words of Irish martyr, Kevin Barry:

Shoot me like an Irish soldier,
Do not hang me like a dog.
For I fought for Ireland's freedom,
On that bright September morn.

Before long, my fears will be greatly aggravated.

We have learnt to look forward to weekends, because the relief warders are invariably ignorant of the special regulations governing our detention. One Friday night, the door that separates our section from the rest of the prison is opened, and a new prisoner brought in.

The quiet of our environment is suddenly broken by the loud and agonising sounds of a man in great distress. For hours on end his voice reverberates far beyond the section in which we are housed. The noise is incoherent and frightening; he makes brief speeches, shouts slogans, sings and bangs on the door, all night long, screaming, crying, kicking the wall.

The man is Zeph Mothopeng, the most senior and highly respected leader of the Pan Africanist Congress after Robert Sobukwe. He has been severely tortured, really brutally tortured, and has suffered a mental breakdown. This is extremely frightening for us, because under ninety-day detention, anything can happen. We have all heard accounts of terrible abuse.

The warders take no notice, but from what we can make out of the man's anguished cries, his main concern, even in his severely traumatised state, is the struggle. He speaks of the devastating effects of police repression on the liberation movement, and on the morale of the oppressed. He says the flicker of hope has been extinguished by the arrest of Sisulu and the Rivonia raid. And our thoughts again turn inwards, to our individual welfare, only now the fear is much compounded.

In the morning, instead of unlocking our cells one by one so that we can go to the bathroom, the warders let us all out together, including Zeph. He is an elderly man, and we are already apprehensive about his welfare after the terrible night, but when we see the burn marks on his fingers from electric shocks, our fear knows no bounds.

Zeph is a lot calmer than he was last night. Most importantly, he is coherent and able to describe his torture. We are absolutely disgusted and horrified at the inhumane treatment that apartheid's police have meted out to him. What makes his ordeal even worse is that, instead of giving him the medical treatment that he needed urgently and so badly, Zeph was put into a straitjacket.

Eventually brought to trial and sentenced to three years' hard labour, Mothopeng would meet us again, on Robben Island. In the interim, he would bring a civil action for damages against the police and the Minister of Justice. His lawyer was a well-known human rights advocate, Dr George Lowen, and when Lowen learnt that I was among those who had spoken to Zeph and seen the torture marks, he would insist that I be called as a witness. This would place the PAC in a quandary. It was 1966, and the PAC was still very anti-Indian, anti-white and anti-communist – and the man Lowen wanted to call as a witness for Zeph was both an Indian *and* a communist! Eventually, after much internal discussion, the PAC group on the island would agree that I should testify, and in the end, three communists, Govan, Raymond and I, would go to Pretoria to give evidence for Zeph.

In solitary confinement, anxiety is greatly increased by an amplified hunger for news. All sorts of ideas pass through my mind about how to get news from outside. I feel certain that my close friend and dear and loyal comrade, Amien Cajee, or Doha, is having similar thoughts. The Cajees took over my flat in Johannesburg when I was arrested.

An unexpected harvest

During this nerve-wracking period, on a very cold day, we are looking forward to the regular supply of food from home. It's a holiday, and we know that a good quantity of victuals will be sent by concerned family and friends. Amien is already a banned person, so his wife, Ayesha, and Sylvia, who has not yet been banned and who has a car, drive to Pretoria to deliver food and clothing for us. Sylvia cannot come in, so she waits in the car while Ayesha delivers the items.

On this particular day, my cell is unlocked and I am told to go and collect my food. But instead of the usual generous parcel, I am given a small paper bag containing an apple, a banana and one orange. My immediate suspicion is that the warders have stolen the food, as they do from time to time, and I am both annoyed and disappointed. 'Is this all they brought?' I ask. 'Who were they? Were they the people who normally come from Johannesburg?' The warder assures me that the same people who usually bring food, left the packet.

I am furious, but some sixth sense stops me from throwing the fruit away in a fit of pique. Knowing the workings of Amien's mind as I do, I somehow realise that by sending this modest packet of fruit in place of the customary substantial parcels, he is trying to convey some message. Back in my cell, I carefully examine the fruit. The apple and orange look normal, but concealed in the ripe banana, I find a sewing needle, thread and a piece of pencil lead. The sign is clear and urgent: Let's start communicating. I don't have to think twice; my mind is already focused on the method.

Amien and Sylvia have sent 'messages' twice before. Knowing that I am especially anxious about her safety, they want me to know that she is safe. On one of her weekly trips to the prison, Ayesha includes a red jersey in my clean laundry. It is newly knitted and beautiful, but it is not a garment that I have ever owned. I examine it closely, and want to jump with relief and joy when I notice that the pattern on the front forms the letter 'Y' – which can only stand for Yasmin, my Indian name for Sylvia!

Sylvia is 'white' and our relationship is prohibited under the Immorality Act. Liaisons between blacks and whites are criminal offences, and a special police unit concentrates on nothing else but trapping and arresting offenders, hence our use of Indian names, like Yasmin. Sylvia knitted the jersey specifically to let me know that she was safe.

Another time, they sent me a jersey with a little 'Yasmin' name tag sewed inside. Both messages brought me huge relief.

And now, thanks to the ingenious camouflage of the banana, I have been given a chance to send a message back. I just have to find the right way to do it.

One advantage, if one can call it that, of solitary confinement is that there is plenty of time to think. Understandably, quite a lot of my time has been devoted to devising a way of reaching Amien and the others, but before I do so, I have to clear a major hurdle. I must consult my colleagues – to do otherwise will be irresponsible. The venture entails risk, and if my subterfuge is discovered, my colleagues will no doubt also be victimised.

With great difficulty I manage to mention my plan to Walter, Govan and Ray. One of them points out the danger and the likely consequences. My response is simple and straightforward. We are facing the death sentence. What difference will a few more months in prison make? They give me their consent.

I conclude that the only method of establishing a two-way communication channel is through my laundry. Using the pencil lead, I write a brief message on a few sheets of soft toilet paper. I say we are well, that I am being interrogated but not assaulted. 'We are in good spirits; you folks outside should not worry.'

I roll up the message and sew it into the girdle of my pyjama pants. Now, how to let Amien know where to look? Under the collar of my pyjama jacket, I pencil the word NARU. It looks like nothing more than an identifying name tag, but in Gujerati, *naru* means girdle.

It will not take any great detective work for Amien to find the message. Every time they collect my laundry, they scrutinise each item for a sign, and it is Sylvia who will find the word. 'Look,' she will say, 'there's something written here!' Amien immediately understands the code, and after that we are able to communicate regularly. Once a week, a message goes out with my dirty laundry, and another comes in with the clean clothes. Those on the outside have the advantage of being able to type notes and conserve space, but they still use soft paper. To my great relief, our system is not discovered, and we use it right up to the end of the ninety-day period.

Every snippet of news, good or bad, is welcome. We learn with joy of the unprecedented escape of Arthur Goldreich, Mosey Moola, Abdulhay Jassat and Harold Wolpe from Marshall Square police station, and receive with sorrow the confirmation of Looksmart Ngudle's death in detention.

I doubt that Sylvia was able to keep those notes I sent. Tensions were running high, and she and Amien probably destroyed them. Decades later, when I met her in Berlin where she had gone to live, she referred to my prison letters and I had the impression that she might have destroyed these early missives. However, she did keep the letters that I wrote her later, while we were on trial.

One week, Amien sends me a jacket that he has found in my flat. What he does not know is that this is an item of clothing we had been preparing for Nelson Mandela, who was arrested last year, as part of our plan to spring him from prison. Concealed in its expertly tailored, bulky shoulders are a false beard and other items that would have served the purpose of disguising his appearance. When I get the jacket, fleeting thoughts of making a daring escape rush through my mind, but I know the odds are stacked against us and that any attempt to flee will simply provide our captors with a good excuse to shoot us.

So I send the jacket back to Amien with the next load of dirty laundry and, though the authorities never detected any of our messages, Swanepoel finds the beard. He is livid and threatens to detain Amien. Eventually, they did arrest him, but by then we would be on Robben Island.

It is more difficult, in some ways, to communicate with those inside the prison than with those outside. Mandela is being held on the first floor, just a few metres below our cells, and there is one warder who occasionally comes to us and says: 'Nelson stuur groete' ['Nelson sends greetings']. We are delighted, and enthusiastically send our salutations back.

So effective was the isolation that we would only discover many months later, when we eventually got together, that Mandela never even knew we were in the same prison until shortly before the end of the ninety-day period. Quite by chance, he recognised some of the farm labourers from Rivonia, who had also been detained. He saw them exercising in a hall, and began to suspect that we might be in the very same building.

The last time I see Swanepoel during my detention is in October. He has me taken to him so that he can inform me that the police have found both my Mountain View cottage and Travallyn Farm.

He is sitting at a desk, his hands clasped behind his head, leaning back in the chair. His ruddy face bears an expression of smug self-satisfaction that is not without a suggestion of malice, of some senseless, primal cruelty. His legs stretched out, feet resting on his desk, he leans back slightly, then spits at me.

'Kathrada,' he says, 'we found the houses without your help. I wanted to save you, but now you can go and hang.'

Part I

Early Life
of a
'Saboteur'

∾ I ∾

A Boy from Schweizer

About 240 kilometres south-west of Johannesburg, in what is now North West Province, lies Schweizer-Reneke, a relatively unknown, dry and dusty little farming town established in 1885 on the site of Mamusa's village. It was named for two soldiers who fell during a raid against the local African tribe.

On 21 August 1929 – the year of the greatest depression in South African history – I was born there, the fourth of six children. Occasionally, the town would rate a mention in the media when rainfall broke its semi-permanent drought, and during the 1990s it was included in maps drawn up by right-wingers as part of their exclusive proposed 'Volkstaat', where white Afrikaners would rule in perpetuity.

But twice in the second half of the last century, Schweizer-Reneke was in the news for other reasons. The first time was when a boycott of Indian traders by whites was raised at the United Nations in New York in 1947. The second was much later, when the all-white town council, in its wisdom, decided to confer the freedom of the town on Eugene Terre'Blanche, leader of the extreme right-wing and fascist Afrikaner Weerstandsbeweging (AWB). Not long afterwards, Terre'Blanche would serve a six-year prison sentence for a racially motivated assault on an unarmed black man, which left the victim mentally and physically maimed for life.

It was not as though the Afrikaners of Schweizer-Reneke were inherently more racist than similar communities elsewhere in the country, but for some inexplicable reason, the town became synonymous with racism.

My father, Mohamed Kathrada, arrived in Schweizer-Reneke in 1919 and opened a small shop. Before that he had worked, among other things, as a hawker in rural Transvaal towns, possibly in Natal as well. Like my mother, Hawa, he was born in a village in Lachpur, India, and they were married before my father came to South Africa to establish himself. He lived in various places, including Nylstroom, before settling in Schweizer-Reneke. We are Gujerati-speaking Muslims, and our family name apparently derives from a special type of rope called *katha*, made along the coast of India for use on ships.

My father was quite a learned man in the field of Islamic religion, and frequently acted as Imam at local prayer services. During his lifetime, and right up to the time when the Indians were moved under the Group Areas Act in the 1970s, prayer services for the local community were held at our house behind the shop. Although not a trained religious teacher, my father conducted the Friday prayers, as well as the nightly prayers during the month of Ramadan, for the small Muslim community on the large verandah of our house. In later years, my brothers had a special prayer hall built in the spacious yard of our second house.

Thus, from early childhood I was exposed to religious influences, aspects of which made a considerable impact on my future line of thought, but although my parents were devout, their children were not forced to practice all the customs and rituals.

We were required to learn Arabic, but only in order to be able to read the Koran aloud, never in the hope of understanding what we read. When I was five years old I started learning the Koran, but we were never taught its meaning, because our teachers themselves did not understand Arabic. We learnt the sounds, the words, without any idea what they were, or what they signified. I am not talking about deeper religious or philosophical significance, but the basic meaning. This lack of understanding was common to my generation and later ones too, I think. There were indeed a few people who went abroad, to universities in India or Cairo and studied Arabic, but by the end of the twentieth century, there was a growing number of well-educated Muslims who spoke fluent Arabic.

At the time of my birth, my father was running a general dealership, selling almost everything: clothing, hardware, blankets, toiletries, over-the-counter medicines, paraffin, cloth by the yard, stationery and groceries. The family was not well off – comfortable, yes, and not struggling, but not rich, and like most Indian retailers in South Africa, living on credit, at the mercy of the wholesalers. In the 1930s, my father acquired another house a couple of hundred metres from the shop. We had white neighbours on three sides – one was the bank manager, and at the back lived the mayor. Relations between the families were always cordial, and other residents and business people set themselves up adjacent to our original premises. One such institution was the exclusively Afrikaner Dutch Reformed Church, and diagonally opposite our house was the agricultural cooperative, whose members consisted entirely of Afrikaner farmers.

Under the land laws of the time, Indians were not entitled to own the premises where they lived. The properties were therefore acquired in the name of a 'Cape Malay' friend, whose 'race group' had not been disqualified from owning residential premises or business sites. Thus, my family occupied the premises as ostensibly rent-paying tenants of our Malay friends.

By 1965, Schweizer-Reneke's population stood at 5 007, of whom 1 661 were white, but in the 1930s, at a guess, the town was home to about 3 000 people, mainly Afrikaner farmers and black labourers. However, we were not the only people of Indian origin in the area. The town had about a dozen shops, most of them run by Indians. The customers were both white and African and, as in the rest of the country, Africans formed by far the majority of the population.

Also in keeping with the rest of South Africa were race relations and attitudes in Schweizer-Reneke. To put it mildly, they were both complex and contradictory, with a discernible distinction between the attitude of a white individual (or family) in personal interactions with 'non-whites', and the attitude of the same individual or family within the broader white community. And, of course, there were always the exceptions.

I never tire of boasting about Schweizer-Reneke's claims to fame. For example, one of mankind's most significant archaeological findings (if not *the* most important) is the Taung skull, found by Professor Raymond Dart in 1924. Before the apartheid government's aberration of creating the 'independent homeland' of Bophuthatswana, Taung fell within the magisterial district of Schweizer. The famous Afrikaans author and poet, Elisabeth Eybers, was not only a 'Schweizer girl', but her family home was next to ours. Sculptor and painter Irma Stern also hailed from 'my' town, where her wealthy family owned a shop.

On a visit to Robben Island, National Party minister of police Louis le Grange, a son of the region, once claimed me as a compatriot, though of course he was stretching the concept somewhat, covering the whole Western Transvaal, and showing a bit of Potchefstroom imperialism!

In 1935, when I was about six years old, one of my father's brothers, who lived in India and had written a number of religious books, came to South Africa on a visit. He was the Maulana Margoub and, at one time, Mufti of Rangoon. I have vague recollections of a man with a reddish beard. By then I could read from the Koran quite fluently, though naturally without any idea of what I was saying. With all the pride and self-confidence of my six years, I proceeded to do just that, in order to impress our distinguished guest. He became animated and excited, urgently addressing my parents in Gujerati, beseeching them to listen to his pleas. He wanted to take me away with him, back to India, to become a Molvi or Imam, but apparently my mother threatened to go on a hunger strike, or some such thing, and I stayed. I have no doubt that my life would have taken a very different path had I gone, but my mother's protests saved me from this fate.

My life as a young South African was smooth, marked by the joy of major celebrations, and the warmth and friendship, the sense of community, of small-town life. To celebrate Eid, we would hold a picnic at the dam, and all the Indian people of Schweizer came, bringing food and soft drinks, sweets for the children, tablecloths and umbrellas and all the other paraphernalia that made picnics colourful and joyous affairs. It was lovely, and I used to race around with the other children, doing the naughty things that children do, getting dirty and thoroughly enjoying myself.

For all our Gujerat origins and the emphasis on Arabic and the Koran, we grew up speaking more Afrikaans than anything else. It was almost my first language. The women in my family still speak Afrikaans, and *boeremusiek,* traditional folk music played on a concertina, still makes me nostalgic.

While I cannot claim that I was politically aware as a child, a number of things made an indelible impression on me. I have a vivid recollection of the 9 p.m. curfew bell being rung, signalling the hour after which Africans required a special pass to be on the streets. I also remember an incident when a white policeman tried to arrest an African on our business premises. My father angrily intervened and ordered the policeman out of the shop.

We had African domestic workers in the house and a Somali cook, Sayed, a tall, taciturn, pitch-black fellow, who used to conjure up the most delicious meals in our steamy kitchen. Because he was a Muslim, he lived in the house with us. My father was very religious, and therefore strict on the question of race. We were never allowed to be rude to any African staff or customers, but because of the religious difference, we did not treat other Africans with the same deference that we showed Sayed.

There was, somehow, a perception that, white or black, a Muslim was superior, different to everyone else, be they Indians, white or African, and though no one would ever say it in so many words, that is simply how it was. My father would never tell me that he, or our cook, was special because he was a Muslim, but we knew that was the case, and it was evident from the behaviour of people within the Muslim community.

Notwithstanding this intangible belief, the first non-family member that I encountered was not a Muslim, but an Afrikaner. The midwife who delivered me was known affectionately to everyone in town as 'Ouma' Oosthuizen, or 'granny'. I do not think she had any formal training, but she was experienced in bringing children into the world, and I was born at home. Ouma Oosthuizen was a daily visitor, a family friend, and she took a keen interest in the welfare of 'her' babies. Naturally, she and her entire family were also customers, and like many of our friends, they came from the poorer group of whites, the very people one would expect to be the most racist.

But Ouma was in and out of our house all the time, and no one ever detected the slightest hint of racism in her attitude and behaviour. She was almost part of the family, but if I were to speculate on her party-political affiliation, I would say without hesitation that, as a matter of course, she and her family would vote for the rabidly racist and oppressive National Party. High among its declared political priorities was making the lives of Indians so intolerable that they would willingly accept repatriation to India.

Ouma Oosthuizen was a sort of godmother to me, and later, when I was away at school and came home for the holidays, I always had to report to her on my progress. I had to show her my school report and answer numerous questions about my health, how I was adjusting to school, my teachers, and city life in general.

I must have been on Robben Island when she died. It is possible that at the time, our letters were so restricted in content and length that I might not have been able to write about her, or I might have deliberately chosen not to do so, because things had become so bad that her family could have been victimised.

The relationship between the Indian trader and the Afrikaner in the rural areas was, and still is, a very special one. Not even the supermarkets that can now be found in small towns have been able to put the Indian traders out of business, because they have always offered a personal touch to their customers.

It still happens that Indian shopkeepers send a truck to outlying areas on pay days, mostly to farms, because the distances are so great, to pick up the workers who want to do their shopping. At the end of the month, when the pensioners get their money, they, too, are provided with transport. Naturally, this is not altruism, it's business, but it is a service, and when the customers arrive at the shop, some are seated and given tea or coffee. When customers are short of cash, credit is extended, another privilege not available from a supermarket.

For more than fifty years, rural whites invariably supported the National Party. In some towns at election time, the party would borrow as many cars as possible from the Indian community, and the campaigners would ask their

Indian friends, '*Vir wie gaan jy stem?*' ['Who are you going to vote for?']. This never changed. Even in the urban areas, the Afrikaners did not seem to know that an Indian could not vote. They could not understand this. They would go to a National Party meeting and applaud the most racist statements, yet be more than willing to act as nominees for Indians trying to get around the Group Areas Act.

When my nephew Enver opened his shop in Carletonville, it was among the first three or four owned by Indians. Today there are about a hundred, and until the Group Areas Act was scrapped, some ninety of them were registered to white nominees. Such arrangements were never formalised by means of written documents, and Enver's nominee, for instance, probably an Afrikaner, but naturally a white person, refused to even accept a Christmas gift, let alone payment for lending his name to the property. In some cases, nominees would accept monthly payments for the privilege, and if they were dishonest, they could claim the whole shop, but I never heard of a single instance where a nominee turned around and did so.

In 1940 or 1941, my father opened another shop on a little farm at Hessie, about twenty-seven kilometres outside Schweizer-Reneke, which was run by my sister's husband-to-be, a cousin and also a Kathrada. Two years later my father died, and my eldest brother Solly became the effective head of the family.

In the early 1950s, my brother Ebrahim also opened a shop, some twenty-two kilometres from Schweizer-Reneke at a place called London Farm. The original family businesses were run by the three other brothers – Solly, until he moved to Johannesburg in the early 1970s, Ismail and Essop, the youngest. Solly, Ebrahim, Ismail, my only sister Amina and her husband are all dead now, but Essop still runs the shop in Schweizer-Reneke.

Shopkeeping never held the slightest attraction for me, and when I was growing up, the family preferred me not to go anywhere near the shops, let alone work in them, as I knew nothing about the business and they thought I might simply give the goods away.

During the depression, there was tremendous hunger and poverty among the poor whites – and others, of course – in South Africa. Since Indians were prohibited from living or even spending the night in the Free State, residents of that province never saw them, unless they travelled to other parts of the country. Many Free Staters had no idea what an Indian even looked like, but this didn't stop them from perpetuating all kinds of myths, not least of which was that an Indian was someone you should run away from.

One such man, named Terblanche, arrived in Schweizer-Reneke after walking all the way from the Free State with his wife and children, seeking work, and food, all along the way. When they got to Schweizer, they went first to the homes of fellow whites, but found no help there. Eventually, hunger and desperation drove them to my father's shop, and he gave them food, not only for that day, but for several weeks, as well as clothes and other items for the whole family. Such action was not uncommon for my father, but Terblanche never forgot his generosity, and he became a lifelong friend of our family.

Among the non-Afrikaner whites in Schweizer-Reneke with whom we had an association was an eccentric old Englishman by the name of Mathias. He was a regular customer at the shop, and lived on his farm with an African woman. He fathered many children, and their relationship outlasted the Immorality Act and all the other discriminatory legislation. His fellow whites had long since given up on him, and so had the police. He was extremely well read and kept up with world events, receiving newspapers from England until he died, but he lived as an African.

There was also a Jewish man, who was a close friend of the family. Mr Slutzkin was a high-class leather worker, and pro-communist, especially after the Soviet Union entered the Second World War. I have no idea how he came by the literature, but throughout the war, he would go out of his way to give me reading matter that I found most interesting. Apart from our family, he had no friends, and I spent time with him whenever I went home, and he often came for a meal with my family.

Khanchacha was a fellow Indian, who lived on a farm outside Schweizer-Reneke. In his early years he had lived in Nylstroom, and was proud of the fact that he had been the barber of staunch National Party member and future prime minister JG Strijdom. When Strijdom died, he sent a letter of condolence to the family and received a very nice reply.

Apart from Irma Stern's family, the only other Jewish family in Schweizer were the Blooms, extremely wealthy and founders of Premier Milling. There must have been commercial competition between the Indian shopkeepers and the rich Jews, but beyond that, there was no relationship at all. I doubt that Slutzkin the shoemaker was any more welcome in the homes of the wealthy Jews than we would have been, so he spent most of his time with the Indians.

For all the racial harmony of my childhood and youth, small-town South Africa could not escape the complexity of the racist politics that characterised the apartheid era. In Carletonville, the mining town where my nephew Enver had opened a shop, a consumer boycott created much tension in the late 1980s. The town lay at the heart of a particularly conservative area, and the town council's decision to declare parks and various other public amenities reserved for whites sparked outrage among the established Indian community. The result was that a certain sector of the white community decided to stop patronising Indian shops. To add insult to injury, the boycott was led by a chap who was Enver's tenant!

On the other hand, during the latter period of my incarceration, the mayor of Schweizer-Reneke was my sister Amina's landlord at their farm shop and house in Hessie, and they had a good and close relationship. In fact, when he had guests, he would often ask my sister to cook a pot of biryani or make samoosas for them. He could have evicted her in terms of the Group Areas Act, but he refused to do so, despite the fact that he later became one of the biggest contributors to the right-wing Conservative Party. As for the fact that I was in jail, I was told that the subject never arose between Amina and her landlord. He certainly knew, but never allowed this to influence his dealings with other members of my family.

But, by the time I reached school-going age, I was forced to come face to face with an animal called 'segregation', as apartheid was euphemistically known before the National Party came to power in 1948.

As in the rest of the country, Schweizer-Reneke had schools for whites and schools for Africans. Being a tiny community, there was no school for Indians, and the law prohibited me from attending the existing schools. As soon as I turned six, my father arranged for the principal of the local African school, David Mtshali, to come to our house in the afternoons and give me elementary lessons in English, arithmetic and other subjects. I had no need of tutoring in Afrikaans, as I had grown up speaking the language.

My three older brothers were sent in turn to the school for Indians in Johannesburg, many hours' drive away. At the beginning of 1938, just a few months after my eighth birthday, I was packed off to distant Johannesburg to stay with a paternal aunt in Fordsburg, and attend the Indian school there.

I don't recall with accuracy how I reacted to this prospect, but it must have been quite traumatic. I do remember that in later years, my brothers teased me about how I quietly tried to hide my tears each time I had to return to Johannesburg at the end of the school holidays.

I suppose that was the first politically flavoured event that affected me directly and recognisably. My young mind simply could not comprehend these prohibitions. After all, our neighbours were white and my godmother was an Afrikaner; the man who taught me the ABC was black, and my playmates were both black and white. How could I possibly understand that I alone had to go to school in Johannesburg, and would only be able to spend time with my family during the holidays?

~ 2 ~

The Dadoo Factor

Go forth, my son, and learn with how little wisdom the world is governed.
– **Count Oxenstierna (seventeenth-century Swedish diplomat)**[1]

M y fate was sealed. Bags were packed, tearful goodbyes were said, the car was loaded. I was ensconced in the back seat next to my father, the driver started the engine and we were off. Of all the farewells, this one was most keenly felt, and the memory remained with me all my life – a little boy pretending not to cry and making all sorts of excuses for his moist cheeks, while my brothers laughed and said, 'This fellow is lying.'

Having never been taught or told that there was any difference between me and anyone else, regardless of colour, I could not understand the strange adult logic that required me to be wrenched from my home and friends and sent to school in far-off Johannesburg. The City of Gold lay at the end of a long bumpy trip along the dry and dusty roads that covered the car in a coat of beige and left travellers coughing and keen to reach their destination.

We arrived on a hot summer's day in January 1938. My first sight of the city was thrilling and scary; it loomed on the horizon full of the promise of a new life, but also as a great indifferent structure and system of huge concrete buildings, busy people and lots of noise.

At my Aunt Fatima's house, the reception was warm but formal. She was a strict and devoutly religious woman, respected in the community. Five or six boys between the ages of eight and fifteen, mostly from farms and rural areas, shared two small outside rooms in the yard of the house in Nursery Road, Fordsburg, where she and her husband lived.

My formal schooling began a week later. Still sulking over being forced to move to the city, I arrived at Newtown Indian Primary with a sense of trepidation. The school was in a large double-storey building on the corner of Bree and Malherbe streets in downtown Johannesburg, and boys – and even a few girls – were streaming into the grounds. Thanks to the tuition of Mr Mtshali, I was immediately placed in a Grade 2 class, but after just one term was promoted to Standard 1. The following year, I again spent only the first term in Standard 2 before being promoted.

My teacher in Standard 3 was Mr N Thandray, a good tutor, but very strict. A few years later he became principal of a school in the Johannesburg suburb of Denver, but for reasons that had nothing to do with education, our paths would cross again, many years into the future.

All Muslim children[2] had to attend Madressa – religious school – every day after normal lessons. To me, the most attractive Indian language is Urdu, which made an indelible impression on me when I learnt it at Madressa. It infused me with a lifelong love of the language and Hindustani music. When I was in prison, I regretted having forgotten much of the Urdu I had known, and I was not allowed to have a dictionary to help me understand the lyrics of the few records we were permitted to have during the later years.

My Arab teacher at Madressa, Mr Siddique, was strict, and his pupils tended to regard him as cruel and oppressive. With his long beard, steel-rimmed glasses and turban, and his humourless expression, his physical presence was enough to make us jittery and nervous before our lessons even began. Unfortunately, this resulted in some of us disliking the subjects he taught, but his four beautiful daughters more than compensated for his own sour countenance. I spent many joyful hours reciting religious texts to Nafeesa, the eldest, on days when her father was instructing the other children.

DR DADOO

It was at about this time, aged nine, that I first heard of Yusuf Dadoo, a guiding light in the arena of political activism. In my child's eyes, he became larger than life. I grew up trying to memorise everything I heard and read about him, and would cling to his every utterance or statement.

It was in 1939 that politics, as opposed to race consciousness, first made an impact on my young mind. This can be ascribed to a combination of things, but foremost among them is what I called 'The Dadoo Factor'. I remember the adults discussing his emphasis on education and his criticism of extravagant weddings. He maintained that the large amounts of money spent on weddings should be used for education instead, and pleaded with parents to send their daughters to school and university so as to facilitate their integration into the broad spectrum of society.

Yusuf Dadoo qualified abroad as a medical doctor. In those years, not even the so-called liberal South African universities admitted students who were not white. The few doctors and lawyers who managed to study outside the country were looked upon with awe, as leaders and role models. But Dr Dadoo was exceptional, even within this illustrious circle. He was charismatic, fiery, frank and bold in his utterances, courageous in his actions and far-sighted in his vision.

More relevant, for me, was his advocacy of the unity and equality of all oppressed people. Was this not the basis of my own upbringing? As time passed, I learnt more and more about Dr Dadoo, but little did I know what impact he would have on my future. During my school years he fulfilled my childhood yearning for a hero, and he would hold that position throughout my life.

A pivotal and revolutionary leader in South Africa, Dr Dadoo had already become a legend by the time I was ten years old. There were other heroes too, of course – cricketers and boxers, film actors, authors, artists, poets and scientists about whom we talked at school, and in the afternoons and evenings. We did all the things that schoolchildren do, playing games, going to the cinema, trying to sing the hit songs of the day, boasting about things we did (and those we did *not* do). We played truant, gossiped about our teachers, were as naughty as any children our age, and got our share of punishment. But even at that early stage, I found myself drifting away from my peers and becoming more interested in the doings and sayings of Dadoo.

Soon I became friends with children whose fathers were his colleagues, and I began to catch sight of him in their homes. It was on one such occasion that he actually spoke a few words to me! Can you imagine what that meant? I believe it was at that moment that the exciting world of political activism, the arena in which one stood up against injustice and oppression, beckoned me.

One of my great friends at school was Essop Cachalia, a shy, clever boy. At his home, I met his uncles, Molvi and Yusuf, also leading political figures of the era. One thing led to another, as if my future had already been chalked out by a force over which I had no control. Of the hundreds of children I encountered in both primary and secondary school, those I befriended all came from politically aware families. My best friend was Mohamed Bharoochi's son, Enver. In their homes, I met leaders such as Messrs Nagdee, Esakjee, Naidoo and Desai who, along with the Cachalias and Baroochis, would play vital roles in both the Nationalist Group and the Non-European United Front, led by Dadoo. Young as we were, we listened to a great deal of political talk, and these were undoubtedly the formative years of our political consciousness.

At the core of Indian politics in South Africa lay the question of ownership and occupation of land, a battle that had been waged since 1885. In 1939, the year that South Africa entered the Second World War, the all-white parliament introduced the Asiatic Land Tenure and Trading Act, aimed at placing further restrictions on the trading and residential rights of Indians.

Dadoo and a handful of his followers formed a radical left-wing grouping within the Transvaal Indian Congress, which at that time was conservative in its outlook and not representative of the community. The Nationalist Group, as it was called, prepared to launch a campaign of passive resistance. This would entail the recruitment of volunteers who would deliberately defy the law and face imprisonment – a radical departure in non-white politics.

For the first time since Mahatma Gandhi left South Africa in 1914, the emergence of Indian leaders who advocated non-violent defiance of racist laws captured the imagination of the people, especially the youth. Even in sleepy Schweizer-Reneke, volunteers, including my eldest brother, Solly, prepared themselves for prison life by sleeping on mattresses on the floor and eating maize meal porridge.

Support for the proposed action posed a threat to the incumbent conservative Indian leadership, which resorted to all means, fair and foul, to scupper the campaign. On Sunday 4 June, hired gangsters invaded a packed and spirited meeting of the Nationalist Group at the Osrins Cinema in Johannesburg, killing one volunteer, Dayabhai Govindjee, and assaulting and stabbing another dozen.

Their real target was Dadoo, but he was saved by the action of a housewife, Mrs Pop, to whose home he had gone after attending to the wounds of some of the victims. Sensing that Dadoo was in imminent danger, Mrs Pop locked him in her house until it was safe for him to leave.

The belief that the gangsters had been hired by TIC officials was effectively confirmed when five of their supporters, including an executive member, were arrested and charged with the attacks. In spite of ample evidence, however, the Attorney-General withdrew the charges.

Far from intimidating the supporters of passive resistance, the violence served to rouse people to action against injustice and stimulate the enthusiasm not only of the volunteers, but of the majority of Transvaal Indians.

Dayabhai Govindjee's house was next to our school, and on the day of his funeral, the principal, Mr Zwarenstein, cancelled the lessons and had the pupils line both sides of the street as the solemn procession, led by Dadoo and his lieutenants, passed. We stood there filled with a mixture of trepidation, excitement and pride.

The image of that funeral became indelibly imprinted on my mind. Little could I then foresee that this would be the first tangible step on the road of political activism that I would follow all my life.

Over the next few weeks, excitement continued to mount, and no one had an inkling of the anti-climax that lay ahead. On the eve of its launch, and much to the disappointment of supporters, the passive resistance campaign was called off. It later transpired that, wanting to avoid embarrassment, South Africa's prime minister and so-called international statesman, General Jan Smuts, had asked the British to persuade Mahatma Gandhi to intervene. Dadoo issued a press statement acknowledging Gandhi's role:

> Mahatma Gandhi has been our guide and mentor in all that the passive resistance council has been doing in this matter, and we shall wholeheartedly await his advice; for we realise that his interest in the cause of the Indians in South Africa has not abated one whit, even though many years have elapsed since he left South Africa.[3]

As it turned out, whatever passed between the British and Indian governments had no effect at all on South Africa's rulers. Gandhi had clearly been misled. Not only would existing racist policies continue, there would be fresh onslaughts on the oppressed, and a number of years would pass before there was any further serious discussion about passive resistance.

Youthful activities

On the domestic front, my aunt was kind to me, but I was homesick. I missed the carefree days in Schweizer, to which I returned for the school holidays. It was on one such visit in 1940, when I was eleven, that my brothers Solly and Ismail taught me to drive a car. We spent many days at the dam and on the back roads, practising with my father's black Oldsmobile. It would be another seven years before I could obtain a driver's licence, but by then I was something of a veteran behind the wheel, so I suppose that was really my first illegal activity.

However, my forte in the field of unlawful acts was political subversion. With typical childhood enthusiasm and bravado, my Johannesburg friends and I were soon distributing political leaflets, putting up posters and writing slogans on walls with lumps of chalk. It was wartime, and with the not inconsiderable experience of ten whole summers behind us, we accepted with alacrity the anti-war party line. How could we not? Was our hero Dr Dadoo not in prison for publicly and boldly opposing what he termed 'the imperialist war'? And had we not learnt of the atrocities being perpetrated by the British imperialists in India?

We distributed copies of the statement that Dadoo made in court, and I learnt snatches of it by heart, reciting it at every opportunity. I accepted without hesitation that in this war, the rich got richer and the poor got killed. All this was well and good, but we needed to do more – something daring in order to display our solidarity with our jailed hero.

A target was easily identified. Those who contributed money for the war effort were given metal plates bearing the words 'Governor General's War Fund', which were screwed to the bumpers of their cars. One night we waited until dark, then pounced on cars parked outside cinemas and the Newtown mosque, removing the metal plates and throwing them away. Our youthful egos were greatly boosted by pats on the back from our elders, and we went to bed with a sense of pride and achievement, happy in the knowledge that by our tiny act of 'sabotage' we had shown our solidarity with Dadoo. Some twenty-five years later, of course, I would be sentenced to life imprisonment for 'sabotage' of a different kind.

Our 'anti-war' activities came to an end in June 1941, when Hitler's armies invaded the Soviet Union. Yusuf Cachalia took me to a conference of the Non-European United Front at the Bantu Men's Social Centre in Eloff Street, Johannesburg, called to review the NEUF's policy towards the war. Communist parties throughout the world, including South Africa, had already categorised the conflict as a 'people's war', and the NEUF decided to end its opposition to the war and renew its demands for the release of communists who had been interned. It also called for the arming of African soldiers and the extension of full democratic rights to all South Africans. Although they faced the same dangers as their white counterparts, African soldiers were not issued with firearms. They drove trucks, dug trenches, carried the wounded on stretchers and performed other menial duties, not unlike those they carried out at home as servants and labourers.

Despite my growing political awareness, I was still only twelve years old, and at my aunt's home I maintained an image of innocence and traditional respect not only for my elders, but for the way things worked in the South Africa of the early 1940s. We lived like any other Muslim family, celebrating the festivals, fasting over Ramadan, not mixing much with outsiders.

The Johannesburg Zoo and the adjoining lake were among our favourite recreation spots, not least because we were allowed to hire the rowing boats on offer. Both amenities were exempt from race restrictions, because a forward-thinking man, Herman Eckstein, had made this stipulation when he donated the land on which they stood to the Johannesburg City Council.

There was a time when Coloureds and Africans were not allowed on the boats, which gave rise to many problems. Indian women in Western dress, for example, were automatically regarded as Coloured, unless they could prove otherwise. But that came later, and during the war we would often pack a picnic on a Sunday and go to Zoo Lake, lazing under the willow trees, rowing our little boat and generally spending many happy hours relishing the fragrances of summer, the buzzing of bees and the joy of being with friends.

There were also many community events, some confined to Muslims and others involving Indians from all religious and social backgrounds. On 7 August 1941, India's greatest modern poet, Rabindranath Tagore,[4] died in Calcutta. Indians in South Africa had a close affinity with the All India Congress's anti-colonial struggle against the British, and, at the time, leaders such as Gandhi, Nehru and Azad were languishing in prison. I had committed to memory a piece of prose by Tagore, 'The Bankruptcy of European Civilisation', in primary school, and it vividly reflected my feelings at the time.

Still, I attended the memorial service at the Gandhi Hall more to hear Dadoo speak than to pay homage to Tagore who, besides one or two poems, was no more than a distant name in my young mind. I remember Dadoo telling the gathering: 'India, poverty-stricken and miserable as she is, has been further impoverished by the death of Tagore.'

Events on the subcontinent continued to inspire and influence the local Indian community. When parts of India were hit by a terrible famine in 1943, South Africans started the Bengal Famine Relief Fund, which operated from the basement under Molvi and Yusuf Cachalia's shop in Market Street. I was in Standard 7, and with a few other boys, I worked in that basement, helping to label envelopes and collect money and goods to be sent to the victims.

It was there that I met one of our community leaders, IC Meer, a student at the University of the Witwatersrand, who immediately took his place, along with Dadoo, in my personal gallery of heroes.

Meer was closely involved with the relief fund. In those years, there was only a handful of blacks at university, and it was a matter of great pride to know a student. I never lost a chance to be seen talking to Meer, especially when he was wearing his Wits blazer!

INSPIRING NEW LEADERS

While inspiring young leaders were emerging, the traditional Indian leadership in South Africa remained inflexible. Following Gandhi's departure in 1914, attitudes among local Indian politicians had become increasingly conservative and subservient. Commitment to the ideals of Gandhi's twenty-one-year stay in South Africa, characterised by passive resistance, defiance of racist laws and the struggle to uphold human dignity, receded more and more into the background.

It was replaced by the politics of expediency. Self-serving leaders ran the TIC's affairs from their business offices and avoided calling elections, their sole aim being to advance the commercial interests of the few. When confronted by anti-Indian legislation and anti-Indian agitation, their invariable response was to appoint deputations and go cap in hand to government officials to plead for the protection of their selfish interests. Not surprisingly, they were not unduly perturbed when the Natal Indians lost their right to vote in 1924 – a mere ten years after Gandhi's departure – or when successive white governments enacted one law after another that eroded the already meagre rights afforded to Indians. It was indeed a shameful period for the leadership of the tiny Indian community, which under Gandhi had put up such courageous resistance to oppressive laws.

However, things had begun to change with the return of Dr Dadoo and Dr Naicker to South Africa in the latter part of the 1930s. Their involvement in community affairs heralded the beginning of innovative and radical approaches to Indian politics.

THE YOUNG COMMUNIST LEAGUE

In 1941, I was drawn into the Young Communist League and Fordsburg Youth Club. Obviously this was not out of any intellectual appreciation of Marxism–Leninism, or any intelligent understanding of its policies on South Africa. It was quite enough for me to know that the YCL was part of the broad struggle against injustice and inequality, and for democracy and non-racialism. Of course, I didn't understand the deeper meaning of those concepts either, but that was what we were told, and what we accepted.

It was at the energetic meetings of the YCL, marked by vigorous debate and a spirit of intellectualism, that I first met Ruth First, Duma Nokwe, Harold Wolpe, Paul Joseph and others. I also recall, during this time, seeing some of the white comrades in army uniform, among them Joe Slovo, Rusty Bernstein, Brian Bunting, Wolfie Kodesh and Fred Carneson. These were all people who would play a definitive role in the struggle against apartheid, and some would pay for their commitment with their lives.

My own attitude towards the war was tinged with ambivalence. Smuts, notwithstanding his public promises and protestations of democracy, continued to pass anti-Indian legislation, especially in 1941 and 1943. Racial persecution was rampant and police brutality continued unabated, such as the killing in 1942 of sixteen African soldiers and policemen who took part in a peaceful demonstration in Pretoria to demand better wages.

My hatred of British imperialism and white racism at home often over-shadowed my belief in the absolute justness of the war against Nazism. Thus, while I would proudly march up to the platform of a pro-war YCL pageant, holding high the flag of one of the allied countries, and diligently attend meetings of the Friends of the Soviet Union and collect coins for Medical Aid for Russia, I would also derive great satisfaction from every blow struck by the Japanese against the British in Asia, and from every setback suffered by white South African troops in North Africa and Italy.

I was as blind in my hatred of British imperialism, and later the American brand, along with racism, as I was in my admiration of the Soviet Union. My young heart would overflow with pride and joy for every crushing blow that the Red Army inflicted on the Nazis at Stalingrad, yet I had the insensitivity to scribble on the blackboard in my classroom: 'We rejoice at the fall of Tobruk'.

The gesture was not only insensitive, but also irresponsible, because it was aimed at Miss Harris, one of the finest and most non-racist of all our teachers – and one of the prettiest. Her brother was with the South African forces in North Africa, and when she came into the classroom and saw my message on the board, she wept. I could not muster the courage to own up and apologise.

In 1941, the Nationalist Group started passive resistance on a small scale against discriminatory licensing laws in Johannesburg. About six stalls, complete with placards bearing appropriate slogans, were set up outside the city hall, magistrate's court, Jeppe hostel and other buildings, where volunteers sold fruit without a licence. Many days after school my friends and I manned the stalls, but while we saw this as an act of bravery, the police simply ignored us, and after a few months the 'campaign' folded.

By 1943, at the age of fourteen, I had been elected to the YCL's Johannesburg District Committee. My growing involvement in political activities coincided with a surge of youthful arrogance and a sense of self-importance. I did not take part in sporting activities of any kind, probably because I had come to regard them as non-revolutionary, or even counter-revolutionary! My duty was to be available whenever 'political matters' demanded my presence.

My meagre political understanding, coupled with a large dose of instinct, would stand me in good stead when I was plunged into a debate in the YCL's District Committee. It would have been relatively inconsequential, if not for the fact that the same debate erupted again ten years later, this time in the ranks of the Transvaal Peace Council. In the YCL it happened in 1945, while two of the most experienced members of the committee, Ruth First and Harold Wolpe, were out of the country, attending the World Federation of Democratic Youth Conference. A comrade from what subsequently came to be known as the 'Doornfontein Group' initiated a move that would have resulted in the radical restructuring of the league.

He argued forcefully that, in order for the organisation to make significant progress in terms of membership and influence, it was necessary to have two YCLs – one for whites and one for other population groups. His proposal was soundly defeated, but a decade later, certain individuals from the same group advocated splitting the Transvaal Peace Council along racial lines.

Apart from various practical reasons they put forward, they argued that whites were not ready for inclusion in mixed groups, and that separation would make it easier to draw white members. Had either proposal succeeded, the impact on not only the YCL and the Peace Council, but on the liberation movement as a whole, would have been enormous. Similar debate within the ranks of the ANC in the 1950s led to formation of the PAC by a breakaway group, and later to the expulsion by the ANC in exile of the so-called 'Gang of Eight' in London.

My political education, as well as my religious development, owe much to Yusuf Cachalia, my good friend Essop's uncle. He instructed me in the Hadis, a set of Islamic law books second in holiness only to the Koran, and took me to meetings of the Left Book Club in Commissioner Street. In addition to stocking a wide range of leftist publications, ranging from Marx and copies of the *Communist Manifesto* to Stalin's speeches and the *World Marxist Review*, the club organised lectures that we sometimes attended. At one, held at the Bantu Men's Social Centre, the speaker was Dr WMM Eiselen, one of the chief architects and philosophers of apartheid, who would later serve as Secretary of Native Affairs under Dr HF Verwoerd,[5] appointed Minister of Native Affairs in 1950.

It was around this time that I encountered another young man who would have a major influence on me. I was a schoolboy, eleven years his junior, and he was a law student when we first met, through my association with Ismail Meer and JN Singh. His name was Nelson Mandela.

The only extracurricular activities that I took part in were the debating society and the historical society, the latter formed because a group of us questioned the political orientation of the debating society's leadership and activities. I contrived to marry my political and school interests by inviting Meer to adjudicate one of our debates. He agreed, and made a huge impression on my schoolmates, which put a feather in my cap. On another occasion, we hosted prominent theatre personality and communist Cecil Williams, who would be driving the car when Mandela was arrested at a roadblock in 1962.

I also involved two more communists, Nat Bregman, a lawyer to whom Mandela was later articled, and Beryl Green in our school activities. Eventually, I was appointed editor of a school publication, *The Historian*, but distribution of the very first issue was halted by the principal because of its 'political' content.

Everything I did rested on a foundation of politics. My Standard 9 class pioneered a farewell function for the matriculants, and even this was given a political flavour by inviting some well-known leftist performers, including Nat and Beryl, to provide the entertainment at what was considered a very successful event.

As my schooldays began to draw to a close, my life became increasingly entwined with that of Dadoo, and over the years a whole spectrum of relationships crystallised between us. He became my leader, my colleague, my father, my older brother, my guide, my mentor and my friend – and I like to think there was an occasion or two when he was even my doctor!

THE COMMUNIST PARTY

Towards the mid-1940s I was admitted into the Communist Party and allowed to join a group – we did not call them cells – on probation. Duties included attendance of group meetings and political classes, house to house visits, selling the *Guardian* newspaper, distributing party literature and staying in touch with the people, acquainting ourselves with their problems with a view to rendering whatever assistance we could.

Such problems included exploitation by unscrupulous landlords, the erratic supply of electricity and water, and the general quality of life. Occasionally, party members were also called upon to settle domestic strife and to arbitrate in gang disputes. One of the major consequences of the war was the dearth of certain foodstuffs, such as rice and sugar, which gave rise to a lucrative black market trade. The party identified the worst culprits and, on an appointed day, organised residents in specific areas to 'invade' their shops and induce the owners to sell the scarce items at the correct prices. While these 'food raids' might not have made a significant dent in black marketeering as such, they did succeed in inhibiting traders from pursuing their malpractices. The raids alienated party members from the guilty shopkeepers, but won tremendous support and respect from the ordinary people.

One of the most exciting Communist Party activities was the weekly Sunday night meeting on the steps of the Johannesburg City Hall. There were the usual hecklers, who were generally harmless and often provided light relief, and the more serious fascist Grey Shirts, self-declared Nazi sympathisers who came specifically to break up the meetings by force. Party members responded by organising themselves into groups to defend the platform and prevent the thugs from disrupting proceedings. We relied heavily on members of the Springbok Legion, a group of ex-soldiers, sometimes in battle dress and military formation, and our side was victorious in almost every fight that broke out, though we did not always go home unscathed.

I also began attending meetings of the Johannesburg West branch of the party, in offices at Chancellor House that would later be occupied by the law firm of Mandela & Tambo. Ismail Meer, JN Singh, Douggie and Alec Lai, Saleh Asvat, Zainab Asvat's brother, Cassim Patel and Krishna Pillay were all members of that branch.

While I had served on the Johannesburg District Committee of the YCL, I remained a rank and file member of the 'senior' party throughout, except for a brief spell on the district and central committees of the reconstituted party in the 1950s and 1960s, operating underground.

My father

The moment of the rose and the moment of the
yew tree are of equal duration.   − TS Eliot[6]

Five years after being uprooted from Schweizer-Reneke, my father died. For that crucial period of my life, I had been outside his sphere of influence, and as a result, I always felt that I never really knew him.

Yet, on the night he died, I had an intensely personal and strangely inexplicable experience.

Although I was home for the school holidays, I hadn't seen my father for some time. He had gone to Johannesburg on business, and, on that fateful night in July 1943, was returning by train. He felt unwell on the journey, and on arrival at the small siding of Coligny, where he had to change trains, his condition deteriorated. After being helped off the train by the conductor, he was driven to the home of close relatives, the Kola family, in nearby Ottosdal.

Knowing none of this, I was asleep in my bed at home when I suddenly awoke to see my bedroom door open, and the figure of a man walk in. I screamed, loudly, and the rest of the family came rushing to my room. There was no one there, of course, and they said I must have been dreaming. I knew instinctively that this was not true, but in the absence of an alternative or better explanation, I eventually accepted their soothing words and comforting assurances.

Everyone went back to bed, lights were turned out, and I once more tried to still my restless thoughts and dull my ears to the night sounds and the rustling of the leaves outside. But I had barely settled down when the door opened again, and I distinctly saw a figure wafting into my room. I screamed again, but once more, there was no one to be found.

The next morning, we received the news that my father had died during the night.

Over the years, many people have asked if my father was associated with Mahatma Gandhi and Ahmed Cachalia. I can say with some certainty that he was not, but, beyond that, I am ashamed to say I know very little about his early life, or my mother's either − one of the unfortunate consequences of being sent away to school at the age of eight, and never really going home again, except for holidays.

While living at my aunt's house in Fordsburg, I formed some firm friendships, and in 1945, when I was in Standard 9, I moved into a flat in Fordsburg with two classmates, Abe Gani and Ahmed 'Dos' Kola, who was also a cousin. It was unusual for three schoolboys to be allowed to set up house on their own with no adult supervision, and of course the experience was liberating and exciting. We relished our freedom, and I grasped the opportunity to become even more involved in politics, but, since food has always been one of my greatest pleasures, I was grateful that I could still enjoy traditional Indian meals at my aunt's house, thus having the best of both worlds.

THE PEGGING ACT

In 1943, the government passed the Trading and Occupation of Land Restriction Act. Known as the 'Pegging Act', it further curtailed the land rights of Indians in the Transvaal and Natal.

In line with their established response, the leaders of the Indian Congress sent a deputation to convey to Smuts their dissatisfaction with the law, and to plead with him to repeal it. They did manage to secure an undertaking that the law would be repealed, but the quid pro quo was the humiliating and spineless suggestion by the Indian politicians that in place of the Pegging Act, the government should set up an Occupation Control Board to regulate Indian residence in white areas.

The board would consist of two Indian and three white members, which meant, in effect, that it could do exactly what the Pegging Act was designed to do, except that Indians would themselves be complicit. The younger leaders in the community once more called for action against the state.

Another sign that the political baton was being passed to the next generation of leaders came in early April 1944, with the formation of the African National Congress Youth League. Among those at the inaugural meeting at the Bantu Men's Social Centre in Johannesburg[7] were Walter Sisulu, Oliver Tambo, Anton Lembede, Nelson Mandela, Robert Sobukwe and David Bopape. As members of the YCL, we occasionally met with the ANC Youth League, but I don't recall encountering any of these political heavyweights at that stage. Later, though, many of them would come to know me as Kathy, the name that just about everyone calls me.

It was my science and maths teacher in Standard 8, Mr Du Preez, who gave me the nickname. For some reason, Afrikaners find 'Kathrada' difficult, and most of them say 'Kathadra'. Du Preez, a humorous man and good at his job, though a bit eccentric, solved the problem by shortening my name to Kathy, and it stuck.

～ 3 ～

Awareness Deepens

A mere twelve months after the Second World War ended, there was widespread expectation of a future in which freedom, equality and peace would flourish, and colonialism, racism and armed conflict would be no more.

In this changed world, South Africa's prime minister, General Jan Smuts, who has been credited with drafting the preamble to the United Nations Charter, set about earning his undeserved reputation as an enlightened international statesman.

In 1946, he was preparing to lead the South African delegation to the UN. His primary aims were to convince the world that his treatment of Indians was fair, and this issue should therefore be removed from the UN agenda, on which it had been placed by India, and to have South West Africa (as Namibia was then called) declared the fifth province of South Africa. He would not only have to satisfy the international community on the correctness of his position, but also the South African Indian community – victims of his government's undisguised racialism.

Smuts was confident that he would have the world body eating out of his hands. He relied on Britain and America to support him, and they did, but he had grossly miscalculated his influence, and failed miserably to achieve either of his goals.

In the hope of mollifying his domestic Indian community, he had added a sop to the Land Tenure Act, which allowed them to elect three members of parliament and two senators – all five of whom had to be white. Two Indians could also be elected to the Natal Provincial Council, and there was to be a partially elected board – an insulting manoeuvre designed to give the impression of genuine representation. It had no powers whatsoever, and could act in a purely advisory capacity.

For the rest, the Smuts government showed a complete disregard and lack of respect for the Indian community's position. In 1946, the worst provisions of the 'repealed' Pegging Act were reintroduced by the Asiatic Land Tenure and Indian Representation Act – the Ghetto Act – that legalised the segregation of Indians in Natal.

The year before, the incumbent conservative leaders of the Natal and Transvaal Indian Congresses had been forced to agree to elections. Dr Naicker and Dr Dadoo were swept into power uncontested as presidents of the two congresses. Dadoo was also elected head of the South African Indian Congress. A new era had dawned for Indian politics in South Africa.

The Dadoo-Naicker partnership mobilised strong opposition to the Ghetto Act, and at the February 1946 conference of the SAIC, public support for resistance to unjust laws was spelt out in a far-reaching resolution. If this discriminatory piece of legislation was adopted, the SAIC would:

• launch a passive resistance campaign;
• boycott the 'representation' provisions of the Act;
• call upon India to withdraw its high commissioner, impose trade sanctions against South Africa and raise the treatment of South African Indians at the UN.

Against the background of a virtually dormant resistance movement, the resolution was initially regarded by many as rather presumptuous and impractical, but, in fact, all of the proposals were successfully implemented.

The end of the Second World War also heralded the start of a new and ominous phase in South Africa's internal security structures with the establishment of the police Special Branch. My first acquaintance with the SB was when they started raiding the passive resistance offices, but the security policemen of 1945 were a very different breed to the brutal thugs that would later swell the ranks of this organisation.

THE PASSIVE RESISTANCE CAMPAIGN

My nature is to join in love, not hate. – Antigone[1]

The passing of the Ghetto Act was a call to action that people around the country responded to with alacrity. However, 'while the Transvaal and Natal Indian Congresses formed resistance councils to combat the "Ghetto" Act, the Cape Indian Congress, under the outmoded leadership of Mr Ahmed Ismail, remained inactive'.[2] Although he was president of the SAIC, which had agreed to the resistance strategy, Ismail did nothing to gain support for the campaign in the Cape, and refused to form a council, even at the request of members of his constituency. In addition, according to Bhana and Pachai, he 'constantly attempted to hinder and harm the movement'. Nonetheless, a Passive Resistance Council was set up in Cape Town under the guidance of Mrs Z 'Cissy' Gool and other leaders.[3]

Across South Africa, the campaign took root and, as history would record, 'the Indians acted alone, though with the praise of the ANC'.[4] A newspaper, *The Passive Resister*, was established to disseminate information on the campaign and related issues, and would be published for the next two years under the editorial stewardship of Ismail Meer.

The principles of passive resistance were based on the philosophy of *satyagraha*, first conceived by Mahatma Gandhi in South Africa in 1906 in response to a law discriminating against Asians by the then-Transvaal government. Roughly translated from Hindustani, the word means 'truth force', but it has come to embody more than that, and is in essence a philosophy of active but non-violent protest against some wrong or inequity in society. The congresses did not adopt the creed of *satyagraha* as a policy, but they did embrace passive resistance and civil disobedience.

The Passive Resistance Campaign office was set up in some of the rooms at Dadoo's house at 47 End Street in the Johannesburg suburb of Doornfontein. Several university students gave up their studies in order to work for the campaign full time, among them Meer, Singh, Zainab Asvat and Abdulhuck Patel. I assisted the Transvaal Indian Youth Volunteer Corps, which would later become the Transvaal Indian Youth Congress, the TIC and the Passive Resistance Council as a driver and in an administrative capacity from the offices in End Street. The campaign opened a new chapter in both my life and Indian politics in general. It was my last year at school and the final examination, known as matriculation, loomed at the end of it, offering the gateway to university.

But in June, Dr Dadoo, IC Meer and JN Singh came to fetch me from my classroom to perform some or other menial task. I never went back. There was tremendous enthusiasm for the cause, and with the abundant wisdom of my seventeen years, cocksure that my contribution was indispensable, I followed suit. In hindsight, I hope we were not viewed as pioneers of the 'liberation before education' syndrome.

The age and education gap between me and the adults seemed to narrow rapidly, and we became friends. I learnt a great deal from them, especially the technicalities of newspaper production.

The increasing amount of time that I spent in End Street introduced me to many pivotal people in my life. That must have been where I met a man for whom I developed the highest regard and the deepest and most loving respect: Walter Max Ulyate Sisulu. His offices were situated close to those of the TIC, and he took an active and enthusiastic interest in the campaign, visiting the offices and forming lasting friendships with many of the people working there.

ACTIVE RESISTANCE BEGINS

It is better by noble boldness to run the risk of being subject to half of the evils we anticipate than to remain in cowardly listlessness for fear of what may happen. – Herodotus[5]

On 13 June 1946, the first batch of seventeen volunteers, led by Dr Naicker and MD Naidoo (who, decades later, would join us on Robben Island), deliberately courted arrest by occupying tents on a plot of land on the corner of Gale Street and Umbilo Road in Durban. It had been designated for the use of 'whites only', and in response to a call by the SAIC, Indian-owned businesses in all the main centres of South Africa closed in solidarity, Indian employees stayed away from work, and children did not go to school. Thousands of people gathered at Red Square in Durban and accompanied the volunteers to the plot of land.

Contrary to expectation, the police did not immediately arrest the protestors, who continued to occupy the tents for a number of days. On 16 June, a band of white hooligans attacked them, while the police looked on, and after that there were nightly assaults, but despite their fear and the threat to their safety, the volunteers stayed on.

On 21 June, the hooligans attacked and killed an Indian bystander, who turned out to be a policeman in plain clothes, but still there were no arrests. In a bid to focus public and media attention on the attacks, a well-known Anglican clergyman, the Reverend Michael Scott, was sent from Johannesburg by the organisers to spend time with the resisters and offer some encouragement and protection.

Scott was tall, good-looking, hard working and deeply committed to opposing any form of injustice. He was utterly committed to his Christian beliefs and the spirit of his religion, but had a great respect for and appreciation of the viewpoints of others. Unselfish almost to the point of being self-effacing, all his actions were aimed at improving the lot of his fellow human beings.

Scott had already made a name for himself with his tireless work for the poor, the elderly, and those affected by the unequal distribution of resources and privileges. He had been in the news for living in Tobruk on the Witwatersrand, one of the first informal settlements in South Africa. He established a church in the shantytown that had walls of hessian, and dedicated himself to drawing attention to the abject poverty and squalid conditions in which people were forced to live.[6]

His fervent commitment to leading a spiritual life based on the values of compassion, commitment to truth and justice, and to challenging the inequities of the South African system was complemented by his striking good looks. Mary Benson, later his assistant in London, was to write of his role in the 1946 passive resistance: 'Gandhi's *satyagraha* – soul force – inspired him. The great dividing line of his life had been his decision to break the law by joining Indians in passive resistance in Durban.'[7]

Scott, who had lived in India before moving to South Africa, had been involved in the formation of the Council for Asiatic Rights, established by progressive whites in Johannesburg in solidarity with the passive resistance movement. On his second night with the protestors in Durban, he was assaulted by the hooligans, and five other people were knocked unconscious. Among those attacked were Zainab Asvat, whose father had been jailed with Gandhi during his *satyagraha* campaign, and Rabia Docrat.

ES Reddy recalls that Scott

felt he could not stand idly by when Indian passive resisters in Durban were being attacked by white ruffians with bicycle chains and other lethal instruments – the police refused to intervene – when several men and women fell unconscious from the blows and one Indian, an off-duty detective, even died.

He stood in the resistance plot with a young Indian woman, a medical student, somewhat in fear as he was jostled. His companion was bleeding, but told him, 'Father, forgive them, they know not what they are doing.' There he learnt a new dimension of the Bible from the Muslim girl – and proceeded to start a crusade against racism in South Africa.[8]

Having taken no action against the ruffians, the police finally began arresting the protestors. Among those sentenced in the first months were Dadoo, Naicker, Scott, Molvi Saloojee, Sorabjee Rustomjee, Zainab Asvat, Suryakala Patel, Dr Goonam, Cissy Gool and Gadija Christopher.

An important aspect of my work during the Passive Resistance Campaign was driving various people to meetings, and this led to my first visit to Durban, and my first sight of the sea, in 1946, with IC Meer and JN Singh. We spent a night or two in Pinetown at the home of Fatima Meer's father, though it would be two years before I met Fatima herself, when she became a student at Wits in 1948.

The highlight of the trip was a night picnic on a boat owned by George Singh. This was the first time we met, and I immediately took a liking to him. That trip on the boat was wonderful – JN, George, Ismail Meer, Ms Radhie Singh and Dr Ansuyah Singh, Ruth First and me, out on the water together, with all the excitement of youth and a picnic basket full of goodies.

Through my work on *The Passive Resister*, I came to know Henry Nxumalo, an outstanding journalist during the 1940s and 1950s, who was known as 'Mr Drum', due to his work on the popular magazine. He had made a name as an investigative journalist, exposing such scandals as the appalling labour conditions on potato farms at Bethal, backyard abortions in the townships of Johannesburg and shameful prison conditions.

When I first met Henry through Ismail Meer in 1946, he was freelancing for the *Pittsburgh Courier* (USA), and occasionally contributed to *The Passive Resister*. We remained good friends right up to his untimely death, and shared numerous experiences together. Struan Douglas writes:

> Mr Drum, Henry Nxumalo, was the first journalist for the magazine, and the first to employ the mass of extraordinary material the polar opposites of South African politics offered the non-white world. He risked everything to bear the truth and maintain the integrity of the exploited people. Mr Drum was the good, fighting courageously and liberally, swallowing tough and dangerous assignments for the cause – to uncover the scoop, provoke change and strengthen the will of the righteous. He was every bit as suave, sassy and heroic as the British Bond, continually at the cutting edge of danger, controversy, mistreatment and inequity. He knew what was going down, and he supplied the details.
>
> 'His working stint on the potato farms rocked parliament, exposing the poor conditions under which Africans laboured. The Clean Up the Reef campaign identified the great area of lawlessness, the 'square mile of sin' and cried for support from the police. He conspired to get himself into Johannesburg central prison, and created an international scoop with the ward conditions and the belittling naked native search. He arrived barefoot and unshaven to beg employment on a farm where an African labourer was flogged to death with a hosepipe. And his investigation into church apartheid was fascinating in its juxtaposition of icy prejudice and the will for 'brotherly love'.[9]

When some of his articles proved too 'hot' for *Drum*, Henry passed them on to Ruth First for publication in *New Age*.

Henry was murdered in the late 1950s, evidently because of his exposures, and to the best of my knowledge his killers were never found.

While many non-white South Africans, especially prisoners, farm workers and labourers, lived under the most appalling conditions, there was a reservoir of innate decency in the attitude of some civil servants towards people of all population groups. One of the early members of the Special Branch was a Sergeant Edelstein, a polite man and a true gentleman, almost apologetic.

Once, when the Communist Party offices in Progress Building, Commissioner Street, were being raided, staff telephoned our office in End Street to warn us. We quickly crammed files that we did not want the police to confiscate into our car, but when I, the designated driver, tried to start the engine, the vehicle would not budge.

The police, including Edelstein, arrived while some of my colleagues were pushing the vehicle, but instead of taking the files, some of the policemen helped push the car, and away we drove! In a twist of fate, I would later encounter Edelstein's brother, a doctor, on Robben Island. He was a callous man, and we often wished his brother had been the one to study medicine.

My work during the Passive Resistance Campaign was largely administrative in nature. At the same time, as chairman of the Transvaal Indian Youth Congress, I was organising meetings and lectures in schools and at community centres, and generally politicising young people regarding the issues of the day.

I had not seen my Standard 3 teacher, 'Murvy' Thandray, since the end of the year spent in his class learning the three Rs and, I am almost sure, receiving my fair share of hidings from him. I say 'almost' because, when this was put to him in later years, he was rather cagey. Nevertheless, he was a wonderful old man, the like of which one would be hard pressed to find among younger generations – a master of discipline, utter selflessness, devotion, courage, rigid morality, modesty, honesty, and with a remarkable sense of sacrifice.

In 1946, he gave up his post as a school principal and a salary of £80 a month to work at the passive resistance offices in End Street for the meagre monthly stipend of £12. In the process he lost his pension, and often did not even receive his stipend on time. On occasion he would walk the six miles home to Denver, and many times there was no food on the table, but he never complained.

Despite the fact that we went to jail together at the end of 1946, Mr Thandray and I never managed to shed our teacher–pupil relationship, and even after his death, I referred to him as 'Mr'.

We spent a month together in Durban prison, and despite many embarrassing moments, our mutual respect endured. On being released, we returned to the passive resistance offices and worked together until we were both banned in 1954.

IMPRISONMENT

No one knows what kind of government it is
who has never been in gaol. — Tolstoy[10]

By December, when I first made the acquaintance of the prison system, there was no longer a need for tents or provisions on the corner plot in Durban. The police would simply arrive and arrest any volunteers who happened to be there. I had travelled to Durban with the specific intention of defying the racist land legislation, and I arrived on a hot and humid summer afternoon. I was in custody by the end of the week.

Prisoners were segregated according to race, but given that the passive resistance campaign was overwhelmingly dominated by Indians, this was not something I gave much thought to during my one-month sentence, perhaps because the few Coloured people arrested at the same time were incarcerated with the rest of us. However, there were no Africans in our section of the prison.

Just before Christmas, rumours started spreading – prisons are great mills of rumour and speculation – that we were going to get all sorts of Christmas treats. Excitement mounted, and we looked forward to manifestations of the Christmas spirit that would cheer our lives.

On Christmas Day, the warders summoned us to 'line up for your Christmas box!' As we stood in the queue, we discussed with anticipation the delicious food we would no doubt enjoy after weeks of dry prison fare. When I reached the head of the line, I was mortified to discover that the generous 'gift' was a mug of black coffee, without sugar. Even in those years, white prisoners got pudding at Christmas.

In later years, when people asked about my feelings during that first spell in prison, I would tell them that it in no way foreshadowed the decades I would spend behind bars. That month in prison was humiliating, but the experience was tempered by the enthusiasm of youth and the sense of being one of thousands fighting for justice.

Harold Solomon, a volunteer in the Passive Resistance Campaign, was under age and could not be sent to prison, but he made his mark in a unique and unusual way.

Harold had arrived at the offices sporting barely visible stubble on his face, a poor excuse for the beard and moustache he had tried to cultivate. An exasperated recruiting officer accepted his application, and soon Harold was off to Durban with a batch of volunteers. They were duly arrested and taken to court, but unfortunately for Harold the magistrate saw through his 'disguise', and instead of imprisonment, sentenced him to six lashes.

A disappointed and downcast Harold returned to Johannesburg with the weals on his buttocks still quite visible. Editor Ismail Meer, forever in search of a good story, had the buttocks photographed and published the picture in *The Passive Resister*. Then he sent the photograph to the SAIC delegation, which was in New York to attend the UN session, and the message came back that it had been circulated among UN delegates and even received some media coverage.

No one was prouder than young Harold, who ceaselessly challenged his peers to do something that would get their faces, let alone their behinds, seen by members of the august body in far-off America!

By February 1947, eight months after the first protestors had pitched their tents on the vacant lot in Durban, 1 586 people had been jailed. Decades later, during the marathon Treason Trial, Professor ZK Matthews would describe the 1946 passive resistance movement as 'the immediate inspiration' for the ANC's 1949 decision to adopt a campaign of civil disobedience.[11]

On 10 March, Dr Naicker and Dr Dadoo returned from a trip to India,[12] and Naicker assured the Natal Indian Congress that India wholeheartedly supported the struggle of South African Indians and opposed any form of surrender. The dynamic leadership of Dadoo and Naicker obviously made some of the more conservative and self-serving members of the Indian community uncomfortable, among them Sorabjee Rustomjee and Ashwin Choudree. I remember *The Passive Resister* carrying a cartoon showing Sorab swimming to America after he had made one of his customarily florid statements in response to a rumoured threat to withdraw his passport.

But in time the spirit of our work would imbue even the early dissenters, and both Sorab and Ashwin would join the procession of activists who passed through Flat 13 at Kholvad House in Johannesburg.

When the Passive Resistance Campaign petered out, the students who had taken part went back to university, and other volunteers returned to their jobs and professions. I, however, had embarked at the age of seventeen on a career as an activist, and would remain one, more or less full time, until I was imprisoned in 1963.

When I went to Durban to take part in the campaign, arrangements were made for me to stay at the home of Fatima and Dawood Seedat, in Hampson Grove. More than twenty years later, Fatima's letters to me in prison would transport me back in time to the wonderful atmosphere and extraordinary people that characterised the Seedat home. They simply exuded warmth, kindness, hospitality, generosity, friendship and love, and everyone, from the grandmother to the youngest child, welcomed visitors and strangers alike with open arms.

Yusuf Dadoo told us often that he could never go to Durban without calling at the house in Hampson Grove, and that he just loved the food, the people and the warmth he found there. In his quiet, unobtrusive way, Dawood symbolised goodness, generosity, unselfishness, devotion and love. When Fatima became a grandmother, she embodied the picture of grannies sketched by so many writers, always busy and involved in the lives of family members, travelling from wedding to wedding, attending the birth of grandchildren, and generally doing everything she could to preserve the closely knit ties. She was an ideal grandmother, and I am sure that she inspired members of successive generations just as she inspired me.

LAKE SUCCESS

There is no limit to extending our services to our neighbours
across state-made frontiers. God never made these frontiers.
– Mahatma Gandhi, 2 October 1920[13]

The boycott of the 'representation' offered by the Ghetto Act was so successful that the government was unable to implement it. No Indian was prepared to take part in the election of white representatives, nor could anyone be found who would agree to serve on the dummy board. I think it can rightly be claimed that seldom, if ever, in the history of the South African liberation movement was there such a successful boycott of a race-based institution.

India recalled her high commissioner, imposed trade sanctions and raised the inequitable treatment of South Africans of Indian descent at the United Nations. India's opposition also contributed significantly towards the rejection of Smuts' efforts to incorporate South West Africa as a province of the Union of South Africa.

That historic session of the UN began on 23 October 1946 at Lake Success in New York. In attendance were 400 delegates, representing fifty-four countries.[14]

South Africa's oppressed people did not need to be educated about the racial discrimination and violence perpetrated by Smuts and his government. Just two months before the UN session, in August, a dozen people had been killed and scores more wounded when police attempted to crush a peaceful strike by African mineworkers.[15] Of course, it was also Smuts who had no hesitation in unleashing the police and army on white strikers in 1922.

As if he was still living in the days of the League of Nations, when international events were dominated by a handful of colonial powers, Smuts audaciously set off for New York, having promised his electorate that he would return with South West Africa as a fifth province. He also assured them that the majority of nations would appreciate South Africa's complex problems and lend an understanding ear to the government's efforts to deal with them.

Smuts did get the backing of Britain, America, Canada and some other countries, but he had not taken account of the influence of member states such as the Soviet Union and India, and even within the countries that supported him, there were voices of dissent. The US Council on African Affairs, for example, was vocal in its opposition to injustice.

India, a year away from independence, was represented by members of its interim government. Political developments in South Africa resonated loudly in New York, and Smuts had not expected to face a situation in which his powerful friends were rendered impotent against the wrath of the majority.

As bright and determined as Smuts was reputed to be, his dedication and wit would wilt in the face of a formidable woman, Vijaya Lakshmi Pandit.

Imprisoned at least three times by the British colonial power in India, she led her country's delegation to the UN in 1946. A year later, she was appointed India's ambassador in Moscow. Her sterling work at the UN and elsewhere would be recognised in 1953, when she was the first woman elected president of the UN General Assembly.

While Mrs Pandit was becoming one of the leading female political figures of the twentieth century, her brother, Jawaharlal Nehru, was preparing to become independent India's first prime minister.

The 1946 UN session also played host to a group of South Africans, including HA Naidoo and Sorabjee Rustomjee of the Passive Resistance Council, AB Xuma, president general of the African National Congress, and Senator HM Basner. They went to New York to champion the cause of democratic rights for all, no doubt contributing to the defeat suffered by Smuts on South West Africa's future status, as well as to international condemnation of the way Indians were treated in South Africa.

On Friday 20 December 1946, *The Passive Resister* commented as follows: 'No one, least of all Smuts, can underestimate South Africa's defeat. For the first time world opinion has rejected the colour bar theory. South African racialists cannot fail to take cognisance of this verdict.' The UN resolution, passed by a two-thirds majority, called on South Africa to conform to the principles of the charter in its treatment of the Indian community, but the Smuts government refused to implement the resolution.

These were exciting times, yet, far from objectively examining their actions and attitudes and taking steps to address the inequalities and inequity of the system, South Africa's white community reacted with anger. By and large, their response was to rally behind the government and stonewall Indian aspirations. This was particularly apparent in the reaction to trade sanctions imposed by India.

BACKLASH

At the time, India was the world's primary, if not only, producer of jute, the raw material from which grain sacks and other bags were made before the advent of plastics on a commercial scale.

When India cut off its supply of jute in the middle of 1947, South Africa's maize farmers were suddenly faced with the huge and unexpected problem of how to pack and transport their crops.

There was no obvious solution, and all along the country's 'maize belt', piles of harvested maize sprang up, which soon became small mountains, exposed to the vagaries of the elements and easily accessible to the many hungry insects and small animals that inhabit the countryside.

With their sense of helplessness, anger and frustration at boiling point, the farmers united with the majority of white society by retaliating against Indian traders – after all, it was at their behest that India had stopped the export of jute.

This anti-Indian campaign started in Schweizer-Reneke, my hometown, and spread, with varying degrees of success, to several other Transvaal towns, especially neighbouring settlements such as Bloemhof and Wolmaranstad.

Seldom before or afterwards were whites as united as during this boycott. The ruling United Party and the opposition National Party, led by Dr DF Malan, found common ground, as did whites from all walks of life. Not surprisingly, the powerful Dutch Reformed Church and local schoolteachers were the main propagandists and organisers of the campaign.

Various factors influenced the white community in Schweizer-Reneke, but the one undeniable economic and emotive factor was the disastrous effect of India's embargo on the farmers. They were hard hit, and some faced ruin. The situation brought to the surface inherent, albeit previously dormant, anti-Indian sentiments, and in 1947, reason, ethics, religion and even personal debts of gratitude to the Indian shopkeeper fell by the wayside.

The farmers also successfully prevented their African labourers from patronising Indian shops. Only those who did not work on farms or for other white employers continued to support the Indian traders.

Some white boycotters were driven by greed. Leaders of the campaign, in particular a Mr Mussmann, promised aspirant white shopkeepers that if they sustained the boycott for six months, the Indians would close their doors and move to India, leaving their businesses open to new ownership.

The Indian shopkeepers suffered greatly during the boycott. Even under normal circumstances, virtually all of them were perpetually in debt to the wholesalers. They enjoyed the trust and goodwill of their suppliers because their business dealings were based on a certain ethos, the almost religious belief that, come hell or high water, debts had to be paid. Bankruptcy was tainted with shame and failure, and was to be avoided at all costs.

The wholesalers in Johannesburg had developed respect and trust for the Indian shop owners and were generous in extending credit and not pressing for payment, but during the boycott much more was needed to keep up the morale of the shopkeepers. No one could foresee how long the boycott would last, and the patience of the wholesalers was not limitless.

The Indians in Schweizer drew some comfort from the loyalty of a handful of whites – the Terblanches, the Oosthuizens, the Pretoriuses, the Van Aswegens and others who refused to join the boycott. Terblanche, who had walked from the Free State with his family during the depression, had meanwhile experienced a reversal of fortune and was running a successful transport business. His customers were all whites, and when he refused to boycott the Indians, his fellow Afrikaners turned against him, not only taking their business elsewhere, but ostracising him and his family. Still he refused to join the boycott, notwithstanding the fact that throughout the Second World War, he had been the local commandant of the right-wing Ossewa Brandwag.

Throughout the apartheid years, there were people like Terblanche, whose personal loyalties were in direct contradiction to the policies of the political party they supported. This remains one of the enduring anomalies of the Afrikaner psyche.

At Ismail Meer's invitation, the Reverend Michael Scott had begun sharing the flat at Kholvad House with us during the Passive Resistance Campaign. At the height of the boycott, he decided to visit Schweizer-Reneke and see if there was anything he could do to normalise the situation.

I drove him from Johannesburg on a dry and sunny winter's day. The Transvaal grasses stretched to the horizon, waiting for either rain or fire. It was as if the parched earth had sloughed off the old year's tired skin of dust and lay still, anticipating spring. We arrived to an atmosphere of weariness and suspense, barely hidden by the quietness of the streets or the comforting warmth of the winter sun.

Shunning the idea of going to the local hotel, Scott preferred to stay at my family's house. From there, each morning, he would go alone on foot from farm to farm and to the homes of other boycotters to talk to them about their 'unchristian' actions. He continued these visits for several weeks, and as a man of the cloth, he was given a polite but generally non-committal reception.

After some months, the boycott began to lose momentum and small cracks appeared in the overall strategy. Many boycotters who had enjoyed favourable credit facilities and friendly personal service at Indian shops had failed to find suitable alternatives. At first they went to Indian shops in neighbouring towns where they were not recognised, but this proved to be time-consuming, costly and inconvenient, and they eventually began to trickle back to the local Indian shops.

However, the boycott leaders, some of whom had vested interests in putting the Indian shopkeepers out of business, were unrelenting. When they failed to dissuade people from breaking the boycott, they decided to intimidate them by deploying pickets and men armed with cameras outside Indian shops.

At this stage, the Springbok Legion entered the fray. This was a left-wing organisation of ex-soldiers who had seen service in the Second World War.

I do not remember how the decision was arrived at, but one Saturday morning I was told to drive one of two cars carrying several of these hefty men to Schweizer-Reneke.

Not having had much to do with military men, my primary experiences with those in service having been with the police, I was rather nervous about the possible outcome of our trip to Schweizer, and when I saw that my passengers were dressed in military uniform, my apprehension increased.

On our journey, I gathered from talk among the men that they intended to physically remove the pickets and cameramen from outside the Indian shops. It all sounded quite exciting, but my trepidation increased even more, and my heartbeat seemed to quicken with every mile we covered.

We arrived in time for breakfast at my parents' house, after which the dozen or so muscular men were just about to set off for the shops when news reached us that some of our equally hefty Afrikaner friends, who had shunned the boycott, had already dealt with the pickets! In the process, they had apparently also grabbed and smashed some of the cameras.

What a relief! And what an anti-climax. The action of the townsfolk put paid to the picketing and harassment, and the brave Springbok Legion volunteers returned to Johannesburg that same day without so much as a harsh word escaping their lips, but the boycott limped on.

By now, it had become a war of attrition between the boycotters and the Indian traders, and the question was, who would weaken first? The Indians had to put up a front of nonchalance, defiance and scorn, and to bolster their bravado they came up with a brilliant and unprecedented idea, one that would also give the impression that they were managing perfectly well financially.

They decided to construct a floodlit tennis court, undoubtedly a 'first' in any rural Transvaal town. Every evening, as darkness offered a welcome respite from the searing heat of the day, the various shop owners would put up the shutters and casually stroll home to change for tennis. Then the entire Indian community would gather around the court, and the players would have a leisurely game under the floodlights, appearing to any spectator to have not a care in the world. As news of this unique phenomenon spread, more and more whites came to witness for themselves this singular nightly event.

And before long, questions were being asked. It was more than six months since Mussmann had confidently predicted that the Indians would leave town and run away to India. Yet here they were, their shops still open, and the only individual who was nowhere to be found was Mussmann, though rumour had it that he was seen in a tiny village near Schweizer.

What precipitated Mussmann's hasty departure was the publication of a photograph in the Communist Party's Afrikaans-language newspaper, *Die Nuwe Stem*. Taken at the opening of the first Indian school in Schweizer-Reneke in

1943, it showed, among others, my father, Mr Cajee, Mr Patel and none other than Mussmann himself, enjoying a cup of tea and Indian savouries!

The newspaper was systematically and widely distributed among the white residents of the town, and ultimately it was a combination of factors that helped the small businessmen to survive and reclaim their niche as important service providers to the community. The patience of the wholesalers, the loyalty of a few white customers, the hypocrisy of boycott leaders and, most importantly, the pervading influence and spirit of the passive resistance movement, all worked to sustain the morale of the victims.

After a while, the trickle of determined white customers returning to Indian shops became a stream, and with the exception of a few hardliners, pre-boycott shopping habits were eventually resumed, but not before reports about the boycott had spread far and wide, even reaching the United Nations.

For the next fifty years, Schweizer-Reneke would remain a hotbed of extreme right-wing Afrikanerdom. Right up to the first democratic elections in 1994, the white voters of Schweizer continued to elect the most conservative elements to represent them in parliament. In the early 1990s, the white community remained stubbornly oblivious to the dramatic changes taking place in South Africa, and continued to harbour hopes that apartheid would remain in place and be entrenched forever.

As life in Schweizer-Reneke returned to its normal rhythm after the boycott, I was entering a new and exciting period, both politically and personally. I had moved into the flat at Kholvad House in Market Street, Johannesburg, in 1947 at IC Meer's invitation. We shared it for a year until he went back to Durban on completion of his law studies, but the flat remained my home until I went underground in 1963.

RELATIONS WITH THE ANC

When bad men combine, the good must associate; else they will fall one by one, an unpitied sacrifice in a contemptible struggle.
— **Edmund Burke**[16]

Through IC and JN Singh, I began to meet an array of interesting personalities, and over the sixteen years that I lived there, scores of politically important people, who would shape the future of South Africa, passed through No. 13 Kholvad House. With nowhere else to meet in a city that was, to all intents and purposes, open only to whites, the flat in Market Street became a hub for activists of other population groups.

From 1947, I began to see more of Nelson Mandela. Broadly speaking we were on the same side, but we differed sharply, especially on tactics. I was in the Young Communist League, while he was prominent in the ANC Youth League and an extreme nationalist, though not a racialist, who did not believe in political alliances with any non-African organisation.

He certainly sympathised with the Indian Passive Resistance Campaign, but as far as cooperation went, he adhered to the Youth League view. This strategic schism was to provide a telling insight into the way of Madiba.

The alliance of the ANC and the South African Indian Congress was greatly strengthened on 9 March 1947 when the Indian congresses of Natal and the Transvaal signed a cooperation pact with the ANC.

The three doctors – Xuma, Dadoo and Naicker – forged and sealed this historic agreement, and my friend and mentor, Ismail Meer, a firm believer in political cooperation between all the people of South Africa, was integrally involved in negotiating 'the Doctors' Pact'.

The agreement strengthened the liberation movement as a whole, and more closely united the oppressed people of South Africa in the struggle against discrimination and racism.

A single example illustrates the impact that the Doctors' Pact had on influencing the attitudes of leading figures towards a policy of cooperation.

> Following a mass meeting to celebrate the signing of the agreement, an enthusiastic Anton Lembede told Walter Sisulu that the Youth Leaguers should accept [the need] to work with other non-Europeans on the basis of equality and independence on matters of common interest. Walter was rather surprised. It had been Lembede who had sponsored a motion (supported by Walter and Oliver Tambo) to exclude communists from membership of the Transvaal ANC unless they first resigned from the Communist Party.[17]

Elinor Sisulu records:

> Walter would later be very embarrassed to admit that on a few occasions, he had also been involved in the breaking up of Communist Party meetings. Walter was never to know whether Lembede's comment on the Doctors' Pact meeting was a one-off comment, or whether it represented a shift in his position on working with the Communists or the Indian Congress. When he walked into Lembede's office on 27 July 1947, he found him writhing in agony. Joined by Nelson Mandela, they called Dr Silas Molema, who had a practice nearby. Molema immediately sent Lembede to Coronation Hospital, where he died on 29 July. 'There are blows from which it is possible to recover quickly; there are others that leave a gaping wound in one's soul for a lifetime.' So wrote journalist and Congress Youth Leaguer Jordan Ngubane in tribute to his friend Anton Lembede. Ngubane's words summed up the feelings of Lembede's friends and colleagues, not least Walter Sisulu, who was beside himself with grief.[18]

MISFORTUNE

A few months earlier, I had been nominated to attend the World Youth Festival in Prague, Czechoslovakia, from 20 July to 17 August, as a representative of the Progressive Youth Council (a coordinating body of a few youth organisations), the Transvaal Youth Congress and the Young Communist League. At that time, travelling abroad was a rare occurrence. People went to India and to Mecca, but very few went to Europe, so there was a great deal of preparation and excitement about my trip. This was enhanced by the fact that among the 'important personalities to be present at the festival [were] Paul Robeson, Ingrid Bergman, Trygve Lie, Albert Einstein, Julian Huxley and Shostakovitch'.[19]

I was scheduled to leave by air on a Sunday morning, but was all packed up and ready to go a few days before. At the same time that the press carried the news that I had been granted a passport for my trip, the ANC Youth League announced that it had elected VT Mbobo, vice-president of the organisation until 1946, to attend the conference as well,[20] but in the end, only Mbobo went.

On the Friday night before our departure, my friend Peppy Ravat and I decided to go to town for some reason or other. We were waiting at the tram stop, and as the tram came into view, we moved towards it. Suddenly, and out of nowhere, a three-wheeled motorcycle travelling at great speed and without any lights on, shot out from behind the tram. Before we realised what was happening, the motorcycle hit me and sped off without stopping. It was the type of motorcycle used almost exclusively by the police, but of course we had no evidence to prove who was responsible, and the culprit was never found.

I was seriously injured. My face was covered in blood and both bones in my left leg were broken. Only the skin held the limb together. I was rushed to hospital and underwent surgery, and when I woke up from the anaesthetic, I was lying in bed with bandages on my face and my whole left leg in plaster. It was well past midnight, and the first faces I saw were those of IC Meer, JN Singh, Dr Dadoo and the Reverend Michael Scott. I was still a minor, and as my guardian, Dadoo had come to authorise the surgery. For the next month in hospital, I was a Very Important Patient, but it took fourteen months before I could dispense with the plaster casts and crutches, a real nuisance.

On the Saturday night after the accident, a chap was brought into my ward with a relatively minor injury, but he cried and made a noise the whole night and kept us all awake. His chief complaint was that he had made plans to take his girlfriend to Zoo Lake the next day, and here he was lying in hospital. I could not help but smile at his predicament, and said to myself, 'Brother, if you only knew where I was supposed to be from Sunday, you wouldn't be making such a fuss.'

THE SISULUS

Real love is so mething beyond the warmth and glow, the excitement and romance of being deeply in love. It is caring as much about the welfare and happiness of your marriage partner as about your own. But real love is not total absorption in each other; it is looking outward in the same direction — together. Love makes burdens lighter — because you divide them. It makes joys far more intense, because you share them. It makes you stronger so you can reach out and become involved with life.

– Reader's Digest, August 1974[21]

Following the Passive Resistance Campaign, Walter Sisulu and I began to form a friendship. It was based on both political commonality and mutual respect. In the late 1940s I met his wonderful wife, Albertina. Like the Fischers and the Chibas, this was a couple that would make a deep and lasting impression on me with their compassion, commitment, depth of sincerity and love, and positive impact on those around them.

In their early years of family life, Albertina continued to work as a nurse, while Walter's mother played an active role in raising the children – Max (born 1945), Lungi (born 1948), Zwelakhe (born 1950), Lindiwe (born 1954) and Nonkululeko (born 1958). The Sisulus also helped raise the children of Walter's sister, Gerald (born 1944) and Beryl (born 1948), and his cousin's son Jongumzi (born 1957).

As would be written about him later, 'Throughout his life, Walter Sisulu showed himself to be a master strategist, an effective mediator, a brilliant organiser and a mobiliser who inspired a devotion and commitment among ordinary people that reflected his own deep, passionate and unswerving dedication to the struggle.' Sisulu was 'a driving force for unity who held together diverse elements that composed the ANC'.[22]

In the last days of January 1948, a year after my release from jail in Durban, we heard that Nathuram Godse had assassinated Mohandas Karamchand Gandhi, Mahatma to the people of India and of South Africa. All Indian shops closed and meetings were held around the country, the largest at Red Square. There was a great sense of shock and loss at this tragedy.

At the beginning of 1948, the Passive Resistance Council decided to defy the Immigrants Regulation Act of 1913, which barred Indians from travelling from one South African province to another without a permit. Batches of volunteers crossed from Natal into the Transvaal in defiance of the law. The campaign lasted only a few months, but by the end of it, some 2 000 volunteers had gone to prison.

I, too, travelled from province to province, but not as part of the campaign. In December 1948, I made my first trip to Cape Town and had my first view of Robben Island from the top of Signal Hill.

A friend, Cassim Amra, had arranged for my companions, three medical students, and I to stay at the home of a wonderful woman, Moms Mohamed, in Keppel Street, Walmer Estate. The house was called The Gem, and both Moms and Pops would become extremely important figures in my life, especially when I was jailed in the Western Cape.

Moms became like a sister to me, and even after Pops died, she continued to make the journey to visit me. But then the security police began to harass her, threatening to withdraw her passport and other dire consequences if she maintained contact with me. Their intimidation worked, and thereafter we could manage only indirect contact through friends and family members.

Another ridiculous consequence of the Immigrants Regulation Act was that a sizeable number of Natal and Transvaal Indians managed to change their classification to Malay or Coloured in order to settle in the Cape. This meant that they could exercise the basic right to freedom of movement, own property and vote, all fundamental liberties that were doled out in South Africa on an arbitrary racial basis, and regarded as 'rights' only for the whites. Many years later, when I was at Pollsmoor Prison, a fascinating and ridiculous debate developed in the prison service about 'rights and privileges'. It raged for years, squandering time, resources and enough paper to remind one of the courts described by Charles Dickens in *Bleak House*.

On that first trip to Cape Town, we tried our best to take a trip to Robben Island, but we could not get permits. Clearly, since I was so keen to get there, the government eventually helped fulfil my wishes, though they took me without a permit, and in an aircraft. I only wanted to visit the island for a few hours in 1948, but I eventually spent nearly eighteen years there!

APARTHEID AND RESISTANCE

Those who imagine that the world is against them
have generally conspired to make it true. – **Anon**[23]

The general election in 1948 tolled the beginning of a new, dangerous, fear-filled and unjust era in my country's history. On 26 May, the pro-Nazi National Party under Dr Daniel François Malan swept to power, defeating Smuts and his United Party. The winning party fought the election under the slogan, 'Apartheid', and their rallying cry was, '*Die Kaffirs en Boesmans op hul plek, en die Koelie uit die land*' ['The Kaffirs and Bushmen in their place, and the Coolie out of the country'].

It is important to remember that racism in South Africa did not originate when the National Party came to power. It started when Jan van Riebeeck landed at the Cape in 1652. But the arch-hypocrite, Jan Smuts, and his South African Party masterminded its most insidious and institutionalised form when the four white-ruled provinces got together and formed a union in 1910. Even in the new, non-racial, democratic South Africa, the disciples of Smuts and the splinter groups spawned by his United Party remained steadfast in their resistance to change and determination to perpetuate white privilege.

In his autobiography, *Let My People Go,* Chief Albert Luthuli eloquently expressed the general attitude of the majority of the South African population to the 1948 election: 'For most of us Africans, bandied about on the field while the game was in progress and then kicked to one side when the game was won, the election seemed largely irrelevant. We had endured Botha, Hertzog and Smuts. It did not seem of much importance whether the whites gave us more Smuts or switched to Malan. Our lot had grown steadily worse, and no election seemed likely to alter the direction in which we were being forced.'[24]

On 3 June, Dr DF Malan became prime minister, and brought together the men who would form his government. Its ideology was based on racist beliefs and its policies were to be overwhelmingly racially motivated. Officially, this government would defend its position as being one of 'separate but equal'. Separation there most certainly was, but so vast was the chasm of inequality that we are still struggling to cross it now, more than half a century later, although great strides have been made.

Repugnant as they were, existing race-based laws were not, in the minds of some white South Africans, harsh enough when the National Party began its reign. The legislation that followed might have been taken straight from Hitler's Third Reich. After all, some of the most prominent members of the NP had unashamedly supported Nazi Germany.

Among the first laws passed was the draconian Group Areas Act, which provided for further and complete separation of ethnic groups into racial ghettoes. At a very personal level, I was deeply affected when this legislation was used to raze my family's shop and houses to the ground in Schweizer-Reneke forty-three years later. Decades afterwards, the unsightly gashes in the surrounding built-up terrain remained as stark and brutal evidence of the callousness of racial engineering.

One of the immediate consequences of National Party government was that the Communist Party's Sunday-night meetings on the steps of the Johannesburg city hall had to stop, since the usual hecklers would have been greatly reinforced by the police. Two years later, the party was banned.

The struggle now faced an extremely vicious enemy, and drastic adjustments had to be made to our strategy.

In early 1949, conflict erupted between Indians and Africans in Durban, and at the height of the riots, I drove a number of TIC officials to the coast. A day or so later, I took Errol Shanley to Clairwood, one of the suburbs in which unrest had occurred. I waited in the car while he went into a house, and when I saw a crowd of stick-wielding, chanting men coming towards the vehicle, I thought my end had come. I crouched under the dashboard and waited, knowing that my Indian skin could put me in a dangerous, possibly even life-threatening situation. Fortunately, the angry mob passed by without looking into the car.

Shortly afterwards, I had to go back to Durban with Molvi Cachalia, who had been given the task of collecting evidence for submission to the Van den Heever Commission, appointed to investigate the riots. His main objective was to gather proof of white incitement and involvement in the unrest, and among the evidence he gathered were photographs that clearly showed whites leading a mob of stick-wielding Africans. However, when Judge Van den Heever ruled that no cross-examination of witnesses would be allowed, the ANC and SAIC withdrew from the commission.

In December 1949 a new ANC leadership was elected. Having realised that all previous attempts to petition and plead for political rights had been futile, the organisation retained its policy of non-violence, which had been in place since it was founded in 1912, but adopted the Programme of Action, which involved new tactics, in the form of mass mobilisation and strike action. The radical Youth League had elected Nelson Mandela and Oliver Tambo to the executive, and Walter Sisulu became the secretary general.

While the ANC was laying the ground for the future, I had to drive Monica Whately, a British woman and UN representative, and Betty du Toit, an Afrikaner and well-known trade unionist, to Basutoland (later Lesotho). The trip was a reminder that the Anglo-Boer War might have ended officially in 1902 but was still raging between the colonial and Afrikaner factions on the ground.

In discussion with Du Toit, Whately simply refused to believe that any territory under direct British control could enforce a colour bar. But when we arrived in Maseru on a cold and rainy night, the hotel manager warmly welcomed the two women, but would not accommodate me. He was solicitous enough, though, to offer me blankets to sleep in the car, and would allow me to use the hotel bathroom in the morning, provided I was up well before any of the guests. The look of triumph on Betty du Toit's face at this manifestation of British 'colour-blindness' was a picture.

We spent two weeks in Basutoland, and encountered yet another glaring example of incipient racism, at a convent, of all places. Asked why the African nuns were not joining us for lunch, the Mother Superior mumbled something about their 'smell'. Whately offered no protest of any kind.

MICHAEL SCOTT

Much of my work at this time involved driving, and in 1949, I made two trips to Bechuanaland (later Botswana). The first was on the instructions of Yusuf Cachalia, and my passenger was the Reverend Michael Scott. Cachalia said Scott would tell me where we were going once we were on the road, and that I was to leave him at our destination and return alone. When I showed some hesitation, not least because of concern over available funds and the reliability of the car, Cachalia advised: 'Go with the spirit of youth, and all will be well.'

So I went, secretly hoping that the road would take us to Cape Town, but when we reached Krugersdorp, Scott informed me that we were on our way to Bechuanaland. Having never been there, I assumed it would be quite a lovely place, but several hundred kilometres further, when a tyre burst, we found ourselves stranded in a desolate landscape with no sign of human habitation.

There was no spare wheel, and after weighing our options, with nothing but Scott's eternal optimism to buoy our spirits, we set off on the long walk to seek assistance. The first person we came across was an old chap reading *Indian Views*. Despite the political interest that his choice of reading material indicated, he was singularly unhelpful and not in the least concerned about our plight. So on we trudged, and some time later we came to a farm.

The owners, whose name was Swart, were taking a Sunday afternoon nap, but when we explained our difficulties, they were most hospitable. While Scott and I rinsed off the dust of our long walk, Mrs Swart made tea and scones, and as we sat down to enjoy them she suddenly asked, out of the blue: 'Do you know Dr Dadoo?' It turned out that she had grown up with Dadoo in Krugersdorp.

Her husband produced a spare tyre and drove us back to our vehicle, and we were soon back on the road. However, our troubles were not over.

There had been heavy rains and the roads were waterlogged, and the car got bogged down in the mud. We pushed and manoeuvred in vain, and just as we were beginning to get despondent, a Jeep belonging to Chief Tshekedi Khama came along, and the driver recognised Scott. In no time at all our belongings had been transferred to the Jeep, and we were on our way to Serowe.

Scott and I stayed at the chief's home for about ten days, during which time we also met the later Sir Seretse Khama. Various chiefs came from South West Africa because they had heard that Scott was on his way to the United Nations, and wanted him to make representations on behalf of their people. They brought money (coins and notes) in small bags for Scott. It was a fascinating experience and I was sad to leave, but Chief Khama's people had pulled the car out of the mud with oxen and I had matters to attend to at home. I was not looking forward to making the trip alone, however, but luckily Scott remembered at the last moment that he had to address a meeting of his diocese that weekend, and accompanied me after all.

This did not meet with Yusuf Cachalia's approval, however, and he insisted that Scott return to Bechuanaland immediately, and resume his journey to New York. To my relief, plans had been made for Scott to fly this time, but it was not to be. At the airport, we were informed that he would be allowed to board the aircraft only if he first surrendered his passport, and since that would mean he could not come back to South Africa, he refused.

So, once again, we set off for Bechuanaland, but this time my friend Peppy came as well, to provide me with company on the return journey.

At about 6 a.m., we stopped by the roadside near Lobatse so that Peppy and I could wash and freshen up, using the large container of water we were carrying in the car, while Scott went off to the nearest hotel to get our flask filled with tea.

As Peppy and I performed out morning ablutions, a police officer rode up on horseback. He questioned us about various things, and was not at all impressed with out responses. Worst of all, although we had passports, they were not valid for Bechuanaland.

Just as Peppy and I began preparing ourselves mentally to being locked up in Lobatse jail, Scott emerged from the hotel. We silently cursed him for appearing at that exact moment, because as a result of his political activism, he was not one of the Bechuanaland administration's favourite people.

Nevertheless, phlegmatic and charming as always, he introduced himself to the policeman, whose entire attitude changed. Not only did his hostility towards Peppy and me disappear entirely, he became decidedly helpful.

Since none of our passports were in order, he suggested we come to his office at 8 a.m., when he would stamp them. Meanwhile, he directed us to the home of the Chands, and told us to say he had sent us. At that time the future capital, Gaberone, was little more than a village, whereas Lobatse was a busy commercial centre, and the Chands had a fairly large shop. We had never met them, but on presenting ourselves with the mounted policeman's compliments, they invited us to share their family breakfast.

Some forty years later, the entire family would be killed in an attack on their home by members of the South African security forces, who believed the Chand home was being used as a transit facility by ANC guerrillas. Even the nightwatchman and the family dog perished in the attack, along with one of the Chand sons, who was mentally handicapped.

Our second journey to Bechuanaland took us close to the border with then Southern Rhodesia, from where Scott boarded a train. Knowing his habits, we specifically asked if he had enough clothes.

'Yes, yes,' he assured us. But when we checked his bags, we found nothing but documents and papers! So Peppy and I gave him all the clothes that we had with us before heading home. That was the last time I saw Scott on African soil, but by the time I got back to Johannesburg, he had sent a telegram, addressed to Ismail Meer and me. It simply said that he could not get a flight to America.

Ismail's reply was unequivocal: 'Proceed to your destination, even if you have to walk.'

Years afterwards, in his autobiography, *A Time to Speak*, Scott vividly described the adventure of his departure from South Africa, when he was driven by two young Indian chaps.

~ 4 ~

A Luta Continua

Apartheid is not just a separation, but a systematic process whereby we are being destroyed.[1]

I was loath to leave my flat. I thought of the many parties and the intense discussions that I had there with Bajee (Reverend Michael Scott), Kathy and Nelson, who had filled the flat with their intelligence, wit and laughter; my neighbours, who never complained; the housewives who sent me delicacies to enjoy. There was consolation in the fact that Kathy took over the flat, and its history would continue with him. **— Ismail Meer[2]**

From 1947 to 1963, my home was a three-bedroom apartment on the third floor of Kholvad House in Market Street, Johannesburg.

Flat 13 belonged to Ismail Meer, who had returned to Durban on completion of his legal studies, leaving me to share what had already earned a reputation as a social and political hub with two medical students.

Coincidentally, Kholvad House had been designed by a talented young architect called Rusty Bernstein, who would later be arrested with me at Rivonia, held in solitary confinement for ninety days and then put on trial.

The last years of the 1940s were a time of increasing political involvement for me, but my passage to adulthood was also marked by a lively social programme and many new friendships. Against the ominous backdrop of growing political repression as the National Party government set about building walls of division on the racist foundations of the past, opportunities to forge bonds with dynamic and committed individuals multiplied. Much of my time was spent at the flat, a gathering place for friends and political allies.

Both Yusuf Dadoo and Michael Scott were regular callers. In fact, Scott had a key to the front door, and often popped in at all hours to bed down before going off again to some remote place or other.

Having left school only a few months before my final exams, I had promised my family that I would take them within a year or so. As time passed, my interest in formal education waned, but fortunately my friend Amien Cajee, and my flatmates, Bis and Cas, kept coaxing me to write the matriculation exam, and eventually I did, passing at the second attempt.

My family harboured some hope that I would study medicine, but I was not fated to be a doctor. For me, it was more important that I dedicate my energy to fighting the unhealthy racism that was increasingly being accepted as the norm for everyday life in South Africa. Racism is a pervasive syndrome that can spread to and poison every part of a system, and in South Africa, everything from the content of newspapers to the use of ablution facilities began to be dictated by discriminatory rules that elevated some people to positions of superiority over others, from the cradle to the grave.

The appointment in 1950 of Dutch-born Dr Hendrik Frensch Verwoerd, the chief architect of apartheid, as Minister of Native Affairs did not bode well for the future.

In early 1950, the police used the Riotous Assemblies Act to issue banning orders against several leaders of the Congress movement, notably JB Marks, Sam Kahn, Dr Dadoo and Moses Kotane.

In protest against the bannings and the imminent passage of the Suppression of Communism Act, the provincial branch of the ANC in the Transvaal, the Indian Congress and the Communist Party organised the Defend Free Speech Convention. May 1 was dubbed 'Freedom Day' and set aside for a strike across the Witwatersrand. It would be the first labour action aimed at the industrial heart of the country, and volunteer groups sprang into action to spread the message.

At a meeting at the Indian Sports Grounds in Benoni, I made our aims plain to the crowd: 'We do not like violence or to take the blood of the white man, we are only demanding justice and to play a rightful role in this country that belongs to us.'[3]

As we prepared for the strike, a small, informal group sprang up that specialised in painting slogans on walls, putting up posters and distributing leaflets. There were six core members – Faried Adams, Mosey Moolla, Herbie Pillay, Solly Esakjee, me, and of course our dear comrade Babla Saloojee – and we took to calling ourselves the 'Picasso Club'. In time, this developed into a cohesive group that would remain active during all the protest campaigns of the 1950s, and even into the early 1960s. Not all the members took part in every activity, but Babla was involved in almost every escapade, every brush with the police and every arrest.

In preparation for the strike, members of the club set off from Flat 13 at about 3 a.m. each day, armed with bundles of leaflets to be handed out at railway stations, hostels and bus stops to thousands of people on their way to work. The downside was that at some point every morning, the police would swoop and arrest us. Fortunately, their powers were still limited, and we were either charged and released on bail, or let off with a warning. Still, in little more than a week, we got to know the inside of police cells at Orlando, Newlands, Jeppe, Marshall Square, Fordsburg, Yeoville and Alexandra.

AN ARGUMENT WITH MADIBA

Although the strike had been organised by the ANC in conjunction with the Communist Party and the Transvaal Indian Congress, the ANC Youth League opposed it. Members argued that it would detract from the ANC's own programme of action, formulated in the wake of the 1949 leadership change, which was more radical and veered towards non-cooperation with other organisations, notably the Communist Party.

It got ugly. The Youth League went as far as disrupting meetings and, on one occasion, Mandela bodily removed Yusuf Cachalia from a public platform. Tensions were running high, and it was in this charged atmosphere that I bumped into Madiba one day in Commissioner Street. After the usual pleasantries, we began talking about preparations for the strike, and our discussion became fairly heated. What began as a friendly exchange developed into a full-blown argument, during which I, with the 'wisdom' of my twenty-one years, made certain utterances to which Madiba took umbrage.

My parting shot was to challenge him, unwisely, to a public debate at a venue of his choice, with the rejoinder: 'I'll beat you!' He got quite angry, and I thought that was the end of it, but it was not.

Although the police imposed severe restrictions on meetings, preparations for the strike went ahead, but political tension escalated dramatically when the police opened fire on crowds of unarmed people who had gathered in several African townships on Freedom Day, killing eighteen and injuring many more. But the strike was a success. The ANC called a meeting of the national executive with the Indian Congress and the Communist Party, and it was during these formalities that I discovered how deeply I had offended Madiba.

To my great embarrassment, he stood up and complained about my disrespect towards him. I was shocked and shamed by the accusation, and expected my mentors to defend me. Instead, Ismail Meer appealed to him not to take this 'hot-headed youngster' seriously and, much to my chagrin, asked Madiba and the gathering to dismiss my behaviour as the intemperate outburst of a 'youngster'. My humiliation was complete. It was a tense moment, but Mandela relented.

Years later in prison, we teased each other about this, and he admitted that he was wrong about the strike. What the incident revealed to me was that Madiba was a man who was not afraid to express himself forcefully, whatever the circumstances, but that he could listen to and accept views that differed from his own.

I recovered from my embarrassment and continued to serve as a Transvaal Indian Youth Congress representative at meetings of ANCYL, as disconcertingly detailed reports from police spies confirm. A confidential report from Inspector Botha to the police commissioner, dated 17 January 1949, recorded my presence, on behalf of the TIYC, at a meeting of ANCYL's Transvaal branch in the Trades Hall, Johannesburg.

Another memorandum, marked 'secret', reflected my contribution to a Communist Party meeting in Sophiatown on Sunday 26 February 1950, as follows:

A Kathrada, subject of NA 706, was then introduced as the last speaker. He stated that the bitter struggle in which the working people are involved, was caused by a government that has gone mad. This situation has been introduced by the government, influenced by the 'Broederbond', who have no interest in non-European affairs. As a result, brutal raids of the police are intensified. Apartheid is not just a separation, but a systematic process whereby we are being destroyed. The colour policy resulted recently in riots and we are not going to stand aside and watch our sisters and brothers being shot by the police. He continued by saying that he was an Indian communist and as such their friend. He compared the Indian and Native situation in South Africa and maintained that they are suffering under the same yoke. The white ruling class is frightened by people like Sam Kahn and Dr Dadoo because every speech by them is another nail in the coffin of oppression. Kathrada concluded by saying that the people will resist any attack on the Communist Party and that Malan must stop before it is too late.[4]

Following the killings of 1 May, a joint meeting of the national executives of the congresses designated 26 June 1950 as a national day of protest and mourning for the eighteen people killed by the police, and the call went out for people to stay at home on that day. The date assumed special significance for the Congress movement, and in 1952 was deliberately chosen for the start of the Defiance Campaign. In 1955, the Congress of the People was also held on 25 and 26 June.

Changing attitudes

At Kholvad House, we realised quite early on that some of the neighbours did not take kindly to the stream of traffic at all hours of the day and night – men, women, children; workers, teachers, doctors, lawyers, students; whites, Africans, Coloureds, Indians, people of every hue and religious persuasion. Racial and religious prejudice raised their ugly heads.

Of course, none of the neighbours spoke to me directly, nor were my visitors openly insulted or abused. Everything was done behind our backs, but in such a way that we would get the message loud and clear. The problem was an old and familiar one: they had been brought up to believe that Africans, and to a lesser extent Coloureds, were prospective robbers, gangsters and rapists, and that all non-Muslims, including whites, were somehow different and inferior.

We simply carried on with our normal life. My friend Ahmed Khota, whom we called 'Quarter', as in 'quarter-pint', made a point of trying to change the attitude of some neighbours by talking to them, and, unbeknown to us, they were watching the comings and goings at Flat 13, and learning.

Chief Albert Luthuli frequently stayed at the flat, and whenever he was in town I gave him a spare key. One Saturday afternoon, around five, I arrived home to find him pacing up and down the passage outside the flat, having forgotten to take his key with him that morning.

He said he had been waiting since about 3.30 p.m. and then, to my complete surprise, added that some very nice people had noticed his predicament and invited him to their flat for tea and cakes.

I assumed it must have been my friend Babla's brother, who lived on the fourth floor, but the chief insisted that he had gone to one of the flats on our floor. I was dumbfounded, and had him point out the exact door.

The occupants were known to us as the most conservative, narrow-minded and racist of all the tenants in the building, yet it was indeed they who had come to the chief's rescue!

In time, all the neighbours shed their ingrained bias, and, without exception, developed excellent relations with the tenants in Flat 13.

My second mother and my Fordsburg aunts

In the absence of my own family, warmth, affection and some wonderful home-cooked meals were lavished on me by the mothers of my friends and fellow activists. My 'Fordsburg aunts' were uncomplicated and humble women, who by no stretch of the imagination could be regarded as political beings.

My 'second mother', on the other hand, the remarkable Aminabai Pahad, had a devotion to her husband and children matched only by her dedicated fight against racism and injustice.

Of course the 'aunts' knew and experienced at first hand the evil of apartheid, and their empathy with those who actively opposed it was both natural and abundant, but they had not the slightest idea that their children were deeply involved in illegal, and often dangerous, political matters.

They did know of my political activity, but not the details, and accepted me into their homes and hearts as a friend of their sons, Tommy, Herbie and Bobby. Their political innocence allowed them to simply ignore the police surveillance of my movements, and their love and support never wavered.

I was friends with both of Auntie Vassen's sons, but especially so with Tommy, the eldest. He and his wife Dela lived in a flat in Park Road, and I visited them often. Our political discussions evidently made an impression on their children that we were unaware of, at least until I walked into their flat one Sunday morning to be greeted by little Delia, aged four, with: 'Good morning, Mr Sabotage!'

Later, when I was placed under house arrest for thirteen hours of each day, and from noon on Saturday until Monday morning, it became impossible for me to visit them or go to the Pahad home for lunch or supper. My neighbours in Kholvad House took it upon themselves – nay, actually vied with one another – to see to my needs, and Aminabai would send food packages every so often. On Sundays, my three 'Fordsburg aunts' insisted on sending me my favourite dishes – fish curry, sheep's trotters, russo (a strong soup which is made in Tamil homes) and sweets.

Their generosity and care continued even when I spent ninety days in solitary confinement in 1963, and throughout my nine-month trial. On my birthday in detention, they sent me special treats, and it was quite the most enjoyable meal I had during that entire period, as much for the food itself as the strong signal that, even in the face of possible harassment and victimisation by the police, our friends remained loyal and steadfast.

Alone in my cell, with nothing to read and no contact with anyone, including the comrades who had been arrested with me, with the prospect of a death sentence eclipsing all other thoughts, it was gestures such as my birthday meal that kept my morale high and boosted my courage, allowing me to successfully withstand the psychological pressure and proffered bribes of my interrogators.

All fear and doubt could be banished by the memory of love and loyalty over many years by the 'aunts', my 'second mother' and many others like them. With such thoughts uppermost in my mind, I would recite my personal mantra: I will resist; I will not break down; I will not betray my comrades; I will not cooperate with my enemy.

Having died at the age of ninety-five, one of my three 'Fordsburg aunts', Kissie Reddy, was cremated in Johannesburg in October 2001. Herbie Pillay, Dr Essop Jassat and I were among the pallbearers.

I was alone in my flat when her niece informed me of her death. I put away my book and sat down at the desk to jot down notes about my association with her. Her two sisters, Auntie Rangee Vassen and Auntie Vengetty Pillay, had died some years earlier in London, where they went to be with their exiled children.

As the memories flooded into my mind, I was reminded anew that, during the long years in prison, whenever I thought about recording my life story, my primary motivation was to pay tribute to two of the most wonderful people I ever knew: Babla Saloojee and Aminabai Pahad, whose love and support began when I was in my late teens and lasted a lifetime, more than compensating for the distance that separated me from my biological mother.[5]

It was, in fact, as a child in Schweizer that I first met the Pahad family. As fellow shop owners, they were friendly with my family before moving to Ophirton in Johannesburg, and then to a flat at 11 Orient House in Bekker Street – diagonally opposite Kholvad House.

I had visited them once or twice in Ophirton, but it was really after I moved to Flat 13 in 1947 that my relationship with the Pahads evolved into a deep and lasting association.

Goolambhai and Aminabai[6] had five sons, Ismail, Essop, Aziz, Nassim and Zuneid, all of them younger than me, when they unofficially adopted me. It must have irked the younger boys tremendously when their mother would berate them for any misbehaviour by saying: 'Why can't you be more like Kathy?'

According to Essop, this was as much an endorsement of my character as approval of my political consciousness.

Though in my late teens, I still felt the absence of a mother, and Aminabai was a wonderful surrogate. My visits to the family became so frequent that if, for some reason, I missed lunch or supper, she would telephone to find out where I was and if I was having a decent meal. When I was laid up with the flu or some other minor ailment, she brought me food and medication and fussed over me as only a mother can.

In return, I would drive her where she wanted to be, occasionally accompany her to social functions, and stay in the Orient House flat when both she and Goolambhai were away.

Aminabai was an exceptional person, warm, friendly, always smiling, generous, compassionate and hospitable to a fault. Her hard work and hospitality became legendary among the countless friends, family members and political colleagues – many of whom were strangers – who visited the Pahads from all over South Africa.

The five Pahad boys and I were always bringing friends, comrades and colleagues to the flat, which was generally filled with people. I was there almost daily and cannot recall a single occasion on which someone was not visiting. Sometimes it would be Chief Luthuli, at others, members of the Dynamos Soccer Club or some of the boys' sporting friends. Often, the visitors were from out of town and had heard about the Pahads from mutual acquaintances or political colleagues.

Their flat at Orient House and mine at Kholvad House served not only as venues where comrades and friends could meet socially and celebrate weddings and other special events, but also as the scene of numerous political meetings. Once, while the Congress leaders were meeting at Orient House, Aminabai sent young Essop to ascertain if we wanted tea or coffee. He was a tall chap, taller than me, in fact, and although he was ten years younger, he looked quite adult. To my chagrin, he addressed me as Uncle Kathy, making me feel so advanced in years that I left the meeting long enough to remonstrate with him: 'Don't call me uncle any more!'

I was young and hot-blooded, but hopefully not overly harsh in meting out discipline to the Pahad boys, whom I regarded as younger brothers. I know I was a demanding political mentor, expecting nothing less than that they sacrifice their personal boyish interests in favour of maximum participation in the mobilisation against oppression.

In the early 1960s Essop – who loved soccer – opted to play a game for Dynamos instead of attending a meeting of the Transvaal Indian Youth Congress, although he was a member of the executive. He never forgot the lecture I gave him on how disciplined and committed an activist had to be! On another occasion, when he was at Wits University in 1961, he arrived at a meeting armed with new ideas from another first-year political science student, and suggested that an organisation be formed in opposition to the National Union of South African Students (NUSAS). I listened to his ill-considered, yet sincere, argument, then stood up and asked: 'What is wrong with Comrade Essop? Why does he come here with Trotskyite rubbish?'

Perhaps I was too stringent in my treatment of these enthusiastic young activists, whom I love as brothers!

One of my more significant contributions to the political education of the Pahad brothers was showing them, by example, that although I was married to the struggle, I nonetheless made time to socialise with friends and family and build a rich and multifaceted life for myself.

In fact, given the impact that my social life must have had on some of my more conservative Hindu and Muslim neighbours at Kholvad House, it's astonishing that they were so tolerant and understanding, even in matters of which they had little experience. They accepted without question the wide diversity of people who visited my flat, and endured without complaint the noise of both political meetings and lively parties. Even the residents of Adams Mansions, the block of flats immediately behind Kholvad House, put up with the racket.

Aminabai and Goolambhai were dedicated activists in their own right, willing to make great sacrifices in the struggle for freedom and justice. She was so much more than a good and gracious housewife, and would be imprisoned on at least three occasions for her political activity, the first time for taking part in the Passive Resistance Campaign. Throughout her life, Aminabai remained fiercely and passionately opposed to any form of racism and injustice.

She was among the first volunteers from the Transvaal to occupy the vacant lot in Durban in 1946, leaving behind her children, of whom the youngest was a mere two years old at the time, and going to prison for a month.

Later in the campaign she was imprisoned again, explaining, perhaps only partly in jest, that she did not want her husband to know the humiliation and ordeal of going to jail, and would rather volunteer in his place.

The Defiance Campaign against Unjust Laws, launched by the ANC in 1952, found Aminabai once again among the ranks of volunteers, and she went to prison once more.

It is almost impossible to measure the influence of activists such as Mrs Pahad. Her name was never to be found among the speakers at political rallies and she played no part in strategy discussions, but in his autobiography, Nelson Mandela wrote: 'I often visited the home of Amina Pahad for lunch, and then, suddenly, this charming woman put aside her apron and went to jail for her beliefs. If I had once questioned the willingness of the Indian community to protest against oppression, I no longer could.'[7]

The generosity, kindness and hospitality of the Pahad family were unprecedented. There was almost never a mealtime when non-family members did not arrive unexpectedly, and, as if by magic, an ever-smiling Aminabai would rustle up enough delicious victuals to feed us all.

The last time I saw her was when she came to the court in Pretoria during my trial in 1964. After this, she and Goolambhai, and their banned sons, Essop and Aziz, went to live first in England and then in India. I was on Robben Island when another son, Nassim, sent me a telegram saying she had been killed in an accident in Bombay. It was a tremendous shock to all who knew her.

My 'Fordsburg aunts' and my 'second mother', along with many, many others like them, never knew what an immeasurable contribution they had made to the struggle in their own small ways, but they are the unsung heroes and heroines of our fight for freedom.

In addition to the mouth-watering meals served by Aminabai and the 'aunts', my friends and I could enjoy a variety of delicious dishes prepared by Thomas, our resident chef. Concerned that as a young bachelor I was not eating properly, my family had sent Thomas from Schweizer-Reneke to take care of me.

One afternoon, under the pretext of having him make dumplings for them, Khatun and Rahima, the wives of two of my friends, persuaded Thomas to spill the beans on our nocturnal activities, and after that, we called him Dumplings.

Thomas was a grand chef, but as a young man with an active social life, I had some qualms about what accounts of my escapades he might be conveying back to my family and the conservative, rural community of Schweizer-Reneke, and used the Treason Trial arrests as an excuse to send Mr Dumplings home.

Of course, it was then up to me, and the many visitors to the flat, to provide meals. Our best friend in the kitchen was a broiler, which required no skill at all, just a little seasoning and a time switch. In any event, we did not cook often. Thanks to the wonderful and generous neighbours, there was a constant delivery of tasty dishes to Flat 13. We were rather lax about returning the containers, though, so the good women of Kholvad House would wait until we were out to descend on the domestic helper and reclaim their crockery.

The friends I spent the most time with were the Vassen brothers, Tommy and Bobby, Aggie Patel, Solly Jooma, Paul Joseph, Herbie Pillay, Amien Cajee, Babla Saloojee and Harry Naidoo.

I like to think that I set a few of my friends on the road to culinary greatness, or at least adequacy. When I was on Robben Island, Tommy Vassen wrote to me from London about a few successful meals he had produced. I replied: 'I'm very proud to learn of your and Harry's culinary achievements and would like to believe that my contribution towards the early training was not absent. Though some cynics would insist that the main contribution came via the inspiration of Chagan.'[8]

From my recollection of our meals together in the days before my imprisonment, the two of them must have improved considerably for Tommy's wife to risk exposing guests to the product of his hands! After all, the fare at Flat 13 was generally simple and straightforward, with the emphasis on quantity rather than quality, and thanks to the little gadget that switched off automatically and simultaneously sounded a warning bell, there was little danger of burnt victuals. I have fond memories of that dear little machine. How majestically it rested on the table – efficient, loyal and an ever-ready ally against any attempt at intrusion by a member of Eve's race. How unobtrusively it helped preserve that little alcove as man's domain.

SOPHIATOWN

It has been my experience that folks who have no vices
have very few virtues.   **– Abraham Lincoln**[9]

I used to spend a fair amount of time in Sophiatown, a vibrant place, highly politicised and militant. Unfortunately many people, especially whites, developed a tendency to romanticise life in Sophiatown, but the true nature of the area can be found in the words and pictures of Can Themba, Peter Magubane and Bob Gosani, among others. Can Themba wrote:

> Somewhere here, and among a thousand more individualistic things, is the magic of Sophiatown. It is different and itself. You don't just find your place here, you make it and you find yourself. There's a tang about it. You might now and then have to give way to others making their ways of life by methods not in the book. But you can't be bored. You have the right to listen to the latest jazz records at Ah Sing's over the road. You can even walk a Coloured girl of an evening down to the Odin Cinema, no questions asked. You can try out Rhugubar's curry with your bare fingers without embarrassment. All this with no sense of heresy.[10]

Some of the Sophiatown characters, like Robert Resha and Joe Modise, were close friends of mine and also involved in politics, so I occasionally spent a weekend there. Other times, when I had to speak at a meeting in Sophiatown, I would stay for the rest of the day.

My Sophiatown friends were highly respected by the gangsters, and I came to know several of them, both in Sophiatown and Newclare. After some Indian shops were burnt down in Newclare, JB Marks and I invited quite a number of the gang leaders to a social gathering at a shebeen, where liquor was served. Several people advised against this folly, but we made it a rule that as soon as the gangsters arrived, they had to surrender their weapons. They were piled in a corner while rival gang leaders enjoyed the party, and afterwards peace was restored.

During 1953 and 1954, I was deeply involved in the campaigns against Bantu Education and the destruction of Sophiatown, which led to me being arrested several times.

The forced removals began in 1955, but it took thousands of armed policemen and soldiers more than four years to relocate all the residents of Sophiatown to the desolate, outlying area that would form the nucleus of Soweto.

THE PICASSO CLUB

My great friend Babla Saloojee was fond of impersonating lawyers, a story we shall come to presently. But he also tried his hand at art, in the form of political graffiti, via the Picasso Club. Near the notoriously dehumanising mine hostels, a road sign bearing the words 'Natives cross here' warned drivers to watch out for pedestrians. I think it was Babla who wittily amended the message by inserting 'very' between the words 'Natives' and 'cross'.

Leaflet distribution was the most mundane and least hazardous of the Picasso Club's duties, but some of us were arrested once for contravening some or other regulation. The options were to admit guilt and pay a fine, or appear in court and plead not guilty. We chose to go to court, but when we were told which advocate would defend us, Babla protested vehemently. He suggested we would be better off representing ourselves than entrusting our fate to this particular advocate, whose court appearances did not reflect his acknowledged brilliant legal mind.

During the discussion that ensued, we persuaded Babla to accept our lawyers, especially as they were not charging for their services. The advocate duly presented the only defence we could possibly offer, but failed to convince the magistrate that we were innocent. It was hard to face Babla afterwards, the more so since the fine we had to pay was much higher than it would have been if we had admitted guilt from the outset!

Putting up posters on walls was not only illegal, unless one had permission from the authorities, but required great effort, along with a bucket of glue, paintbrushes and, most important, lookouts to keep watch. One cold winter's night, Mosey, Esakjee, Babla and I had successfully put up all our posters but one, and were ready to go home and to bed.

Then Babla suggested that a fitting end to the night's work would be to stick the last poster on the wall of Gray's Building, headquarters of the security police. 'You haven't got the guts,' Esakjee challenged Babla.

'I'll do it,' he replied.

'You won't do it,' argued Esakjee.

'Drive there,' ordered Babla.

Mosey and I found ourselves agreeing to this foolhardy proposal, and I drove past Gray's several times until we were satisfied that the coast was clear. Babla jumped out with bucket, brush and poster, and in record time, stuck up the poster and came running back to the car, mission accomplished. Or so we thought.

We were a block or two away when we heard the ominous wail of a police car's siren. I don't know what went through my mind, but I decided to make a dash for it. After a high-speed chase, we were blocked at the intersection of

Eloff and Commissioner streets. It was about two in the morning, and bitterly cold. Although we were dressed in warm clothes, the thought of spending the rest of the night in police cells was most unappealing. Two white police officers came towards us, guns at the ready, and ordered us out of the car with our hands up. I can still picture Esakjee slowly emerging with his hands in the air, saying, 'You've got me covered.'

The police were not quite as affable, but when the sergeant heard my name, he immediately asked where I was from. On hearing 'Schweizer-Reneke', he underwent a metamorphosis, and turned out to be yet another friend of the family!

While we stood there, waiting to be arrested, all he wanted to know was how the various members of the Kathrada clan were doing. Eventually, he waved us on our way with an avuncular piece of advice: 'Chaps, please – next time you put up posters, don't put them on government buildings. Put them up anywhere else, and contact us when you need … when you're in trouble or anything.' With that, we bade the officer goodnight, and went home.

Less than a decade later, Babla would return to Gray's, but the outcome would be tragically different from events on the night of our poster prank.

The Picasso Club's true forte lay in slogan writing. All of us, but Babla in particular, were constantly on the lookout for suitable walls to convey, in the briefest and most effective manner, the particular campaign message of the time. The underlying idea was to gain maximum exposure, not only on the wall, but hopefully also in the press.

Our best work included 'We Won't Move' (during the Sophiatown anti-removal campaign), 'Asi khwelwa' (during the bus boycotts), 'Free Mandela' and 'Asinamali' (during the trade union campaign for higher wages).

One night during the anti-removal campaign, we went on a slogan-painting mission in Sophiatown, Martindale and Newclare. Herbie was the designated 'scribe', while Babla and I were the lookouts. Unlike Faried, who had mastered the art of painting huge letters with clarity and speed, Herbie was meticulous and slow. When the police descended on us with a suddenness that made it impossible for Babla to issue a warning, Herbie remained oblivious, carefully crafting each letter, then stepping back to admire his handiwork and ask for my opinion.

The police said nothing until he was finished, at which point one of them assured Herbie that it looked very nice, adding: 'Now you're under arrest; come with us.'

During our campaign for public libraries in our residential areas, Babla discovered a new paint, and told us excitedly that it was far more effective than what we had been using. It was pitch-black tar paint, and we wasted no time trying it out.

Our target was the long wall of the Johannesburg public library, which was open to whites only. I lived just a few blocks from the building, but had never been allowed inside.

The Picasso Club painted 'Let Us Black Folk Read' along the length of the wall, and a few days later we learnt just how effective the paint was through a report in *The Star*, in which municipal officials complained that it had proved impossible to remove the slogan by any of the usual methods, and they had to resort, at great cost, to sandblasting the wall to get rid of it. The publicity did our campaign no harm, of course, and after a while we returned to the newly pristine wall, this time painting the message: 'We Black Folk Ain't Reading Yet'.

It was impossible to gauge how much of a contribution our slogans made to people's lives, but they must have had some effect, as it wasn't long before a public library, to which we had access, was opened in Fordsburg.

The Picasso Club's activities, started during the Passive Resistance Campaign in 1946, continued all through the Treason Trial, and even into the early 1960s.

SOLLY JOOMA

One of the regular guests at Flat 13 was Solly Jooma, both a political ally and close friend. He lived in Middelburg, about 150 kilometres from Johannesburg, but as a travelling salesman, he spent a great deal of time in the city and often stayed at the flat. But on a fateful Saturday night in the mid-1950s, Solly slept at the home of Aggie Patel instead.

We had been to Reggie Vandeyar's wedding, a truly festive occasion, with dancing, eating and surreptitious consumption of alcohol. Like just about all our social functions, the wedding was non-racial.

As the party drew to a close, an uninvited guest named Leon arrived and immediately started acting in a provocative manner, picking arguments with guests and making politically hostile remarks. The Congress movement had introduced a boycott against a certain brand of cigarettes – I forget why – and Leon deliberately took out a pack of the offending cigarettes and smoked one after another.

After a heated argument when we closed the party with the singing of 'Nkosi Sikelel' iAfrica' and Leon loudly interrupted to demand that we sing 'God Save the Queen' instead, Aggie Patel invited a few people to his flat nearby for coffee. Solly Jooma went as well, and by the time everyone else left, it was so late that he decided to sleep at Aggie's flat.

The early morning quiet was shattered by a loud banging on the door, followed by policemen breaking it down and forcing their way into the flat. Leon was with them, having reported seeing white women and Indian men entering the building together.

That was enough, in the bigoted minds of apartheid's minions, to warrant a raid under the Immorality Act. Solly, sleeping in the passage, was the first to be knocked down. As Aggie emerged from the bedroom, the police grabbed and beat him, badly.

When his wife, Khatun, walked out into the passage, Sergeant Visser's worst fears were automatically confirmed. Although Indian, Khatun's complexion was light enough to suggest that she was white, and Visser, enraged by this 'evidence' that there had been intimacy across the colour bar, assaulted Aggie so severely that he broke his jaw.

The three frightened Patel children witnessed this brutal attack on their father, which might well have been far worse if not for the unexpected arrival of Dr Moosa. He had been passing the building on an early morning house call, heard the commotion and came to investigate.

Like Khatun, Moosa was light-skinned, and his presence infuriated Visser even more, since he was clearly just another 'kaffirboetie'[11] hampering the work of the police. Visser promptly assaulted Moosa too, and only when he demanded the names of everyone in the flat did it dawn on him that they were all Indians.

Not even this stopped him, however. He arrested Aggie, Solly and Moosa, took them to the Fordsburg police station and charged all three with resisting arrest and assaulting police officers. A terrified Khatun and a neighbour walked two kilometres to my flat to get help.

At the police station, I was shocked by the severity of the injuries that were obviously causing Aggie, Solly and Dr Moosa great pain. I found them sitting on a bench, no attempt having been made to provide medical attention. The police insisted that they would have to pay bail before being released, and even though the sun was not yet up, I knocked on the doors of friends and colleagues to raise the necessary amount.

Before taking them to the hospital for treatment, I had photographs taken to record their injuries. Aggie's were the most serious, and for a considerable period, while his broken jaw healed, he had to take all sustenance in liquid form, through a drinking straw. Ruth First lent the Patels her liquidiser.

When they appeared in court a few weeks after the assault, their defence advocate was one of the finest in the country, Vernon Berrangé. The magistrate rejected Visser's claims that the police had been attacked, and acquitted all three accused. The verdict was greeted with spontaneous applause from the public gallery, along with shouts of 'Afrika' and the ANC salute. From where I sat, I had a clear view of Visser, who was visibly angered by the verdict.

But we were so jubilant at the outcome that we paid scant attention to his scowling face and barely suppressed rage, and even less to his threat: '*Ek sal julle kry*' ['I will get you'].

Aggie, Solly and Dr Moosa sued the government for damages. The case was settled out of court, and the three of them received a sum of money. It was a rare victory for us, and one that provided much satisfaction.

With that, we thought a nasty chapter had been closed, but Molvi Cachalia, either much wiser or relying on some kind of premonition, warned us to be careful and to avoid dark streets late at night. We should have taken him more seriously.

Some weeks later, I was awakened by an urgent knocking on my front door around 4 a.m. I opened the door to find some policemen and Molvi's younger brother, Yusuf. Well aware of my natural antagonism towards apartheid's law enforcers, Yusuf urged me to stay calm before giving me the terrible news.

Solly had been killed. He had been bludgeoned to death, his face smashed almost beyond recognition, his body left in the gutter of Goch Street, Newtown, in the rain.

The police wanted me to go with them to corroborate Yusuf's identification of his body, but I was in a state of shock, my head reeling, my heart racing. I had never before experienced such feelings. I sat down and told the police that I could not bear to see my dear friend in that state. 'No, let somebody else go and do that,' I pleaded. They could see how upset I was, and left.

At Solly's funeral in Middelburg, attended by a large crowd, I managed to pluck up enough courage to look at his dear face for the last time. It was swollen, and barely recognisable.

'What sort of human being,' I asked myself, 'what sort of mentality, is responsible for an act of such savagery?'

Solly had not a single enemy in the world. He was loved and respected by all who knew him, and none of his friends could think of anyone who hated him as deeply as this brutal attack indicated.

I told the investigating officer, Sergeant Ackerman, the same thing when he visited me in the course of the investigation. There was not a single person I suspected, not even remotely. But Ackerman was persistent, urging me: 'Even if you think it is far-fetched, just give us the names.'

At length, and after some incisive probing by Ackerman, I mentioned the Visser affair, but immediately said I honestly did not think he could be involved in Solly's death.

But he was. Not long afterwards, Ackerman came to the flat one evening to inform me that he had arrested Visser, who would be charged with Solly's murder. There was ample evidence, Ackerman said, linking Visser to my friend's death. I was shocked.

After a preparatory examination, Visser was ordered to stand trial before Justice Rumpff[12] and two assessors. While Visser was giving evidence in his defence, the judge asked him why, after killing Jooma, he found it necessary to repeatedly crush the dead man's face with the heel of his boots. Visser replied that he wanted to give the impression that Jooma was killed by 'kaffirs', because he believed that only 'kaffirs' killed people in that manner.

Found guilty of culpable homicide, Visser was sentenced to ten years in prison and six lashes. In passing sentence, the judge described the murder as most cruel and brutal. He made some scathing remarks about the police, and said that he believed Visser should be given the death sentence, but the assessors had found grounds for leniency.

Within a matter of days, Enver Matthews and Barney Desai happened to see Visser, with his wife and child, outside a department store in Cape Town. They rushed off to find photographer Howard Lawrence,[13] who worked for the *Cape Argus*, but the editor refused to publish the photographs he took, probably because, at the time, English-speaking white South Africans had either actively thrown their weight behind the policy of apartheid, or chose to remain silent.

Knowing that there was still one newspaper with the courage and integrity to expose the injustices of apartheid, regardless of the consequences, Enver, Barney and Howard took the damning evidence to the weekly, *New Age*. The very next issue carried a front-page story about Visser, along with the photograph proving that he was not in jail. When Congress of Democrats member Len Lee Warden raised the matter in parliament, the Minister of Justice, CR Swart, denied the allegations in the *New Age* report, and dismissed it as 'typical communist propaganda'.

His reaction gave rise to some doubt and concern among the staff of *New Age*. Fearing that they had made a mistake, they sent the photographs to various people who had previously seen Visser face to face. We confirmed the identity of the man in the photograph and made affidavits to this effect.

Armed with this corroboration, Len Lee Warden raised the matter in parliament again, and this time Swart could not simply dismiss it. He grudgingly agreed to investigate, and after a while reported back that Visser had been sent from prison to Valkenberg, a psychiatric hospital in the Western Cape, and was released from there by mistake.

He was allegedly rearrested, but if he went to prison at all, it could not have been for long, because he was back on the streets of Johannesburg before we were arrested in 1963.

ACTS OF IMMORALITY

If you want to understand life, stop believing what other people say and write, but observe yourself, and think. — **Anton Chekhov**[14]

So the miscarriages of justice continued, with countless innocent people falling victim to the arbitrary application of the law and state-sponsored violence directed on all levels at the non-white population of the country. Men, women and children were affected. And, in 1956, the women rose up in protest.

The infamous pass system had roots dating back to 1896, when it became compulsory to carry Transvaal pass badges to discourage desertion from the mines. More stringent legislation on identity documents was introduced in 1946, but the National Party government's decision in 1955 to include urban African women among those subject to the hated pass laws evoked widespread resistance.

In 1956, more than 20 000 women staged a historic march on the Union Buildings in Pretoria, the very seat of government, in protest against the injustices of the pass system. By the following year, discontent was rife, and in Johannesburg alone, more than 2 000 women were arrested for defying the pass laws. They were defended in court by the legal firm of Mandela & Tambo.

It was a time of heightened emotions, with political activity increasingly focused on the anti-pass campaign, but we still found time to have fun.

One Saturday night, after sharing a meal at my flat, Tommy Vassen, Harry Naidoo, Quarter and I went downstairs to my car, so that I could drive them home. It was around midnight, and we were surprised to see a well-dressed white man sitting on the pavement across the street, apparently waiting for a bus.

We strolled over to inform him that there were no buses running at that time of night, and, to my astonishment, I recognised him as a senior prosecutor at the Johannesburg regional court.

He was clearly drunk and not very coherent, and my instinctive reaction was to find a way in which we could exploit the situation and cause maximum embarrassment and harm to the system we despised.

In an offer devoid of any shred of altruism, I asked the man if he would like to come up to my flat for a drink, after which I would drive him home. He accepted, and we all went back upstairs, turned on some music and poured nightcaps. All the time, however, I was furiously trying to think of how we could turn the situation to our advantage, but it was the prosecutor himself who offered the solution.

Sprawled on the couch, a glass in one hand, cigarette in the other, his head thrown back slightly, his eyes glazed, the man asked us to arrange a sexual encounter between him and an African woman! This was better than anything I might have envisaged, but we had to act fast.

I made a few frantic telephone calls, hoping to find a photographer who, even at such a late hour, would be interested in capturing a 'scoop' on camera. Finding no one, I left our guest in the capable hands of my friends and drove to the offices of the *Sunday Express*. The night editor could hardly believe his luck, and agreed to send a photographer to my flat immediately, but I also extracted a solemn undertaking that he would not publish the photographs until he got the go-ahead from me.

Next, I had to find someone to play the part of a 'loose woman'. I quickly tracked down the person I had in mind at a party in Fordsburg, and explained what she would have to do — all, of course, in the interest of the struggle. I assured her that there would be no untoward behaviour.

When 'L', as we shall call her, arrived at my flat, she took a seat next to the highly intoxicated prosecutor, and before long he had his arms around her and was enthusiastically kissing and fondling our 'bait'.

The rest of us had taken up positions that allowed the photographer to hide behind us, and he took some great shots. As soon as he had enough, we manoeuvred 'L' away from the amorous suitor and someone drove her back to her party.

It had been an unexpectedly eventful night and we were tired, but it took a fair amount of persuasion to coax our unwitting victim downstairs and to my car. He kept asking what had happened to 'L', but by this time he was decidedly unsteady on his feet and two of us had to support him. As we lurched out of the building, the photographer took another shot, using his flash. This had not been part of the plan, and the sudden burst of light penetrated the prosecutor's befuddled brain. It took some fast talking on our part to persuade him that no one had taken a photograph and that he had merely seen a flash of lightning, but eventually we got him into the car.

He kept on asking for 'L', and refused to tell us where he lived until we promised that we would arrange another date for him. Strangely, he also urged us to stand together, and promised his help in return for our favours.

A few hours later, still not sure what we should do with the damning photographs, I drove to Nelson Mandela's house to boastfully inform him of our 'scoop'. Not only was Madiba defending the pass offenders against our wayward prosecutor, but he was at the forefront of the struggle, and I felt confident that he would appreciate the political capital that could be made from our compromising photographs.

Questions of ethics and propriety had not entered my mind, but during the course of my discussion with Mandela, I was forced to consider the morality of the crafty plot that I had engineered. He made no judgment, but he did put the situation into perspective.

'We know this man supports the National Party,' said Madiba, 'but as a prosecutor, he is scrupulously fair. Should we destroy him simply because he is a Nat?'

With the seed of doubt planted in my mind, I went to see two more of my lawyer friends, Joe Slovo and Harold Wolpe. They both knew the prosecutor and, like Mandela, held him in high esteem. The consensus was that he was not someone we should target for destruction.

The next step was to ensure that the incriminating photographs did not fall into the wrong hands. Fortunately, the senior manager of the *Sunday Express* was a friend of Joe's, and he agreed to destroy both the photographs and the negatives.

The prosecutor's indiscretion was never exposed, and a short time afterwards, he was promoted to the post of magistrate.

In hindsight, I was overcome by shame and embarrassment. My plan, born of political immaturity, was unworthy of the proud traditions of the political movement in which I was deeply involved, and it was thanks to the wisdom and foresight of Mandela, Slovo and Wolpe that I was prevented from sinking to the venal depths that characterised the very system we opposed.

The segregation laws not only caused animosity and resentment between the various racial groups, but also stirred up deep and conflicting emotions, sometimes to tragic effect. One evening, a young Indian boy, the son of a friend of mine, arrived at my flat with an attractive young Afrikaner girl. They had fallen in love and been charged under the Immorality Act, but were out on bail.

I was surprised to see them, but we made tea and sat down for a chat, during the course of which it emerged that the two young people were extremely depressed by the thought of going to prison for no other reason than that they loved each other.

They had, it seemed, decided that death would be a better option, and essentially, wanted to jump from my third-floor window. Naturally, I talked them out of it, and later drove them home, but it was deeply disturbing to me that a cruel and indifferent system could drive young people to such desperate lengths.

Later, I would experience the heartlessness of the Immorality Act at first hand. After nearly ten years on Robben Island, someone I loved very much sent me a Christmas card from England. She signed it Yasmin, the name by which I referred to her in letters to mutual friends, and under which one or two of her letters had previously slipped through the prison censorship net.

However, by 1973, the authorities had established her true identity and knew that she was "*n blanke vrou*' ['a white woman']. It would be thirty years before I knew it, but in a memorandum dated 10 January 1973, the prison censor ordered that I was not to be given the card, but that it was to be placed in my file, as it was 'not in the interest of national policy for a white to be corresponding with a non-white'.

So perverse was the Immorality Act that when my friend Dr Paul Hendrickse, a medical specialist, visited South Africa in 1962 from Nigeria, to which he had emigrated, he and his British wife were obliged to take separate accommodation.

Throughout this period of political tension and inequity, Flat 13, Kholvad House, was a refuge for a wide range of people determined to change the system that oppressed us. Alex La Guma once wrote a column about Flat 13 in *New Age*, and Dennis Brutus and Richard Rive were inspired to compose poetry about my home and the variety of personalities who passed through it.

On the last night of 1962, a large group of my friends gathered at the flat while we debated where best to see in the New Year. Some opted for the Danube, but in the end we went to Ophirton, and had a wonderful time.

Little did we know that this would be the last time we would be there together, or that none of us would ever again be as carefree as we were that New Year's Eve. For some, 1963 would bring marriage, children, a new life in England. For me, the watershed year that changed so many of our lives would lead to Rivonia and Robben Island.

Oppression Knows
No Boundaries

*It was the same shame which we knew so well, which submerged us after
the selections, and every time we had to witness or undergo an outrage ...
the shame which the just man experiences when confronted by a crime
committed by another, and he feels remorse because of its existence, because
of its having been irrevocably introduced into the world of existing things,
and because his will has proven nonexistent or feeble and was incapable
of putting up a good defence.* — **Primo Levi**[1]

The twentieth century was a definitive time for the planet, challenging
human beings spiritually, ethically, intellectually and on a broad range of
issues. While we advanced technologically and mechanically, and entrenched
systems for managing our societies bureaucratically, many of the new political

ideologies presented inflexible and even cruel approaches to dealing with our fellow creatures.

The polarities of human belief found expression in the battle to shrug off the yoke of colonialism; the struggle to wrest power from the hands of the few and distribute resources to the many; the crusades against racism, sexism, exploitation, anti-Semitism and xenophobia. Ideology, as well as the more skilfully disguised motives of profit and power, shaped global conflict.

The recurring theme of man's inhumanity to man reverberated around the world at different times, from the Anglo-Boer War in South Africa at the start of the century, to the Cold War in the middle, and heinous acts in Bosnia, Rwanda and Afghanistan during the death throes of those 100 years.

In some respects, the atrocities and carnage of the Second World War, the premeditated cruelty that it exposed us to, encapsulates the great moral tragedy of the twentieth century. It is one thing to hear about war crimes from others, be touched by their shadow through books and films, but it is another thing entirely to enter the belly of the dead beast yourself and be surrounded by the voiceless bones of those it has devoured.

In 1950, the year in which Paul Robeson, Pablo Neruda and Pablo Picasso shared the International World Peace Prize,[2] the National Party government in South Africa introduced the Suppression of Communism Act, the ominous Group Areas Act, the Immorality Act and the Population Registration Act.

Having completed my matric at the insistence of friends, I enrolled at the University of the Witwatersrand for a Bachelor of Arts degree. One of my co-students was Ismail Mohamed, who would later become Chief Justice of South Africa, while Harold Wolpe was my sociology lecturer. I joined the Students Liberal Association, which I represented at the 1951 congress of the International Union of Students in Warsaw.

I would also attend the third World Festival of Youth and Students in Berlin as an Indian Youth Congress delegate, and work at the Budapest head-quarters of the World Federation of Democratic Youth for three years.

TRAVELS ABROAD

The rule for travelling abroad is to take our common sense with us, and leave our prejudices behind.   **– William Hazlitt**[3]

History is a vast early warning system.   **– Norman Couping**[4]

Foreign travel was still something of a novelty when I was young, and a large crowd of well-wishers turned out to wish me bon voyage. Joe Matthews, son of Professor ZK Matthews, drove me to the airport.

Flying to Europe from South Africa was an exciting experience in the days before jet travel. We made five stops – at Livingstone, Nairobi, Wadi Halfa, Athens and Rome – before reaching London. It was late at night when we landed at Wadi Halfa in the Sudan to refuel, and the passengers were allowed to disembark and stretch their legs. As I emerged from the aircraft, it hit me, for the first time, that I had left South Africa. All my fellow passengers were white, and it was wonderful to see that all the airport officials, from the lowliest cleaners to the customs and immigration officers, were pitch-black Sudanese.

As I paced up and down, an airport official called me aside and said there was someone who wanted to see me. He took me to an office and introduced me to a middle-aged man, dressed in short pants and sandals, who turned out to be a local magistrate.

Somewhat embarrassed by the fact that while the rest of the passengers had to make do with water, I was served with snacks and a hot beverage by the Sudanese officials, I also felt vindicated. All my life I had been on the receiving end of racial discrimination, and now, as an African and a Muslim, I had been singled out, in an African and predominantly Muslim country, for special treatment. It was as if the magistrate was deliberately impressing on my fellow passengers that beyond South Africa's borders, being white did not automatically translate into superiority or privilege.

Brief stops at Athens and Rome helped acclimatise me to another strange phenomenon that I would encounter, first in England and later on the continent menial jobs being done by white men and women.

In London, I was able to renew my friendship with the Reverend Michael Scott, but he was too busy, and not well enough, to accept an invitation as guest of honour at the Berlin Youth Festival in 1951. I also met Rajani Palme Dutt, a leading British communist and walking encyclopaedia, and his friend Harry Pollit, secretary of the British Communist Party.

A couple of weeks later, I took a flight to Prague, and was struck by the fact that as one moved from Western to Eastern Europe, not only the politics but the landscape itself changed. From the hills surrounding the capital of Czechoslovakia the view is dominated by the many churches, and it is easy to understand why Prague, the 'city of a hundred spires', is renowned for its beauty, its architectural wonders and the unique perspective it offers on the history of Bohemia and European life, dating back more than a millennium.

The eye drinks in the panorama of the town and is drawn to the winding course of the Vltava River, segmented by a variety of bridges built at different times in the city's history. Inevitably, one's gaze is drawn to Prague Castle, the great structure of Hradcany that watches, ever vigilant, over the landscape. From this viewpoint, Franz Kafka's disturbing visions and interrogation of modern life whisper loudly into the receptive ear.

It was in Prague that Gauleiter Reinhardt Heydrich – *Der Henker*, or the Hangman – was assassinated on 4 June 1942. Thoughts of the bloody and cruel retribution exacted by his henchmen darkened the edge of my consciousness as I walked the city streets.

The Nazis had accused residents of the little village of Lidice of hiding the assassins. On 9 June, the SS rounded up all the villagers, and the next morning 170 men were shot while their mothers, wives and children looked on. A number of women were also shot on the spot, or as they fled in terror. The rest were sent to Ravensbrück concentration camp, where most perished. Some 100 of Lidice's children were clinically placed with families throughout the Reich, to be raised as Germans. The village was burnt to the ground.

The Nazi killing machine was so efficient that soldiers returned several days later to round up men who had been working in the mines on the day of the massacre. They were taken to Prague and hanged. Surveying the scene of such merciless destruction, I recalled how bravely Julius Fucik had continued to write his last words, almost up to the very moment of his execution. Fucik symbolised resistance to Nazism, and his words, published as *Notes from the Gallows*, took their place in a body of literature that would inspire future generations.

From Prague, we travelled north-east to Budapest by train, a journey set against the magnificent backdrop of the Carpathian Mountains to our left, and the rolling fields and farmlands of rural Hungary unfolded on the right.

Budapest was the headquarters of the World Federation of Democratic Youth, an international organisation founded in London at the end of the Second World War to promote peace.[5] Thanks to my work as secretary of the Transvaal Indian Youth Congress, I was supposed to spend the next three years with the WFDY.

Budapest is a thrilling city, and I soon established a cosmopolitan circle of friends. I lived at the Hotel Duna in Buda, the older section of the two cities separated by the Danube, resonant with the history of conquests and empires. Pest was a hive of activity and industry, abundant with coffee bars, shops and shows, which we attended at night.

Hungary was a novel experience, and I wallowed in all the attention and unsolicited privilege bestowed on me, almost certainly because, in the early 1950s, Indians were virtually unknown in Central and Eastern Europe. Everywhere I went – at cinemas, theatres, restaurants, pleasure resorts – I was ushered to the front of the queue. Some kind soul would spontaneously take my hand and lead me right to the front, while the rest of the patrons looked on in approval. The people were generally aware of race discrimination in South Africa; this was their way of displaying sympathy for a victim.

Budapest also presented me with the opportunity to purchase books and political texts that were either not available or would not have been allowed in South Africa. I posted many of them home to the Cachalias, Joe Matthews and Madiba.

The World Festival of Youth and Students for Peace and Friendship took place in East Berlin over a two-week period in late 1951. Sonia Bunting and sixty other young activists flew from South Africa and England (where many of them were studying) to attend the festival, and I was nominated leader of the group.

There were some moving events that I shall never forget, social gatherings where young people met and talked, sang, danced, ate, drank, kissed, embraced and pledged everlasting friendship. Thus Vietnamese met the French, Koreans talked to Americans, and Israelis consorted with Germans. In a gesture of solidarity, delegates sent postcards to Paul Robeson and Jomo Kenyatta, who personified the fight against racism and all forms of discrimination.

I spent a couple of nights at what remained of the Adlon Hotel, Hitler's favourite Berlin hostelry. Like many other structures in the city, it had been badly damaged. The entire landscape was pockmarked with piles of rubble and the skeletons of once grand buildings, and throughout Germany, the ravages of war were still apparent. On our journey through the lands fed by the Elbe River, about thirty kilometres from the Czechoslovakian border, we had passed through Dresden, and for many years afterwards the ruined town became synonymous in my mind with District Six, Sophiatown and other areas razed to the ground in the name of ideology.

Delegates at the conference made a special effort to offer their hands in friendship to the German people, overwhelmed by massive collective guilt, amid pledges that never again would there be a war such as the one that had ended six years before. The festival was a tremendous success, not least thanks to the friendliness, hospitality and warmth of the German people, especially the youth. I was made an honorary member of the *Freie Deutsche Jugend*, and returned home with my blue shirt of membership.

After the festival I headed for Warsaw, where I was to participate in the Conference of the International Union of Students. On a visit to a Polish farm, two young Turkish girls suddenly stopped in their tracks to gaze at an animal. We could not understand their amazement at first, but it turned out that they were seeing a pig for the first time in their lives. One girl was the daughter of the acclaimed and politically persecuted Turkish poet, Nazim Hikmet. I remember reading how Hikmet, persecuted for much of his life before he went into exile in the USSR, survived solitary confinement in a filthy latrine by singing. I, too, took great solace in music during my time in solitary confinement.

When we went to what had been the Warsaw ghetto, I was reminded of the Nazi atrocities in Czechoslovakia. The Jews who rose up in Warsaw had been crushed as ruthlessly as the villagers of Lidice.

Confined to an area of the city behind a wall eighteen kilometres long and almost three metres high, the beleaguered Jews had been warned by one of the rare escapees from Treblinka that extermination waited at the end of a nightmarish rail journey in closed cattle cars.

Led by Mordecai Anielewicz, the young and the brave rose up against their captors on 19 April 1943. By 8 May, the uprising had been crushed, and rather than be taken prisoner, Anielewicz and others took their own lives. In a gesture symbolic of the annihilation of a people and a culture, the SS general in charge ordered the destruction of the Great Synagogue of Warsaw, and reported to his Nazi masters that 'The ghetto is no more.' When I visited the site of this blot on humanity, only a modest monument marked the murder of tens of thousands of Jews and paid tribute to the handful who fought back and died. One hopes that in dealing with the long-suffering people of Palestine, the leaders of modern-day Israel find enough resonance with the treatment of their fathers and grandmothers to act humanely and with compassion.

Of all the post-war images recorded on my European odyssey, the one that became indelibly printed on my mind was a visit to the former concentration camp at Auschwitz. I could never obliterate the sight of the trench in which dogs mauled and savaged people to death; the gas chambers and incinerators; the lamp shades made of human skin, the pillows stuffed with human hair.

Auschwitz is arguably the most poignant reminder to mankind of the evils of racism. It is all but impossible to describe the emotions that surged through me as I walked on the fragments of human bones littering the street near the incinerators. My friend Johan broke down and wept, and I doubt he ever forgot that visit, or the vow he made there.

Knowing that such horrors should never be forgotten, I carefully collected a handful of bone fragments and brought them back to South Africa when I returned, as a reminder of the consequences of racism. Some years later, the police found them during a raid on my flat. When I explained what they were, and where they were from, one of the policemen callously remarked: '*Dit was seker net Jode nê?*' ['They were probably just Jews, not so?'].

During my stay in Budapest, I sent a great deal of communist literature to Nelson Mandela, who was a voracious reader. I knew that although he had close relationships with communists such as Joe Slovo and his wife Ruth First, Yusuf Dadoo, JB Marks and Moses Kotane, Marxist thinking had been anathema to Mandela since his early days in the ANC Youth League. He considered it a foreign notion, and not what Africa wanted or needed, but nevertheless made the effort to read and understand as much as possible of this and other political viewpoints. He accepted the need for the ANC to have a balanced foreign policy vis-à-vis the socialist East and capitalist West.

When we were on Robben Island together, we 'veteran' communists discovered, to our shame, that we knew far less about Marx and Engels than Mandela did. This did not make him a communist, but typically, if any subject was important enough, he made it his business to master it.

Prior to my departure for Europe, I was as good as engaged to a young woman, and for a while we stayed in touch by correspondence. Then I did a despicable thing. Having decided that I did not, after all, want to get married, I simply stopped writing to her – without a word of explanation or apology, then or even after I returned to South Africa. I deeply regret the pain and humiliation my unilateral decision caused her.

Before the end of 1951, news reached me from home about plans to launch a joint defiance campaign, including strikes, boycotts, non-cooperation, civil disobedience and rejection of 'dummy' apartheid institutions designed to represent the voice of the African people. The underlying motivation was to transform the ANC into a people's organisation as a prelude to mass action.

According to Mandela he, Walter Sisulu and others were influenced by Gandhi's non-violent struggle in India, and by the South African Indian Congress's 1946 Passive Resistance Campaign, in their efforts to promote the programme of action. Two critical events in 1946, he wrote, 'shaped my political development and the directions of the struggle'. The mineworkers' strike and the Passive Resistance Campaign 'forced me to recast my whole approach to political work. The Indian campaign became a model for the type of protest that we in the Youth League were calling for. It instilled a spirit of defiance and radicalism among the people, broke the fear of prison.'[6]

In far-off Budapest, I became restless and increasingly homesick. I was all of twenty-three, and smitten by the bug of self-importance and an exaggerated sense of what I could contribute to the unfolding drama. The urge to go home became almost an obsession, but I realised that my personal feeling of 'indispensability' would not be enough to convince the WFDY to cut short my planned three-year stay. It was important for them to have me there, because I was the only person from the entire African continent at WFDY headquarters. In desperation, I resorted to a strategy that, in retrospect, was at the very least unethical.

I asked my friend and comrade, Amien Cajee, to have the Youth Congress write and say they needed me to come home. I cannot recall my feelings when the letter arrived, but more than half a century later, it occurred to me that I might have benefited from staying in Budapest for the full three years. There was so much to learn.

But letters from home and clippings from the *Guardian* conveyed an unprecedented thrust towards a head-on confrontation between the liberation movement and the apartheid regime, and I yearned to be part of the action.

In June 1951, the ANC's National Executive invited the SAIC and the Franchise Action Council (a Cape Town-based organisation established to mobilise people against the proposed disenfranchisement of the Coloureds) to discuss a joint campaign of passive resistance and a general strike.

On learning this, my thoughts reverted to events surrounding the Freedom Day Strike in 1950, when ANCYL vigorously opposed cooperation with the other congresses and the Communist Party. Barely a year later, the ANCYL leadership had undergone a metamorphosis, and was enthusiastically embracing the sentiments expressed by ANC treasurer general, Dr SM Molema, at the opening of the SAIC conference: 'Only so long as the white man can succeed in making us believe that non-European destinies are antagonistic or incompatible will he succeed in destroying us one by one. If we realise the identity of our lot and combine to do relentless battle for our legitimate and common rights of life and liberty, we shall save ourselves and our children, and no power on earth can prevent our success.'

My journey home began in May 1952, via Prague and London, but this time I was anxious to reach my destination, and spent little time admiring the sights and sounds of these magnificent cities.

THE RETURN HOME

If most of us are ashamed of shoddy clothes and shoddy furniture, let us be more ashamed of shoddy ideas and shoddy philosophies.
— Albert Einstein[7]

I travelled home by sea, and it was on board the *Carnarvon Castle* that I experienced apartheid as practised by the British shipping line, Cunard. I had a cabin to myself on the upper deck, with a porthole through which I could observe the endless sea.

Among the passengers was a single Coloured family. They were allocated a table on their own in the dining hall for the entire journey. But the stewards were in a quandary about where to seat me, though it was obvious that there were plenty of empty chairs at various tables.

Eventually, they placed me with a kindly and elderly Englishwoman at a small table on the edge of the main dining area.

My companion, Harriet Goddard, was not politically active, but she had enjoyed a comfortable upbringing and felt it her duty to spend the next few years doing charitable work among the poor in South Africa. For once, I was thankful to apartheid. It was responsible for me finding myself at the same table as a warm and caring human being, who went out of her way to ensure that my voyage was pleasant.

But there was an unexpectedly naughty side to Harriet, which caused me great embarrassment. In keeping with tradition, passengers were expected to don fancy dress for the party when the ship crossed the equator, and I was to be her escort.

Naturally, I went to her cabin to fetch her, and when she opened the door, I was shocked beyond belief. Harriet had decided to go as Eve, and the apparition that greeted me was the last thing I would have expected. Nevertheless, we went to the party, and I somehow survived the stares and sniggers.

I had also befriended the few South African students who were on board, but it was noticeable that the closer we got to Cape Town, the more aloof they became. By the time the ship docked, they had reverted totally to the habits of a lifetime as white South Africans.

Walter Sisulu, Duma Nokwe, Alfred Hutchinson, Henry 'Squire' Makgothi and Paul Joseph would attend the next World Youth Festival for Peace in Bucharest, Romania, in 1953, with Walter the guest of honour. All except Sisulu and Nokwe were smuggled out from Cape Town on a ship, and I arranged to get Walter and Duma to Europe by air. The only airline prepared to take them was El Al.

Local festivals were held in Cape Town and Johannesburg. The latter, over two days at Mia's Farm, was hugely successful. We had planned for 500 participants, but three times as many turned up.

I had managed to find a travel agent prepared to help us send people abroad without passports, and this arrangement worked well for quite some time until the government passed legislation making it a criminal offence.

Because I had successfully smuggled Michael Scott out of South Africa a few years earlier, my political leaders had used my services in this regard again. In 1949, I witnessed the arrangements for Dr Dadoo to go to London, from where he would continue his political work, and I facilitated attendance of the Bandung Conference in Indonesia by Moses Kotane and Molvi Cachalia.

Duma and Walter were the first to benefit from my clandestine arrangement. They were followed by Leslie Messina in 1954, to attend the WFTU conference, and Lilian Ngoyi and Dora Tamana, who went to the international women's conference. In 1953, I was elected to the WFDY executive in absentia, but I never managed to attend a single meeting.

After the festival, Walter and a few of the others travelled to some of the communist countries, including the Soviet Union, which made a deep impression on him. In a tribute published when he died in 2003, *The Star* recorded:

Being of working-class origin and a member of the oppressed masses, the Soviet visit was an unforgettable experience. Here he was, meeting people of different nationalities, who were once oppressed by tsarist rule. He was invited to speak on Radio Moscow.

In the meantime, at a rally in Johannesburg to mark the 36th anniversary of the October Revolution, Ahmed Kathrada announced that Sisulu and his colleagues were in Moscow celebrating the November 7 anniversary. The announcement caused a sensation to the packed Trades Hall and much annoyance to the Special Branch.[8]

It was undoubtedly a political coup for our festival committee, but the matter was highly sensitive and potentially explosive. It was the first time in decades that an ANC leader had visited a communist country, and by its very nature the entire exercise had needed to be handled clandestinely. Not even the most senior ANC leaders could be consulted in advance. Time and secrecy were of the essence, and at the same time, preparations had to be made to minimise the anticipated damage when the news broke.

I had turned to Madiba for support and assistance. Without hesitation he not only reiterated his support for the Sisulu trip, but undertook to convey the news and explain it to Chief Luthuli and the ANC's National Executive. He assured me that if it became necessary, he would take full responsibility for the action.

In the process, we were afforded a glimpse of Mandela's thinking on the armed struggle a full decade before he would present it to the ANC. He asked Walter to go to China, which had been under communist rule since 1949. Walter discussed with the Chinese leaders the idea of an armed struggle in South Africa, and the possibility of securing a supply of weapons. They lent a sympathetic ear, but advised against an armed struggle on the grounds that it was premature and required considerable political and practical preparation.

My own travel was curtailed even before I stepped off the *Carnarvon Castle* in Cape Town in the middle of 1952. When the ship docked, I was told to wait in my cabin, and in due course a couple of immigration officers, accompanied by members of the security police, entered and informed me that they had instructions to confiscate my passport, which they duly did.

Harriet Goddard, who had waited in the cabin with me, was outraged, and burst into tears. When we parted she extracted a promise from me that I would write, and for a while I did, but after a few months I stopped corresponding with her.

Our paths would cross once more, purely by accident, and she immediately took me to task for having stopped writing. I promised anew to stay in touch, but I didn't, and I never heard of Harriet again.

∾ 6 ∾

Defiance

From the Cape Town docks, Brian Bunting took me to 'The Gem', home of my friends, Moms and Pops. After a day or two I went to Schweizer-Reneke and spent a little time with my mother and family, and then it was back to Johannesburg.

The South Africa to which I returned in May 1952 was a country struggling under increasingly stifling legislation – the National Party was making good on its racist election promises of 1948. The Native Laws Amendment Act restricted and controlled the movement of people in urban areas even further. Without proof of employment, Africans were not permitted to remain in a town or city for longer than seventy-two hours. African men had to carry passes at all times and were only permitted to stay in designated areas. The government's next step would be to extend the iniquitous pass system to African women.

In an atmosphere of heightened political activity, there was much support and enthusiasm for the planned Defiance Campaign. Nelson Mandela was appointed national volunteer-in-chief, with Molvi Cachalia as his deputy.

Addressing a UN seminar in 1989, ES Reddy would sum up the campaign's significance as follows:

> It was the Defiance Campaign of 1952 that promoted wider consciousness of apartheid and led to the establishment of organisations to educate public opinion and assist those persecuted in the struggle against apartheid (e.g. Defence and Aid Fund and Africa Bureau in London, and American Committee on Africa in New York). That campaign – which showed that the African people could organise and lead a civilised mass resistance against a brutish regime – inspired many people in the West, including prominent pacifists and humanists.[1]

A joint planning council had been established to plan and prepare the masses for the campaign. Dr JS Moroka, president of the ANC, headed the council, with Walter Sisulu, JB Marks, Yusuf Dadoo and Yusuf Cachalia as members. The council's final declaration emphasised the need for cooperation and reiterated the 'firm conviction that all the people of South Africa, irrespective of race, colour or creed, have the inalienable and fundamental right to participate directly and fully in the governing councils of the state … the Nationalist government, in its mad desire to enforce apartheid, has at every opportunity incited the people to racial strife and has attempted to crush their legitimate protests by ruthless police action.'

Six laws were to be defied: the Group Areas Act, the Separate Representation of Voters Act, the Suppression of Communism Act, the Bantu Authorities Act, the pass laws, and the stock limitation and rehabilitation schemes. Five of the six had been passed by parliament with simple majorities, but because the Coloured vote was entrenched in the constitution, disenfranchisement under the Separate Representation of Voters Act required a constitutional amendment, and this, in turn, demanded a two-thirds majority in parliament.

The Nats were hell-bent on getting this legislation passed, because it would remove a vital stumbling block to their goal of abolishing the Coloured vote in the Cape. Their first efforts were declared illegal by the Supreme Court, which in those years was staffed by judges who were bold and independent, and did not shirk from unpopular judgments. In order to attain the two-thirds majority, the government eventually resorted to enlarging the senate which, together with the lower house, gave them the required majority.

The ANC and SAIC conferences in December 1951 and January 1952 endorsed the decisions of the Joint Planning Council, albeit with reservations by some leaders of the Natal Indian Congress, Chief Luthuli, Professor Matthews, Dr Njongwe and others. Mandela once again expressed his opposition to the joint campaign with the Indian Congress. He argued that he had only recently been elected as the national president of the ANCYL, and believed that the campaign should be exclusively African. In his auto-biography, he recalled:

'While I had made progress in terms of my opposition to communism, I still feared the influence of Indians ... I raised the matter once more at the national conference ... where the delegates dismissed my view as emphatically as the National Executive had done. Now that my view had been rejected by the highest level of the ANC, I fully accepted the agreed-upon position.'[2]

Mandela's acceptance of the majority view would be the hallmark of his political style. Over the lengthy period we were incarcerated together on Robben Island and at Pollsmoor, I found him to be a democrat par excellence, so much so that, on occasion, I teased him about taking democracy too far.

Reservations about the Defiance Campaign were also expressed by Manilal Gandhi, son of the great Mahatma. He was the editor of *Indian Opinion*, started by his father, and a member of the Natal Indian Congress. Attending the ANC conference as an observer, he asked for permission to speak and, according to Walter Sisulu: 'Gandhi argued that *satyagraha* involved an understanding of certain principles, such as non-violence and discipline. He thought that Africans were not ready for that. His lengthy speech annoyed everybody.'[3]

Gandhi continued to press his views. He visited Walter at his offices and 'continued to argue that the Defiance Campaign was inadvisable. Walter patiently spent hours trying to allay Manilal's fears that the ANC and the campaign were led by communists, but he disagreed with Manilal's view of passive resistance as a quasi-religious tenet. The ANC leaders saw passive resistance as a tactic and not an inviolable principle ...'[4]

It was nothing new for Manilal to be at variance with Congress policy. He was often at odds with the official stance, and instead of working towards consensus, he chose to act unilaterally, with scant regard for the principle of collective discussion and decision. Inevitably, his utterances and actions attracted considerable media attention.

As early as 1946, when the first tentative plans for the Passive Resistance Campaign were being discussed, Manilal was negative. Not content with trying to dissuade Indians in South Africa from supporting the plan, he took his one-man opposition to the Mahatma, knowing the high esteem in which he was held by members of the SAIC.

His primary objection was that communists, including Dr Dadoo, were leading the passive resistance movement. The Mahatma reportedly admonished his son sharply, reminding him that since Dadoo had been democratically elected, it was Manilal's duty to support and serve under him.

Someone, or something, caused Manilal to have a change of heart, and by December 1952, he and Patrick Duncan jointly led a group of volunteers into Germiston location, where they were arrested.

CORRESPONDENCE WITH THE STATE

On 21 January 1952, the ANC issued a written ultimatum to the prime minister, Dr DF Malan, stating that 'the ANC has, since its establishment, endeavoured by every constitutional method to bring to the notice of the government the legitimate demands of the African people and repeatedly pressed, in particular, their inherent right to be directly represented in parliament ... and in all councils of state'.[5] The government was given until 29 February to repeal the six offensive laws. Failure to comply would see mass protests taking place on 6 April – the three-hundredth anniversary of Jan van Riebeeck's arrival in South Africa – as a prelude to the Defiance Campaign.

The ANC made it clear that 'the struggle which our people are about to begin is not directed against any race or racial group but against the unjust laws which keep in perpetual subjection and misery vast sections of the population'.[6]

In his reply, Malan's private secretary, M Aucamp, stated that correspondence from the ANC should be addressed to the Minister of Native Affairs and not to the prime minister. He went on to defend all aspects of the apartheid system, and attempted to justify its laws as benevolent and beneficial for all racial groups in South Africa. 'It should be understood clearly that the government will under no circumstances entertain the idea of giving administrative or executive or legislative powers over Europeans, or within a European community, to Bantu men and women, or to other smaller non-European groups,' said Mr Aucamp. 'The government therefore has no intention of repealing the long-existing laws differentiating between European and Bantu.'[7] If the ANC went ahead with the Defiance Campaign, the government would use all the machinery at its disposal to quell any disturbances and deal with those responsible, he warned.

The Secretary of Native Affairs, Dr Eiselen, maintained that 'many resisters don't understand "unjust laws". The term is a complete misnomer. These laws are vital to our common existence in this country.'[8]

The SAIC also sent a letter to Malan, expressing support for the ANC's ultimatum. In keeping with the government's stance that South Africa had no place for Indians, a 'foreign and outlandish element' that should be sent back to India, there was not even an acknowledgment of receipt.

While the government refused to recognise the SAIC, it enthusiastically promoted a tiny group of Indian conservatives. These were the men who had previously run the SAIC from their business premises, and who had been ousted from leadership positions in the 1945 Congress elections. They later formed the South African Indian Organisation (SAIO) in order to perpetuate their collaborationist practice of begging for crumbs of concessions from the apartheid table, with the sole aim of protecting their own business interests. The SAIO soon faded into oblivion, but some of the founder members would resurface, decades later, in that political aberration known as the House of Delegates.

In reaction to the letters from the ANC and SAIC, the government invoked the Suppression of Communism Act to issue strict banning orders against five senior Congress leaders. JB Marks, Yusuf Dadoo, Moses Kotane, David Bopape and Johnson Ngwevela were the first individuals banned under this legislation, which forced them to resign from all liberation organisations and prohibited them from taking part in any activities of these organisations, or public meetings. Communist Party members Sam Kahn and Fred Carneson were also expelled from parliament and the Cape Provincial Council respectively, and the popular liberation newspaper, the *Guardian*, was banned.

THE DEFIANCE CAMPAIGN TAKES OFF

The 26th of June had been chosen as the date of the formal launch of the Defiance Campaign, but on 31 May, the Joint Planning Council announced that four of the banned leaders would defy the government by attending public meetings, thus inviting arrest. On 2 June, Moses Kotane addressed a public meeting in Alexandra township, and was arrested. Dadoo and Bopape were taken into custody during a meeting at the Lyric Cinema in Fordsburg, which I attended. Along with Marks, all three went to jail for defying their banning orders.

The campaign kicked off as planned on 26 June in Johannesburg, Boksburg, Durban and Port Elizabeth, and soon spread to other centres. I was among those who gathered in Boksburg to lend support to the first fifty volunteers, jointly led by Walter Sisulu, secretary general of the ANC, and Nana Sita, president of the Transvaal Indian Congress.

Walter was a last-minute replacement for the Reverend Mr Tantsi, acting president of the ANC in the Transvaal, who informed Mandela at the eleventh hour that he was feeling unwell and had been advised by his doctor not to court arrest. Walter later revealed that Tantsi had admitted he wasn't ill at all, but had decided he was not in a position to go ahead as planned.[9]

Tantsi's change of heart was a severe setback, the more so because in all major anti-apartheid action, the Congress movement's practice was that leaders led from the front, not by virtue of issuing instructions from the comfort of their offices. However, Madiba's choice of Walter as a substitute for Tantsi was inspired.

After a rousing send-off, accompanied by the singing of freedom songs and shouting of slogans, the volunteers entered Boksburg location without the requisite documents, and were promptly arrested. That night, another fifty volunteers, led by Flag Boshielo, defied the curfew that demanded all Africans be off the streets from 11 p.m. They, too, were arrested.

It was an auspicious start to a campaign that would see close on 10 000 volunteers imprisoned over the course of the next year.

Just before his group was sentenced, Walter made a statement in court spelling out the background to the Defiance Campaign and reiterating the determination of volunteers to resist unjust laws. Since its birth in 1912, he pointed out, the ANC had stood for the abolition of all laws that discriminated against the African people, and had exhausted all constitutional means at its disposal. With each new law introduced by the government, the rights and freedom of Africans were eroded even more.

'As an African, and national secretary of the African National Congress,' he said, 'I cannot stand aside in an issue which is a matter of life and death to my people. I wish to make this solemn vow and in full appreciation of the consequences it entails. As long as I enjoy the confidence of my people, and as long as there is a spark of life and energy in me, I shall fight with courage and determination for the abolition of discriminatory laws and for the freedom of all South Africans, irrespective of colour or creed.'[10]

It was vintage Sisulu. During the more than fifty years that I worked with him, he fought the good fight, remained true to his pledge and his solemn vow, offered his quiet, unwavering courage and determination, his unequalled maturity and foresight, in order to witness the ushering in of democracy and see the great strides towards the non-racial, non-sexist, democratic South Africa for which he had sacrificed everything.

THE TRIAL

In August, the police arrested twenty leading activists, including Mandela, Sisulu, Dadoo, Nana Sita, Yusuf Cachalia, Ntatho Motlana and Molvi Cachalia, under the Suppression of Communism Act. I was caught in the net as well. We were charged with organising and leading the Defiance Campaign with the aim of 'bringing about change in the industrial and social structure of the country through unconstitutional and illegal methods'.

On the first day of our trial, the court reverberated to the deafening chant of slogans and freedom songs and the magistrate found it impossible to proceed. The police admitted their inability to silence the crowd, which included a significant number of schoolchildren, organised by the Indian Youth Congress to demonstrate outside the court. This was twenty-four years before June 1976, and the police had not yet become so brutalised as to open fire on and kill protesting schoolchildren.

The magistrate had a reputation for being tough, and he was much feared by activists, as most of his rulings were tainted with racial overtones. That morning, however, he resorted to the only solution, and asked two of the accused – Dr Moroka and Dr Dadoo – to appeal to the demonstrators to allow the case to continue. The demonstrators obeyed and moved to a nearby public area, where some of us addressed them during the lunch adjournment. Among the protestors were Essop and Aziz Pahad, Mosey Moolla, Herbie Pillay, Faried Adams and Essop Jassat.

The preparatory examination ended with the magistrate committing us for trial in the Supreme Court, where we appeared before Justice Rumpff. As expected, most of the testimony came from police officers, but there were a few surprises waiting for us.

The ANC had been infiltrated by members of the Special Branch. One, known to us as Makanda, spent virtually every day in Walter's office, and was ever ready to run errands and clean the premises. He even offered to polish people's shoes. He would regularly buy food, fish and chips, mostly, and share it with everyone else in the office. He played in a band and readily offered to play at official functions. In fact, he and his band had performed at the function in Johannesburg on 26 June when the first volunteers were sent on their way.

Now here he was in the witness box, under his real name, a detective sergeant in the security police. Given the amount of time we knew he had spent in and around Walter's office, there was little in his testimony that we were not aware of.

Another Special Branch officer turned out to be extremely adept at short-hand, and quoted many of our speeches verbatim to the court. Our defence counsel, advocate Vernon Berrangé, had failed to find anything substantially wrong in his notes, but at one point, while testifying about one specific speech that had been made in a mixture of English, Afrikaans and *tsotsitaal* [gangster slang], the witness punctuated his account with numerous '*blanks*'. For example, he would say 'This *blank* government is now playing with fire. The Boers are going to *blank*.'

The magistrate insisted that the witness fill in the blanks, but after hearing just the first two or three of the crude swear words and vulgarities that had been used, he stopped the flow of profanity and said he had heard enough. It's worth recording that the accused who was being quoted went on to become a well-known professional and successful businessman.

The same witness also testified about some of my speeches, a couple of which were subsequently included in the book *Passive Resistance in South Africa*, by Leo and Hilda Kuper. When I read them many years later, I felt thoroughly ashamed of myself. They were a combination of youthful bravado (because I knew the police were taking notes), arrogance, immaturity, bad politics and, worst of all, some racial slurs.

The most disturbing aspect of our trial was that Dr JS Moroka broke ranks and offered extremely damaging testimony against us. Mandela later wrote:

> The trial should have been an occasion of resolve and solidarity, but it was sullied by a breach of faith by Dr Moroka. The day before the trial I went to see [him]. He said the matter that disturbed him more than any other was that by being defended with the rest of us, he would be associated with men who were communists. I remonstrated with him and said it was the tradition of the ANC to work with anyone who was against racial oppression. But Moroka was unmoved.
>
> The greatest jolt came when Moroka tendered a humiliating plea in mitigation to Judge Rumpff. Asked whether he thought there should be equality between black and white in South Africa, Moroka replied that there would never be such a thing. We felt like slumping in despair in our seats. His performance was a severe blow to the organisation, and we all immediately realised that Dr Moroka's days as ANC president were numbered. He had committed the cardinal sin of putting his own interests ahead of those of the organisation and the people.[11]

Sadly, Moroka's testimony foreshadowed other betrayals. It was the evidence of turncoats that sent Comrade Vuyisile Mini to the gallows. Bartholomew Hlapane and Piet Beyleveld would be responsible for Bram Fischer being sentenced to life imprisonment, and Bruno Mtolo was deeply complicit in the outcome of the Rivonia Trial.

In hindsight, we should probably not have expected from Moroka the same level of militancy, political understanding, acumen and foresight shown by men such as Luthuli and Dadoo. We should have remembered that Moroka had been a leader of the rival All African Convention, and joined the ANC virtually on the day of his election as president general. As such, he had no appreciation of the historical background and internal dynamics that preceded the Defiance Campaign.

Still, Moroka's newfound anti-communism was nothing more than his attempt to rationalise his decision to distance himself from his co-accused in order to impress the court. How soon he had forgotten that, just a year earlier, in the face of an anti-communist campaign, he had publicly endorsed the election of JB Marks – a communist – as president of the ANC in the Transvaal.

Although as hurt and disappointed by his action as everyone else, I could not harbour ill feeling towards Moroka forever. We had sat next to one another for many weeks during the trial, and I had come to know him quite well, so, a decade later, while on my way to Basutoland, I called at his home in Thaba N'chu to pay my respects.

Throughout our trial, the Defiance Campaign had continued in a peaceful and disciplined manner. But, little more than a month before we were sentenced, riots broke out. The unrest began in Port Elizabeth on 18 October, and within three weeks had spread to Johannesburg, Kimberley and East London. The only 'weapons' in the hands of the angry crowds were stones, while the police retaliated with bullets. About forty people were killed, including six whites who fell victim to the rioting crowds. Hundreds of people were wounded and there was extensive damage to government buildings and some churches. The killing of the six whites evoked hysteria in the newspapers, with the *Eastern Province Herald* deploring the 'ill-considered return to jungle law', and the government mouthpiece, *Die Burger*, commenting: 'For a while, primitive Africa was stripped of the veneer of civilisation and escaped from the taming authority of the white man.'[12]

The ANC laid the blame squarely at the doors of the government and the police, and strongly denied that it was responsible for the riots. The respected academic and sociologist, Professor Leo Kuper, supported this view, stating that there was 'no evidence to connect the resistance movement with the disturbances, nor was violence at any time advocated by the resisters as a means of struggle'.[13]

Of greater significance were the words of Judge Rumpff when passing sentence on us. He said that although the Joint Planning Council had envisaged 'a range of acts from open non-compliance of laws to something that equals high treason', he accepted the evidence that we had 'consistently advised your followers to follow a peaceful course of action and to avoid violence in any shape or form'.[14]

As December began, all twenty of us, including Moroka, were found guilty of contravening the Suppression of Communism Act, and sentenced to nine months' imprisonment with hard labour, suspended for three years.

Rumpff's judgment added a new dimension to South African law. Having found us guilty as charged, he ruled that we would now fall into a special category of political offenders – Statutory Communists. At the stroke of his judicial pen, avowed non-communists such as Moroka, Molvi Cachalia – a Muslim priest – and Nana Sita, a Gandhian, were turned into Statutory Communists on whom the police could impose the type of banning order that had previously been reserved for listed members of the Communist Party.

Neither the judge nor any of us could have envisaged that we would meet in a courtroom again just four years later, when Rumpff would head the panel of judges for the Treason Trial.

THE CAMPAIGN ENDS

At various stages of the campaign, approaches were made to the leaders to call it off. The South African Institute of Race Relations was among the first to call for an end to the campaign, advancing reasons that were unacceptable to the leadership. Not surprisingly, the most disingenuous appeal came from the United Party, then under the leadership of JGN Strauss. Two of the leading party members tried to persuade Sisulu and other leaders that if the UP could publicly claim it was responsible for persuading the congresses to call off the Defiance Campaign, its chances of winning the 1953 general election would be greatly enhanced. In return, if it won the majority vote, the UP government would repeal five of the six unjust laws at the heart of the campaign. The pass laws, however, would have to stay.

Either the United Party was naive and ignorant, or typically hypocritical and opportunistic. The pass laws were the most pernicious, humiliating and punitive of all the racist laws. Hundreds of thousands of Africans had been jailed under these laws, and offenders continued to be arrested daily. The Congress leadership was well aware that the UP represented the interests of big business, and the mining houses in particular relied very much on the pass laws to ensure a constant supply of cheap migrant labour. Retention of the pass laws ruled out any possibility of the leadership agreeing to the UP's call.

Former ANC president general Dr Xuma made a similar appeal, although Mandela and Sisulu differed in their recollection of this situation.

Walter suspected that Xuma's approach was linked to that of the Institute of Race Relations. Xuma insisted that it was his personal initiative, and said he was sure that if the campaign was ended, arrangements could be made for Sisulu and Mandela to meet with the prime minister. Walter replied that they were not interested in meeting the prime minister, only in having him repeal the six offending laws.

According to Madiba, Xuma told them that the campaign would soon lose momentum, and it would be wise to halt it before it fizzled out altogether. 'As it was, we continued the campaign for too long. To halt the campaign while it was still on the offensive would have been a shrewd move. Dr Xuma was right: the campaign soon slackened, but in our enthusiasm and even arrogance, we brushed aside his advice. I argued for closure but went along with the majority. By the end of the year the campaign floundered.'[15]

Even with the campaign in its death throes, some of us would not see the writing on the wall. At about this time, the government passed two vicious pieces of legislation, the Criminal Laws Amendment Act and the Public Safety Act. Under the former, anyone protesting against any law by using illegal means risked whipping, imprisonment of up to three years, or both. The Public Safety Act provided for nothing less than the declaration of martial law and detention without trial.

With the best will in the world, it became impossible to breathe new life into the flagging campaign. Early in 1953, Chief Luthuli formally announced that the Defiance Campaign had been called off.

In 1958, I attended a joint meeting of the Congress executives and the South African Congress of Trade Unions to discuss possible protest action to coincide with the forthcoming general election. A strike was under consideration in order to highlight our demand and struggle for universal franchise. Some SACTU comrades insisted that the working class would be satisfied with nothing less than a week-long strike. After much discussion, agreement was reached on a three-day stayaway. As it happened, the response was so poor on the first day that it was called off immediately.

It is true that in respect of several campaigns, we did not recognise the point at which they peaked and should have been called off, but this should not be perceived as failure. At the very least, each protest action stimulated personal contact between activists and the masses, a sine qua non for the success of any liberation organisation.

Although the Defiance Campaign petered out, the positive results far out-weighed any negative perceptions:

- The ANC membership catapulted from a mere 7 000 to more than 100 000, with a large number of functioning branches all over the country.
- It was the first major act of defiance against the apartheid regime and gave concrete meaning to the 1949 programme of action.
- It was the first action of its type and scale conducted jointly by the ANC and SAIC (in the spirit of the Dadoo-Xuma-Naicker Pact).
- For the thousands of volunteers, and many thousands more, it helped remove the stigma and fear of prison.
- It made huge strides in winning global support for the plight and struggle of the oppressed.
- It influenced the formation of the Congress of Democrats to carry the policies and message of Congress to the white sector of the South African population, and paved the way for the Congress Alliance (with SACTU and FEDSAW as adjuncts).
- Most importantly, it gave rise to a new breed of leaders who recognised that the struggle called for courageous actions, which entailed danger and sacrifice. This would pay dividends, especially when the ANC was banned and forced into exile.

In November 1952, Chief Albert Luthuli was stripped of his chieftainship by the apartheid state. A year later, he was elected president of the ANC.

In 1953, I was recruited into the reconstituted South African Communist Party, operating underground. I was happy to once more be serving my principles in my capacity as a member. Harold Wolpe and Joe Slovo telephoned and arranged that we meet in a car parked on Becker Street, and I was assigned to the district committee and a unit of three or four people. We would meet at my flat, or in a motor car. By and large, the units dealt mainly with our work in the Congress movement. For the SACP, we engaged in political education among ourselves and looked for potential recruits.

Amazingly, the party functioned underground without any casualties. While security was always an issue, party members were also members of Congress, which was still legal. In the 1950s the ban on gatherings was not too strict. We did take basic precautions to protect documentation and material, but for the most part, if the security police saw a fellow communist in my company, they simply assumed we were on Congress business. Even when someone was caught with a Marxist publication carrying the party line, *Inkululeko*, the police did not realise that the SACP had been revived.

In 1953, too, the Separate Amenities and Bantu Education Acts were introduced. From then on, all public facilities were segregated and the state was in control of the education of all its citizens.

In its determination to curb, obstruct or prohibit all anti-government activity, the Special Branch applied various tactics, ranging from indiscriminate raids on the homes of certain ANC leaders to accosting them on the street, often under the flimsiest pretext, such as checking that their 'passes' were in order.

One of the most frequent victims of this harassment was Walter Sisulu. His nemesis was Sergeant Dirker, undoubtedly one of the most active and overenthusiastic of the Special Branch's members. He would accost Walter anywhere and at any time and demand to see his passbook. It was just the sort of petty harassment that often resulted in arrests and court appearances, and caused severe disruption to both the domestic and political life of an activist – all of which Dirker knew only too well.

～ 7 ～

Congress of the People, Permits and Prison

Initially, banning orders were issued only against a handful of leaders. One possible reason for this was that the police hoped that by making an example of certain individuals, others would be intimidated. The more plausible explanation, however, is that the legislation in place at the time limited the power of the police.

The Suppression of Communism Act made provision only for people to be banned from attending public gatherings and confined to specific magisterial districts. More drastic action could only be taken against those individuals either listed as having been members of the Communist Party or who had been convicted of an offence under the Act.

In 1953, the government instituted new laws against passive resistance, as well as the Reservation of Separate Amenities Act, Public Safety Act, Criminal Law Amendment Act and the Bantu Education Act.[1]

PROVINCIAL PERMITS

The world is a looking glass, and gives back to every man the reflection of his own face. Frown at it, and it will in turn look sourly upon you; laugh at it and with it, and it is a jolly, kind companion; and so let all young persons take their choice. **– William Thackeray, *Vanity Fair*[2]**

Indians wishing to travel from one province to another for any reason and length of time required a special permit. Failure to produce one was a criminal offence, carrying a sentence of up to three months with no option of a fine.

The Orange Free State prohibited residence by Indians altogether, however temporary. Most Free Staters – white and African – had never even seen an Indian, but this didn't stop them from subscribing to the myth that we were thugs and ogres at best, cannibals at worst.

Indians in possession of the necessary permits were allowed to travel through the Free State, provided they did not stop anywhere for any length of time. The restrictions on interprovincial travel applied only to Indians, though Africans, of course, were subject to the limitations of the pass laws and influx control measures. Coloureds and whites were free to move around the country as they pleased.

The inevitable consequence was that many Indians living in the Cape Province managed by some or other means to acquire 'Coloured' identities, even though this necessitated a change of name in many cases. As race classification became entrenched, this trend spread, with Africans named Ndlovu adopting the surname Oliphant[3] overnight, in order to take up residence in the Western Cape.

Once the security police had blacklisted Indian activists, they could not obtain interprovincial travel permits but, although the apartheid regime was heavily influenced by Nazi and fascist ideologies, the Nats were never able to attain the thoroughness or level of inhumanity and barbarism of the Nazis in their efforts to harass and persecute opponents of the regime. This enabled us to exploit loopholes in the system in order to circumvent the provincial travel regulations.

I had been travelling without permits for many years, but the first time I ran into trouble in this regard was in 1953, in the Eastern Cape town of Uitenhage. Essop Jassat and I had gone to represent the Indian Youth Congress at a joint meeting of the executives of the SA Indian Youth Congress and the ANC Youth League. During a break we stepped outside the hall, and I was promptly accosted by a security policeman, Sergeant Minnie, who politely asked if I had a permit to be in the Cape Province.

Of course I did not, but I managed to whisper hurriedly to Essop that he should say he was a Malay. Since this group was officially classified as Coloured, the travel rules did not apply to them.

To our surprise, Minnie accepted Essop's claim without question. He apologised to me, but made the point that although he had the power to arrest me, he was not going to do so, since he realised I was there specifically to attend the meeting, and he had no wish to disrupt our business. We could carry on, and he would send me a summons to appear in court at a later date on a charge of being in the Cape without a permit.

The meeting ended with the formation of the Joint Youth Action Committee, primarily to facilitate contact with the World Federation of Democratic Youth. I was appointed secretary, with Duma Nokwe as president. As a key member of the Youth Action Committee, I was responsible for coordinating the activities of the youth wings of the African and Indian congresses.

Some weeks later, the summons duly reached me. Despite advocate Harry Bloom's excellent defence, I was found guilty and sentenced to three months imprisonment, suspended for two or three years. Of course, my name was placed on the blacklist, and any further travel permits were out of the question.

VISIONS OF A NON-RACIAL CONGRESS

In his presidential address at the ANC's Cape conference on 15 August 1953, Professor ZK Matthews proposed that a Congress of the People be convened. The National Executive agreed, and in May 1954, Chief Albert Luthuli issued a call for participation by means of leaflets, published in several languages and distributed throughout the country by more than 10 000 'freedom volunteers'. They canvassed support and collected demands from numerous representative groups and organisations.[4] In time, these contributions would be collated by a team, including Rusty Bernstein, and form the template of the landmark Freedom Charter.[5]

While attending a secret meeting in Tongaat to plan the congress, we were alerted to the presence of the police, and managed to destroy incriminating documents just in time. However, I was in a difficult situation. I had travelled to Natal without a permit, and with the suspended sentence hanging over me, I knew that if I was caught, I would have to go to jail for at least three months. There wasn't much time to think and few places to hide, so I did the only thing I could, and hid in one of the motor vehicles until the raid was over.

A couple of months later I was elected as a delegate to the SAIC conference in Durban, a major national event that would attract attention from both the media and the police. I dared not go without a travel permit, but in order to get one, I would have to resort to subterfuge.

Using the address of a friend who lived in the area, I submitted an application to the magistrate's office in Benoni and, to my relief, a permit was issued without any difficulty. Delighted to have outwitted the bureaucrats, I went to the conference, and when the police predictably raided the proceedings, they were more than somewhat deflated when I produced a valid travel permit.

When a petty tyrant is thwarted, he invariably dredges the deepest recesses of his mind to find a way of getting his own back. The police were obviously annoyed that they had no grounds for arrest, and I sensed a determination to see me behind bars one way or another.

A few weeks later, I was summonsed to appear in the Benoni magistrate's court on a charge of perjury, emanating from using a false address in order to obtain a permit.

In order to secure a conviction, the Crown had to show that I had lied under oath. Their chief witness was a magistrate who falsely testified that I had sworn the contents of my application were true. My lawyer, Harold Wolpe, argued that nothing in the statutes prevented an applicant from setting up a special address for the purpose of obtaining a permit. The court agreed, and I was discharged. Having found the weak link in the system, I continued to obtain travel permits in various outlying areas.

But the authorities were determined to put a stop to our activities, and when they realised that the selective banning of leaders had neither dampened the spirits of activists nor curtailed the activities of the various organisations, they widened the net.

BANNINGS AND RESTRICTIONS

On 22 October 1954, I was served with a two-year banning order that not only prohibited me from attending gatherings, but also demanded my resignation from thirty-nine political organisations. Some of them were bodies that I had no connection with at all, while others, such as the Unity Movement, were actually politically opposed to the Congress movement. The real problem, however, was that this section of the banning order was applicable for life. I would never again be able to legally take part in any political activity.

Needless to say, I did not comply, and nor did most others who received similar orders, but these draconian conditions heralded a change of tactics by the security police that would culminate in the widespread practice of detention without trial, torture and state-sponsored murder.

Despite the banning order, I carried on with my work in preparation for the Congress of the People. Of course, I could not physically attend the congress but, like many other banned persons, was able to follow the proceedings from premises adjoining the venue.

My two-year banning order expired towards the end of 1956, but I was almost immediately served with another, this time for five years. In addition to the previous restrictions, I was now also confined to the magisterial district of Johannesburg.

Shortly after my perjury case, Babla Saloojee and Solly Esakjee had cleverly managed to obtain a three-year interprovincial travel permit for me. These were only legally issued to Indians born before 1913 and who met certain other criteria. Armed with this valuable document, I went to Knysna in 1955 for the wedding of Ismail Pahad and Rokeya Kajee. Afterwards, Salim Saleh, Baboo Dadoo, Aggie Patel and I went on to Cape Town.

One night, at a party at the home of Jack Tarshish in Rondebosch, the security police barged in, demanding to know if I was there. Aggie immediately panicked and tried to escape by jumping through a bathroom window, straight into the arms of a waiting policeman. The house was surrounded, and the police had obviously received information about our movements. They soon singled me out from the rest, wanting to know what I was doing in the Cape. Imagine their surprise when I proudly produced my three-year permit!

However, they immediately confiscated it, but not before I insisted on a receipt. I must have had some notion that I could offer the receipt as proof of my right to travel around the country.

The first test of my ingenuity came towards the end of the year, when Aggie, Salim and I went to Bloemfontein with Dr Ike Moosa.

Early one Saturday morning, as we waited for coffee at a restaurant in the Coloured township of Heatherdale, the security police arrived, demanding to see our travel permits. Both Aggie and Dr Moosa had Indian fathers and Malay mothers and were classified as 'Coloured', so they had no problem. Salim offered some or other explanation for not having a permit, and I confidently produced my receipt, explaining that the actual permit was already in the hands of the Special Branch in Cape Town. It made no difference, and we were driven to the police station without further ado.

Tall and middle-aged, the station commander was a decent man, who obviously spent much of his time in the sun. He looked as if he should have been out farming the land, but instead here he was, upholding the law. He had never seen or spoken to Indians in his life. He looked at us and shook his head in wonder and perplexity. Not only did these mythical ogres look much like him, they all spoke Afrikaans!

But he had a major problem. He had cells for whites and cells for Africans. He had no cells for Indians, and his standard rules and regulations were silent on the matter of where we should be held. Eventually, he turned to us for advice, and we informed him that since we were regarded as non-European, he should lock us up in the African cells.

Just as we were settling down for the night on our sleeping mats with some none-too-clean blankets to ward off the cool night air, the cell door opened. In

came the station commander, carrying a stool to sit on. Having seen the inside
of a cell quite often by then, I fell asleep fairly quickly, but Dr Moosa and our
custodian talked long into the night, in Afrikaans, of medical matters. It seemed
the station commander's wife was ailing, and had consulted numerous doctors
without success. Now he had a doctor, albeit an Indian, in his custody, and he
could discuss his wife's condition free of charge.

The next morning, the station commander went to the restaurant in
Heatherdale where we had been picked up, and arranged for food and coffee
to be sent to us. We had made a friend, it seemed, and for the rest of the
weekend, three meals a day were delivered to us from the restaurant.

On Monday morning, events took yet another unexpected turn. The police
had accepted that Aggie and Dr Moosa did not need travel permits. Salim's
case was even more astonishing.

His grandfather, it seemed, hailed from the French colony of Mauritius,
which entitled his direct descendants to the same rights enjoyed in South
Africa by all French citizens. So, although Indian to the bone, the vagaries of
South African law had suddenly transformed Salim Saleh into a Frenchman,
with all the privileges of the whites! His Mauritian name was Alphonso Joseph
Jacquesson, and he was registered as a voter in France. This amused all of us no
end. Salim could not speak a word of French and had been to France only
once, in 1951.

I was thus the sole offender. After a brief court appearance, I was transferred
to the Bloemfontein Prison and spent a few nights there before being released
on bail.

My lawyer was Joe Slovo. Over the next few months, we travelled to
Bloemfontein several times for the case, and I found myself in a ridiculous
situation. The court required my presence in Bloemfontein to face trial, but
the law of the province barred me from staying overnight. The security police
insisted that I obtain special permission from the Minister of Justice, but no
one knew if he even had the authority to grant a dispensation of this nature.
In the end, Joe advised me to simply ignore the situation and attend the court
sessions as required. If the police decided to arrest me, we would deal with it.

Of course, the handwritten receipt for my three-year permit would hold no
water in court, and it could not be denied that I was in the Free State without
a valid travel document, so we had to find a legal loophole through which I
could escape further punishment.

The charge sheet claimed that having entered the Orange Free State without a permit, I had failed to report my presence to the police at the earliest
opportunity. Joe argued that I had passed through many other towns before
reaching Bloemfontein, and there was no evidence before court showing that
I had not reported to the police somewhere along the way.

It was not a strong argument, and the state could have knocked it down quite easily, simply by checking with the police stations along the route, but the magistrate accepted Joe's scenario and discharged me on the main count of being in the Free State without a valid permit.

He did, however, find me guilty of being in the Coloured township of Heatherdale without a permit, and fined me 10 shillings. Four decades later, Free Staters would actively woo Indians to settle in their province!

OLD SHARP

In the early summer of 1954, the police swooped on the Transvaal Indian Congress offices and arrested Paul Joseph, Mosey Moolla and me. They took us to security police headquarters in Gray's Building, on the corner of Von Wielligh and Marshall streets in central Johannesburg.

We were rudely ushered out of the police van and up to the sixth or seventh floor. No sooner had we arrived, than Paul indicated that he had an urgent call of nature. The police were in a quandary: the one available toilet was reserved for 'whites only'. The junior officers looked at their seniors for guidance, the seniors looked at one another. What were they to do?

It was Sergeant Dirker who came up with a solution.

'Where does old Sharp piss?' he asked his colleagues.

And Paul was taken to the toilet used by so-called Coloured Sergeant Sharp.

It wasn't long after this that I was served with my five-year banning order, which restricted my movement to the Johannesburg magisterial district. I made up my mind well in advance that when this banning order expired in January 1962, I would take a long holiday in Cape Town.

CONGRESS OF THE PEOPLE

Although we hardly ever celebrated our birthdays, Eid often saw us getting together at Aminabai Pahad's home. We celebrated Diwali with Jasmatbhai or Narsibhai as our hosts, and spent Christmas with Nelson or the Sisulu family in Soweto. Part of our established Christmas tradition was to visit Helen Joseph. It was wonderful – friends called all day long to convey good wishes, take some refreshment and depart. I was pleased to learn that Helen spent Christmas Day in exactly the same way every year until her death in the early 1990s, with one difference. Helen always set a place at an empty chair, in honour of those of us in prison. What an indomitable lady!

In March 1955 the South African Congress of Trade Unions was formed, adding strength to the United Front alliance under Chief Luthuli. It was the only non-racial federation of unions.[6] The chief's call in 1954 for freedom volunteers had raised a small army of young people, and planning for the Congress of the People became a priority.

The congress was seen as a major and definitive step in shaping the political future, and the ANC, for example, hoped that the impact and legacy of the Kliptown congress would rival that of its founding conference in 1912. The Congress of Democrats, an organisation comprised of left-thinking whites, including Rusty and Hilda Bernstein, Helen Joseph, and Bram and Molly Fischer, saw the COP as an opportunity to forge stronger bonds with sister organisations in the struggle, and to highlight the plight of the majority of the country's citizens for other white South Africans, many of whom were oblivious to or uneducated about the harsh realities of life for non-whites in South Africa.

The two other key organisations involved in planning the Kliptown congress were the Indian Congress and the South African Coloured People's Organisation, SACPO, under the leadership of Stanley Lollan and George Peake, the president. SACPO was closely aligned with the thinking of other struggle organisations and, in fact, Oliver Tambo and Yusuf Cachalia were speakers at its founding conference.

New Age, one of several successors to the *Guardian*, announced on its front page on Thursday 9 June 1955, that the Isithwalandwe Awards, to be presented at the Congress of the People, would go to the Reverend Trevor Huddlestone, Chief Luthuli and Dr Dadoo 'for outstanding service in the name of the liberation movement and the oppressed people of South Africa struggling for their rights'.[7]

I served on the general purposes committee, which was responsible for technical matters such as the fencing of Kliptown Square, erection of the platform, electricity, toilets, water and food. On 25 and 26 June, the atmosphere at Kliptown was tense. Due to my banning order, I could not attend in person, but I had a clear view of events from a vantage point in a nearby storeroom. Officially, 2 844 delegates from all over South Africa attended, but there were also some 3 000 observers.[8]

The security police kept a close eye on proceedings through their field glasses, and took notes of all the speeches. On the Sunday afternoon they moved into action, searching and taking the names of everyone present, ostensibly investigating possible treason charges.

The historical significance of this people's assembly is beyond question. The Freedom Charter became the beacon of the liberation movement and represented the cornerstone of demands by the Congress movement for decades to come.

As one of the guest speakers when the square was renamed in honour of Walter Sisulu forty-seven years later, I recalled the importance of the Congress of the People: 'The demands called for the people to govern and for the land to be shared by those who work it. They called for houses, work, security and for free and equal education. These demands were drawn together in the Freedom Charter, which was adopted at Kliptown on 26 June 1955.["9]

HALFWAY TO ASIA

By the mid-1950s, the government was trying to move Indians to Lenasia, an area bordering Soweto and some distance from the centre of Johannesburg. When people refused to go and live so far from the city, they were threatened with legal action in terms of the Group Areas Act and the demolition of houses, ostensibly as part of slum clearance. One of the crudest manoeuvres was closure of the Booysens High School towards the end of 1954, followed by construction of prefabricated classrooms in Lenasia as the only alternative.

Parents refused to be intimidated, and obeyed the TIC's call for a boycott of the Lenasia school, which found itself with twelve teachers and very few pupils. At the same time, plans were being made to establish a private school in Fordsburg.

With Molly Fischer as principal, the Central Indian High School was probably the first in South Africa with a multiracial staff. Teachers included my erstwhile teacher, Mr Thandray, Alfred Hutchinson, Duma Nokwe, Michael Harmel, Joan Anderson, Dan Tloome, Mr Moosajee, Diza Putini and Sheila Morrison.[10] I served as secretary of the CIHS Parents' Association until my arrest at the end of 1956, while Narsibhai Parbhoo was chairman.

The school nurtured a number of pupils who rose to prominence, including Abdul Minty, and Essop and Aziz Pahad. However, the initial enrolment of 400 soon outgrew the available facilities, and the only option was the school in Lenasia. This, in turn, led families, albeit reluctantly, to move to the new suburb to be closer to their children's school. At a meeting in 1956, I spoke out strongly against the resettlement of Indians, while a fellow speaker, a Greek communist, made the ironic observation that Lenasia was so far from the centre of Johannesburg that it was 'halfway to Asia', hence the name, since 'len' was the Greek word for 'half'.

The Indian community in South Africa remained a prickly thorn in the government's flesh. A report on 23 June 1956 in the *Natal Witness* quoted WA Maree, Minister of Indian Affairs, as follows: 'After the effect of the Group Areas Act has been felt, Indians will be only too pleased to get out of South Africa. The [National] Party holds the view that Indians are a foreign and outlandish element which is unassimilable. They can never become part of the country and they must therefore be treated as an immigrant community.'[11]

Supreme Court judge and chairman of the Group Areas Board, De Vos Hugo, was even more crass, dismissing Indians as 'a band of robbers who won't part with their ill-gotten gains unless forced to do so'.[12]

NO TYRANNY OF NUMBERS

On 5 June, just less than a year after the Congress of the People, Chief Luthuli responded to attacks by journalist Jordan K Ngubane with a statement that had timeless resonance:

> The African National Congress is not interested in making its African majority a tyranny to other groups. It appreciates that the essence of true democracy lies in the majority seeking, through discussion rather than in the mere counting of heads, to accommodate to the utmost the legitimate wishes of the minority. The African National Congress has no desire to make the African majority the tyranny of numbers. It is only interested in establishing a bond of true friendship among all sections of the South African population on the basis of true democracy.
>
> [To suggest otherwise] is unfair to people in the other racial communities who have sacrificed for freedom in our land, as proved by those who partici-pated in the 1950 Protest Day and in the great Defiance Campaign of 1952. In these campaigns, all racial groups in South Africa actively participated and made sacrifices deserving of praise, and not scorn, by anyone genuinely desiring the liberation of Africa. I have said it in the past, and I repeat it here, that to me Africa is a land for all who are in it, who give it undivided loyalty, whatever their racial origin might be. I believe in and work for the acceptance of the concept of all in Africa being known as Africans and merely differentiating, if such a differentiation must be made, by referring to their racial origin.[13]

Six months earlier, the government had made it compulsory for African women to carry passbooks. The move had been five years in the making – as far back as April 1950, I had told a meeting at the Indian Sports Grounds in Benoni: 'The government has decided to introduce a pass law for women: I want to tell Dr Malan that we will die before we will allow this pass law to be introduced. He is dealing with a new generation and not with the non-European of twenty years ago. We are not against the white man in general; we are prepared to work with those who work with us.'[14]

On 9 August 1956, some 20 000 women marched on the Union Buildings in Pretoria, and presented the prime minister with a petition containing hundreds of thousands of signatures in support of demands for the withdrawal of passes for women and the repeal of the pass laws. The preamble proclaimed: 'We are women from every part of South Africa. We are women of every race, we come from the cities and the towns, from the reserves and the villages. We come as women united in our purpose to save the African women from the degradation of passes.'[15]

My banning order was fairly lax at the time, so I was able to drive Aminabai Pahad and some of her friends to Pretoria and observe the march. The leaders were Lilian Ngoyi, Rahima Moosa, Helen Joseph and Sophie Williams, who presented a petition signed by thousands of women to the prime minister's office. It was with great sadness that I learnt of Lilian's death while I was in prison. I was able to attend Helen's funeral, but unfortunately missed Rahima's. Sophie and I became close friends, and I watched with pride as she rose from a rank and file activist to a leading position in the Coloured People's Congress. When she returned home from exile, she served on the Gender Commission and became an active member of the ANC Women's League. After the 2004 election she was elected to the Gauteng Provincial Legislative Assembly.

TREASON!

My first banning order expired in October 1956, but rumour was rife that arrests on treason charges were imminent. The Minister of Justice, CR Swart, had already indicated that the Congress of the People and the drawing up of the Freedom Charter would lead to detentions, and by late 1956, the story doing the rounds among activists was that a number of cells in the Old Fort were being whitewashed and prepared for occupants.

The police swooped on 5 December. The security police arrived at my flat with a search warrant and confiscated a number of documents and books, including personal letters. Later that morning they returned, armed with a search warrant for Babla Saloojee's possessions. I told them he was not staying with me, and when their search proved fruitless, they left.

The third time they came, they were looking for Ebrahim Moola, and on their fourth and final visit of the day, it was Amien Cajee they wanted. Neither of them was living at the flat, and the police did not arrest me.

But the next morning, we learnt that 140 leading activists had been apprehended throughout the country. The effect was summed up by Lionel Forman, who observed wryly: 'On the night of December 4, I went to bed as an ordinary activist. On December 5, I woke up as a leader.'

The detainees were flown to Johannesburg from Durban, Port Elizabeth and Cape Town, and taken to the Johannesburg Fort. A group of those who had escaped arrest immediately formed a support committee, and set about arranging food and toiletries for the prisoners, and organising a meeting in Sophiatown to demand their release. Numerous posters and banners were printed with the slogan, 'We stand by our leaders'.

A huge crowd gathered at Freedom Square in Sophiatown on the Sunday morning. Among the speakers were Michael Harmel, Barney Ngakane, David Bopape and me. Also on the platform was Sampie Malupe, acting as interpreter. While the meeting was in progress, a contingent of armed police surrounded the square, and a group of security policemen, led by Colonel Spengler, made their way to the platform in a provocative manner, manhandled Sampie to the floor and arrested him.

A few days later, it was my turn. The security police arrived at the flat early in the morning and told me indifferently to collect my personal belongings. They took me to police headquarters at Marshall Square, where Walter Sisulu, Joe Slovo and Rusty Bernstein were already in custody.

When they transferred us to the Fort, we were reunited with those who had been arrested in the initial swoop, including Mandela, Chief Luthuli, Professor Matthews, Dr Naicker and Dr Motala. Inexplicably, a number of other leaders, such as Dr Dadoo, JB Marks, Molvi and Yusuf Cachalia, Nana Sita, Es'kia Mphahlele and Dr Njongwe, were not among the victims.

∾ 8 ∾

We Stand By Our Leaders

*High treason is a capital offence under South African law and may carry
the death penalty.*   **– Helen Joseph, *If this Be Treason*** [1]

For the next five years our lives would play out against the grim backdrop of
the Treason Trial. It would be one of the least focused, most time-consuming
and bureaucratically complicated cases in the annals of South African justice.

Helen Joseph wrote: 'The course of the trial appeared bewilderingly complex
because of the great bulk of the evidence, the seemingly endless series of
further particulars and amendments to the indictment, the discharge without
explanation of two-fifths of the accused, the split of the remaining accused into
separate groups, the court's dismissal of the indictment against one group, and
anomalies in the inclusion of some persons and exclusion of others among
those arrested, discharged, or regrouped.' [2] The London *Times* highlighted the
trial's fairness as its 'one bright spot', and said that 'for the rest, darkness and
confusion prevail'.

Briefly, the proceedings unfolded in the following phases:[3]

- The preparatory examination, held in the Johannesburg Drill Hall from the time of our arrest in December 1956 to the beginning of 1958, when the magistrate ruled that there were sufficient grounds for a trial on charges including high treason. We were granted bail soon after being arrested. In January 1958, the Attorney-General withdrew all charges against sixty-five of the 156 accused, including Chief Luthuli.
- The trial of ninety-one accused by a panel of three judges in Pretoria from August to October 1958 on the first indictment. The accused were divided into three groups and only thirty were ultimately prosecuted.
- Legal argument on the second indictment of thirty defendants, including Mandela, Sisulu and me, from January to June 1959.
- The trial on further charges, from August 1959 to March 1960. The prosecution called 150 witnesses, with one, Professor Andrew Murray, staying in the witness box for almost six weeks.[4] The state closed its case on 10 March, and the defence began presenting its case on 21 March – the day of the Sharpeville massacre.

The state of emergency was declared at the end of March, and the trialists were arrested anew. The court adjourned until the end of April, when the defence counsel withdrew at our request. On 18 July, one of the lawyers returned, and by the beginning of August most of the defence team was back.

We were released on 31 August when the state of emergency was lifted, but the trial continued until 7 October. Judgment was given in March 1961.

THE PREPARATORY EXAMINATION

Long ago Cicero had discovered the profound difference between justice and morality. Justice was the tool of the strong to be used as the strong desired. — **Howard Fast, Spartacus**[5]

During the 1950s, all charges that carried the death penalty had to first be tested in a preparatory examination, presided over by a magistrate who had the authority to either commit the accused for trial, or withdraw the charges.

In our case, the chief magistrate of Bloemfontein was appointed to conduct the preparatory examination, which took a year. The majority of the accused were from the working class, but there were also seven lawyers, six doctors, two architects, three ministers of religion, a professor, teachers and nurses. At our first appearance, a large crowd of supporters gathered outside the court, singing and chanting struggle slogans and demanding to be allowed in.

We could hear the commotion outside and were greatly upset by the sound of gunfire when the police attempted to disperse the crowd.

The Crown called hundreds of witnesses and presented thousands of exhibits, ranging from books on Marxism to placards reading 'Soup With Meat' and 'Soup Without Meat', confiscated at the Congress of the People. Other documents included a Russian recipe book, an Indian school magazine, a statement by one of the accused explaining to his lawyers why he wanted a divorce, a letter stating that a cheque had been lost and another reporting that it had been found.

That was the calibre of evidence designed to prove that we were involved in a conspiracy to overthrow the government by violent means and install a communist regime based on the Freedom Charter. Day after day, for months on end, we had to sit through repetitive and monotonous evidence that had the effect of inducing sleep.

But first we had to dispense with the specially constructed cage in which the 156 of us were to be confined throughout the hearing. Our lawyers refused to consult with us through the wire fence, and the magistrate ordered the structure dismantled.

The Crown led the interminable evidence of security policemen who had confiscated documents and literature during raids on our homes, and taken notes of speeches made at hundreds of public meetings. Then they called their star witness, Solomon Ngobose.

By then, the testimony had become so tedious that we were scarcely paying attention. Helen Joseph caught up with her administrative work or did crossword puzzles in the dock, Ruth First and Rusty Bernstein read, and many of us simply nodded off. Public interest had dwindled to a handful of people.

So we were surprised to arrive at court one day and find the gallery filled to capacity, with some of the most senior security police officers, Tiny Venter, Sampie Prinsloo and At Spengler, in the front row. Other dignitaries, government officials and ambassadors were also present, the press was out in force and the atmosphere was pregnant with foreboding. The defence team had no idea what was going on until the prosecutor, permanently dour and unsmiling, informed the court triumphantly that he was about to demonstrate what we had really been planning under the guise of non-violent protest.

Ngobose, in his late forties, testified that he had graduated from Fort Hare University with a BA degree before going on to study law. He even produced a photograph of himself on graduation day. We were still puzzling over what any of this had to do with the trial, when the prosecutor dropped his bombshell.

With all the confidence in the world, Ngobose claimed he had been elected provincial secretary of the ANC in the Eastern Cape, and that on 18 October 1952 he was instructed by the provincial executive to lead a riot at the New Brighton railway station in Port Elizabeth. This was part of a 'well-planned' campaign of violence by the ANC, and several people, black and white, had been killed, said the witness. Those who had been aware of the plan included Walter Sisulu and ANC treasurer general Dr Letele.

As the prosecutor finished leading this damning evidence, he glanced over at Tiny Venter and his colleagues for a nod of approval, collected his papers with a flourish and sat down.

On the defence side of the courtroom, there was stunned silence. Not one of the accused, including the Eastern Cape leaders, had ever even heard of Ngobose, much less involved him in any campaign such as the one he described.

The court adjourned for several days so that our lawyers could prepare for cross-examination. When we returned, Ngobose faced Vernon Berrangé, who had a razor-sharp mind. I had previously seen inveterate gangsters and hardened policemen crumble under cross-examination by this master of the art. His opening salvo was blunt and to the point:

'Solomon Ngobose, I put it to you that you are a cheat, a liar, a thief and a robber. What do you say to that?'

Ngobose denied being any of these things.

'I put it to you that every bit of evidence that you gave to this court has been a pack of lies. What is your comment?'

Another denial.

'I put it to you that you never spent a single day at Fort Hare as a student, you never graduated, and your so-called graduation photograph represents nothing else but a falsehood. You were not even a member of the ANC, let alone its provincial secretary.'

Denial, again.

Then Berrangé delivered his *coup de grâce*.

'Mr Ngobose, you have been in and out of prison for many years. And on the night of 18 October 1952, when you claim to have led the riot in Port Elizabeth, you were in fact a prisoner in Durban Central Prison, where you were serving a sentence for one of your many crimes. Before you deny this also, I want to show you a letter, in your handwriting, dated 18 October 1952, posted from prison, with a prison date stamp, and addressed to Advocate Hassan Mall.'

It was deathly quiet in the courtroom. The prosecution was squirming, and the senior police officers had slipped out of court one after another during Berrangé's attack on the state's key witness to trumped-up charges of violence.

But the prosecution doggedly carried on, just as the apartheid juggernaut pushed forward relentlessly. Over the next two years, new and harsher measures became law: house arrest, ninety-day detention, the Sabotage Act, the Terrorism Act. Torture and death in detention became almost routine, and the courts were clogged with cases against activists. Many, many years later, it would be possible for us to remember Solomon Ngobose and others of his ilk as comical interludes, but, in fact, they represented the blind determination of a government to convict us, by hook or – quite literally – by crook.

THE 'EXPERT' WITNESS

Men who distrust the people and the future may overwhelm us with their learning, but they do not impress us with their wisdom, thank God. — **Gerald Johnson**[6]

To show that our struggle was rooted in a sinister communist conspiracy, the Crown imported an expert from Switzerland – a clergyman by the name of Professor Bohensky. Analysis of more than 10 000 documents was entrusted to Professor Andrew Murray of the University of Cape Town.

However, when Bohensky could find nothing 'communistic' in the documents, it was left to Murray to make the Crown's case, both at the preparatory examination and the later trial, when advocate Issy Maisels, QC, was unleashed on him.

First, Maisels established that Murray had a master's degree from Stellenbosch University in philosophy and psychology, and that his thesis had been titled 'The political aspects of miscegenation in certain groups in the Transkeian territories'. Next, he confirmed that at Oxford University, Murray had studied literature and written another thesis, this time on the philosophy of James Ward, while his doctoral dissertation dealt with the philosophy of Charles Bernard de Nouvaea.

None of these, the professor acknowledged, had anything to do with communism or political theory, though he did maintain that since De Nouvaea was a political reformer in nineteenth-century France, that thesis had dealt with political philosophy.

Maisels then turned to Murray's expertise in the use in documents before the court of certain words or phrases which, he had testified, denoted adherence to the communist doctrine. Among them were 'war-mongering American imperialists', 'fascist', 'anti-imperialist', 'police state' and 'anti-capitalist'. Murray held up one excerpt – 'full confidence in the ultimate triumph of Africa' – as 'an example of the communist doctrine of historical materialism'.

Also 'typically communist' was Chief Luthuli's call for closer cooperation with trade unions, and 'for the establishment of a united front to challenge the forces of reaction', the Crown's expert claimed.

Murray, and the Crown, should already have realised during the preparatory examination that they were on dangerous ground. Berrangé had sought the professor's comment on the following passage: 'In the industrialised state, the instruments of production are usually in the hands of the dominant group … this has a three-fold result …'

Murray had confidently replied that it was 'straight-from-the-shoulder communism'. Asked if he could identify the author, Murray was unable to do so, leaving Berrangé to feign surprise.

'You can't? Will you be very surprised to hear that you are the author? Do you deny it?'

The hapless professor responded: 'Not if you say so.'

During the trial, Maisels had his own fun at the professor's expense, pointing out that some of the expressions he had identified as 'communist' were, in fact, used by such eminent persons as American president Woodrow Wilson, and South Africa's prime minister, Dr DF Malan.

Seven days into cross-examination, Maisels told the judges: 'This witness is not qualified to give the evidence that he has, by virtue of his ignorance of many topics ... and the opinions that he has given are calculated to or may possibly mislead the court'.

Walter Sisulu later described our defence team as 'without doubt, the finest assemblage of legal talent ever banded together in one place'. All our lawyers were dedicated human rights advocates with proud records of defending activists in the apartheid courts, and every one of them appeared on our behalf at greatly reduced fees. The instructing attorney was the brilliant and flamboyant Michael Parkington, while the advocates were Maisels, Bram Fischer, Sydney Kentridge, HC Nicholas and Rex Welsh, all of whom were Queen's Counsel, Vernon Berrangé, Tony O'Dowd, John Coaker, Chris Plewman and David Osborne.

THE TRIAL OF THE FIRST BATCH OF THIRTY

In August 1958, thirty of us went on trial in Pretoria. Rather than travel to and from Johannesburg by bus, Madiba and I often cadged a lift with Helen Joseph. As we drove through the plush suburbs north of the city, we would joke about which of the grand houses we would one day live in. Helen recalled, 'We chose a home for Kathy, the young Indian bachelor, so gay, who often travelled with us. His was a handsome villa with a large wing on either side for all his Moslem wives!'[7]

The trial was so boring, at times, that some of us resorted to discreet forms of entertainment in court, including books of cartoons. One day, Stanley Lollan and I decided to circulate an *Andy Capp* book among our co-accused and observe their various reactions. Some were obviously amused, some indifferent, and a few simply could not fathom what was going on. A few hours later I received a note. 'Comrade,' it said, 'what has all this to do with Marxism-Leninism?'

One of the most welcome diversions was the delicious refreshments provided daily for all the defendants by Mrs Thayangee Pillay.

On 19 October 1959, one of our co-accused at the preparatory examination, Lionel Forman, died while undergoing open-heart surgery. His two outstanding characteristics were his immense foresight and his readiness to express critical views on political matters not always consonant with mainstream thinking. On behalf of the Treason Trialists, Leon Levy and I wrote to his widow, Sadie: 'Our deep feelings of sorrow are not easy to express, for we knew Lionel for almost half our lives and shared the pleasure of working in the movement where he stood as a giant above us.'[8]

SHARPEVILLE

With reasonable men I will reason; with humane men I will plead; but to tyrants I will give no quarter. – **William Lloyd Garrison**[9]

On Monday 21 March 1960, Chief Luthuli was testifying for the defence. The entire court listened with rapt attention as the ANC's highly respected president slowly and clearly spelt out every aspect of the organisation's policy and goals. Never before had distinguished members of the judiciary been afforded so much insight into the African continent's foremost liberation movement. Little did we know that not two hours' drive from the courtroom, a tragedy was unfolding that would have an irrevocable impact on South Africa's history.

It was during the morning tea break that we learnt with shock and horror that the police had opened fire and killed a large number of unarmed protestors staging a peaceful protest against the pass laws in the township of Sharpeville. Later, we would find out that sixty-nine people had died in the hail of bullets, and many more were wounded. Most of the dead had been shot in the back.[10]

Of course the trial continued, but the shootings jolted us into realising that the ANC's declared policy of non-violence had become an anachronism. How could we support peaceful protest against a regime that was as ruthless as it was brutal?

When the court adjourned for the day, the ANC's national leadership met in an emergency all-night session and decided:

- to declare Monday 28 March a national day of mourning and protest – in effect, a countrywide strike;
- to call upon people to burn their passes;
- to send the secretary general, Oliver Tambo, out of the country to set up a structure in exile in anticipation of the ANC being banned.

On Saturday 26 March, ANC leaders, including Chief Luthuli, Walter Sisulu, Nelson Mandela and Duma Nokwe, publicly burnt their passes, never to carry them again. Two days later, hundreds of thousands of people responded to the stayaway.

PARTINGS AND ARRESTS

Dig a well before you are thirsty. – **Chinese proverb**[11]

On the evening of 27 March I was among a handful of comrades who assembled at a house in Johannesburg's northern suburbs to say goodbye to Oliver Tambo, affectionately known as OR.

His wife Mama Adelaide was a nurse, and was on duty at the general hospital. It was my task to take her to the house in Houghton to bid OR farewell before he was driven to Bechuanaland in the dead of night. It was not until a few days later, when we received word that he had arrived safely in Dar es Salaam, that we could sigh with relief.

It would be thirty years before I saw OR again, in a hospital in Sweden, where he was recuperating after a stroke.

Arrangements were also made for Yusuf Dadoo to leave the country. Although we were in detention when he left, I remember my last meeting with him. We chatted and laughed for a while, and then he was gone. In the weeks after Sharpeville, many lives were changed forever.

On 28 March, while masses of people came out on strike, the government tabled the Unlawful Organisations Bill in parliament, which would allow them to crush any resistance organisation. The next day, the ANC's National Executive met and decided that if the organisation was banned, it would go underground, and a statement to this effect would be issued. It was the Muslim festival of Eid, and along with Madiba, Helen Joseph and Walter Sisulu, I had lunch with some friends in Pretoria.

That evening, I received an urgent but enigmatic phone call from Madiba, and rushed to his house in Orlando to make sure I had understood him correctly. He was alone, his face grave, his eyes resolute. He told me that he had been tipped off by a contact in the Special Branch that the government intended declaring a state of emergency the next day, and that 'activists throughout the country will be arrested and detained without trial'. In the face of this new threat, the ANC leadership had taken certain decisions that had to be conveyed to those concerned without delay.

This was decades before the advent of mobile phones and computers, and many people did not even have access to their own telephone landlines. Yet I had to find a way of reaching as many of our co-accused as possible, with instructions that we were to go to court as usual, and allow ourselves to be detained.

Before dawn, however, leaders such as Moses Kotane, Dadoo and Michael Harmel would go underground.

At 5 a.m. on 30 March, I was one of thousands of activists arrested in

Johannesburg after the state of emergency had been declared. We were transferred to Pretoria, where I shared a cell with my fellow Treason Trialists Joe Molefe, Mosey Moolla, Faried Adams and Stanley Lollan.

That day alone, 1 500 activists were arrested in countrywide swoops, but the figure would reach 20 000 over the ensuing days.

On 31 March, we were taken to the Pretoria Prison, where most of our fellow Treason Trialists were waiting. Only then did we realise that none of the defendants from the Eastern Cape had been arrested. They were staying at various houses in Soweto, and the police did not know where to find them. Neither did we!

Oblivious to our arrests, they had boarded a bus for Pretoria that morning as usual, and must have been thoroughly bewildered to be met on arrival at the Old Synagogue, where our trial was being held, by a throng of stern-faced policemen. Their freedom had not lasted long.

In a classic example of security police bungling, they refused to arrest Wilton Mkwayi, despite his insistence that he was one of the accused. Eventually, they became so angry that they threatened to charge him with obstruction of justice, and Wilton, for once more than happy to obey a police order, fled.

He lost no time in crossing the border into Basutoland. With Raymond Mhlaba, Steve Naidoo, Patrick Mthembu, Joe Gqabi and Andrew Mlangeni, he was among the first members of MK to undergo military training in China. The next time I saw Wilton was three years later at Liliesleaf farm in Rivonia.

Wilton was a great believer in the power of *muti*,[12] and never doubted that it was his *muti* that had 'blinded' the police and saved him from detention during the state of emergency. He took his traditional medicine all the way to China, and no one could ever persuade him that it was anything but *muti* that kept him away from Rivonia on 11 July 1963.

THE TRIAL CONTINUES

When the Treason Trial resumed after our arrests, the witness, Chief Luthuli, was absent. We knew that warders had assaulted him soon after his arrival at Pretoria Local Prison, and we were seething with anger because we were powerless to do anything about it.

The prosecutors offered some lame excuse for the missing witness, but Justice Rumpff was having none of it, and ordered the police to bring the chief to court without delay.

Although apartheid's security police were a law unto themselves, some semblance of the rule of law still existed in 1960. The prosecutors knew that failure to produce Chief Luthuli would expose their allies, the security police, to a charge of contempt of court.

As soon as he appeared, it was apparent that the chief had been assaulted. Ironically, just eighteen months later, he would be awarded the Nobel Peace Prize.

Once our legal team had addressed the assault, they raised the question of conditions in the prison where we were being held. The food was not only of an appalling standard, but served in line with racial policies. White prisoners received white sugar and bread, while Indians and Coloureds were given brown sugar and bread. Africans were given no bread at all, due to the absurd premise that they did not like bread, which was a 'more sophisticated or Western taste'.[13]

Incidentally, Madiba was as disciplined about food as about anything else. However tasty a dish, I never once saw him eat more than a modest quantity, or heard him complain that he had overeaten.

When Sydney Kentridge raised the question of prison food, Madiba told the judges that it was not fit for human consumption.[14] Rumpff decided to put this to the test, and later that day asked that a dish of prison food be brought to him in court. He took a few bites, pronounced it quite tasty, and suggested that it should be served warm, and that better eating utensils be provided. The situation remained unchanged until a few weeks later, when JB Marks and Yusuf and Molvi Cachalia were among detainees transferred to Pretoria Prison from Johannesburg. The warders told us that their luggage filled a couple of trucks!

Because of the sizeable number of Muslims (including two spiritual leaders) in this group, the first demand was for *halaal* food. The prison authorities decided to set aside one kitchen, in which the Muslims could prepare their own food. Our request that all the political detainees be fed from this kitchen was turned down, and the authorities supplied only enough raw ingredients to cater for the Muslims. However, the warders had great difficulty monitoring which prisoners were Muslim and who went in and out of the kitchen, so we were able to exploit the concession after all.

Among the chief cooks were Yusuf Cachalia and Suliman Esakjee. It was a case of history repeating itself, since their fathers had been prison cooks during Gandhi's passive resistance campaign in South Africa in the first decades of the twentieth century.

The arrival of the new detainees injected a strong sense of spiritual need into our prison community, and attendance of Sunday services was greatly encouraged. JB Marks, a political orator of note, led the prayers, which were heavily spiced with political messages. Molvi Saloojee did the same during Muslim prayers. As soon as the authorities realised what was happening, our services were halted, and henceforth only members of the clergy who were registered with the prison were allowed to feed our souls.

When our trial began, we were anxious about one of the three judges, Justice Kennedy. In an earlier trial, he had sentenced twenty-two political prisoners to death in Natal. On the day that all but one of them was hanged, we 'fasted the whole day in demonstration against this mass hanging'.[15] Understandably, we were not at all happy that the 'hanging judge' would be involved in deciding our fate.

But, in a strange twist of fate, Kennedy's sister was his clerk, and a few days after our detention, we were surprised to receive a message from 'Mrs K'. She conveyed her intention of providing home-cooked food for Chief Luthuli as long as he was detained. It never occurred to her to discuss this arrangement with our lawyers; she simply decided, as the good and kind person that she was, to do it.

And there were other caring gestures. On Helen Joseph's birthday, Mrs K brought her a bunch of flowers. When one of the defendants, Elias Moretsele, died suddenly of a heart attack, she sent a wreath to the family. While I believe Mrs K was a warm and generous soul in any event, I couldn't help feeling that she had been influenced, to some extent, by Chief Luthuli's exposition of the ANC's aims.

To our even greater surprise, her brother seemed to undergo a metamorphosis during the trial. Initially openly hostile towards us, he gradually became unexpectedly reasonable, to the point where we actually began to like him. He also had an amazing memory for detail, and an uncanny ability to keep track of the documents placed before court.

Originally, the three judges assigned to the trial were Rumpff, Kennedy and Ludorf. While we had misgivings about Kennedy, we were truly horrified at the appointment of Ludorf, a known supporter of the National Party, who had acted for the government on numerous occasions before being promoted to the bench. At the outset, therefore, we suggested that our lawyers should apply for Ludorf to recuse himself.

They cautioned us to consider our options well, running through the list of possible alternatives and pointing out that we might end up with someone even more biased in the government's favour, such as Hiemstra.

We never intended presenting a purely legal defence. Our strategy was to include our political beliefs and an exposition of the struggle at every opportunity, and there was no room in our plan for lack of courage or conviction. By refusing to be tried by Ludorf, we would send a strong message to our supporters, so Issy Maisels went ahead and made the application. To our great surprise, Ludorf agreed to step down, and was replaced by Judge Bekker.

He was not only competent and highly regarded for his impartiality, but was also a decent human being. He went out of his way to ensure that our trial was fair, and was without a doubt our favourite judge.

Our legal fees were paid by the Treason Trial Defence Fund in South Africa, and the International Defence and Aid Fund in England, which contributed most of the money to pay our lawyers and provide assistance to our families, since the prolonged proceedings meant that many of the accused were unable to generate any income of their own.

The South African fund concentrated on getting donations of food and clothing, and various addresses were publicised as collection points.

One Sunday night, quite late, the occupants of one house where donations could be dropped off heard their gate being opened, followed by footsteps on the path. Guessing that someone was coming to deliver contributions, they waited for a knock on the door. There wasn't one, but almost immediately the family realised that the visitor was leaving again.

The man of the house opened the front door to investigate, and caught a clear glimpse of the anonymous donor just as she got into her car. He recognised her as Judge Bekker's wife, and she had left a carton of men's clothing on the verandah.

Ever since our arrests, the prison authorities had denied us access to newspapers or other sources of information. Our conversations with visitors had to be confined to 'family matters' – a precursor for the rules imposed on us at Robben Island.

But staying abreast of current affairs is the lifeblood of political activism. Depriving us, through the long years behind bars, of access to news was one of the cruellest forms of punishment our jailers could inflict on us.

During the Treason Trial, we managed to bypass the news blackout by hinting that our lawyers might bring the daily newspapers to court and 'forget' them on their table. This worked reasonably well, and we also struck up a relationship with one of the journalists covering the trial, the court interpreters and even some of the African policemen, all of whom managed to supply us with the newspapers we so sorely needed to read.

The situation improved considerably when Bram Fischer asked me one day what the possibilities were of smuggling a small transistor radio, which he would provide, into the prison. I discussed the suggestion with some of my colleagues, and we agreed that it was worth taking the risk, provided Bram would not be compromised.

Because our return to prison at the end of each day often coincided with the warders' shift change, we were rarely searched. The day staff were in too much of a hurry to get home, and the night staff assumed that their colleagues had done their duty.

Bram also gave Helen a radio. Getting it into her cell was no problem, but there was the question of fresh batteries every now and then. She solved the problem by tucking them, one at a time, into her trademark bun. The African court orderlies we had befriended kept us supplied with batteries.

We had to find a safe hiding place for our radio, of course, and there were few options. However, experience of many raids on our homes had taught us that the one item white policemen never touched was the footwear of people, which their inherent racism suggested were unclean. Gambling that the prison warders would have the same mentality, we concealed the little radio in a dirty sock and stuffed it into a well-worn tennis shoe.

Not only did the radio escape attention throughout our detention, but I continued to use it for about three years afterwards. It was eventually confiscated when the police raided my Mountain View cottage, and I never saw it again.

Sometimes, our secret news sources offered wholly unexpected information, such as the Tuesday afternoon when Justice Rumpff announced that, due to Judge Kennedy not feeling well, the court would not sit the following day.

Imagine our surprise a few days later when we opened one of our contraband newspapers and saw a photograph of all three judges, taken at a horse-racing track on the very day that Kennedy had been 'ill'!

The Sharpeville massacre, and the state of emergency that followed, changed the entire zeitgeist in South Africa. We were genuinely concerned that, in the prevailing atmosphere, we would not get a fair trial. Our lawyers sought a postponement until the state of emergency was lifted, but this was refused. We discussed the matter among ourselves, and came to the conclusion that the only way to drag out the proceedings until the political climate became less volatile was to instruct our advocates that they were to withdraw from the case. We would retain the services of our attorney, and conduct our own defence.

When Issy Maisels informed the court of our decision, Justice Bekker was genuinely shocked, and asked if we fully appreciated the earnestness of what we were doing. There was not a murmur of dissent from any of the defendants, and we took over our defence immediately.

This meant that we each represented ourselves. The two qualified lawyers in our ranks, Mandela and Duma Nokwe, advised the rest of us on how to proceed. One way of utilising the court's time was to call each other as witnesses.[16]

While Accused No. 1, Faried Adams, was leading the testimony of Accused No. 2, Helen Joseph, he ran out of questions. Rather than admit this, Faried asked the court for an adjournment, on the grounds that he was 'feeling very tired, My Lords'.

It didn't work. Rumpff reminded us that we had been warned to think carefully before dismissing our advocates, and instructed Faried to carry on.

This proved to be the catalyst for the first murmurs of discontent among us. That night, some of our co-accused questioned the wisdom of our unanimous decision, and it took some convincing for them to agree that we would stand by it. However, this early experience of dispute resolution would stand us in good stead during our long imprisonment later, when it served as a model on numerous occasions.

Naturally, we insisted that the authorities provide us with all the facilities and equipment needed to prepare our case. Apart from a cell in which we could consult with one another, we needed a typewriter, legal tomes and access to all the court documents.

The typewriter and carbon paper were immediately put to use for compilation of a daily 'news bulletin', containing snippets gleaned from our secret newspapers and the transistor radio. We called it *Naledi*, which means 'morning star', and for as long as the state of emergency lasted, we kept our fellow detainees informed about events outside the prison walls.

Inevitably, the authorities planted informers among the hundreds of political detainees, and when we returned from court one afternoon, our cell had been ransacked. Fellow prisoners told us they had overheard warders say they were hunting for our radio, but just about the only item that had not been touched was the grubby tennis shoe in which it was hidden.

The facilities at our disposal to prepare our case were far from adequate. Madiba described them to the court as follows:

> In size, My Lords, the cell is approximately fourteen by seven paces. In the cell, My Lords, there was one table, a shelf containing records of the case, no chairs or benches were provided and the accused had either to stand, squat or sit on bare cement. Later during the day mats were provided for all the accused. There were sanitary buckets, which appear to us to have been used by other persons. They had not been emptied and the whole atmosphere was reeking with stench. Because of dim lights, the cell was dark and dingy.[17]

Justice Rumpff listened patiently to Mandela's complaints and assured us that they would be attended to. Of necessity, we had sought permission to hold consultations in the evenings with co-accused Helen Joseph and Leon Levy. Because they were white and held in a different section of the prison, this presented a major problem for the authorities. Certain prison regulations were cast in stone. Consultations at night, even with lawyers, were almost unheard of. The idea of a white male prisoner being taken to the non-white section was repugnant enough. For a white woman to enter that area was simply unthinkable, and would require nothing less than the permission of the minister.

Just three years later, the political ether in South Africa would have become so contaminated that virtually no judge would entertain complaints of any nature from political prisoners, who were routinely referred to as 'saboteurs', 'Poqo' and 'terrorists'. Amid widespread torture and abuse, the judiciary, for the most part, would turn a blind eye to the evils of apartheid's security apparatus.[18]

Astonishingly, however, we were granted permission to consult with Helen. She would later describe this breakthrough as 'epoch-making'.[19]

I believe it was Tolstoy who observed that prison officials have *rules* where the *heart* should be. His words often came to mind during our subsequent consultation sessions in the visitors' room. Nelson, Duma, Faried and I were separated from Helen and Leon by a metre-wide passage, a sort of no-man's land between two rows of chicken wire. In addition, to comply with the strict rule against physical contact between men and women, a wooden partition was erected to keep Helen and Leon apart.

The situation was absurd. We sat next to one another every day in court, with no undue restriction on our personal interaction, but inside the prison, apartheid was religiously adhered to.

I was Accused No. 3, and I called Molvi Cachalia as my first witness, to testify about the oppressive laws that applied particularly to Indians. I seriously considered having him give evidence in Urdu or Gujerati, as a delaying tactic, but Justice Rumpff saw through my strategy and ruled that Molvi was more than competent to testify in English. Still, I managed to keep him in the witness box for the best part of a week, and then called Stanley Lollan.

Among the detainees in Pretoria Local Prison were a number of members of the ANC's National Executive Committee, including Chief Albert Luthuli (president), Walter Sisulu (secretary general), Nelson Mandela (deputy president), Dr Wilson Conco, Leslie Messina, Lilian Ngoyi and Duma Nokwe. Some NEC members were also in other prisons, such as Professor ZK Matthews in East London and treasurer general Dr Arthur Letele in Kimberley.

The suggestion was made that we should explore the possibility of holding a mini-NEC meeting in prison. After much consideration, we realised that since we were conducting our own defence, we had the right to call any witnesses we chose, and applied for Professor Matthews and Dr Letele to be transferred to Pretoria.

Needless to say, the 'legal consultation' was nothing more than a meeting of the ANC's most senior leaders in detention. Historians will no doubt assign this meeting its proper place in the annals, but for me, it stands as yet another example of the ANC's tenacity and the ability of its leaders to turn even major obstacles into advantages. Given the bannings and prohibitions in place at the time, it is highly unlikely that so many NEC members could have been together at the same time in any other place but prison!

Shortly afterwards, we heard a radio news report indicating that Verwoerd would lift the state of emergency at the beginning of September. We recalled our full legal team without delay.

The Minister of Justice had banned both the ANC and the PAC on 8 April 1960, forcing the ANC to implement a long-standing contingency plan to continue functioning as an underground movement. Mandela had anticipated that this situation would arise since 1952, when a banning order prevented him from attending the ANC conference:

Along with many others, I had become convinced that the government intended to declare the ANC and the SAIC illegal organisations, just as it had done with the Communist Party. It seemed inevitable that the state would attempt to put us out of business as a legal organisation as soon as it could ... I approached the National Executive with the idea that we must come up with a contingency plan for just such an eventuality ... They instructed me to draw up a plan that would enable the organisation to operate from underground. This strategy came to be known as the Mandela Plan, or simply, M-Plan.[20]

On 9 April, the day after the liberation movements were declared illegal, a fifty-two-year-old white farmer, David Pratt, tried to assassinate the prime minister, Dr Hendrik Verwoerd.

Verwoerd had just finished making a speech at the Rand Easter Show when, according to the police, 'a man stepped up ... a shot was fired at virtually point-blank range from a .22 automatic pistol. A second shot was fired into his right ear. The arrest was made so quickly and the removal was done so quickly that an angry section of the crowd was frustrated from assaulting the detainee ... David Pratt ... was soon thereafter hurried to Marshall Square.'[21]

Verwoerd survived the attack and was back at his desk within two months. At his trial, Pratt, a father of three, claimed he had been attacking 'the epitome of apartheid'. His hour-long statement from the dock 'ended with an indictment of apartheid, which he called a slimy snake that was gripping the throat of South Africa'.[22] The court found that Pratt was 'mentally disordered and epileptic', and he was committed to a mental hospital in Bloemfontein, where he hanged himself on 1 October 1961.

After four long years, the Treason Trial finally ground to a halt on 29 March 1961 with a unanimous verdict of 'not guilty'. The judges must have been as weary of the process as the accused, since they cut short the closing argument by the defence in order to deliver their findings.

The prosecution had relied heavily on the alleged use of violence by the Congress movement to secure our conviction. It was, perhaps, the fatal flaw in their case, particularly as Justice Rumpff had previously ruled that the Defiance Campaign had in no way been linked to violence.

MR WHITE AND MRS SWARTBOOI

After months in prison and in court I needed a break, but my banning order restricted me to the magisterial district of Johannesburg. Permission to visit my mother in Schweizer-Reneke had already been refused, so it would certainly not be granted for a trip to Cape Town. The only thing to do was take a chance and hope for the best.

Ahmed Kathrada outside the family store   At school in Johannesburg

With friends Naomi Shapiro (right) and Dorothy (left), Cape Town, 1948

Amina Pahad (left); Goolam Pahad (above) with his five boys: (from left to right) Essop, Nassim, Juneid, Aziz and Ismail

Dr Yusuf Dadoo, Nelson Mandela and Molvi Cachalia (foreground), during the Defiance Campaign trial

Chief Albert Luthuli

JN Singh

The Defiance Campaign, 1952. Ismail Meer is leading his batch,
at the Berea Road Station, Durban, just before their arrest

Nelson Mandela met Oliver Tambo on his journey abroad in 1962

Reverend Michael Scott

Alfred Nzo and Mrs Nzo, Yusuf Dadoo, Indira Gandhi,
Mrs Cachalia and Molvi Cachalia in India

Ahmed Kathrada was known for arguing with the police

Disguised as Pedro Perreira,
the day after the Rivonia arrest

Police presence at Rivonia Trial

Bram Fischer

Yusuf Dadoo and Joe Slovo with banners
at a demonstration in London

The only person I told about my plan was Bram Fischer. He was a friend, political colleague and lawyer, and in case of trouble, I would need all three. On the first day of the Easter weekend, Harry and Ahmed Kosadia and I set off in Ahmed's new car. By the time we reached Beaufort West, the car was giving trouble, but it was the Saturday morning of a long weekend and all the garages were closed.

The prospect of spending the rest of the weekend in the little Karoo town was not a happy one. The hotel manager suggested we approach Bobby White, a local mechanic. He warned that White normally refused to work over weekends, but thought he might take pity on us, as he had previously lived in Johannesburg.

I introduced myself to White as Mr Mohamed, and was stunned, during our conversation, when he suddenly asked if we knew 'Kathy Kathrada'. We mumbled something vague, but when White left the room, quickly decided that we should tell him the truth, as much in the hope that this might induce him to repair our car as to save him from any possibly embarrassing revelations about his 'friend'.

As I owned up to my true identity, White became quite animated. 'Don't you remember me? I was at the airport when you went to Europe in 1951!'

I later determined that he had, indeed, been among the well-wishers who had come to see me off, but I have a terrible memory for faces and did not recognise him at all. Nevertheless, Bobby White agreed to fix our car, but insisted that we first meet the woman in his life, Mrs Swartbooi, whose complexion was as fair as his own was dark!

MADIBA GOES UNDERGROUND

Shortly before the Treason Trial ended, the All-In African Conference met in Pietermaritzburg and decided to send an ultimatum to the government in response to plans to declare South Africa a republic.

The conference demanded that a national convention be called, representing all the people of South Africa, with a view to drawing up a new constitution. If the government did not accept this proposal, a three-day countrywide strike would take place.

Mandela, whose ban had expired, made a surprise appearance at the Pieter-maritzburg conference, but shortly after our acquittal, he went underground.

This heralded a sea change in his life. He would no longer be staying at home with his wife and children; in fact, he no longer had a place he could call home, and was constantly on the move to avoid detection.

I was a member of the small committee charged with facilitating Madiba's day-to-day activities. We had to find safe houses where he could stay and meet with ANC comrades. Some were also used for occasional visits from his family. We also had to arrange special venues where journalists could interview him from time to time. For security reasons, these premises were never used again. We also had to acquire motor vehicles that were unknown to the security police, in which he could be moved from place to place. Looking after Mandela placed a daunting responsibility on us. We dared not fail.

As the date of the promised strike approached, members of the organising committee also made preparations to go underground. With less than ten days to go, we received our orders to disappear. I was going to disguise myself as a Muslim priest, and had a long robe, fez and false beard for this purpose.

With a suitcase containing my disguise, I left my flat at 6 a.m. to pick up Molvi Cachalia. I was driving my Volkswagen Beetle, not yet known to the police and therefore relatively safe. But, as luck would have it, when I stopped at an intersection in Fordsburg, the nemesis of all activists, the notorious Sergeant Dirker, accompanied by Lieutenant van Wyk, crossed my path.

Dirker was an uncommonly zealous security policeman, frequently to be found driving around at all hours of the day or night in the hope of spotting an activist engaged in some or other illegal activity. His primary quarry was Walter Sisulu, but he would happily arrest any of us, given an excuse.

That morning, Dirker informed me that he had a warrant for my arrest because I had broken my banning order by going to visit my mother in Schweizer-Reneke five months before. When he found my disguise, he became extremely excited.

A new law allowed the courts to order someone detained for twelve days without being charged or granted bail. When I was taken to court after spending forty-eight hours in the cells at Marshall Square, Dirker told the magistrate that the security police had reason to believe I was planning to skip the country. My disguise was offered in support of the argument, and bail was not only refused, but I was charged under the Suppression of Communism Act and became the first person detained in terms of the twelve-day detention law.

I spent the first few days at Marshall Square and Modderbee Prison on the East Rand before being transferred to the Johannesburg Fort. My tiny cell, in the punishment block, was made of iron. When I lay down, my feet touched one wall, my head another. If I raised my arms above my head, I touched the ceiling. The light was dim and, since it was May, it was already bitterly cold. The only thing I could do was keep all my clothes on and wrap the thin blankets around my body.

At my next court appearance, bail was again refused and the case was transferred to Schweizer-Reneke. In all, I spent about six weeks in several police stations and three prisons.

Dirker, Van Wyk and 'Coloured' Sergeant Slabbert drove me to Schweizer-

Reneke. When we stopped in Klerksdorp to get petrol, out came a parcel of food they had brought, and a flask of hot coffee, which they shared with me. While I drank from the same plastic cups that Dirker and Van Wyk used, Slabbert – the Coloured sergeant – was unceremoniously told, '*Kry vir jou 'n blik*' ['Get yourself a tin can'] and, without a word of protest, he went off to find an empty jam tin from which to drink his coffee.

Both Dirker's instruction and Slabbert's compliance were entirely in keeping with apartheid's pecking order. The structure of every sphere of South African society was whites at the top, followed by Indians, then the Coloureds, with Africans at the very bottom. In the Cape, Coloureds were one rung higher than Indians, but only in certain respects.

Many of the policemen in Schweizer-Reneke knew my family, and some of the older men even remembered me as a child. Because the cells at the police station were made of corrugated iron and were decidedly uncomfortable, they offered to clear one of their offices and convert it into a cell for me.

Dirker refused, insisting that this 'dangerous terrorist' had to be kept in a proper prison. The nearest facility was in Christiana, a good hour's drive away, and that is where I was to be taken.

But, before we left, the sergeant decided to take me home to see my mother. I was unshaven and somewhat dishevelled, and she promptly fainted, convinced, from my appearance, that I had been subjected to ill treatment and torture. When she regained consciousness, I assured her that I was physically fine, apart from an attack of gastritis, and she gave the police something to eat before we set out for Christiana.

Halfway between the two towns, we were met by policemen from Christiana and I was formally handed into their custody. I stayed in prison there for about a month, but after just a few days, I realised that one of the African prisoners who had been transferred from Schweizer-Reneke at the same time was paying special attention to me. Every morning, for example, he brought me a bucket of hot water for shaving and washing, which was most welcome in mid-winter.

Eventually, I struck up a conversation with him. I asked him how long his sentence was, and he said three years. I asked him why he had been sentenced. He replied: 'I broke into your brother's shop.'

Dirker had issued instructions that I was not to receive any visitors or newspapers, but had grudgingly conceded that as an awaiting-trial prisoner, I could have food brought in from outside. The Nanabhay and Bhikoo families earned my eternal gratitude by sending food to me each day.

The monotony of prison life was made bearable by the two faithful literary companions I had taken with me, *The Oxford Book of English Verse* and *The Complete Works of William Shakespeare*. One dreary afternoon, a bored young guard sidled up to my cell to make conversation. He noticed my reading matter, and after a few inane comments about the bard, left me with what he obviously perceived as a profound observation: 'Man, that Shakespeare wrote some nice recitations!'

Although I am a Muslim, another diversion was found in attendance of the Sunday church services led by the Dutch Reformed minister. He was clearly delighted at what he must have seen as my conversion, and at the very first service I attended, gave thanks to the Lord 'for the coolie who is in our midst'.

By far the most amusing incident during my stay at Christiana was an unexpected visit from my 'lawyer', who turned out to be none other than my good friend Babla Saloojee. Babla had passed only Standard 7 at school, and his English was mediocre, to say the least. But he had a rare talent for impersonating lawyers, and his performance totally fooled the prison officers.

He said he came from the legal firm of Bhoolia & Bhoolia, and that they were preparing a bail application to be heard in the Supreme Court. He even went so far as to bring along a sheaf of legal documents, as well as a petition that I had to sign.

Then he had me swear an oath before a warder, who was also a commissioner of oaths, and reeled off the names of several judges, one of whom, he claimed, would hear my application. However, he solemnly warned, there was no expectation of a sympathetic hearing, and I should be prepared for a lengthy stay in prison.

The next day I had more visitors. The security police wanted me to make a statement about my 'lawyer'. Sensing trouble, I reminded them that as an awaiting-trial prisoner, they were not entitled to question me, and refused to disclose the identity of my legal representative.

As it happened, the petition Babla had me sign was genuine, and had been drawn up by a real attorney. In an ironic twist of fate, the Supreme Court bail application was heard by Judge Quartus de Wet, the very man who would later sentence me to life imprisonment, but who, on this occasion, criticised the state for their unwarranted persecution of me, and granted me bail of £50. Babla came to fetch me from Christiana, and the case was eventually heard in Schweizer-Reneke, where I was given a lenient sentence of six months, suspended.

No sooner was I home than I had a new responsibility.

Mac Maharaj was studying law in England when the Communist Party sent him to East Germany for training. His expertise was in communication, printing and intelligence, but he also underwent a course in urban guerrilla warfare. In 1961 or 1962 the party sent him back to South Africa to carry out some of the underground movement's most clandestine tasks.

Only four or five people throughout the country even knew of Mac's return, and Rusty Bernstein, on behalf of the Communist Party, entrusted his safety and well-being to me. On arrival, Mac stayed with his sister in Springs, but I quickly had to find another safe haven for him.

It was difficult, but I decided the home of Indres Naidoo was a good choice. There was a constant stream of people through the house, and no one, including the Naidoos, would realise that Mac was involved in politics.

But he also had to have a social life, so I arranged with the Vassen brothers and Herbie Pillay that they would play bridge with him. Of course, they had no idea who he was or why he was in Johannesburg either, but as friends of mine, they agreed to entertain him as best they could.

Shortly after they had spent an evening playing bridge at Suliman Esakjee's house, I was contacted by an enraged Tommy Vassen.

'Who the **** is this guy? He quarrels all the time!' Tommy bellowed. 'Who is this chap? He's so damn argumentative! We are going to **** him up!'

All I could do was plead with them not to do anything silly, but it took some effort to restore the equilibrium between my friends and Mac. Fortunately, he was able to carry out all the tasks expected of him successfully, right up to the time of his arrest in 1964.

THE SPEAR OF THE NATION

... who will deny that 30 years of my life have been spent knocking in vain, patiently, moderately, at a closed and barred door? What have been the fruits of my many years of moderation? Has there been any reciprocal tolerance or moderation from the government? No! On the contrary, the past 30 years have seen the greatest number of laws restricting our rights and progress until today we ... have almost no rights at all.
– Chief Albert Luthuli

If the government reaction is to crush by naked force our non-violent struggle, we will have to reconsider our tactics. In my mind, we are closing a chapter on this question of a non-violent policy.
– Nelson Mandela, May 1961

The words of Chief Luthuli summed up the frustration and suppressed anger of the people in the face of increasing oppression and relentless onslaughts on their dignity and humanity.

But it was Mandela, during a press interview while he was underground, who gave the first public voice to the previously private views of a considerable number of ANC leaders who were contemplating a move away from the traditional policy of non-violence. His statement unquestionably portended the formation of Umkhonto we Sizwe, or MK, but the first seeds of the armed struggle had been planted as far back as 1953.

In general, there is a tendency to either downplay MK's contribution to the struggle, or to grossly romanticise it. Due to the publicity it attracted, Dr Percy Yutar's histrionic claim, during the Rivonia Trial, that we had been plotting 'a violent and hellish revolution' was accepted by many without question, but the truth is, during the time I stayed at Liliesleaf, I witnessed nothing that could even vaguely be described as advanced preparations for an uprising. There was a lot of talk, and much shuffling of papers, but the only weapon I ever saw was a single little pistol, and it had long since jammed! Various studies have, in fact, confirmed that at the time of the Rivonia raid, the only weapon MK had at Liliesleaf was an airgun.[23]

In truth, MK's contribution was admirable, and needs no embellishment to take its place in the annals of the struggle. Where discrepancies occur in accounts of MK's role, it should be borne in mind that even people involved in the same event remember the details differently, and amnesia is no friend of accuracy.

I was struck, for example, by a section in Rusty Bernstein's excellent book, *Memory Against Forgetting*, which not only states that I was never an MK member, but also ascribes to me 'a principled objection to violence'.

The facts are just the opposite. Not only was I among MK's earliest recruits, I also served on the regional command that identified potential targets even before the official launch of the armed wing on 16 December 1961.

Furthermore, I was a member of a unit that carried out modest acts of sabotage with the dual purpose of assessing the targets and testing the efficacy of our equipment. At no time did I object in principle to the decision to move to an armed struggle, and I have never harboured the slightest regret about MK's formation.

I did, however, terminate membership of the regional command during the first half of 1962, after discussing certain reservations with some of my senior comrades. Not all men are born to be soldiers, and I realised at a fairly early stage that my aptitude lay in the political rather than the military field. My view was in no way at odds with the policy of either the ANC or the South African Indian Congress. Indeed, at the joint meeting where they agreed to form MK, it was explicitly spelt out that this should not be at the expense of our political work.

But there were two incidents that strengthened my reservations about being an active member of MK.

The regional command met a few weeks before the official launch of MK to finalise the targets where bombs would be placed on the night of 16 December. One of them was the Portuguese Labour Office in Market Street, earmarked in protest against the slave-like treatment of migrant workers from Mozambique, employed by South African mines.

Kholvad House, where I lived, was right next to this building, and I knew that children played on the pavement outside, sometimes until late at night. To avoid exposing them to danger, I suggested that we find an alternative target, and I was greatly taken aback when one of my colleagues – let's call him Comrade X – responded: 'This is war, and we must accept that people will die.'

His attitude was in direct contradiction to what I understood MK's policy to be, namely that every effort would be taken to prevent human injury, and that attacks would be launched against symbols of apartheid, such as government buildings and military installations, as well as power plants and communication lines.

After some discussion, the regional command agreed that an incendiary rather than explosive bomb would be used at the labour office. My unit was given the task and indeed, as I had predicted, there were children playing outside until well after dark, and we had to wait until they had gone home before placing the device.

The second incident also involved Comrade X. Some friends and I decided, on the spur of the moment, to visit him one Sunday afternoon, and what we found shocked me beyond belief. He was in his living room, openly assembling a bomb, oblivious to the need for even the most elementary security, and quite unconcerned about whether or not my friends were members of MK.

Comrade X was my senior in the movement, and it would have been impertinent of me to say anything, but the combination of these two events forced me to confront my own fears and misgivings. Some years later, on Robben Island, an MK colleague accused me, during a fairly heated discussion, of having been too scared to remain an operative. There was a certain element of truth in his indictment, but I was genuinely concerned that the reckless disregard for security shown by Comrade X was not confined to him alone within MK ranks, and that the possible consequences for the underground movement as a whole were dire.

As the sabotage campaign progressed, there were more incidents that seemed to confirm my belief, and in due course I was greatly relieved to learn that others shared my concerns, which were amply illustrated by the Rivonia raid and certain evidence produced at our trial.

On two occasions during 1962, at Chief Luthuli's request, I had to drive Moses Kotane in utmost secrecy to the tiny village of Groutville in Natal, to which Luthuli was restricted in terms of his banning order. Our journeys offered wonderful opportunities for us to discuss certain matters freely. Moses and I had known one another for a long time, and he was one of the most senior, experienced and respected struggle leaders.

On one of the trips, he revealed his displeasure about some of the developments within MK, and singled out Comrade X for harsh criticism, using words such as 'reckless' and 'adventurism'. Of course, I endorsed his opinions completely, but one of the fundamental lessons I had learnt over the years from persons of the calibre of Kotane, Bram Fischer, Yusuf Dadoo, Walter Sisulu and Madiba was that while comrades were entitled to criticise one another when necessary, and in the most severe manner, this should never be allowed to dilute or destroy our interpersonal relations with one another.

So my dealings with Comrade X remained as congenial as ever, and we never discussed what I saw as his dismissal of security measures, or my reservations about MK. After the first bombs exploded on 16 December, the police swiftly narrowed down the likely suspects to a handful of us. Among the dozen or so who were raided the next day were Comrade X and me. Later, we were both placed under house arrest, I for thirteen hours a day and he for twenty-four. Soon afterwards, he and a number of others who had been placed under house arrest went into exile, and, several years later, he died abroad, never to see his beloved South Africa again.

❧ 9 ❧

High Roads and Low Ebbs

*Shall I tell you the secret of the true scholar? It is this: Every man I meet
is my master in some point, and in that I learn of him.*
— Emerson, *Letters and Social Aims*[1]

After the Treason Trial, I spent a good deal of time traversing South Africa, banning orders notwithstanding. I had learnt to drive at the age of eleven, and covered thousands of kilometres over the years, yet just about the only thing I knew about a car was how to change a flat tyre!

Although it was illegal to do so without a permit, I often visited Soweto, or at least Dube and Orlando, which was what the sprawling township consisted of at the time. On the way home from there one Sunday evening, Stanley Lollan and I were waved down by a group of white youngsters whose car was stuck at the side of the road. Given the political climate and increased polarisation between the races, there was a very real danger that they could be attacked, so we stopped to help them.

They had run out of petrol, and we offered to take them to the nearest garage that would still be open, in Mayfair, ten kilometres away. It was a tight squeeze, but they all jumped into my car.

Their conversation was sprinkled with references to 'this damned Group Areas Act', 'this bloody government' and the like. I assumed they were just putting on a show for us because we had done them a favour, but as we drove, one of the youngsters mentioned that his father was having problems with the authorities after selling a plot of land to an Indian.

It turned out that his father was in Delareyville and that my brother, Ismail, was the buyer!

The five-year banning order that confined me to the Johannesburg magisterial district expired at midnight on Monday 15 January 1962. Fully expecting it to be renewed immediately, I stayed away from my flat for about ten days prior to that date and, having learnt from past experience that the best hiding places were the homes of political activists, I stayed at Rusty and Hilda Bernstein's house.[2]

At the stroke of midnight, Tommy Vassen, Dennis Brutus and I set off by car for Schweizer-Reneke, our first stop on a journey to Cape Town. We reached my sister's farm in the early hours of the morning to find various of my family members waiting anxiously to warn us that the police did, indeed, want to serve me with a new banning order, and were looking for me. We cut short our visit and got back on the road as soon as possible.

I spent several weeks in Cape Town without any harassment from the police, but subsequently realised they'd had me under surveillance the whole time.

On one of our excursions with my good friend Barney Desai, we went to the top of Signal Hill, from where there is a panoramic view of the city, the sea and, on a clear day, Robben Island, which had been recommissioned as a prison for 'non-white' male political prisoners the year before. As we gazed out across the cold Atlantic Ocean, Barney laughingly pointed to the island and joked: 'That's Kathy's future home.'

To my surprise, nine months would pass before the police issued my next banning order. I used the time productively, travelling twice more to Cape Town, to Port Elizabeth and East London, about half a dozen times to Durban, and driving to Swaziland, Bechuanaland and Basutoland. All my movements were monitored, obviously in the hope that I would lead the security police to activists who were engaged in illegal activities, but they were disappointed.

Twice during this period I drove Moses Kotane to Natal to meet with Chief Luthuli. We stayed at the home of my friend, George Singh, one of the pioneers in the field of non-racial sport in South Africa. His hospitality was renowned, his generosity a legend, and when we left, he gave Moses an expensive bottle of Scotch as a farewell gift.

Moses was no more than an occasional drinker, and I coveted that bottle of whisky. All the way back to Johannesburg, I tried to persuade him that it would be better off in my flat than at his home in Alexandra, given the law against 'non-whites' possessing or partaking of liquor.

But Moses was having none of it.

As we made our way to Alexandra along Louis Botha Avenue in the early morning hours, a car behind us began to hoot loudly and persistently. I slowed down and signalled that the driver should overtake us and he did, stopping almost immediately. It was the police flying squad, and both Moses and I had visions of being arrested for having the contraband whisky.

As the occupants of the police car walked towards us, thoughts of spending a night in prison flashed through our minds, but to our astonishment, the sergeant, most apologetically, explained that he had recognised the car's registration plate, TR, and simply wanted to chat to us because he, too, was from Schweizer-Reneke, and was feeling homesick.

When I told him my name, he became quite excited, telling me that his family had been clients at my sister's shop for years. We must have spent a good thirty minutes talking about mutual acquaintances before the sergeant cheerfully sent us on our way.

In a democratic South Africa, free of all discrimination, it isn't easy for those who did not experience it at first hand to comprehend life under petty apartheid. We could not sit down to a meal in a restaurant, and at many retail outlets in white areas, assistants served us only grudgingly. Buying snacks in Hillbrow one night, I was left to wait while the clerks served one white person after another, despite the fact that they had come in long after me. Eventually I lost patience and asked angrily if my money was black.

While I criss-crossed the country during my nine-month reprieve, Walter Sisulu was under severe restriction and Madiba had disappeared from the public eye entirely. Some of their children were at school in Swaziland, and shortly before the end of a term, Walter asked me to fetch them for the holidays. Rumours had been circulating for some time that there were plans to abduct some of the children, and the Mother Superior flatly refused to release them into my care.

As I was about to leave, having failed to persuade her that I really was a trusted family friend, Walter's daughter Lindi, aged seven or eight, saw me through a window and came running to greet me, happily calling my name. The good sisters relented and I was able, after all, to drive Lindi, Madiba's eldest daughter Maki and Duma Nokwe's niece home.

THE BLACK PIMPERNEL

By this time, the press had dubbed an elusive Mandela the Black Pimpernel. The police were hunting him relentlessly, and it was almost a full-time job to ensure that he stayed out of their clutches. At the same time, it was vital for ANC supporters to know that he remained dedicated to the cause, and one way of keeping this message alive was through the media. From time to time Mandela gave telephone interviews to reporters, and on rare occasions met them face to face.

A British television journalist, Brian Widlake, had come to South Africa to conduct a prearranged interview with the prime minister, Dr Verwoerd. For some reason, Verwoerd cancelled the interview and Widlake, not wanting his trip to be wasted, made it known via a few South African anti-apartheid colleagues that he would like to talk to Mandela instead.

Having determined that Widlake was no security threat, the committee responsible for Madiba's safety selected a safe house in the Johannesburg suburb of Cyrildene for the interview. My task was to get Widlake to the venue without being followed.

I kept a close eye on the rear-view mirror to make sure there was no car tailing us, but not far from the appointed house, I took a wrong turn and spent several panic-stricken minutes trying to find my way back. Eventually I found the house, where Madiba was already waiting, and to my surprise, Widlake commended him on our excellent security precautions. The poor man thought our circuitous route was all part of a plan to lose anyone who had us under surveillance!

That was the only television interview Madiba gave while he was underground, but we did arrange a number of print interviews for him. One of the British journalists he met, Patrick O'Donovan from the *Observer*, wrote after the Rivonia Trial: 'It seemed odd that he should not have been caught, but the tyranny was at that time mitigated by inefficiency and coarse stupidity.' Having recognised in Madiba the makings of a great leader, O'Donovan also wrote: 'He had that inexplicable serenity, which he shared with Chief Luthuli, that seems special to the South African intellectual.'[3]

When Mandela moved to Liliesleaf Farm he assumed the identity of a labourer, David Motsamayi, wearing overalls and spending many hours tending the vegetable garden. He lived in one of the rooms in an outbuilding, and at night pursued his intensive study of armed struggles in countries such as the Philippines, China and Cuba, as well as the struggle of the Boers against British colonial rule in South Africa.

His presence at Liliesleaf brought with it vastly increased security considerations. Due to his position at the heart of the liberation struggle, he was South Africa's 'most wanted' fugitive, and every time he left the farm to attend secret meetings, he faced the threat of capture. In addition, leaders such as Sisulu, Joe Slovo, Rusty Bernstein, Ruth First and Dan Tloome were frequent visitors to the farm, while Madiba's wife, Winnie, and their daughters sometimes spent weekends there. We took every possible precaution, and throughout Mandela's stay, nothing untoward happened. In light of the later raid, this may have caused us to become complacent, or perhaps we allowed our vigilance to lapse once Mandela had departed.

At the beginning of 1962 we smuggled Mandela out of the country, so that he could attend the Addis Ababa conference of the Pan African Freedom Movement for East, Central and Southern Africa and mobilise support for the ANC and MK. Amien Cajee was given the sensitive and dangerous task of driving Madiba across the border into Bechuanaland.

From Africa he travelled to London, where he met Milton Obote, prime minister of Uganda, David Astor, editor of the *Observer*, and the Reverend Michael Scott. On his way back to South Africa, Mandela met with General Aboud, president of the Sudan, Ethiopian Emperor Haile Selassie and the Algerian head of state, Achmed Ben Bella. He also underwent training at a military camp near Morocco under Lieutenant Befikadu.

My flat at Kholvad House continued to serve as a venue for political meetings, though our activities became increasingly clandestine. When an Israeli journalist requested an interview with Walter Sisulu in April, the flat was the logical choice of venue.

Under the pretext of a social gathering, Ben Turok brought the journalist to the flat and we had tea. Just as the interview was starting, the security police arrived and arrested Walter, Ben and me on charges of attending an illegal gathering. Despite my protestations that my banning order had expired, they kept us in the cells at Marshall Square and the Fort for a few days. I subsequently sued the Minister of Justice, BJ Vorster, for wrongful arrest, and was paid £100 in an out-of-court settlement.

THE NET TIGHTENS

Adversity is a state in which man most easily becomes acquainted with himself, being especially free from admirers then. **–Samuel Johnson**[4]

On 27 June the Sabotage Act became law and the government introduced house arrest. On 30 July, 102 individuals were listed as 'banned'. The state also invested in a campaign to sow dissent within the liberation movement. 'Informers were recruited at an unprecedented rate in the early sixties. The police went so far as to issue a public appeal for spies through a black newspaper, *World*. "Any reliable informer can be assured of making a comfortable living by giving information" it promised. "A man with attentive ears can easily net something in the neighbourhood of R250 per month as an informer. We treat all information confidentially and protect the identity of informants. It is essential for the men who volunteer to deal only with the white staff." Since the average township-dweller earned between R24 and R42 for a month's work, it was not surprising that [some] came forward ... to assist the police.'[5]

In preparation for Madiba's return to South Africa, Walter Sisulu and I were sent to Bechuanaland to ensure that everything was in order for his aircraft to land. Cecil Williams had recently acquired a new car, and because it was still unknown to the police, he would drive Madiba back to Johannesburg. Everything went according to plan, and by the end of July, Mandela was back in our midst, albeit still underground.

The police search for him had moved into high gear. Nine months of following known activists, frequent raids and numerous roadblocks had failed to turn up any trace of the Black Pimpernel, and the authorities were not pleased that he continued to evade arrest.

After briefing the ANC leadership at Liliesleaf, Madiba's top priority was to report to Chief Luthuli in Natal. He was impatient to do so, and our committee was instructed to accelerate arrangements. While abroad, reports had begun to surface that Madiba had deviated from the ANC's historic policy of non-racialism after encountering opposition to this stance from some of the African leaders. He wanted to clarify the position without delay.

The committee was strongly opposed to the suggestion that Cecil Williams and his car should be used again to transport Mandela to Natal. We assumed that the police in Bechuanaland would have given their South African counterparts a full account of Madiba's return. The ANC leadership overruled our objections, and Mandela went to Natal posing as Cecil's driver. He met with Chief Luthuli and the Indian Congress leaders, and was on his way back to Johannesburg when the car was stopped by the police at Howick.

Mandela's seventeen months as South Africa's most wanted outlaw came to an abrupt end on 5 August 1962. I was appointed secretary of the Free Mandela Committee, and while he was awaiting trial I saw Madiba several times. Joe Slovo, his lawyer, informed the prison authorities that he needed me to be present during consultations, as I would probably be called as a witness.

During one session, Madiba asked Joe if the documents that he had left at Liliesleaf had been removed. The next time they met, Joe assured him that, to the best of his knowledge, all the documents had been secured and stored elsewhere. Liliesleaf, he had been told, was 'clean'.

It was not until the Rivonia Trial that we discovered this information was false. In fact, all of Mandela's documents, including his diary, were exactly where he had left them, and the prosecution had a field day with them.

In October 1962 I saw JN Singh and Ismail Meer in Ladysmith for the last time. By then, I was becoming concerned that if the police didn't serve me with a new banning order soon, some of my colleagues might start thinking I was an informer. Already there were signs that certain people were avoiding contact with me, and the police were actively stoking the fire of suspicion. Helen Joseph later wrote: 'By this time, most of the 30 accused [in the Treason Trial] had been banned. Kathrada, the Indian Youth Congress leader, said that if he didn't get banned soon, people would begin to suspect him!'[6]

It was deeply painful to hear from loyal comrades that some of my 'friends' had warned them that I was cooperating with the police. Fortunately such malice fell, by and large, on deaf ears, and I was by no means the only one targeted by such hurtful mendacity.

The 'dirty tricks' perpetrated by the security police knew no bounds. Walter Sisulu received an anonymous telephone call from 'a concerned comrade' who wanted to alert him to the fact that I was having an affair with Madiba's wife, Winnie. No one was immune to the toxic effects of a system that perverted justice on a daily basis and institutionalised lawlessness as a means of ridding the state of its enemies, real or perceived.

One of the early victims of this calumny was my friend Johan Oosthuizen, known to all as Oosie.

I first met Oosie during the 1950s when he covered a meeting in Sophiatown as political correspondent for an Afrikaans daily newspaper, *Die Vaderland*. Oosie, whose father was a school principal and belonged to the elitist Afrikaner secret society, the Broederbond, was almost certainly a member of the National Party at the time.

But what he saw at the protest meeting a few days after the first Treason Trial arrests in December 1956, including the police roughly wrestling an interpreter off the stage, caused Oosie to drastically review his political beliefs. He befriended Patrick van Rensburg, a former South African consul in the Belgian Congo, and soon afterwards they both joined the Liberal Party and struck up friendships with ANC and SAIC members.

But Oosie's newfound political views were more in line with those of the Congress of Democrats, and despite being acutely aware of the repercussions, he became a member. His family ostracised him, his wife divorced him, former friends and colleagues shunned him, and the security police placed him under surveillance. He changed jobs, joining the staff of the *Rand Daily Mail*, but even this avowed liberal publication was not comfortable with his political alliances.

His editors and colleagues were thoroughly intimidated by visits from the security police, who advised that this 'undesirable' person should be removed from their midst as soon as possible.

In August 1962 I asked Oosie to accompany me to Durban, where I had to attend an SAIC executive meeting, and then to Cape Town for a few days. On our return, the security police gave his editor a full report on the trip Oosie had taken with a 'dangerous communist', namely me, and he lost his job.

His social circle now consisted primarily of Congress members. To make matters worse, a few members of the Congress of Democrats treated him with suspicion, believing that as an Afrikaner, he must be an informer.

As the malicious stories about Oosie's loyalties spread, he began drinking heavily. In less than a year he had lost everything, and found nothing but rejection. On 5 October, the cleaners at the block of flats where he lived found Oosie dead, his head in the gas oven. Before he died he wrote several letters, one of which ended with the words, 'Long live Mandela'.

I had lost a comrade, and I was shaken by his death, which was an indictment of some of his new comrades, gripped by fear and paranoia, as well as the security police, who hounded and harassed him until he could take no more.

HOUNDED

For you were a man only when you could be the things you were and face up to the truth without flinching or denying it. The truth was that in life on earth there was no such thing as happiness without pain, victory without defeat. There were joy and enchantment and beauty to be garnered on the path, but at all times too there were burdens to be borne.
— **Paul Gallico, The Lonely**[7]

Oosie's death heralded the beginning of a bleak period in my life. Three weeks later, while attending an underground conference in Johannesburg, Wolfie Kodesh paid me a midnight visit with a copy of the *Sunday Times* carrying the banner headline, 'Police Hunt For Sisulu And Kathrada'.

Walter and I quickly discussed the situation with our comrades, and it was agreed that he should slip away to Bechuanaland, where a conference of the ANC in exile was imminent. It was also decided that as secretary of the Free Mandela Committee, I should make an appearance at Madiba's trial in Pretoria on Monday 22 October.

I quietly slipped into the Old Synagogue where the trial was being held, but the ubiquitous Sergeant Dirker noticed me almost at once. When he beckoned me to follow him outside I ignored him, and during the tea adjournment, made my way quickly to the dock to speak to Mandela. Dirker followed and tried to thrust the house arrest order at me, but I insisted that he read each restriction out loud. It was a deliberate act on my part, designed to humiliate Dirker, whose English was appalling, and perhaps it was petty, but at the time it was at least one way of getting back at him for all the grief that he had caused.

He struggled through the document, then ordered me to return to Johannesburg immediately. I was confined to the Johannesburg magisterial district, prohibited from attending any gatherings or communicating with any other banned or listed individuals, and had to report to the police daily.

And so I became the second victim of the new house arrest laws, Helen Joseph being the first. I could no longer have any visitors at my flat, not even my mother. I was confined to the flat for thirteen hours on weekdays, and around the clock on holidays and weekends. I needed to have someone come and stay with me, both for company and, in the event of visitors arriving, to convince the security police that they were not my guests, but his.

Amien Cajee was the perfect candidate. We had been friends for many years and he had stayed at the flat before. A few months earlier, however, he had taken a job as a bookkeeper in Wolmaranstad, about 200 kilometres away. Just how loyal a friend he was, he proved when it took just one telephone call from me for him to board the next train to Johannesburg and move in.

No sooner had he arrived than the security police threatened to arrest both of us, Amien for staying in the flat illegally and me for breaking my banning order. We consulted one of South Africa's pre-eminent human rights lawyers, Advocate Sydney Kentridge, who assured us that the police had no grounds for arresting either of us. So Amien stayed, but just as we were getting used to our shared way of life, I received instructions to abandon the flat and go underground.

On 7 November, Mandela was sentenced to five years' imprisonment. After some time in Pretoria Prison, he was sent to Robben Island.

GENEROSITY

We make our friends; we make our enemies; but God makes
our next door neighbour.   – **GK Chesterton**[8]

The women of Kholvad House had taken care of the bachelors in Flat 13 as though we were family members for years. Sarabai Mogalia, who lived above me, was especially kind and generous, and when I was placed under house arrest, her ministrations became even more important.

Every evening a stream of neighbours' children, some of them just toddlers, would come to the flat bearing a bowl or plate of something good to eat, one bringing a *roti*, another delivering a *puri* or samoosa. I started keeping a supply of chocolates in the flat so that their nightly trips would not go unrewarded.

I had always been fond of children, and those little ones gained a special place in my heart, along with their thoughtful mothers. Prevented from having adult company, no one could possibly take issue with a group of pre-schoolers, or accuse me of breaking my banning order by consorting with children. Their visits brought a ray of light into a life over which dark clouds were ominously gathering.

BANTUSTANS

There is a pleasure in being mad, which none but madmen know.
– Dryden, quoting one of the Greek philosophers[9]

The first month of 1963 saw apartheid tighten its iron grip on the lives of millions of people in South Africa with the birth of the Bantustan. On 23 January, Verwoerd announced that the government was to 'grant the Transkei self-government'.[10]

The Promotion of Bantu Self-Government Act of 1959 had laid the legislative framework for the traditional home of the Xhosa to become the first Bantu homeland, with a legislative assembly that could take no decision unless it was first approved by Pretoria.

In order to demarcate areas where Africans could 'rule' themselves, apartheid's architects carved up the country, consigning the overwhelming majority of people to 13 per cent of South Africa's least productive soil while the rest, including the fertile and arable farmland and the industrialised urban centres, remained the province of the whites.

The advent of the Bantustans marked the beginning of what would be an eventful year in South African politics. On 17 April three members of an MK unit – Reggie Vandeyar, Indres Naidoo and Shirish Nanabhay – were arrested while attempting to plant a bomb. Later that night they were joined in custody at Marshall Square by Isu 'Laloo' Chiba and Abdulhay Jassat.

Indres had been shot, and when the police took him to his house to search it, his wound had not yet been attended to. Throughout that night I received telephone calls from anxious family members, but there was little I could do about the situation until 7 a.m., when my house arrest order allowed me to leave the flat.

Joe Slovo, Harold Wolpe and I agreed that attorney Jimmy Kantor was the best candidate to gain access to the detainees. By mid-morning, we received the devastating news that the police had refused Jimmy access to all five of the men, and that he was consulting colleagues with a view to bringing an urgent application in the Supreme Court.

We could not wait for the law to run its course. Ama Naidoo was beside herself with worry about Indres, and we had no idea what the police might be doing to the other four men in the meanwhile.

We turned to Babla Saloojee in a desperate attempt to gain access to our comrades at Marshall Square. All he wanted was five packs of toiletries, a few new shirts and some cash.

He did it! After giving the police on duty some or other sob story, he presented them with the cash and the shirts, and they allowed him to talk, briefly, to all five detainees. His news, however, was not good. Chiba, Shirish and Jassat had been severely beaten and tortured with electric shocks. Indres had a gunshot wound, and Reggie had a broken shoulder after being clubbed with a rifle butt. He would have trouble with that shoulder for the rest of his life, while Jassat would suffer from seizures resembling epileptic fits.

According to the Report of the Truth and Reconciliation Commission,

> General Hendrik van den Bergh, head of BOSS at the time, appears to have been personally involved in the interrogation of these activists. Reggie Vandeyar described his encounter with the man he believed to be General Van den Bergh: 'At one point, I heard them saying that the "big boss" was coming and they stood to attention when this tall figure came in. He was an erect man, wearing a suit and a Homburg hat. He appeared very severe. He walked straight up to me. I was leaning against the wall. He grabbed my hair and smacked my head against the wall. He shouted, "Who sent you?" I did not respond. He walked straight out without saying anything. The police saluted him and Major Brits went after him. I suspect this man was General Van den Bergh, the head of BOSS, but I am not certain.'[11]

When the five were taken to court forty-eight hours later, I was shocked to see their physical condition. They were among the last of the activists to be brought before a court so soon after arrest. The Sabotage Act and ninety-day detention law had just come into effect, and Reggie, Indres and Shirish became the first MK members to be charged under the former, and sentenced to ten years imprisonment each, while Laloo and Abdulhay immediately fell victim to the latter.

UNDERGROUND

Two roads diverged in a wood, and I –
I took the one less travelled by
And that has made all the difference. — **Robert Frost**[12]

I did not want to go into exile, but shortly after Reggie and the others were arrested, I was instructed by the SACP leadership to go underground. I was given four hours to vacate the flat I had lived in for sixteen years, abandon everything I owned, including my car, and go to Rivonia.

Bob Hepple, a recently co-opted member of the Central Committee, drove me to Liliesleaf Farm. In contrast to the constant hum of Market Street, it was quiet and peaceful.

The property covered twenty-eight acres on the northern outskirts of Johannesburg and, in addition to the main house, had a number of out-buildings. It had been bought through a front company, set up for this very purpose, by the SACP. The 'official' occupants were well-known architect and artist Arthur Goldreich and his family, while farming activity was under the supervision of Thomas Mashifane, a long-standing SACP member who had recruited a group of young labourers from rural Sekhukuniland. They had no inkling that Liliesleaf was anything but a private home.

Security surrounding the farm was strict, and apart from the Central Committee, only a few people even knew it existed. When the first MK cadres returned to South Africa after receiving military training in China, Raymond Mhlaba and Wilton Mkwayi stayed at Liliesleaf while MK was looking for suitable headquarters. Govan Mbeki had been at the farm since November 1962, when he defied a banning order that demanded he return to Port Elizabeth from Johannesburg. From time to time, Walter Sisulu also stayed at Liliesleaf.

Goldreich, who was in charge of creating effective disguises for the under-ground operatives,[13] helped me change my appearance and I assumed the identity of Pedro Perreira, a Portuguese. I stayed at the farm until 2 July, when Bob Hepple drove me to my new hideout, a garden cottage in Mountain View, tucked between the grand homes in Houghton and the more eclectic suburbs of Yeoville and Observatory.

Denis Goldberg, who was on his way out of the country, was already at No. 10 Terrace Road when I arrived. Before going into exile, he had been given the task of buying several vehicles and another farm, Travallyn, for the ANC.

One is invariably edgy when living underground, but I felt fairly safe at the Mountain View cottage and inconspicuous as Pedro Perreira. My comrades living at Travallyn, outside Krugersdorp, were equally comfortable about their security.

However, a number of us had started feeling uneasy about the continued use of the Rivonia farm. We were well aware that the need-to-know principle had not applied to Liliesleaf for some time, and that far too many people – one of whom was Bruno Mtolo, a saboteur from Durban and leader of the Natal branch of MK – had visited the farm.

But there was no avoiding one final meeting in Rivonia. In the days leading up to this crucial gathering, I became more agitated and afraid. The only person with whom I could share my misgivings was Walter Sisulu, whose views coincided with my own. I also had a lengthy discussion with Ruth First on one of her visits to the farm, and was pleased to find that we shared the same opinion of the High Organ's plans. She, too, was concerned about security, and in desperation I asked to see Yusuf Cachalia, briefed him on what was happening at Liliesleaf and conveyed my concern about the flouting of security.

Rusty Bernstein summed up my feelings succinctly: 'In retrospect, it is evident that the "safe house syndrome" was at work. Liliesleaf Farm seemed to be the easy option for every hard choice. It was, after all, "safe". I began to sense that, in the top MK echelons, there was a growing gung-ho spirit of recklessness – though in their cloak and dagger operations they would probably have called it necessary boldness. It was not shared by those of us who still lived and moved about in fear in the real world outside the fence.'[14]

OPERATION MAYIBUYE

Because of the controversy surrounding the recently drafted and widely rejected 'Operation Mayibuye', it was a matter of priority that we examine alternatives, such as those suggested in a document drawn up by Bernstein.

A few weeks before, on the explicit understanding that it was merely a draft document, the Central Committee had allowed Joe Slovo to take the Operation Mayibuye plan abroad in order to canvass the views of the leadership in exile. On Saturday 6 July, members of the High Command and a few others, including me, met at Rivonia to discuss Rusty's critique of the plan.

We ran out of time, as Rusty had to rush home in order to comply with his banning order, and it was to complete this meeting that we went back to Liliesleaf.

Despite a National Executive Committee decision that such a radical policy shift would only be made after thorough consultation with the national leadership, a stance supported by the Central Committee, the High Command initiated the proposed move from sabotage to guerrilla war. The wisdom of this strategy would be debated for decades to come, throughout the Rivonia Trial and long afterwards on Robben Island. Mandela would later write: 'As far as I was concerned, Operation Mayibuye was a draft document that was not only not approved, but was entirely unrealistic in its goals and plans ... I did not believe that guerrilla warfare was a viable option at that stage.'[15]

Walter Sisulu did not support the plan either. '[He] explained that he was at a meeting of the High Command when the Operation Mayibuye document was discussed. Some supported it and others did not. He himself felt that guerrilla warfare was not a feasible proposition at that stage. By the time of the Rivonia arrests, no decision had been taken on the issue of guerrilla warfare.'[16]

According to Bernstein, the chief proponents of Operation Mayibuye were Govan Mbeki, Joe Slovo and Arthur Goldreich. His own objections were that the document 'lacked political depth' and was premised on a wholly inadequate analysis of the real balance of power in the country, glossing over sober considerations of both the government's strengths and weaknesses, and ours.

It seemed to me to be founded in military-style thinking, slicked over with a political gloss. It was based on a fairly simplistic military assessment of the logistic problems of guerrilla warfare rather than on a social and political programme which also encompassed armed force ... I have long had a contempt for military thinking and its obsession with numbers and with things ... Operation Mayibuye seemed to me to be military thinking at its worst ... Its political content was simplistic, quite inadequate as a basis for such a serious and irrevocable action as it would commit us to. I disliked everything about it, and said so. It is my clear memory that the document had still not been endorsed by anyone other than the MK command.[17]

At his trial in March 1966, Bram Fischer described Operation Mayibuye as 'an entirely unrealistic brainchild of some youthful and adventurous imagination. If ever there was a plan which a Marxist could not approve in the then prevailing circumstances, this was such a one ... if any part of it at all could be put into operation, it could achieve nothing but disaster.'[18]

The document was divided into six parts, of which the following were among the salient features:[19]

- 'The absence of friendly borders ... are disadvantages. But more important than these factors is the support of the people who in certain situations are better protection than mountains and forests ... In the rural areas ... the over-whelming majority of the people will protect and safeguard the guerrillas.'
- 'The active hostility towards [South Africa] from the world ... [and] particularly ... from almost the whole of the African continent and the socialist world may result in such massive assistance in various forms, that the state structure will collapse far sooner than we can at the moment envisage ... even armed international action at some more advanced stage of the struggle are real possibilities.'
- 'The following plan envisages a process which will place in the field, at a date fixed now, simultaneously in preselected areas, armed and trained guerrilla bands, who will find ready to join, the local guerrilla bands with arms and equipment at their disposal: Simultaneous landing of four groups of 30 based on our present resources whether by ship or air – armed and equipped in such a way as to be self sufficient ... for at least a month ... thereafter, there should be a supply of arms and other war material to arm the local population. On landing, a detailed plan of attack on preselected targets with a view to taking the enemy by surprise, creating the maximum impact on the populace, creating as much chaos and confusion for the enemy as possible. Before these operations take place, political authority will have been set up in a friendly territory with a view to supervising the struggle ... It is visualised that this authority will in due course of time develop into a Provisional Revolutionary Government.'

Part IV dealt with internal organisation: 'Our target is that on arrival the external force should find at least 7 000 men in the four areas ready to join the guerrilla army in the initial onslaught.'

Part V required the Intelligence Department to identify 'points along the coast which would be suitable for landing of men and supplies and how these are going to be transferred from the point of landing to the area of operations'.

Day after day I listened to comrades excitedly formulating the plan, and as the deliberations proceeded, it dawned on me more powerfully than ever before how isolated one can become in one's thinking, even if one lives just a short distance from the people of the townships. Were my comrades living on a different planet? They were certainly living in a world of their own, completely divorced from reality. Theirs was a world of fantasy, romanticism, impatience and intolerance, but the problem was, they sincerely believed in what they were writing and planning. They were in a hurry to implement it, and did not take kindly to any criticism.

During discussions of Operation Mayibuye on Robben Island, I often expressed the view that our arrest had really been a blessing. Had the plan been implemented, we would almost certainly have gone to the gallows. But our retrospective discussions lacked the heat of those at Liliesleaf and often included some good-hearted banter. Nevertheless, it was only on Robben Island that I learnt how annoyed my colleagues at Rivonia had been by my opposition to Operation Mayibuye, and my criticism of the lack of security. Some of them were so angry that I was regarded as obstructing the revolution, and one of my best friends, Wilton Mkwayi, was actually preparing a stick with which to beat me up!

RAIDED

It was around 3 p.m. on Thursday 11 July that, as the officer in charge reported telephonically to his superiors, the police 'hit the jackpot'. They had hoped to capture Walter Sisulu, and finding the rest of us with him was a bonus.

Warrant Officer CJ Dirker would later testify: 'I jumped out of the van and ran in a westerly direction towards the main house. I went into the kitchen, where I met two of the employees, Solomon and Thomas. Solomon was busy making ice cream, which he said he was preparing for Pedro. I have known Sisulu since 1952. Kathrada also since 1952. On that day, when I saw them, I found it difficult to identify them. I looked at Kathrada several times before I recognised him. Kathrada had a black moustache [it was actually red]. His hair was long and a reddish colour. He was peculiarly dressed, with a long coat.'

Dirker's evidence was peppered with lies. He claimed to have taken each of us around the property while making notes of what we said, which was untrue. He also claimed to have opened the bonnets of vehicles belonging to Bob Hepple and Rusty Bernstein, and established that the engines were cold. In fact, Rusty had installed an anti-theft device that would have let off a high-pitched alarm had the bonnet indeed been lifted.

According to the court record, Lieutenant WP van Wyk testified that my disguise was so effective that, 'I asked people, "Who is the white man?" Then he asked me, "How do you like my coat?"'[20] Detective Sergeant Kennedy said it was 'very difficult' to recognise me, and that I asked him: 'Would you have recognised me if you saw me in the street?'

There are many theories about how the security police learnt of the farm in Rivonia. One story is that an anonymous informer contacted Van Wyk and claimed to know the location of the ANC's headquarters. When they met, on a dark night, with Van Wyk in an unmarked police car, the informer was heavily disguised behind dark glasses and a scarf, and they drove around the dusty Rivonia roads for several hours looking for the farm in vain. The story goes that they returned the next night, and the night after that.[21]

Bernstein wrote that the Central Committee 'had never intended to turn the place from a "safe house" into MK's semi-permanent headquarters. Boldness and daring were necessary qualities for the cloak and dagger nature of their activity, but they seemed to encourage a casual, almost reckless disregard for security at Liliesleaf. Things which need not have been done there, were, because it was easy and available. Things that should never have been kept there, were; and people who should not have known of its existence were taken there. Unconsciously, MK was turning our safe house into a place of peril.'[22]

Not only had the farm become the headquarters of MK, but the half-dozen or so members of the National High Command had assumed the role of the national leadership of the ANC and SACTU. Only the Communist Party's Central Committee, albeit with a depleted membership, continued to function independently.

Sisulu was the most senior of the ANC leaders in the country, and he was also the political commissar on MK's High Command. I was a full-time functionary of the Communist Party and I was at Liliesleaf on the instructions of the party. My primary task was to do party work, to carry on with my work among Indian Congress activists and generally be available for any other political tasks.

Because I was no longer a member of MK's Regional Command, I tried as best I could to be out of earshot when the High Command held its meetings or when there were sensitive informal discussions relating to MK. The problem, however, was that we were effectively confined to a single room, where we slept, ate and met. Because there were no assistants, I frequently had to type and encode, or cyclostyle, correspondence and other documents for the party, the ANC and the High Command. Much of the MK work I did was more out of duty and discipline than conviction. It also kept me occupied.

I was not alone in worrying about our increasingly lax security. Our 'foreman', Thomas Mashifane, also expressed concern. But what worried me the most was what I perceived to be the harebrained talk and planning at formal and informal discussions between members of the High Command.

The police claimed that they'd had the farm under surveillance for some hours before the raid. Why, then, did they not detain the dentist who had come to take an impression of Walter's mouth, and who left the property barely thirty minutes before the police swooped? And why was the dentist allowed to emigrate, unhindered? He was the only outsider who knew that Walter would be at the farm that day.

The truth is, we never found out who or what led the police to Rivonia that day. Every version that has been bandied about over the years is based on nothing more than speculation.

The government crowed in triumph. In a front-page report in the *Rand Daily Mail* on 13 July, the police commissioner confidently stated: 'We are following up clues which will undoubtedly lead to the end of all subversive elements.'[23] He described our arrest as 'a major breakthrough in the elimination of subversive organisations'.

Over the next ten years he would be proved correct, but the state's success went hand in hand with torture, detention without trial, betrayal and dirty tricks.

Under Yutar's cross-questioning, Thomas Mashifane testified that among the most regular customers for the fresh produce from the farm were the officers at the Rivonia police station!

ESCAPE FROM MARSHALL SQUARE

It was towards midnight on Saturday the 11th of August that the four men slipped out of Marshall Square and disappeared into the night. This was the most dramatic jailbreak in the history of the South African prison service. — Joel Joffe[24]

A few hours after the raid, Arthur Goldreich was arrested when he returned to Liliesleaf from work, suspecting nothing. He, his wife and fellow activist Harold Wolpe[25] were held at Marshall Square, while the rest of us, including Denis Goldberg, were taken to the Fort and transferred to Pretoria the next day. Abdulhay Jassat and Mosey Moolla were also being held at Marshall Square.

A young warder, Johan Greef,[26] was somehow bribed to help Wolpe, Goldberg, Jassat and Moolla escape. In the weeks that followed, all four had the luck and cunning to successfully escape the dragnet set up for their recapture. Their escape was deeply humiliating for the authorities.

Arthur and Harold hid out in my Mountain View cottage for a week, hardly daring to breathe, let alone talk. They kept the blinds down and the lights off, and made their way out of the country as soon as they could. Abdulhay and Mosey also escaped across the border. The security police finally raided the cottage on 5 September.

⊷ Part II ⊷

Another Terrain

of the

Struggle

Invictus

Out of the night that covers me,
Black as the pit from pole to pole,
I thank whatever Gods there may be
For my unconquerable soul.

In the fell clutch of circumstance
I have not winced nor cried aloud.
Under the bludgeonings of chance
My head is bloody, but unbowed.

Beyond this place of wrath and tears
Looms but the Horror of the shade,
And yet the menace of the years
Finds, and shall find, me unafraid.

It matters not how strait the gait
How charged with punishments the scroll,
I am the master of my fate:
I am the captain of my soul.

— WE Henley

~ 10 ~

The Rivonia Trial

Fools live to regret their words, wise men to regret their silence.
– Reader's Digest[1]

On 6 October 1963 we emerged from our ninety days of detention to be fingerprinted and formally charged. After three months of strict solitary confinement – filled with robust interrogation and threats, anxiety and fear – it was a huge relief to have our status changed to 'awaiting-trial prisoners'. At last we were allowed contact, albeit restricted, with the outside world – with our lawyers, our families and friends. Equally important was the opportunity we now had to access newspapers and books.

Thanks to the secret messages from Sylvia and Amien we were not entirely ignorant of developments, but we had no idea that the build-up to our trial had commanded so much attention. Government spokesmen, the press, the SABC, the police and other defenders of the state had waged a well-orchestrated campaign to rouse public opinion against the ANC and its 'revolutionaries', with the result that long before the first witness was called, we had been tried, convicted and even sentenced by white South Africa.

On 7 October we had the first consultation with our lawyers, though it was really more of an introductory session than a formal discussion of our defence. Bram Fischer, Vernon Berrangé and George Bizos I already knew, but I had not previously met Arthur Chaskalson and Joel Joffe, a young advocate and attorney respectively, whom Bram had brought into the team.

He said of Arthur Chaskalson that he was 'the new Issy Maisels', and we were instantly impressed with the commitment and enthusiasm of the newcomers. We never doubted that every member of our legal team would go the extra mile in pursuit of truth and justice on our behalf, and we were right.

The meeting was also the first time the eight of us had spoken to one another for months. I had last seen Mandela on 22 October 1962, when I was served with my house arrest orders while attending his trial.

As a sentenced prisoner, he now wore the humiliating prison uniform of short pants and sandals. It was painful to see him in this attire, which reflected the demeaning and universal white South African custom of referring to all African men, irrespective of age, as 'boys'. Even little children spoke heedlessly of the 'garden boy' and the 'kitchen girl'.

That first meeting was somewhat chaotic. We had so many questions, so much to say to one another, but we did at least manage to pair up advocates and accused. I was to be represented by Vernon Berrangé.

One other item of significance was the revelation by Bob Hepple that he had been asked, under interrogation, if he was prepared to turn state's evidence and testify against us. We were rudely jolted when he admitted that instead of categorically rejecting the suggestion, he was giving it some consideration. He attended no more of our consultations, and we were left to wonder what he would decide.

When we parted that day, it was with an earnest caveat from our lawyers: Be prepared for the worst.

The spectre of the gallows had loomed large in our minds since the moment of arrest, and we had effectively resigned ourselves to the inevitable. Even at my most bold and blunt during interrogation by Rooi Rus Swanepoel, I was concealing my innermost and deepest fear. Now our lawyers had spelt it out in the clearest possible language.

Our strategy from the outset was to treat this as a political trial and to conduct ourselves with pride and dignity. The eyes of our people, and the world, would be on us, and we dared not show weakness. We could not rely on the Appeal Court to overturn a death sentence. Only the struggle and international solidarity could save us from the gallows. Therefore, in the event of a death sentence we would not lodge an appeal. We prepared ourselves for the worst.

We had no idea what specific charges we would face, but we were determined to force the prosecution to prove each and every allegation levelled at us, and challenge every shred of fabricated evidence they placed before the court. We would make admissions or volunteer information only if this was politically expedient.

And, regardless of the consequences, we would not apologise for our political beliefs or activities.

TO COURT

Violence in the voice is often only the death rattle
of reason in the throat. — John F Boyes[2]

On the opening day of the trial we were ferried to the historic Palace of Justice in Pretoria under arguably the heaviest armed escort ever to accompany prisoners to a South African court. The anti-ANC hysteria that had been whipped up by Dr Percy Yutar, the lead prosecutor, permeated proceedings from the start.

Yutar's high-handed, histrionic and arrogant attitude gave credence to a story that had reached us, namely that he had specifically asked the Minister of Justice, BJ Vorster, to let him try the case. His motivation, according to the grapevine, was that he was Jewish, and because the defendants included some adherents of this faith, he was ideally positioned to demonstrate to the world that not all South African Jews were 'communists' or 'terrorists'.

As white South Africa united behind Yutar, our supporters bravely demonstrated solidarity with the accused, while international protests and anti-apartheid campaigns burgeoned. By 106 votes to one, the United Nations adopted a resolution condemning the Verwoerd government for its 'repression of persons opposing apartheid', and called upon South Africa to 'abandon forthwith the arbitrary trial now in progress, and grant an unconditional release of all political prisoners and to all persons imprisoned, interned or subjected to other restrictions for having opposed the policy of apartheid'. The sole dissenting voice was that of South Africa.

On 30 May the UN representatives of thirty-two African states appealed to all countries that shared diplomatic relations with South Africa to 'take all necessary measures to prevent the execution of African nationalist leaders now on trial in Pretoria'.[3] By the time we were sentenced, this group had grown to fifty-six members, who issued a joint statement expressing 'profound indignation' at our punishment.[4] The Soviet Union, Czechoslovakia, Morocco, Nationalist China, Sierra Leone, India and Liberia used a meeting of the Security Council to speak out against the court's decision.[5]

When we learnt that we were to be tried by Judge Quartus de Wet, my thoughts flashed back to 1961 when he had granted me bail and lambasted the security police for persecuting me. I hoped this would augur well for us.

Yutar and his team had taken three months to draw up the charges against us, but although copies of the indictment were released to the newspapers in advance, the first time we, or our legal team, saw the voluminous document was in court, after the judge had taken his seat.

Bram immediately asked for a six-week postponement so that our lawyers could study the indictment. The judge allowed three weeks. *State vs Nelson Mandela and others*, more commonly known as the Rivonia Trial, had begun.

THE TRIAL BEGINS

Dulce et decorum est pro patria mori.   **– Horace**[6]

When the court reconvened, Bram led the attack on the indictment. In his book, *The Rivonia Story*, Joel Joffe later wrote: 'He is the complete lawyer … painstaking, clear, precise. Unlike the public concept of a lawyer, he is no orator … his performance here might be crucial for the whole future, perhaps even for the lives of the people in the dock. The men in the dock were not just his clients. They were colleagues with whom he had worked for years, many of them close personal friends.'[7]

One of the most glaring deficiencies in the state's case was that some of the charges against us related to incidents that took place before the Sabotage Act was passed. Nelson Mandela was implicated in 156 acts of sabotage, all of which had occurred while he was in prison.

'Either the state knows who committed the acts, or it does not,' Bram argued. 'If it does not know, then it should not charge them with the acts. If it does know, it should tell us.'

'With his voice rising with a rare passion and anger, Bram declared that the state had decided that the accused were guilty. It had further decided that, since they were guilty, a defence would be a waste of time.'[8]

Before responding, Yutar dropped a bombshell. All charges against Bob Hepple had been withdrawn, he told the court, and he would be called as the state's first witness. Hepple, who had said nothing to us, left the dock and walked out of court a free man.

The judge quashed the original indictment, telling Yutar:

> The whole basis of your argument, as I understand it, is that you are satisfied that the accused are guilty. And you are arguing the case on the assumption that they are guilty. A preliminary matter like this must be approached on the assumption that the accused are not guilty. The accused are assumed to be innocent until they are proved to be guilty. And it is most improper, in my opinion, when an accused asks for particulars in regard to an offence which is alleged to have been committed, to say to him: 'This is a matter

which you know all about.' That presupposes that he is guilty and he will not be told anything about the offence.[9]

Astonishingly, despite the prosecutor's pleas, the rest of us were also set free – but only for as long as it took Rooi Rus Swanepoel to rearrest us, right there in the courtroom.

Two weeks later, Yutar presented a new nine-page indictment. While it had been amended, the state's case remained substantially the same, and was based on 193 acts of sabotage that had allegedly been perpetrated by the accused or 122 of their agents.

Yutar argued that although we were charged with sabotage, 'this is nevertheless a case of treason par excellence. It is a classic case of the intended overthrow of the government by force and violence with military and other assistance of foreign countries.'[10]

This time, the judge accepted the indictment and the state prepared to call its first witness the following day.

But Yutar's troubles were not yet over. Bob Hepple had fled the country, and was out of his reach in Dar es Salaam – because, the prosecutor claimed, he had been threatened and intimidated by the accused.

Since Swanepoel had questioned me relentlessly during my ninety-day detention about the location of my hideout, I was intrigued to hear Yutar claim that Hepple had cooperated fully with the police, and had led them to the cottage in Mountain View. I felt hurt, betrayed and angry, and it was quite some time before I was ready to give Bob any credit for leaving the country in order to avoid testifying against us. One thing that helped ameliorate my feelings about Bob was a statement he issued from Dar es Salaam in which he made it clear that the only threats he had received had come from the police, and not from us or any of our supporters.

THE VOICE OF THE STATE

I wouldn't say that this was the most important police work in the country. I just carried out my ordinary duties.   – **Warrant Officer Dirker**[11]

Almost the whole police force was there on the 12th.
– **Lieutenant WP van Wyk, leader of the raid on Liliesleaf**[12]

Before Yutar could deliver his opening address, Bram intervened to ask the judge whether it was in order for this speech to be broadcast live by the SABC. Of course, Yutar pleaded ignorance to the presence of the broadcaster's microphones, but we were sure he had stage-managed this unprecedented publicity stunt. The prosecutor loved the fact that our case had turned the media spotlight on him, and was quite crestfallen when the judge ordered the SABC to remove its recording equipment from the court.

The newspapers, of course, had a field day. After we were sentenced, the *Daily Mirror* castigated them as follows:

> The government-controlled South African press is cock-a-hoop and exults thus: World opinion must itself stand condemned before the bar of international justice if it now favours a campaign for the release of the prisoners convicted after a fair trial of the most fundamental crimes against their fellow countrymen. [But] the apartheid laws of South Africa are loaded against the accused in just the same way as the Nazi laws were loaded against people in Hitler's People's Courts. How South African lawyers can practise and continue to brag about the system of justice that permits indefinite arrest and imprisonment without charge is a miracle of moral agility.[13]

The international press was often sympathetic to the cause of South Africa's oppressed. Among the newspapers that condemned the 'white supremacist government'[14] were the *Washington Post*, the *Los Angeles Times*, the *New York Times*, the London *Times* and the *Guardian*, which said that the accused included 'men who would be among the pillars of a just society'.[15]

With Hepple gone, Yutar opened his case by calling the labourers and domestic staff from Liliesleaf. Thomas Mashifane, the foreman, was not a young man to begin with, but by the time he took the stand, he had visibly aged. When his evidence was concluded, he sought and was given permission by the judge to ask a question. He described how, in solitary confinement, he had been made to take off all his clothes and then been beaten and kicked as he ran naked around a table.

'I just want to know,' he said in his soft voice, 'why I should be assaulted like that when I was not committing any offence. I just want to know why they were hitting me?'

The judge told him to report the assault to the police, assuring him that it would be investigated. Mashifane replied: 'I did complain to the police, and at that time pus was still coming from my ear. Nothing was done.'[16]

Mashifane's closing words ruptured the hush that had fallen over the court. 'When a person is being "killed" he can't speak as he would have wanted to speak if he had not been suffering pain. A man speaks better when he has not been hit.'

The testimony of Eva Hlongwane, who had worked for my landlord in Mountain View, was equally poignant. 'I was arrested in September. I don't know why. I was released on 23 December. I told Lieutenant Swanepoel everything I knew. Then I was still kept after that for three months. Lieutenant Swanepoel kept on asking me questions. For a month I was quite alone.'[17]

Next came testimony about the purchase of Liliesleaf and Jimmy Kantor's legal practice, especially as this related to visits by some of us to his law partner and brother-in-law, Harold Wolpe. Kantor had been arrested on 21 August 1963 – my birthday, spent in solitary confinement – after Wolpe escaped from Marshall Square.

It was one of many grievous blunders by the security police. Kantor was a debonair young lawyer with a circle of fashionable friends, married to a beautiful model, who liked nothing more than to relax over weekends at Hartebeespoort Dam near Pretoria, where he kept a small boat. He was not a political activist and there was no evidence whatsoever linking him to anything illegal. In his book, *A Healthy Grave*, he disclosed that he came close to a complete emotional breakdown while in solitary confinement.

Detective Sergeant van Rensburg testified that when Kantor's office was raided and numerous files and books removed, he asked the lawyer where Wolpe and Goldreich were.

'He said he made it his business not to know. He expressed hope that they escaped,' Van Rensburg said.

Yutar handed in hundreds of documents, most of them found at Rivonia, including Operation Mayibuye, Mandela's diary, leaflets and correspondence. The court also received the draft of a secret radio broadcast I had been working on and a pamphlet I had compiled to mark the commemoration of 26 June. I would also be grilled on a section of the Mandela diary.

By the time Yutar called his last witness, the feeling within the defence team was that his case against me, Rusty Bernstein and Raymond Mhlaba was so weak that we might even be acquitted.

LETTERS TO SYLVIA

For the longest time I had adhered to a conscious decision not to fall in love across the colour line, knowing full well that both the personal and political consequences could be devastating. How, then, had Sylvia Neame, with her blonde hair and blue eyes, become the most important person in my life?

As the state tightened its noose on political opponents in the early 1960s, my circle of friends shrank steadily, until only the closest and most trusted few remained. Detention and banning orders made normal communion all but impossible and, simultaneously, my political work was becoming increasingly dangerous.

I was thirty years old, and lonelier than at any other time in my life. I needed someone who was more than a friend, someone with whom I could share love, companionship and camaraderie and, perhaps most importantly, from whom I could draw courage when my own wavered.

Sylvia was at the University of Cape Town when we met, but soon afterwards, as though in answer to my prayers, she was awarded a scholarship to study at Wits and moved to Johannesburg.

I threw caution to the wind, and by the time I was instructed to go underground, Sylvia and I were so close that the Communist Party decided she would act as my courier and driver.

We could have gone into exile together, but some inner conviction prevented me from leaving, and from a political point of view, I never rued that decision.

Throughout the trial, Bram Fischer smuggled out my letters to Sylvia and brought back replies. They were members of the same underground Communist Party cell, and it was Bram himself who suggested that we should write to one another, offering the services of his wife, Molly, and their teenage son Paul as couriers.

Prudence and common sense ought to have dictated that I forego my personal interests and decline Bram's kind offer rather than risk exposing one of South Africa's finest advocates to professional censure. But it is possible that some of us had become rather self-centred and had developed the exaggerated and arrogant idea that the world somehow revolved around us, simply because we were prisoners, and had forgotten that we were merely spokes in a single wheel of the liberation struggle. We had fallen into the trap of indiscriminate and often disproportionate entitlement – a malady that unfortunately continues to ensnare and even corrupt some erstwhile freedom fighters.

At a certain point, however, I was overcome by guilt and shame at having inveigled Bram and Molly into this subterfuge and so, with great reluctance, I suggested to Bram that we should abandon our illegal activities. A few days later, he brought me a message from Molly: Under no circumstances should Sylvia and I stop writing to one another. Molly liked being the link between us, and Paul had just been given a new bicycle 'and simply loves riding it to play postman'. There was to be no further discussion of the matter, Molly said.

And so, thanks to the kindness and courage of Bram, Molly and Paul, Sylvia and I were able to communicate until just a few days before I was sentenced. Then she herself was detained and the letters had to stop.

About three months earlier, I had written to her: 'As long as they don't hang us, I am confident we won't have to remain in jail for a very long time.'

Sometimes my letters were more political than personal:

It is most encouraging to hear that the affected people have recovered their equilibrium and shed a bit of their fear. Best of all is the report of the optimism about the future. While one hates to dampen the spirit in any way, it is always good to be at all times fully aware of the reality of things. While there is some cause to engender optimism, we must not forget the struggle is not going to be easy. Much hardship still lies ahead which will require a great deal of sacrifice and courage. I have no doubt you are fully conscious of this, but would suggest you slip in this reminder whenever people tend to run away with themselves. We must try and avoid mass disillusionment, which can easily be caused if we don't hold our feet on the ground. Please don't get the impression that I am feeling any less confident. On the contrary, everything makes me feel more and more optimistic. I am still as sure in my mind as ever that we will meet sooner than we think. And this can only be as a result of a change which I feel is imminent.

Other letters to Sylvia bore testimony to our optimism. Even in the shadow of the gallows, thoughts turned to a life beyond the prison walls, regardless of the laws that made it impossible for a white woman and an Indian man to have an open relationship:

All this brings me face to face, however reluctantly, with the reality of thinking of us as two separate individuals, two separate lives with two different futures. At any rate insofar as the immediate future is concerned. We can be under no illusion that at the very best I must expect to be indisposed for a considerable time. What about you? And, without hesitation, I want our relationship to be as close and strong when you reach this goal, to share the sense of achievement and joy. But is it possible? Is it fair to even expect it? Some time ago you said you would like to wait for me. Do you still feel that way? Would you not be depriving yourself of maybe years of what would be a happy and normal life? I have expressed my wishes before and they are still the same today. To me it will always be a tremendous source of strength and encouragement to know that if and when I walk out of here one day, you will still be there. Needless to say, this knowledge would make life so much easier. But I have said this was being very selfish. So please, darling, do not let this factor cloud your judgment. For I might tell you, if you are going to depend on me in order to help you arrive at a decision, you will always get the same response as above.[18]

Of course, when I wrote to Sylvia during a court recess at the end of March 1964, neither of us could possibly have envisaged that it would be thirty years before our optimism was realised. On 18 and 19 April, I was still looking ahead:

So you see, yours truly does not face exactly a happy future – not the immediate future at least. But, *alles sal regkom* [everything will be all right] and I have great faith in it. It certainly won't be too long. Don't you worry, lovey, we will really make up for all this. These hardships and separation will only make more enjoyable the days and years we will yet spend together. Nobody is going to be able to stop that. No matter how things may look, don't ever allow yourself to get disillusioned.

On Sunday 7 June, I wrote:

The question was again put to me by someone this week. Is all this suffering really necessary, when you can easily live a comfortable life outside? And the usual jazz about how well off we are in South Africa compared to the conditions in the rest of Africa and Asia. Simple as all that – in SA all can be well clothed, fed and roofs over their heads, and schools and sports etc etc. But how could I explain my feelings to him, for he just won't understand. Of what good are these things to me when I haven't got dignity? And what is life without dignity?

By the time the defence began presenting our case, I was missing Sylvia terribly.

I want to come back to you. If only you know how much you have come to mean to me. How much I value your closeness and courage and loyalty … I can only wish time flies so fast so that we can be united once again and make up for the hardships of this enforced separation. Tonight I feel very close to you. I wish I can express my feelings somehow. You have entered my life when I needed you most … The bell has gone. I still have an hour, but I'm going to leave off to finish my book … Goodnight my darling. After many weeks I have just heard Sikelel'iAfrika again. Not many voices but nevertheless most welcome. Obviously political chaps. In so many jails throughout the country these songs must be sung every evening. Wish those in Govt can only know they just cannot succeed in crushing the spirit of the people.

On the Monday that the defence team closed its case, I tried to be as light and encouraging as possible:

I think we'll be sent off to the island after sentence. I suppose it will be nicer there – work outside, my fondness for the sea, the weather etc. Just you be patient – we will yet do a lot of things together we've been talking about. Not the least of which will be the holiday at the seaside cottage – just the two of us. I can almost smell the sea.

Drum wanted to know if they could publish a picture of me taken by the police the day after our arrest. People say I looked like King Farouk while I was in disguise. This is hardly complimentary. I am very ashamed. On the [other] hand I'm sure you and many others will want to know how I did look, so it might not be a bad idea to give them permission. I have indicated that other than the fact that I am ashamed, I have no objection in principle.

A month before the trial ended, I wrote:

I wish I could transplant my feelings to your heart and to the hearts of all my dear colleagues and friends. I remain as optimistic as ever about our struggle. In fact, I feel more confident than I did a year ago. I am happy that I have been able to make some contribution. There is no such thing as defeat in our struggle. And this is certainly not the time to even think of it. No matter what happens to us who are on trial at present; no matter how many of our former comrades have fallen by the wayside, and no matter how many will still leave us before we achieve our goal, the invincibility of the cause is becoming clearer by the day. It cannot possibly be otherwise. I want you to remember this, for I am certain it will help to lighten the burden of waiting.

In the week when our advocates presented final argument to the court, it was impossible not to extol the virtues and many talents of our defenders:

We've had a lovely day today. What a pleasure to listen to such brilliant argument. Even if the court eventually rejects it all, it makes one feel good after listening to it. And another thing, I hope it will teach Yutar a lesson in teamwork. He was the prima donna and just didn't want to give his colleagues a chance, in case they push him out of the limelight. Mr Chaskalson who spoke for the whole day today, is the most junior member of our team, yet he was given the opportunity to start off the defence argument. What a brilliant mind. I've heard of him for some years but only realised today his real calibre. He will certainly go a long way in his profession and obviously has the makings of another Maisels. What a tribute to a brilliant legal team, with such an outstanding leader. I don't think we could have done better.

My last letter to Sylvia from the Pretoria Prison was by way of farewell. On the eve of the verdict being pronounced, I was beset by uncertainty, confusion and doubt. As is evident from the content, I had no idea whether or not I would be able to communicate with her again:

The case seems to have taken quite an unprecedented turn for me, as you most probably must have gathered from the newspapers. If the remarks and general attitude of the judge during the defence argument are an indication of his state of mind, then Bernstein and I should expect to be acquitted. And perhaps Mhlaba as well. Since the very first day of our arrest I had made up my mind that I'd be convicted, although I had no doubts at all about my innocence.

Ayesha wasn't too sure whether my folks will be coming on that day. You never know, they might even be able to give me a lift back … I love you very much and will long for you no matter where I am and what I do. Goodbye sweetheart. On matters of principle there can be no compromise or weakening. Bye bye my love and keep well.

Also to everybody else, friends of mine and others who have been so wonderful all these months. I shall always be looking forward to being with them all again.

Chief Albert J Luthuli, president general of the ANC, was also writing letters. He was petitioning international leaders and organisations to address the human rights crisis that had developed in South Africa. Sadly, it was to be another three decades before any significant changes for the better became a reality.

On 9 March 1964, Chief Luthuli wrote to the UN Secretary-General, U Thant:

> Dear Sir,
>
> I write to you most urgently today to stress that whatever hope there still remains for a negotiated and peaceful settlement of the South African crisis will be lost, possibly for all time, if the United Nations does not act promptly and with firmness on the vital matter which has moved me to make this urgent appeal.
>
> You will also be aware that the last months of the year saw the bringing to trial of nine of the country's foremost liberation leaders, in the so-called Rivonia Trial in which the leaders are charged with allegedly plotting a war of liberation against the government. The nine include Nelson Mandela, who was arrested shortly after his return from a tour of independent African states in 1962, and who was taken from his prison cell, where he was serving a five-year prison sentence. There is the grave danger that all or some of the nine leaders on trial will receive the death sentence. Such an outcome would be an African tragedy. It would be judicial murder of some of the most outstanding leaders on the African continent. It would have disastrous results for any prospects of a peaceful settlement of the South African situation and could set in motion a chain of actions and counter-actions which would be tragic for everyone in South Africa as they would be difficult to contain.
>
> I address myself to you with the utmost urgency to urge that you use your good offices to avert the tragic crisis threatening South Africa.
>
> Yours sincerely,
> AJ LUTHULI
> President General[19]

We never learnt what the Secretary-General's response was.

Mandela and Sisulu speak

The Chinese word for crisis contains two characters:
one means danger; the other, opportunity. — **Anon**[20]

The court and the country had eagerly awaited the start of the defence case. On 23 April, as expected, Nelson Mandela was called as the first witness. However, Bram informed the court that instead of answering questions, he would read a statement from the dock.

Yutar was furious. He had been preparing for months to grill and humiliate Madiba, and he did not take kindly to being denied his chance. His appeal to the judge to warn the witness of the diminished value of a statement evoked from De Wet the terse response that the defence advocates had more than enough experience to advise their clients, without any advice from the prosecutor. Bram pointed out that as a qualified lawyer himself, Mandela fully understood what he was doing.

For the next five hours, Madiba owned that courtroom. He outlined his political history, dealt with the plight of the oppressed people and their desire for equality, justice and full voting rights. He admitted his role in the founding of MK and that he had undergone military training abroad. He spoke of the readiness of some African states to offer training in guerrilla warfare to MK cadres should the necessity arise to move from sabotage to armed resistance.

The dramatic peroration succinctly encapsulated the determination of an oppressed people to be free:

> During my lifetime, I have dedicated myself to this struggle of the African people. I have fought against white domination, and I have fought against black domination. I have cherished the ideal of a democratic and free society in which all persons live together in harmony and with equal opportunities. It is an ideal which I hope to live for and to achieve. But if needs be, it is an ideal for which I am prepared to die.

Of course we had read the address beforehand, discussed and unanimously approved it. We understood its implications.

That statement from the dock stands as a memorable beacon in our history. In political matters, Madiba was unhesitatingly selfless. He had led the argument for an ideological defence and was the first to suggest that if we were sentenced to death, there should be no appeal. This was an extremely difficult decision for all of us, but Madiba reasoned that for the sake of the people, their morale and the success of the struggle, we could not allow the trial to end on an anti-climax.

With Mandela having eschewed cross-examination, Walter Sisulu became the key defence witness. Having been denied the opportunity to question Mandela, Yutar was fully expected to direct all his frustration against Walter, and even our own lawyers were concerned about how well a man who left school at the end of Standard 6 would stand up to blistering interrogation by a doctor of law.

But we knew Walter, and we had every confidence in his abilities. He did not let us down, dealing with even the most complex of questions calmly and brilliantly. Only once did he come close to losing his temper, when Yutar challenged his testimony about indiscriminate persecution by the security police.

> Yutar: How do you know they arrest people indiscriminately?
> Sisulu: I know. They arrested my wife; they arrested my son. That was indiscriminate. I have been persecuted by the police. If there is a man who has been persecuted, it is myself. In 1962 I was arrested six times. I know the position in this country.

Yutar: You do?

Sisulu: I wish you were in the position of an African. I wish you were an
African.[21]

'Walter defied all odds by producing a virtuoso performance in the witness
box. "Only one phrase could describe his performance – absolutely brilliant!"
enthused Kathrada. "At the end of it all, Walter emerged from the witness box
as cool, as calm and unruffled as when he had entered it. Our lawyers and even
the accused were amazed at his composure, his phenomenal memory and the
masterly manner in which he acquitted himself."'[22]

Joel Joffe was deeply inspired by the way Walter handled challenging questions
and Yutar's irrational and insulting behaviour and statements. 'Walter in the
witness box had been a triumph. The way he came through revealed his real
qualities of stability, calmness and certainty in himself which had made him a
leader in his organisation, and which had ultimately made him Secretary General
of the African National Congress. His colleagues who had persuaded us beforehand that he would be more than a match for Yutar had understood him well.'[23]

'Dr Yutar had tried to take on Walter in the political arena and Walter had
just destroyed him. I have never in my experience as a lawyer, seen a witness
perform better under extreme pressure.'[24]

'The whole court, I think, had been impressed by this simple man of meagre
education but of tremendous sincerity, calm, conviction and certainty. To sentence
such a man to death would not be easy for any judge.'[25]

After several days of gruelling cross-examination, badgering and insults,
Walter emerged triumphant and unscathed. To a man, we were proud of him.

THE THIRD WITNESS

There is no truth existing which I fear, or would wish
unknown to the whole world.   – Thomas Jefferson[26]

I was the third witness. Advocate Ismail Mohamed, a friend since the early 1950s
and someone I trusted without reservation, had been asked by our defence
team to help me prepare my evidence.

Within the parameters of our defence strategy, I had to grapple with the
question: Exactly how much do I disclose to him? Knowing what scant evidence
the state had against me, the omission of certain incriminating information
could be not only personally advantageous, but crucial to the outcome of my
case. My colleagues knew my position vis-à-vis MK and agreed that I should
abide by the group strategy, namely not to volunteer any information that the
state did not already have. But I still had to decide whether this non-disclosure

should extend to my own advocate or not. Was this an ethical or a political problem, or both? And which consideration should take precedence?

Even though it all happened more than forty years ago, it is historically important to record the facts. I did not disclose my full involvement in MK or consideration of Operation Mayibuye to Advocate Mohamed or the court. I rationalised that since I owed no allegiance to my enemy, I could tailor my evidence to my own best advantage.

So I admitted to having been informed of MK's formation by Mandela, but denied having been a member. Nor did I volunteer that while at Liliesleaf, I had carried out a number of administrative tasks on behalf of MK.

Joel Joffe later wrote:

> The case against Kathrada was extremely weak. [He] was quite a different character. Only 34 years old, he had been active in the South African Indian Congress since he was a schoolboy. He was essentially one of the doers, the organisers, the men who get things done. He did not claim to be a policy-maker or a theoretician. In discussions he seldom expounded an opinion at any length. But what he did with remarkable effect was to heckle pointedly, with biting and pertinent interjections, and often with a great deal of sarcasm and humour. Dr Yutar cross-examined in an aggressive fashion and this acted as the spur to the aggressive sarcasm so characteristic of Kathrada in discussion. Yutar found it hard to keep his temper with Kathrada, especially when he refused to answer questions about other people and their activities.[27]

The case against me was based mainly on the following:

- I had hired taxi owner Essop Suliman on several occasions to smuggle MK trainees to Bechuanaland. The police detained him and 'persuaded' him to give evidence against me. He began testifying on Friday 20 December. Because of inconsistencies in his evidence in other trials, he was not believed by Judge de Wet, but, in fact, Suliman was telling the truth. I had dealt with both him and his brother, sending people by taxi from Johannesburg to Lobatse, from where they would go to Kenya and Tanganyika to train as MK soldiers. Suliman testified that on one occasion he transported people to the border and met with Joe Modise at the Morabi Garage, where Walter had told him to go. In September and October 1962, I had engaged him to transport people to the Bechuanaland border, he said. After Suliman's release from detention he sent me messages apologising for his revelations. Both he and his brother had been severely tortured, and the brother committed suicide after being released.

- The notorious Sergeant Dirker testified that he once saw Duma Nokwe and me in Sisulu's office, although all three of us were banned and prohibited from communicating with each other. We could not fathom the relevance of this evidence and it was not true. If Dirker had seen us, he should have arrested us.

• Abel Mthembu, an MK member who turned state's evidence, testified that he saw me at Rivonia when he went to discuss matters with members of the High Command. It was true that we had seen each other there, but I had taken no part in the discussions. The state tried to show otherwise:

Yutar: Supposing you were present when Slovo spoke [to Mthembu] about MK. You wouldn't tell us about it?

AMK: I assure you I wouldn't do what Mthembu has done.

Yutar: Abel Mthembu has come over here and taken the oath to tell the truth and the whole truth!

AMK: That's what I saw him do.

Yutar: And you're not prepared to do what he did?

AMK: I wouldn't divulge matters that took place in confidence.

Yutar: You regard him as a traitor?

AMK: I do.

Yutar: To whom?

AMK: To the cause of the freedom of the non-European people.

Yutar: And what do you do with traitors?

AMK: My Lord, I want to repeat what Mr Sisulu said, that if and when the time comes, I hope they will be tried and dealt with.

Yutar: By whom?

AMK: By the machinery set up, when the people of this country run this country.

Yutar: The provisional revolutionary government?

AMK: You can call it that.

Yutar: Were there any traitors among your own people, the Indian people?

AMK: I suppose there are. There are traitors among all people, Indians, Jews, South Africans, Afrikaners, the lot.

Yutar: And what were you going to do with the traitors, let's deal just with your people, the Indian people?

AMK: My Lord, when it comes to traitors, they are traitors. Whatever colour they are, they are traitors. I hope they will all be dealt with similarly.[28]

• Bruno Mtolo, another MK man who turned state witness, said he saw me when he asked to meet members of the High Command at Rivonia. In the presence of Wilton Mkwayi and me, Mthembu had asked Govan Mbeki if it was all right to bring Bruno. He said 'Okay'. Bruno had arrived the next day and testified that Walter, Govan, Wilton and I were there. 'I was introduced to Sisulu as Ala, Mbeki as Dlamini and Kathrada as Pedro.'[29] He had discussed MK matters with Mbeki. The next day, he saw me typing and duplicating an ANC leaflet issued on 26 June, which he identified as Exhibit R10.

I admitted typing and duplicating this leaflet, but Bruno lied when he said he saw me typing and cyclostyling it. Bruno showed no remorse about testifying against us. In fact, he seemed almost self-righteous about his betrayal. Perhaps this was the result of having been held in solitary confinement – an experience that affects some men in strange ways. Although he implicated me in various activities, I don't believe it was Bruno's evidence that condemned me to life in prison so much as one of the sentences in Exhibit R215, another leaflet: 'At Addis Ababa, the prime minister of Algeria, Ben Bella, called for a blood bank to aid our struggle. No longer with words alone, but with deeds.'[30]

• A transcript of my draft broadcast in reply to a speech by a member of the cabinet, Dr Eben Donges:

Yutar: This proposed broadcast of yours in response to the speech of the
    minister of finance … I'm suggesting to you it's a very vicious document.
AMK: I don't agree with your description of the document. I agree it was
    immoderate language, but I don't agree that it's vicious. I think what the
    minister was saying was vicious.
Yutar: You have called them among other things criminals!
AMK: That's what they are.[31]

• Most of the labourers and domestic staff testified that they had seen me at Rivonia, doing typing, duplicating, and other such work. This was true.
• When the police raided Liliesleaf, they found me in the same room as Sisulu, Mbeki, Bernstein, Mhlaba and Hepple. A copy of Operation Mayibuye was found in the same room.

From previous experience I knew that cross-examination would extend well beyond the evidence presented against me in the current trial. This had been emphasised by Sydney Kentridge when I consulted him about bringing a claim for damages against the National Party mouthpiece, *Die Transvaler*. The newspaper had carried a front-page report which, although not naming me, clearly identified me as having been responsible for the bombing of the pass office situated around the corner from my flat.

I had first seen Yutar in action against Communist Party leaders in the 1946 sedition case following a strike by African mineworkers, and regarded him as a cog in the regime's repressive machinery. Extracts from the court record illustrate clearly that ours was not a meeting of the minds:

Yutar: Wolpe was a communist?
AMK: He's a listed communist
Yutar: He was a communist, I said!
AMK: Well, he is a listed communist as far as I know.

Yutar: I repeat for the third time … never mind about the word listed, he was in fact, a communist?

AMK: Well, I repeat that he was a listed communist as far as I knew him.

Yutar: You are not prepared to say as far as you knew him he was a communist, apart from being listed by the government?

AMK: I knew his beliefs to be communistic.

Yutar: Now Sisulu has given evidence under oath?

AMK: Yes.

Yutar: And as has indicated, as you have done, that you are not prepared to mention names which implicate others?

AMK: Correct.

Yutar: You are quite prepared to exculpate people who are appearing in this trial? You know what I mean?

AMK: I don't.

Yutar: You're not attaching any blame to accused in this case, for example, No. 6, Bernstein.

AMK: Ask me a question. I might be able to answer it.

Yutar: Where you can exculpate Bernstein, when you can remove any blame from him, you do so?

AMK: If that is a fact, that may be so, but I'm prepared to tell the court the truth.

Yutar: By the way, your oath was to tell the truth, the whole truth, and nothing but the truth?

AMK: I'm aware of that.

Yutar: But when it comes to giving evidence which might implicate somebody either in this court, or outside this court, then you're not prepared to give that evidence?

AMK: I'm honour bound not to.

Yutar: Honour bound to whom?

AMK: To my conscience, to my political colleagues, to my political organisations to which I owe loyalty.

Yutar: And what about being honour bound to your oath to the Almighty?

AMK: I am not telling lies.

Yutar: You're not honour bound to that are you?

AMK: Well, I don't know if the police are doing the Almighty's work. I am not prepared to give the police anything that might implicate other people.

Yutar: And the political colleagues include the communists?

AMK: Naturally.

Yutar: And the political organisations include the Communist Party of South Africa?

AMK: It does.

Yutar: And you're not prepared to give any evidence which might implicate any members of the Communist Party, or the party?

AMK: I am aware that I have implicated myself to a great extent [by admitting that I was a member of the Communist Party]. I am not prepared to implicate anybody else.

Yutar: And this political organisation to which you owe this loyalty includes the African National Congress?

AMK: Yes.

Yutar: And also includes MK?

AMK: If I knew anything about MK, I would not tell you.

Yutar: Then how am I to test your story, what you're telling us?

AMK: I feel very sorry for you Doctor, but I am unable to help you there.

Yutar: I don't need your sympathy Kathrada. How is his lordship to test the accuracy of your evidence?

AMK: I'm afraid I have no suggestions.

Yutar: I'll leave that to his lordship. And you know what strikes me as very peculiar? You say you owe a loyalty to the Communist Party. It's an anti-religious party, is it not?

AMK: I don't know it as being such.

Yutar: So you are loyal to the Communist Party, which is anti-religious and doesn't require you to take the oath of allegiance?

AMK: I have never been asked to forsake my religion or my beliefs. Throughout the years in which I was a member of the Communist Party, I know of nobody who has been asked to forsake his beliefs.

Yutar: Were you told by the Communist Party leadership that you were not to implicate anyone?

AMK: Nobody has to tell me that, that is basic ... [it is] common to everybody who is fighting for freedom.

Yutar: Why did you play not only white, but play Portuguese? Weren't you ashamed to play the part of a Portuguese? Even a Portuguese name, Pedro Perreira!

AMK: I was ashamed to have to be placed in a position of playing white altogether in my own country.

Yutar: And was Cajee's name and your address used as a secret address for the receipt of publications from overseas?

AMK: That's almost laughable. My address to be used as a secret address? The police are at my flat I don't know how many times. They know my flat since 1946, and they know it's always been occupied by politicians. That would hardly be a secret address.

Yutar: Do you know a gentleman named Suleman Saloojee?

AMK: Yes. There are two people by that name that I know.

Yutar: Well, tell me what two do you know?

AMK: Well, tell me which one you want to know about. I am not going to tell you which two I know! You tell me which one you want to know about, and I'll decide whether to answer about him or not. I won't tell you what the address is. I won't tell you their business activities.

Yutar: Why not?

AMK: I want to know what you know about them, because I see members of the Special Branch sitting here.

Yutar: Did the African National Congress speak on behalf of 12 million non-whites?

AMK: They certainly do.

Yutar: Although its membership at its highest, if even that is to be accepted, is 120 000?

AMK: If you knew the conditions under which these organisations have to function, 120 000 is a very high membership.

Yutar: We are going to make a submission to his lordship, and we're going to support it with evidence, documents and otherwise, that you are nothing else but a communist agitator!

AMK: That's your opinion. I don't know what you mean by a communist agitator.

Yutar: That you are a member of the Communist Party and that your job is to agitate people to make them believe that they are oppressed and trying to incite them!

AMK: My lord, I thought we had solved this problem already. We don't have to make any non-Europeans believe that they are oppressed. [They] know they are oppressed.

Yutar: Your organisation, the South African Indian Congress, was one of the allies [of the ANC]?

AMK: That's right. And the Communist Party.

Yutar: Because you belonged to 39 organisations, didn't you?

AMK: My lord, I did not. That is one of the farcical things about these banning orders. I was banned from the majority of organisations which I did not even belong to. Some of which I was opposed to.

Yutar: And you hope to achieve that 'freedom in our lifetime' in your lifetime?

AMK: Certainly, even in your lifetime.

Yutar: Did you ever paint slogans protesting against the removal of the Bantu from Sophiatown?

AMK: I did.

Yutar: Yes, and you incited them not to move to Meadowlands?

AMK: I called upon people not to move.

Yutar: Which do you prefer, Sophiatown or Meadowlands?

AMK: I prefer to live where I would like to live, not where somebody in parliament tells me to live.

Yutar: Right, but of the two places, Sophiatown with all its slums and
shebeens, or those beautiful garden houses in Meadowlands? Which
do you think is the better place of the two?

AMK: Sophiatown with its comparative freedom, rather than Meadowlands
which has got 101 restrictions, permits, where your own mother can't
come and visit you without a permit.

Yutar: Is it not a fact Kathrada, but for the timely intervention of the police
[during the Durban riots in 1949] there would have been a bloody
massacre of the Indians by the Bantu?

AMK: My lord, we who lived through those days were of the opinion that,
but for the timely intervention of the Marines, not the police ...

Yutar: By the way, have you been to India?

AMK: No, I have not been.

Yutar: Do you know about the suffering of the people of India?

AMK: I know of the suffering of the people of this country, where I was
born.

Yutar: You've never been there and you've never done any research?

AMK: I have read about India.

Yutar: And don't the people suffer there?

Yutar: As a result of years and years of British oppression, people do suffer
in India.

Yutar [Do you know] George Naicker?

AMK: George Naicker I know. I don't know him to have held any position
in the South African Indian Congress.

Yutar: And he is a co-religionist of yours?

AMK: Co-religionist? He's a Hindu and I'm a Moslem.

Yutar: Oh yes, but an Indian?

AMK: Yes. Two different religions.

Yutar: Billy Nair?

AMK: I know Mr Billy Nair.

Yutar: Also an Indian?

AMK: Also an Indian.

Yutar: Yes, and?

AMK: And a human being.

Yutar: If you're trying to be smart with me, I'm prepared to take it.

AMK: I don't know why you keep on saying co-religionist and Indian.

Yutar then questioned me about the bomb planted in the Rissik Street Post
Office, for which Ben Turok was sentenced to three years' imprisonment. He
asked if I knew that the structure was made of wood:

AMK: I don't know if it's made of wood. I know it's made of stone as far as
I can remember.

Yutar: Look, there's a lot of woodwork inside. What would have been the effect of a bomb exploding in such a building, the possibility of loss of life to people working in the building?

AMK: It all depends on when it explodes, I suppose.

Yutar: An innocent man posting a letter over there, an innocent child, maybe even a young Indian girl! Or a little Indian child!

AMK: I don't know why the Indian comes into it.

Yutar: I said maybe?

AMK: Maybe, it may be a Jewish child too.

Yutar: By the way do you know of any similar provision in any other countries in the world, for detention without trial?

AMK: Remind me and I might be able to confirm it. Offhand I don't.

Yutar: Kathrada, do you know that India has a three-year-detention no trial law?

AMK: Quite likely.

Yutar: Did you ever voice any protest against that along the same lines as you do against the 90-day detention no trial law in South Africa?

AMK: I have not. I live in South Africa, I suffer from the laws in South Africa, and my objection is to what goes on to me and my people.

Yutar: You were trying to get assistance from Ghana. Do you know that Ghana has a five-year detention no trial law?

AMK: That is correct. I'll get assistance from the devil, provided it is for my people in this country, and the freedom of my people.

Yutar: But you choose to attack the country of your birth!

AMK: I choose to attack it and I will go on attacking it, till things are put right.

Yutar: Are you sometimes referred to as 'K'?

AMK: I am not referred to as 'K'. I don't know anybody who refers to me as 'K'.

Yutar: Do you know anybody else who goes under the initial of 'K'?

AMK: Yes, Mr Khrushchev.

Everyone in court, including the judge, laughed, but Yutar was not amused. Next, he turned to bombs planted by MK in Johannesburg and other urban areas, and asked if I had confidence in 'these people'.

AMK: I have said that I regard the leadership of the African National Congress as a responsible leadership. I have said that those who are in MK have been forced to resort to these methods. I have the fullest admiration for their courage, and when you talk of responsibility, I also know that members of the Ossewa Brandwag committed acts of sabotage when they had the vote, and when they had every other means of expressing themselves – and some of them are in the government today.

Yutar: By the way, as a matter of interest, as a communist, which brand of communism do you follow now, Khrushchev or China?

AMK: I follow my own brand of communism and that is freedom in South Africa from oppression. That is what I follow.

Yutar: You are a member of the Communist Party? A loyal follower of the Communist Party?

AMK: I am.

Yutar: Whose aim and object is to secure freedom for what you call the oppressed people in this country?

AMK: For what are the oppressed people in this country.

Yutar: And to that doctrine you subscribe fully and unequivocally?

AMK: Fully and unequivocally.

Yutar: And you were determined to see the fulfilment of the policy, the aims and objects of the Communist Party!

AMK: I still am.

Yutar: Which involved the overthrow of the government of South Africa?

AMK: That is so.

Yutar: By force and violence if necessary?

AMK: When and if necessary.

I cannot claim that everything I said in my evidence was true, but when I said I did not belong to Umkhonto we Sizwe, I was not lying.

In a letter to Sylvia while I was on the witness stand, I wrote:

Calling me as the third witness was almost as great a surprise to me as it was to the other side. I felt a bit nervous for the first hour or so, but thereafter felt okay. In fact, every too often when under cross-examination, before I answered a question I thought to myself: How would she have liked me to answer? The prosecution was quite shocked, I think, at the frankness with which I dealt with my involvement. But I always felt that while fully and frankly stating my attitude towards Umkhonto, I was not going to pull my punches or withhold my beliefs. I know that quite a few of my friends, and you too, will have been surprised to learn that I had connections with Umkhonto.

Raymond Mhlaba, Rusty Bernstein, Govan Mbeki and Denis Goldberg testified after me, while Elias Motsoaledi and Andrew Mlangeni emulated Mandela and merely read statements from the dock.

VERDICT

We do not err because truth is difficult to see. It is visible at a glance. We err because this is more comfortable. — **Alexander Solzhenitsyn**[32]

On 11 June, Judge de Wet summed up all the evidence against each of the accused. '[He] said that he had recorded his reasons for the conclusions that he had come to and would not read them out. The judge dealt more fully with evidence given by Kathrada than with that of the other accused.'[33]

What he said was: 'Now it is clear that Accused No. 5 was an active supporter of the so-called liberation movement. The question to be considered in the case of this accused is whether he has been proved to have been an accomplice of the other accused. It is the existence of criminal intent in each of those who jointly committed a crime which entails on each a criminal responsibility. I think his conduct in relation to document R10 might be sufficient to justify me in finding that he is an accomplice, but there are additional factors.'

The judge itemised those as:
- My role in the Free Mandela Campaign.
- My 'almost daily contact with Goldreich' and the other accused 'who were actively associated with the affairs of the Umkhonto. He admits discussing these affairs with them and must be presumed to have expressed his opinion and given his advice and in this way he associated himself with these activities.'
- The transcript of my planned broadcast, *The ANC Calls Upon The Indian People*.
- The transcript of Walter Sisulu's broadcast on 26 June, which I had typed, and from which the judge cited the following sentence: 'In the face of violence, men struggling for freedom have to meet violence with violence.'

On the basis of the evidence, De Wet said, 'I am satisfied that the state has proved that Accused No. 5 was party to the conspiracy alleged in Count 2, and I find him guilty on this count. I am not satisfied in regard to his guilt on the other three counts and he will be found not guilty on these three.'

Nelson, Walter, Raymond, Andrew, Elias and Denis were each found guilty on all four counts. Rusty was acquitted, but was promptly rearrested on other charges.

Aggrey Klaaste was in court that day, and in the next edition of *Drum*, he wrote that he would never forget 'the expressions on the faces of the accused men when the verdict of guilty was given – Nelson smiling to his wife; Walter Sisulu waving; Kathy Kathrada shrugging his shoulders'.[34] The day after the verdict was handed down, *The Times* of London reported that sixty British members of parliament, led by representatives of the Labour, Conservative and

Liberal parties, 'joined a march down Whitehall to South Africa House to protest against the Rivonia Trial verdicts'.[35]

The *Washington Post* got it wrong, though, reporting: 'Kithrada [*sic*] was found guilty of planning a violent revolution and an invasion of foreign military units.'[36] On the very day that we were found guilty, Dr Martin Luther King and thirteen supporters were arrested in St Augustine, Florida, 'during an attempt to integrate a restaurant'.[37]

Our lawyers were certain that a higher court would overturn the verdict against me, and pleaded with me to appeal. I refused. Not only would such action have set me apart from my colleagues, but I would only have been arrested for something else, such as breaking my banning order, and sentenced to at least ten years in prison.

Once the verdict was in, all the anxiety and fear that had been a part of my life for eleven months were condensed into the twenty-four hours that remained before we knew our fate. Would we face the gallows or many years of incarceration? Through the longest night of my life, I prayed for the strength to endure the waiting, and for the hope and courage that had sustained me during my ninety-day detention.

In the morning, as we gathered to go to court, we drew fortitude from one another, reminding ourselves anew of our responsibility to our struggle and our suffering people. Thousands of supporters lined the streets around the Palace of Justice and gathered on Church Square, some bearing placards with messages such as, 'You will not serve these sentences as long as we live', 'A milestone of freedom has been reached' and 'We are proud of our leaders'. Hundreds of policemen, many with dogs, formed a human barricade around the court building.

First there were the pleas in mitigation of sentence. Bram Fischer had approached Harold Hanson, a specialist in the field, who had agreed to argue on our behalf despite the fact that his reaction to Mandela's statement had been that we seemed to be actively courting the death sentence.

He was eloquent in appealing for clemency, pointing out that it was not our political aims that had been criminal, 'only the means to which they resorted'.[38] Furthermore, said Hanson, 'the accused represent the struggle of their people for equal rights. Their views represent the struggle of the African people for the attainment of equal rights for all races in this country.'[39]

George Bizos and Bram had approached at least three people to testify on our behalf, but they all refused. Liz Lewin, in the throes of a divorce from her husband Hugh, who would in due course be jailed for his involvement with the African Resistance Movement, had asked author Alan Paton to testify in mitigation[40] and he had agreed.

'Even more moving was the appearance of Alan Paton, the well-known author and president of the South African Liberal Party. He said he had come to ask for clemency because of the future of the country. He described Mandela, Sisulu and Mbeki as men of sincerity and a very deep devotion to their people.'[41]

To a belligerent question from Yutar, Paton responded: 'I am a believer in the removal of any racial discrimination whatsoever, also economic discrimination. I am in favour of a reconstructed society [in South Africa], in favour of some measure of the redistribution of the land and wealth of this country and the removal of the grosser inequalities.'[42]

Paton came under savage attack from Yutar, who demanded of him: 'Are you a communist? Are you a fellow traveller?'

Designed to discredit Paton, such questions merely exposed Yutar's abysmal ignorance. Paton was an avowed humanitarian and anti-communist. 'Denis Goldberg, Accused No. 3, almost laughed out loud when Dr Yutar implied that Sharpeville was engineered by the African National Congress.'[43]

SENTENCE

There has been, there is, no silence like the silence in a court when the judge lifts his head to hand down judgment. All other communication, within and without, is stilled; all is ended. This is the last word.
— Nadine Gordimer, *The House Gun*

Uppermost in my mind that morning was the warning of our lawyers at the very first consultation: 'Chaps, prepare for the worst.' They had certainly done everything possible to protect us from that 'worst', putting up a relentless and legally brilliant fight. But would it be enough?

The court was packed with supporters, friends and relatives, their faces tense, their eyes betraying their anxiety. Aggrey Klaaste described the way that some of us looked that day: 'Nelson Mandela in new, dark suit, taking notes, notes, notes; Sisulu, fined down to thinness; Denis Goldberg, cheerful and almost chubby; Govan Mbeki, listening, listening, listening, hand cupped to ear; Raymond Mhlaba staring at the proceedings.'[44] I do not believe that any of us showed outward signs of fear, though the death penalty must have been at the forefront of our thoughts as Justice de Wet bent his head towards his notes:

> I have heard a great deal during the course of this case about the grievances of the non-European population. The accused have told me, and their counsel have told me, that the accused, who are all leaders of the non-European population, have been motivated entirely by a desire to ameliorate these grievances. I am by no means convinced that the motives of the accused were as altruistic as they wish the court to believe. People who organise a revolution usually plan to take over the government, and personal ambition cannot be excluded as a motive.

The function of this court, as is the function of a court in any country, is to enforce law and order, and to enforce the laws of the state within which it functions.

The crime of which the accused have been convicted, that is the main crime, the crime of conspiracy, is in essence one of high treason. The state has decided not to charge the crime in this form. Bearing this in mind, and giving the matter very serious consideration, I have decided not to impose the supreme penalty which, in a case like this, would usually be the proper penalty for the crime. But consistent with my duty, that is the only leniency which I can show.

The sentence in the case of all the accused will be one of life imprisonment. In the case of the accused who have been convicted on more than one count, these counts will be taken together for purposes of sentence.

He spoke the crucial words, 'life imprisonment', almost in a whisper, then hurried from court. A deep hush enveloped the courtroom, followed by an audible sigh of relief – not shock, as one would normally expect at the prospect of a life sentence, but relief, because it was not a death sentence.

We turned and smiled at the packed public gallery and Denis, I think, shouted: 'Life sentence!' The enormity and full implication of the sentence would sink in soon enough, but for that moment, there was only jubilation that we were not going to be hanged.

The press lost no time pressing home some salient points. The *New York Times* wrote: 'To most of the world those men are heroes and freedom fighters, the George Washingtons and Ben Franklins of South Africa. If disaster is to be averted in South Africa, those who now hold the reins of power there must re-examine the policies that are sowing the seeds of holocaust.'[45] Stanley Uys, one of my favourite journalists and also an acquaintance, pointed out in the *Observer* that 'the 3 500 000 whites do not really know what the 13 500 000 non-whites think of the trial verdict. This is a particularly dangerous kind of *apartheid*.' He also offered revealing statistics about political repression in South Africa in the preceding eighteen months, 'best revealed by the official figures: 1 162 members of Poqo have been charged and convicted. A further 269 members of the banned African National Congress or of its associated organisation, "The Spear of the Nation," have been convicted of sabotage. Seventy-eight Africans have been found guilty of political murders and 44 have been sentenced to death.'[46]

In time, we would learn that one of our lawyers, Arthur Chaskalson, had been told by Harold Hanson even before the court convened that morning that the death penalty was not going to be handed down. Asked how he knew this, Hanson replied, 'I asked the judge. I went in to see the judge this morning and I said, "Are you thinking of the death sentence?" And the judge said no.'[47]

It was a Friday, and the authorities told our loved ones to come back the next day for the last visit, and to collect our clothes and other belongings. They also made an appointment for our lawyers to see us the following Tuesday.

And then we were taken back to Pretoria Local Prison in a large police van. I remember how hot it was, all of us crowded into the same space, the smell of sweat and dust, the fear and aggression on the policemen's faces, the reek of diesel, the personal silence, and the swell and fall of the roar and murmur of the assembled crowd. We were transported to the prison at great speed and non-stop. Road signs, stop streets, traffic lights, speed limits – all were ignored in pursuit of locking us away, returning us to our cells. Traffic police led the convoy, with sirens wailing at full blast. It was all very dramatic.

On each day of the trial, the police had taken us along a particular route to and from the courthouse. This was the pattern to which our supporters and the crowds of spectators had become accustomed. On the day of our sentencing, in a gesture designed to confuse the crowd, the lead car suddenly veered right as we left the court parking lot, and took off in the opposite direction from where our supporters, family, journalists and others patiently waited. We had a brief glimpse of Mama Sisulu standing at the side of the street, and then our vehicle thundered away from the waiting throng. This unexpected change of routine was yet another example of the petty manoeuvring of the authorities in the psychological battle to prove who was in control.

The eight of us had been housed in single cells ever since our arrest and throughout the trial, but that night the prison officials moved us into a communal cell together, except for Denis, who was taken to the white section of the prison. Regulations stipulated that Indians, Coloureds and Africans were also to be segregated from one another, but strict separation according to race was a costly exercise, and there were always staff shortages, and that policy was hardly ever applied in the prisons where I spent time, but the whites were always separated.

We had to change into prison uniforms, and they told us we would remain in Pretoria for some time. Then they said, look, even though you are now sentenced prisoners, you may finish off the food that you have received from outside. From the time of my arrest, Ayesha Cajee, Amien's wife, and others used to bring me the most delicious food. I can still remember those home-cooked meals. She even brought prawns a couple of times! To have such delicacies in jail was unthinkable, but they really spoilt me with their kindness. That night, we ate the last non-prison food that we would taste for a very long time. After a few hours of small talk, we went to bed around 9 p.m. It was bitterly cold.

Around midnight, or perhaps 1 a.m., we heard footsteps on the concrete floor. Suddenly, the lights came on, the gates were unlocked and we heard metal grating on cold steel as the key turned in the sturdy lock. The heavy door swung open and a whole group of warders walked in. We awoke to their looming bulk, their surly faces, an unexpected interruption in this long, dark night. 'Get ready,' said one. 'Take all your belongings.'

'Where are we going?'

'We don't know. You will see. And hurry up,' came the terse reply.

The prison clothes were all the same – we most likely had long pants and felt jackets, but I recall that they were not warm enough, that the icy air crept up on us, sliding cold fingers around our legs and torsos, insinuating itself against our skin. We did have shoes, and socks, too.

We took our time getting ready, of course. Not that we had many belongings, mainly a few books. As previously convicted prisoners, Mandela and Sisulu had already accumulated some effects – study materials, textbooks and so forth. The rest of us, newly sentenced, were not allowed to take anything except a book or two. I had my loyal companions, the *Oxford Book of Verse* and the *Collected Works of Shakespeare*. We were also told to take two blankets each.

As soon as we were ready, they shackled us and handcuffed us one to the other, in pairs. Govan and I were joined together at the wrists and ankles. Then we were moved to a truck and, accompanied by a huge escort of police, military and prisons personnel, we were driven to a military air base outside Pretoria.

It was dark, and cold. I remember the grey of the concrete and the belligerent and nervous faces of some of the men escorting us. We were taken to an aircraft standing on the runway, each step hampered by the leg-irons and handcuffs that bound us in pairs.

No one told us so, but we had already guessed that we were on our way to Robben Island. We had been looking forward to seeing our families on the promised visit later in the day, and our lawyers on the Tuesday, but the authorities had lied to us. We were angry, and disappointed, but such broken undertakings were typical of what we came to expect. By 14 June, when our families learnt that we were to serve our sentences on a tiny island in the icy Atlantic Ocean, the headline in the *Sunday Express* blared: 'Already There. Rivonia Men Flown in Secret to Robben Island'.

The aircraft was a military transport, bare and bitterly cold, and it was full. In addition to the seven of us, there were numerous policemen and warders, about three to each one of us.

We were not tense or overly nervous, but we were so very, very cold. The two blankets we had each brought were not nearly enough to keep us warm. Our escorts, of course, were well clad, with heavy overcoats and more.

Another terrible thing about the trip was that some of us got airsick. My partner, of course, was Govan, and when he got sick, he had to drag me with him to the toilet, because they would not unlock the handcuffs. That and the cold are what I remember most about the trip.

We did talk, to one another and to our escorts. They were neither nasty nor brutal. In fact, the colonel who was in charge gave us something to eat, his own food, from his own lunchbox. If I remember correctly, he was Colonel Aucamp, the head of prison security.

Not long after he was released from prison, Mandela, speaking at a public meeting, recalled that journey, and related a conversation between Van Wyk, the security policeman who had led the raid on the Rivonia farm, and me. I had quite forgotten Van Wyk's assurances, as we flew through the darkness that night, to the effect of: 'Oh, no, you fellows won't serve your full sentence, you'll be out in five years, and you being a bachelor, all the girls will be waiting for you.'

There was a strange atmosphere on the aircraft, a cordiality from the officials that we would not experience again for many years. They treated us with respect, although there was great fear and anxiety among the authorities of widespread violence, attempts to free us, insurrection. Clearly, they would be far happier and sleep more easily at night once we had been installed on the island.

At about 8 a.m. on Saturday 13 June, after a cold and uncomfortable flight, the drone of the Dakota's engines dropped in tone, the aircraft circled, touched down, and the engines were still. We had landed on Robben Island. Our life sentence had begun.

~ II ~

Outpost of Oppression

We exited the aircraft to an icy drizzle and buffeting winds, to be met by guards armed with automatic weapons. The atmosphere was tense and subdued. They took us from the airstrip to the prison in a vehicle, still handcuffed to one another until we went into a very old building. B Section, which would be our eventual 'home', was still under construction.

One of the bureaucratic idiosyncrasies was that with each transfer to a different prison, one had to change clothes. Those in which you arrived had to be returned to the former prison, so that their stocks would tally. So now we were issued with Robben Island uniforms, and we were shocked and angry when we saw them.

I was the youngest of the Rivonia 7. Mbeki was almost twenty years my senior, Sisulu seventeen, Mandela eleven. But I was given long pants and socks, while they got short pants and no socks. We all got a canvas jacket, shirt and jersey. They were not supposed to get shoes either, because at that time, African prisoners wore sandals made from old motor-car tyres, but a concession was made, possibly because of their age, but more likely because of who they were. One little favour in a litany of degradation.

Freshly attired, we were taken to the reception office in the administration block where all new arrivals were processed. We were fingerprinted, allocated prison numbers and given cards bearing our names, numbers and thumbprints. These would be our primary identity documents for the next eighteen years. My number was 468/64 – I was the 468th prisoner admitted to Robben Island in 1964, and it was only mid-June.

It was starting to get light. The soft rays of the Cape morning, dimmed by the persistent drizzle, were touching this windblown island off the southern tip of Africa. That cold, wet dawn heralded the beginning of a different life for all of us, one we had never envisaged.

The only other prisoner in the old jail was George Peake, and he really tried to make us comfortable. He smuggled some news and a little sustenance to us, because he had already made some connections. When you switch over from normal food to a prison diet you don't feel like eating anything for a while. You take a little food, but you are really too tense to eat, and George knew this and tried to ease our introduction to the prison fare.

He was a popular fellow, who had adjusted fairly quickly to this harsh new environment. He had been there for about two years, he knew his way around, and until our arrival he was the only political prisoner in the old jail.

George was in his forties and had been a member of the Cape Town City Council and president of the Coloured People's Congress. At that time, Coloureds and Indians were allowed to vote in the Cape municipal and parliamentary elections and were also allowed to serve as elected officials. He had been sentenced to only three years, because the Sabotage Act had not yet been passed when he was caught trying to blow up part of the Roeland Street Jail, and he could be charged only under the Explosives Act.

We stayed in the old prison until 25 June, working for eight hours a day, with a lunch break from 11 to 11.30 a.m. Supper was from 3 to 3.30 p.m., because the warders changed shift at 4 p.m. They worked in three eight-hour shifts around the clock.

Our labour was to break stones. Each of us sat on a low boulder with a piece of slate in front of us that had to be chopped with a very heavy metal hammer into ever-smaller pieces, until they were about the size of gravel. Most of us found it tough, and I even had difficulty handling a wheelbarrow loaded with the gravel. Not only was this hard labour that none of us was used to, but there is an art to pushing a barrow laden with stones. I almost tipped the heavy wheelbarrow, but Madiba, who had been doing a lot of physical exercise outside, and had been a boxer and was strong, ignored the watching warders and stood up to demonstrate what I should do.

It is this type of refusal to bow to the petty indignities of small-minded people that characterises his life, both within the prison walls and in the freedom of the world. When we were not working, we were locked up. Our only breaks were for meals and cold showers in the morning. The showers were icy and the water harsh and salty; the food was badly prepared, overcooked and of poor quality. Much to our annoyance and disgust, the petty discrimination in attire was applied to meals as well.

On our twelfth day on the island we were told to pack up our belongings, loaded on a truck and taken to the 'new' single cells in B Section, where we would stay for nearly two decades.

Less than two weeks before, we had learnt that our fate was to be not death, but life. As the aircraft from Pretoria passed over what I imagined was Schweizer-Reneke, town of my birth and my home, I had thought of my family below, sleeping, unaware that I was being taken away, powerless to change the course of events dictated by that 'life imprisonment' ruling. But even then, I don't think I really considered that I would not see Schweizer for another thirty years, or that so many members of my family would no longer be alive by the time I gained my freedom.

Nor could I possibly have realised that it would be two decades before I would see a child again, or that we would have to adapt to living with grown men in conditions where I could never see the stars in the night sky or know the joy of celebrating birthdays, Diwali, Eid or Christmas with family and friends.

Nothing could have prepared me for the enormity of losing all choice in such mundane matters as deciding when to wake up and when to sleep, or comprehend that minor joys such as letter-writing and meetings with family and friends would be so severely curtailed and controlled, and that fundamental human rights would become privileges that had to be earned and were always under threat of removal.

No bread for Mandela

God, when we don't have food to suit our taste,
then give us a taste to suit our food.   **– Anon**[1]

Indian and Coloured inmates were fed according to the prison department's D diet. Africans ate what was stipulated in the F diet. In the morning, the distinction lay in something as petty as the amount of sugar sprinkled on the porridge that we all received. We also got a mug of soup and a mug of coffee, unsweetened. Everything was cold by the time it reached us, and some prisoners would mix their coffee with the porridge to try to make it more palatable.

For lunch, the Africans were given plain boiled mealies and boiled turnips.

Now raw turnip can be fairly tasty, but boiled, it is the most awful vegetable. Nevertheless, for months, if not years, those were the only vegetables we got. Indians and Coloureds were given mealie-rice or samp instead of whole mealies, and sometimes they would give us what they called peas, but were more likely lupins, and quite inedible.

The third meal of the day was porridge and a mug of soup for the Africans, while Indians and Coloureds also got coffee and a chunk of bread, roughly spread with white margarine. Meat or fish was added to the mix three times a week, Africans getting less than Coloureds and Indians.

There was no bread for the Africans, and how people missed that. Govan Mbeki would later say that one of the things he missed most in prison was that simplest of all sustenance, bread. Even after concerted protest, it took some years before African prisoners were granted the magnanimous concession of being allowed to buy a single loaf of bread once a year, at Christmas.

The first period on Robben Island was the toughest. The rules were harsh and by and large the warders enforced them rigidly. One of the biggest challenges was communication, even among ourselves. Silence in the cells was strictly observed, and one of the few chances we had to speak to one another was during the daily ritual of cleaning the toilet buckets from our cells. The warders kept their distance while we performed this task, and we seized the opportunity to exchange views and discuss ways of improving our conditions.

In time, the prison authorities came to realise that political activists were a different breed than other prisoners, and that the discipline they imposed on common-law prisoners simply did not work with those incarcerated for their ideological beliefs.

We constantly objected to the discriminatory diet, but when one of the Coloured prisoners wrote a letter of protest to the authorities, the response was that if he was unhappy, he could apply to be 'reclassified as a Bantu, and get Bantu food'. Mandela had warned us that head-on confrontation was likely to result in equality according to the lowest denominator, when in fact we should be striving for standardisation at the highest level, so until we came up with a better strategy, we continued to eat what we were given and wear the clothes we were issued with.

The bread was about the only food that I found tolerable, but I even got used to the porridge, and, in fact, preferred the whole mealies to the mealie rice. Our cells were on opposite sides of the same passage, and it was extremely uncomfortable to witness my political leaders getting even more frugal fare than I was. Whenever possible, we smuggled our bread to them, and once the prison routine relaxed a little, we all pooled our daily rations so that everyone ate more or less the same.

LOSS

One writes of scars healed, a loose parallel to the pathology of the skin,
but there is no such thing in the life of an individual. There are open
wounds, shrunk sometimes to the size of a pinprick, but wounds still.
– F Scott Fitzgerald, *Tender is the Night*[2]

Our first visitors, on 25 June, were our lawyers Bram Fischer and Joel Joffe. The wind was howling, it was bitterly cold and the island felt especially stark and gloomy.

We all had a special fondness for Bram's wife Molly, whose kindness had supported us through many difficult times, and one of the first things Walter asked was how she was. Bram answered: 'Walter, Mo ... Molly is all right. Molly is all right.'[3]

My friend Amien Cajee had sent a message, asking me to suggest a name for the baby his wife was expecting later in the year, and I chose Djamilla, in honour of Algerian freedom fighter Djamilla Boupacha, who showed enormous bravery, courage and conviction, and was severely tortured by the French.[4]

Towards the end of our meeting, Mandela again mentioned Molly, and 'Bram just walked away, it seemed almost rudely.'[5]

After the lawyers had left the island, one of the officers, Major Visser, called Mandela to his office, and what he told him not only explained Bram's uncharacteristic brusqueness, but spoke volumes about his strength and integrity.

On the Saturday that we arrived on Robben Island, Bram and Molly had decided to drive to Cape Town from Johannesburg. They had planned to take a holiday after the stress of the trial, and on learning that we had already been moved, Bram decided to combine a visit to Robben Island with the celebration of their daughter Ilse's twenty-first birthday.

Molly had worked as tirelessly during the trial as Bram, catering to our needs, acting as our researcher and, of course, shuttling secret correspondence between me and Sylvia. That night, travelling through the Free State, as Bram approached a bridge, a motorcyclist travelling in the opposite direction suddenly swung out to pass a car. Bram swerved to avoid hitting the motorcycle head-on, but in the process his car left the road and plunged into water ten metres deep. Bram and Liz Lewin, who was with them, scrambled out through the front windows, but Molly was pinned in the back seat, and despite Bram's repeated efforts to save her, she drowned.

Bram and Molly's marriage had been one of the happiest I ever knew. Losing Molly after thirty years of sharing their lives extinguished a spark of vitality in Bram. Her funeral service was attended by hundreds of people of all races and colours and from all walks of life, a fitting tribute to the unique position that the Fischers held in the hearts and minds of people of all political persuasions, from all occupations, from the highest in the land to the lowest. They were among only a handful of South Africans, at the time, who could genuinely count among their friends people from every population group. In lieu of flowers, the family asked that contributions be sent to the Rivonia Trialists.

When Bram came to the island, his wife had been dead for less than two weeks, yet he came to discuss our loss of freedom rather than his own devastating personal loss. 'By sheer effort of will, he put his grief aside.'[6] Of Molly's death, Fischer's biographer Stephen Clingman eloquently wrote: 'Now she, who loved water, had suffered death in a dark pool surrounded by dry land, while his comrades had been sentenced to life on an island surrounded by sea. He had helped save their lives but could not save hers. They had been sentenced to a living eternity, she to some other kind, and he to a future without all of them.'[7]

We were shaken to the core by Molly's tragic death and deeply moved by Bram's sheer selflessness in dealing with our situation, despite his own pain and grief. So we were grateful that the authorities allowed us to write a letter of condolence and let Bram know that we shared his sorrow.

Cruelly, the prison authorities never posted the letter, and Bram never received it.

Two months later, almost to the day, Bram himself was charged because of his work for the Communist Party. Sylvia was arrested on the same day.

To the single cells

It was on the day of Bram and Joel's visit that we were hurriedly moved to the single cells. The 26th of June is a significant day for the ANC, as both the anniversary of the Congress of the People at Kliptown and the date on which the Defiance Campaign was launched in 1956. Perhaps the authorities anticipated trouble and moved us to the most secure section of the prison, despite the fact that the grey paint was not quite dry, the ablution facilities not yet functioning.

These were the single cells in which some of us would spend the next eighteen years of our lives. There were thirty of us and we were the sole inmates, totally isolated from 1 500 common-law and other political prisoners on the island, though in time we would develop a number of innovative ways to communicate both with them and the outside world.

Some of the cells faced a courtyard and others, including mine, the sea. If I stood on a bench and pulled myself up by holding onto the bars across one of the two small windows, I could just see the sky and the ocean, some distance off. It was tiring, but I spent many hours gazing through that tiny window on the outside world. On a clear day I could see clear across to Bloubergstrand, and sometimes I could distinguish the outline of cars moving about on the mainland. At night, there were the myriad flickering lights that delineated the coastline.

In all the years I spent on Robben Island, I only once looked up at the night sky from outside my cell. It was on the night of the earthquake in the Western Cape, when all our cells were unlocked and we were moved outside into the courtyard.

My cell had two windows in the outer wall, each the size of a briefcase, and one larger window facing the inner passage. To our great irritation, the warders or visiting prison officials would peer at us through the passage windows as though we were some species of strange and dangerous animal. A single naked light bulb in the centre of each cell burnt all night and most days. We were under twenty-four-hour observation, warders patrolling up and down the passage. At night, some of them would take off their shoes and pad about in their socks, especially after our study time was up. Of course, many of us continued to read surreptitiously under the blankets, but if we were caught, the punishment was spare rations for several days – rice water to drink and nothing to eat.

The floor was rough, grey cement, and we slept on it on a sisal mat. Later, they gave us a thin felt sleeping mat as well. There was nothing else in the cell except three blankets, an ablution bucket and a basin of water for drinking, shaving and washing. To break the monotony and add a personal touch to our cells, some of us used to polish the floors. The walls, the ceiling and the bars on the windows were painted grey. The sills were plain cement. One of the terrible things about life in prison is that you see no colour. One yearns for a splash of brightness and natural light. The doorway had an iron grille that opened into the cell, behind which was a wooden door opening into the passage.

The light in the ceiling was really far too dim to read by, but in the 1970s they installed fluorescent tubes. We were not allowed to turn off the light, although we could reach the switch by stretching an arm through the bars and along the passage wall.

Most of us adopted the bad habit of pulling the blankets over our heads when we slept. We weren't supposed to, of course, as the warders could not see our faces that way, but the alternative was to sleep in the light. It took me many, many years to break the habit of sleeping with my head under the covers.

The warders who came on duty in the morning were supposed to turn off the lights, but sometimes they did not bother to do so. At other times they were deliberately nasty, switching the lights off on the dull and rainy days when we could not go outside.

Only two prisoners in our section had a table and a stool – Mandela, because he had been imprisoned on Robben Island even before the Rivonia Trial and was already registered as a student, and George Peake. In September 1965, when George was released, I inherited his furniture. The rest received stools and tables later.

The warders had been thoroughly indoctrinated about who we were and seemingly considered us dangerous. Each time we went to the exercise courtyard or to the bathroom, our cells would be unlocked only once there was a warder in position on the catwalk above, his rifle trained on us. I spent eighteen of my twenty-six years in prison in the B Section of Robben Island. During the first months after our arrival, groups of warders visiting from other prisons would stand at the passage windows of our cells and stare at us as though we were animals in a zoo.

In the early years we were sometimes locked in our cells for days on end, and some especially sadistic warders would insist, at such times, even in the dead of winter, that our blankets were placed outside the cells.

There was nothing in the cell. Bibles were allowed, but not the Koran or literature pertaining to any other religion. Muslim prisoners were assured that all meat served on Robben Island was *halaal*, but of course there was no way of verifying this.

COLD COMFORT

Among the formalities of prison life is seeing the doctor on admission, with the emphasis on 'seeing'. Stripped naked, we had to line up in the corridor outside the prison hospital, our backs to the wall, in silence. The doctor did nothing more than ask if anyone had health problems, and irrespective of the nature of complaints, the universal panacea was instructing medical orderlies to dispense castor oil or Epsom salts. There was no physical examination or individual attention at all.

Two of the political prisoners, Pascal Ngakane and Masla Pather, were qualified medical doctors, but instead of using their expertise in the hospital, the authorities put them to work with picks and shovels in the limestone quarry, leaving routine health care in the hands of orderlies who had some training as nurses, and common-law prisoners assigned to the hospital.

A fortnight after we arrived, Bernard Newman, an international author and 'authority' on prisons, came to the island. We were given new uniforms and, on the morning of his arrival, taken to another section of the prison, where the showers worked, and allowed to perform our first full ablutions. Never afraid to speak his mind, this concession prompted Mandela to tell Newman that he should come to the island more often, as not only were we given new clothes, but we had also been allowed to take a shower.

Newman later told the London *Times* that Mandela was 'in a cell by himself, at his own request, in a partly built new block', and that the physical conditions were 'better than in a good many prisons' he had visited in Russia and Britain. Mandela 'and others' had complained of 'cold and damp, of lack of bath facilities, of sanitary arrangements, and of the roughness of the prison food', Newman said, but 'no one had produced information on alleged atrocities'. It was his opinion, Newman said, 'that under the present prison governor, appointed last February, it is unlikely that atrocities would be permitted'.[8]

Newman must have been an apologist for the South African government, or he would not have been allowed access to the prison, and for us, the only consequence of his visit was a typically vindictive response to Mandela's comments about showering.

The very next morning, in the middle of winter and with rain bucketing down, the warders woke us at 5.30, yelling that since we wanted so badly to bath, they were going to let us do so.

They took us to the old section of the prison and made us all take ice-cold showers. No one was excused, and this 'punishment' was repeated daily until the facilities in B Section were completed.

By August, the worst of the winter was behind us, though it was still cold at night. I wrote to friends that my health was fine, my morale high. I had lost a fair amount of weight, but it was excess that I needed to shed, anyway. The major challenge, for me, was getting used to the brackish drinking water. I could barely stomach the salty taste, and for the first ten years on the island, that was all we had to drink.

We were each given a litre of water at 4 p.m., and that had to last until we were unlocked the next day. Laundry was a major challenge, as garments washed in the brackish water dried stiff and rough, and had an unpleasant odour. It was also impossible to rinse the white coating of dust from our bodies after a day in the quarry – the water was simply too hard to be really effective.

Even the most rudimentary needs turned into a battle. In June 1965 I wrote to the commanding officer: 'A little while ago we were told that we would no longer be allowed to order facecloths. The towel issued to us is really not absorbent enough and adequate for both washing and drying purposes A face-cloth is essential to remove the fine lime dust and dry ourselves thoroughly. With washing and showering the prison towels hardly have time to dry. This is much more so during the cold season when we often find ourselves having to put on our clothes over semi-dry bodies.' We were allowed facecloths some years later.

The prison kitchen once tried using the brackish water for cooking, but the result was so inedible, even by prison standards, that it caused a major hunger strike, and they never used it again.

If I had to use a single word to define life on Robben Island, it would be 'cold'. Cold food, cold showers, cold winters, cold wind coming in off the sea, cold warders, cold cells, cold comfort. Decades later, many of the former prisoners retained a heightened sensitivity to cold. Walter Sisulu felt it so badly that, in later years, a special heating system was installed in his home in an attempt to make him more comfortable. It was as if the cold had somehow permeated our very bones, and we never quite managed to thaw out again.

Punishment for the slightest infraction, real or imagined, took various forms. The most severe penalty was solitary confinement for weeks or even months, and there were many cases of prisoners being physically assaulted by warders, but the most common form of punishment was dietary. Awful as the food was, it was all we had, and necessary, so being deprived of three consecutive meals, the maximum that warders up to the rank of warrant officer *could* withhold, was a dire sacrifice.

Higher-ranking officers had the authority to withdraw six meals, but prisoners had the right in later years to opt for a hearing instead, with warders acting as magistrate and prosecutor. In serious cases, court officials would be summoned from the mainland and the prisoner could be represented by a lawyer. For some time, this was the only way inmates could have contact with lawyers.

Contact of any kind with the outside world was minimal. In the period immediately after our incarceration we were permitted to write and receive one letter every six months consisting of 500 words each, and have one visit during the same period. Both incoming and outgoing mail were cut ruthlessly, and it generally took a month or more for correspondence to be delivered.

When the warders wearied of counting the words, they told us we could write a page and a half per letter. My handwriting was always tiny, so I was able to cram anything from 1 000 to 1 500 words into the available space.

All our letters were censored with indiscriminate fervour, and it was only once we were able to access our prison files that we realised how much of the correspondence sent to us was simply never delivered.

The very first letter from my brother was withheld from me, allegedly because its contents were objectionable. I was given the letter eighteen years later, on the day I was transferred to Pollsmoor. The 'objectionable' parts were sentences about a change of government in Britain. Harold Wilson and the Labour Party were now in power ...

Letters written in African languages were sent to Pretoria for censoring. Some of the Robben Island censors could speak African languages, but none, for example, knew anything about the indigenous languages spoken by SWAPO prisoners. Letters in any 'foreign' language were immediately filed, and those whose loved ones were unable to write in a language known to the warders, just never got their letters.

The censors wielded their pens and scissors with unnatural enthusiasm, and even the letters we did get were often mutilated to the point of being meaningless. The correspondence was diligently scoured for any 'objectionable' content, including mention of certain people, or even an oblique reference to someone the warders thought we should not know about.

When we arrived on the island, a senior officer assured us that within five years we would have been forgotten by anyone we cared about. He was wrong, but the trickle of censored correspondence we received, the long periods between communication, added immeasurably to our sense of isolation.

One of the state's most effective instruments of emotional torture was the infamous Black Book. It contained an amorphous and ill-defined list of names that served as the prison's index of people with whom we were allowed no contact at all. They included whites in general, former prisoners, anti-apartheid politicians, political activists, journalists, lawyers who were not directly involved in one's case, members of various religious and welfare organisations, medical doctors who were not also family members and just about anyone else the authorities declared 'undesirable' on a whim.

At a fairly early stage, I wrote to my family: 'Don't bother to phone and leave a message for me – we are never told about telephone calls.' We were allowed no newspapers, radios, clocks or wristwatches, and warders deliberately concealed the dials of their own watches lest, perchance, we note the time of day.

Until the early 1970s, few prisoners were taken to the mainland for medical treatment, however serious the ailment. In 1964, 'Robben Island was without question the harshest, most iron-fisted outpost in the South African penal system'.[9]

June and July were the bleakest months.[10] From 8 a.m. to 4 p.m. each day we sat on concrete blocks in the courtyard of our cellblock, breaking stones. The gravel was used by the construction crews, so that, in effect, the prisoners built their own jail.

Allocation of cells seemed random, at best. In my section, there were ANC leaders such as Mandela and Sisulu, the rest of the Rivonia Trialists, some junior members of the ANC and three illiterate peasants from the Transkei, who had launched an abortive attempt to assassinate Chief Kaiser Matanzima.

Yet some senior ANC members, even provincial leaders such as Harry Gwala and George Mbele from Natal, were in the grossly overcrowded communal cells. We were not allowed to fraternise with prisoners from outside B Section, though two common-law prisoners were housed in our section, ostensibly to clean the corridors and ablution block. Their chief tasks, however, were to spy on us and plant contraband in our cells for the warders to find during raids, so that they could mete out punishments to us. This did not turn out quite as planned, however. We befriended the men, and one of them not only joined the ANC when he was released, but went abroad to receive MK training.

Unfortunately, one day he was caught smuggling a newspaper into Mandela's cell, and served the rest of his sentence in the communal section. This also led to the other common-law prisoner being moved from our section, which was a pity, as they had more freedom of movement, sometimes even working in the warders' homes, where they were able to lay their hands on newspapers and the occasional magazine, which they would trade for soap and tobacco from us.

Our next official visitors were a reporter and a photographer from London's conservative *Daily Telegraph*. The day after our sentencing, the newspaper had carried an editorial headed 'South Africa on Trial', which read, in part: 'It cannot be disputed that yesterday's convicts had a fair trial' and extolled the 'independence and scrupulous impartiality of the court', concluding that there had been 'no miscarriage of justice'.[11]

However, the newspaper had gone on to qualify its stance, stating that a number of complex moral issues merited further attention, and ending with: 'It is the tragedy of the Republic that it provides no way but violence for such a man to influence its fortunes.'[12]

At the time of their visit we, of course, had no way of knowing what they had written, but we were all familiar with the conservative politics of the paper. The first inkling we had that something was afoot was one morning, when instead of being given our usual mallets to break the rocks, we were issued with little sewing kits and a pile of old uniforms to mend. Around lunchtime, the commanding officer brought his English guests to our courtyard to witness our 'sewing circle'.

Unbeknown to us, they took secret photographs of Mandela and Sisulu speaking to one another, which were widely publicised abroad, though we only heard about this many years later. They also took a larger group photo of all of us. In it could be seen the front row of prisoners working with hammers, and our row sewing. Hardly had the journalists reached the harbour than our sewing garments were taken away, and back came the hammers. This photograph was distributed widely to show that Mandela and the Rivonia men were doing light labour.

All of us developed and honed coping mechanisms to deal with the harsh prison conditions, the isolation, the sheer boredom and frustration, but I would be lying if I claimed that our many years on Robben Island stole nothing from us but our time and our lives. Our deepest personal pain was not something we shared with one another as a rule, partly because we all knew that there were many, many others undergoing even worse privation than we ourselves, and partly because we respected one another's privacy, as far as it is possible to do so under communal living conditions.

BABLA SALOOJEE

Each visit, no matter who the fortunate recipient, was a joyful event for all of us. It was a tangible reminder that there was still a world outside our prison, and if we were lucky, we would glean some snippet of information, however small, on what was happening in our country. More importantly, it was one of the few ways in which we could get news of loved ones and comrades.

So it was with great excitement that we waited, one Saturday afternoon in September, for Walter to have his first visit from Mama Albertina, his wife. We had been on the island for three months and waited eagerly for Tshopo, as we affectionately called Walter, to return and tell us everything.

We could see at once that he was upset, and the news he brought shocked us into silence. Suliman Saloojee, my dearest friend Babla, was dead, killed by the police.

This most gentle of men, this inveterate prankster, my comrade and source of strength, had been picked up under the ninety-day detention law, brutally interrogated and tortured to death – by the sadistic Rooi Rus Swanepoel – then flung from a window on the seventh floor of Gray's Building, Johannesburg headquarters of the security police, on Wednesday 9 September 1964. His death, and the nature of it, filled me with grief and rage such as I have seldom known, and I would never again think of Babla without an echo of the utter horror that passed through me that Saturday afternoon.

Not surprisingly, the so-called inquest accepted the police version that Babla had committed suicide by jumping to his death. I have never doubted, however, that he died under interrogation, and that his body was then thrown out of the window.[13]

Babla died just two months after being detained on 6 July with Laloo Chiba and Sylvia. The magistrate found that 'nothing in the evidence suggested that Saloojee had been assaulted or that the methods of interrogating him were in any way irregular. He found that no one was to blame for his death'.[14]

Mary Benson was later to recount a poignant meeting that she had with Bram Fischer on his last trip out of South Africa. 'Bram described the effects of police torture. Suliman Saloojee, a young Indian held in solitary, had somehow managed to smuggle a message to his wife. "Pray for me," he'd appealed. Bram could hardly contain his wrath and grief as he explained that Saloojee was not a religious man and that, a day or two later, while being interrogated in security police headquarters, he had fallen seven storeys to his death.'[15]

I wrote to Babla's wife, Rookie, in October, and in November I wrote home. There had been a change of staff on the island and I was deeply frustrated at being unable to trace whether the letters were even posted.

Over the years, we never stopped talking about Babla. At least a dozen of the thirty or so inmates in my section had known him, but none so well as I. We had been friends since the late 1940s, he had stayed at my flat for a lengthy period and I loved him like a younger brother. I simply could not come to terms with Babla's death. He was too young, too vibrant, too loved by his family and friends to be gone. I dreamt about him many, many times – alive, laughing, teasing, mischievous, a restless spirit, never sad or depressed. I could not conceive of Babla dead, and throughout my prison term, it was the memory of his life I clung to.

As soon as possible after my release, I stood silently by his grave, overwhelmed by my memories of this remarkable man.

INTEGRITY

That song whose breath
Might lead to death,
But never to retreating.   – O'Casey[16]

While Vuyisile Mini, a convicted MK cadre and a fellow Treason Trialist was on Death Row, he was approached to testify against Wilton Mkwayi, Mac Maharaj, Laloo Chiba and others facing terrorism charges. If he agreed, the state would commute his sentence to life imprisonment. Mini turned down the offer. He was the first MK cadre to be hanged in Pretoria and, like John Harris, who planted a bomb at Johannesburg's Park Station, he went to the gallows singing. The words of 'Nkosi Sikeleli'Afrika' poured from his soul as the trapdoor opened and he dropped to his death.

Vuyisile Mini made a choice. He could have sold out his comrades, and lived. He could have abandoned his principles, and lived. He opted instead to follow the path of integrity, remain true to his beliefs, and vanquish the ignoble manner of his death with the greatness of his honour and courage.

Decades later, when the river of time had washed away so much, and so many people had been swept along in its course, when fresh waters of freedom and liberty had baptised a brutalised country with a future of hope, peace and tolerance, Mini's family endeavoured to recover his remains from an unmarked grave and give him the hero's burial he deserved. It was 1997, but their efforts were thwarted by Pretoria City Council officials.

In January 1965, Mac Maharaj and Laloo Chiba came to the island, Mac to serve twelve years and Laloo eighteen. Both had been severely tortured with electric shocks and beatings, made to stand on the same spot for days on end and verbally abused. It disturbed us greatly to hear how Mac, desperate not to break under this onslaught 'of the most sadistic and obscene nature',[17] had tried to slit his wrists with shards of broken eggshell. It was not until Laloo testified before the Truth and Reconciliation Commission that I realised how much he had suffered, but neither man betrayed their comrades.

After being sentenced in December 1964 they spent about two weeks at Leeuwkop Prison north of Johannesburg, arriving on Robben Island on 5 January. They were shackled for the duration of the trip to Cape Town in the back of a truck, along with Raymond Nyanda and three other prisoners. Nyanda, Mac and Laloo were placed in single cells in our section, but a few weeks later, Nyanda was transferred off the island. In all probability, he had been deliberately planted in our midst as a spy – an insidious ploy favoured by the authorities to sow dissonance in our ranks. Later this led to some serious consequences in the ANC and MK training camps.

A GENEROSITY OF SPIRIT

There are verily, two sweet fruits in this poison-tree of the world: one is the taste for good literature, and the other, the company of good people.
– Sanskrit aphorism[18]

While I was still in Europe in 1952, Laloo Chiba followed his mother and sisters to India, where he found a bride, Lakshmibehn, and brought her back to South Africa.

After being recruited into the movement, we kept him out of the public eye, so much so that uninformed people sometimes criticised him for not being politically active. In the period following Sharpeville, his involvement deepened, and on 16 December 1961 he was a member of one of the first MK units to commit sabotage. Under the leadership of Wolfie Kodesh they planted bombs at the post office and at the Bantu commissioner's office in Fordsburg, and at the pass office in the centre of Johannesburg.

On 17 April 1963, Laloo and Abdulhay Jassat were arrested, tortured and held at Marshall Square. Laloo was pivotal in planning the escape of Harold Wolpe, Arthur Goldreich, Mosey Moolla and Abdulhay Jassat, and when he was finally released after ninety days in detention, he immediately went underground.

We had been arrested in the interim, and Wilton Mkwayi was trying to form a new National High Command for MK. He asked Laloo to serve on it, and before long he was arrested again. At Pretoria Central he joined Mac Maharaj, Paul Joseph, Steve Naidoo and Ahmed Bhaba, and a few months later, Wilton was captured as well.

During what became known as the Little Rivonia Trial, they were represented by George Bizos and Joel Joffe. Lionel Gay led the band of state witnesses who testified against them, his evidence grossly exaggerated to the point where he claimed they had been members of an execution squad. No such unit existed, but along with the evidence of other turncoats – Piet Beyleveld, a member of the SACP's Central Committee, Patrick Mthembu and Ahmed Bhaba – it was used by the court to convict them.

Beyleveld's greatest perfidy was the testimony he later gave against his friend and mentor, Bram Fischer. On 30 January 1965, *The Times* of London reported that Mr MH Festenstein, chairman of the Johannesburg Bar Council (and, incidentally, a former member of the SACP!), 'said the council had decided to start proceedings to remove Mr. Abram Fischer, QC, from the roll of advocates'. Bram, having been released on bail of £5 000, had 'failed to appear in court on Monday, where he was to face charges with 13 other whites of belonging to the banned Communist Party'.[19] When Bram was rearrested, it was Beyleveld, and others, whose testimony sent him to prison.

Wilton Mkwayi was the consummate optimist. Every year without fail he would predict: 'Next year, we are going home.' He was a unique character, extremely popular across the political spectrum, capable of brutal frankness and enormously generous. He had little formal education, but brought a wealth of experience in politics and trade unionism to the movement. Mac Maharaj was a most astute politician, highly intelligent and brave.

SYLVIA

If I could live my life over – I think that I would have pondered more on the human heart, the emotions, feelings, those strange, perplexing guests who come uninvited to live with us, and who sometimes take control. And I would have pondered on love. – **Marcus Aurelius**[20]

Not least among the challenges of Robben Island for me was my insatiable need for contact with Sylvia.

As I had conveyed to her in the closing days of the trial, it was unrealistic and selfish to expect that she would wait for me while I served my sentence, but in my heart I must have secretly hoped that she would.

I had reiterated my view to her via mutual friends in London after arriving on the island, and though not said lightly, it took me several years to come to terms with the full implications of releasing her from any commitment.

Fortunately, by the time she let me know that she was getting married, I had accepted the reality of our situation and could genuinely wish her well.

We hadn't been on the island long when I received news that Sylvia had been detained and was a co-accused with Bram. His apprehension was a devastating blow to the underground movement, of which he was the most senior member at the time. When I learnt of his arrest, I was transported back to an exchange between Bram and Percy Yutar during our trial, when the prosecutor – in a quite jocular manner – told our advocate: 'In this briefcase, I've got enough evidence to send you to jail for life.'

Bram, Sylvia and thirteen others were charged with wanting to establish 'a despotic government based on the dictatorship of the proletariat'. In April 1965 they were sentenced to prison terms ranging from one to five years each.[21]

In an unprecedented move, given the times and the charges against him, Bram was granted bail to allow him to conclude a civil case in London. Being the honourable man that he was, he duly returned to South Africa and was on home soil when he decided that he would not stand trial, and became a fugitive from justice.

Sylvia was interrogated relentlessly by my arch enemy, Rooi Rus Swanepoel. Though the security police had never revealed this to me, they had known about our relationship for some time, and they used this knowledge against her in detention, with Swanepoel at some point raging that she must have wanted to give birth to 'mongrels'.

During the latter half of the 1990s, one of Sylvia's co-accused, Jean Middleton, testified about the conditions at the women's prison in Barberton, Mpumalanga, where they were incarcerated:

> When you speak about Barberton, what you really have to speak about is the brutality of the place. Through a window, we used to see women, black women prisoners, carrying things sometimes. However fast they tried to run, the wardresses would urge them on by whipping them with those long leather straps attached to their keys and sometimes there would be a baby on a woman's back, so the baby got whipped.
>
> Worst of all were the shirts we used to wash. Those came from the men's jail, they used to come in every Monday and at least one shirt and one pair of shorts every week (and they only got one clean shirt a week and they did very hard work, it seemed, in a hot climate) would not be stained with blood, but caked with blood from clogging and that sulphur ointment, caked.[22]

With Sylvia imprisoned at one end of the country and me at another, without Bram to act as an intermediary, without daring to use her name in any of my letters, I had no idea how I would cope.

From Robben Island, contact with Sylvia was taboo on three levels: she was white, she was a communist and she was a political prisoner. In correspondence with Amien and Ayesha Cajee, she could be referred to only by one of several Indian names – Yasmin, Sakina and Khala among them. With the help of my loyal friends, a few letters and messages did get through.

So, for example, I wrote: 'Tell Amien that I was most distressed to hear of my Khala's indisposition again. I fervently hope and pray she is up and about again and in perfect health. This causes me constant anxiety and worry. Please also ask him to convey my dearest love and fondness. I still recite the passages from Shakespeare daily, which bring back a host of pleasant and cherished memories. She is uppermost in my mind.'

As soon as she was released from prison, Sylvia went into exile in London, where she quickly made contact with Tommy and Bobby Vassen, Herbie Pillay, and Essop and Aziz Pahad.

I was thrilled to be sent a photograph of my 'Fordsburg aunts', with Sylvia right in front, dressed in a sari, her distinctive blonde hair covered with a scarf. I spent hours in my cell gazing lovingly at that photograph perched upon my bookshelf, secretly relishing the fact that it had escaped the attention of the censors.

Then one day I was given an envelope containing a photograph of Sylvia without her Indian disguise. There was no indication of its origin. I was naturally suspicious, but also grateful to receive it, though of course I could not put it on display.

A few weeks later, my cell was raided by a pair of warders. They removed both photographs of Sylvia and marched me off to Lieutenant Fourie's office, where he slowly and deliberately tore the precious images into tiny pieces, not even bothering to hide his pleasure at destroying these symbols of racial defiance.

Much, much later, I discovered the Orwellian truth behind this incident. PJB van Wyk, the prime minister's security adviser from the Bureau of State Security, had sent a memo to the commissioner of prisons in January 1970, informing him that Sylvia Neame, who had served a prison sentence because of her communist activities, 'writes to Kathrada under the guise that she is a family member, and jokes that she has sent him a photograph of herself, clad in a sari'.[23]

However, what the warders did not know was that I had a third photograph of Sylvia, cut from a newspaper and used in a collage of various Hollywood stars and a few more photographs of friends, including Joe Slovo and Ruth First.

That collection escaped the warders, but they refused to let me have a photograph of Phyllis Naidoo, taken on a city street, for no other reason than that a completely unknown white woman was visible behind her. Similarly, I was denied photographs of Essop and Aziz Pahad with their new brides, both of whom were white.

CONDITIONS

When Jock Strachan was released from prison in Pretoria in 1965, he defied the law that prohibited publicity about conditions in South African jails and approached the *Rand Daily Mail* to disclose the most appalling accounts of how prisoners were being treated. Jock's revelations appeared in three instalments during June and July, and 'effectively blew open the entire archaic structures of the South African prison system, and conditions for all prisoners, indomitably thereafter monitored by Helen Suzman, were never the same again.'[24]

There were repercussions, of course. Journalist Benjamin Pogrund and editor Laurence Gandar were charged with contravening the Prisons Act, and Strachan found himself back behind bars fairly quickly.

Improvements in the food and clothing for prisoners that followed publication of the articles didn't last long, but for once the prisoners fought back, and 1966 saw our first hunger strike.

B Section, where we were housed, was so isolated that the inmates in the communal cells had already started their strike when the prisoners who brought our breakfast whispered the news to us. We agreed unanimously to take part in the protest, and although he supported the decision, it placed Mandela in a difficult position.

He had already initiated discussions with Major Kellerman with a view to possible improvement of various conditions, and it didn't take Kellerman long to chastise Madiba, in our presence, for jettisoning talk in favour of action.

When the strike was called off after six days, some inmates were charged with endangering their own lives and had an additional six months added to their sentences. In apartheid's prisons, inmates were 'owned' by the state, and damage to government 'property' was a serious offence.

From 1965 we were put to work in the lime quarry with picks and shovels. It was a welcome change, but some of us, especially Madiba, would suffer damage to our eyes from the bright glare of the sun against the white limestone cliffs.

At first they drove us to the quarry in the back of a truck, but after a few days, we walked. It took about twenty minutes, and I relished the warmth of the sun on my body, the exercise and, above all, the opportunity to see some of the many small wild animals that inhabit the island. In due course, our daily walks would also offer other benefits.

The physical separation of supporters, even within the same facility, made communication vital if the movement was to survive. We soon realised that the route taken by inmates from the main section crossed our path to the quarry. More importantly, the ground was littered with empty matchboxes, discarded by warders while they watched us work. It was Mac who suggested that we should pick up as many empty boxes as we could. That was typical of Mac – even if he had no immediate idea of how such items could be used to our advantage, he never let an opportunity to forage anything pass, just in case it came in handy.

Laloo devised a way of creating false bottoms for the boxes, and he and Mac, both very good at writing in miniscule yet legible script, compiled messages to our comrades in the general cells. We somehow managed to explain the plan to them, and before long we had a two-way communication channel going. The 'message boxes' would be dropped on the ground and casually picked up by our comrades from the kitchen while they were delivering our lunch to the quarry.

Work at the quarry was tough, but not nearly as bad as chopping stones had been. We were given a daily quota at first, but we simply ignored it, producing whatever quantity we could, and this came to be accepted, along with our refusal to call the warders 'boss', run when we were called or refuse to obey certain orders. The warders had never come across prisoners who defied them on such things before, but they learnt, eventually, that political detainees and other prisoners were two entirely different breeds.

Studies and communication

When two merchants exchange their products, each one gives up part of his possessions, but when students exchange knowledge, each keeps his own and acquires the other's. Can there be a better bargain than this?
— Simon ben Lakish[25]

Writing materials were highly prized. Registered students had to buy their own, and were not permitted to receive such items from outside. If a well-wisher sent a pen, for example, it would generally be returned, or placed with our personal effects until we were released. Once in a while, a warder with a heart would bend the rules and allow the recipient to keep such items.

Once permission to study was granted, we could acquire some stationery, but, for example, when my ballpoint pen ran dry, I had to exchange it for a new one. Failure to produce the used pen meant that I could not get another one. As more and more prisoners became students, the warders found themselves spending too much time acting as pen and paper clerks, so the rules were relaxed to the point where we could draw three, then six, ballpoint pens at a time. I gave my surplus pens to fellow prisoners who could not afford to pay for their studies.

The three Transkeian peasants incarcerated with us, two of them quite elderly, were completely illiterate, but keen to learn how to read and write. But they had no money, nor the means of obtaining any, so they could not register as students. It was virtually impossible for us to smuggle pens and paper to them, but someone managed to slip a pencil or a ballpoint pen to one of them. They still had no paper, but then one found a wrapper for Palmolive soap, and started practising to write the alphabet and his own name.

He was caught by the warders and placed on spare rations for three meals.

Undeterred, the trio used their working hours at the quarry to practise their letters in the sand, and by the time they left the island, all three were literate.

Apart from three months at Wits University in 1951, I had done no studying since matric. When I decided to remedy this situation on Robben Island, I wrote to my family: 'So when Ma or anyone else starts worrying about me, they must just imagine that I'm not in jail but at university. Only now can I really appreciate how hasty and unwise I was to give up my studies eighteen years ago. And if I wasn't in jail I wouldn't have had an inclination to go back to the books. So please be very firm with all the children who are neglecting their schoolwork. Do not let them give up.'

Prison regulations encouraged study, but our jailers deliberately misinterpreted this provision and took it upon themselves to convert studying into a privilege, and consequently a weapon in their arsenal of punishments.

They simply ruled that only prisoners who were funded by immediate family would be allowed to study. Books and money sent to me by NUSAS, for example, were promptly returned. On one occasion, funds sent from home were frozen until the authorities had verified that the donors were indeed my siblings.

Although I applied for permission to study soon after our arrival on the island in June 1964, it was not until the day before registrations closed on 31 March 1965 that I was told I could go ahead and enrol with the University of South Africa.

Unisa was the biggest correspondence course university in the world at the time, with thousands of students across the globe. By special arrangement, prisoners paid only R10 per course, a third of the normal fee, and even this was more than many people behind bars could afford. That didn't stop the authorities from lobbying the university to introduce a standard fee for everyone, however. They also obstructed the number of textbooks we could have, allowing the prescribed works but not the recommended additional reading. Sometimes, we were able to borrow these from the university library.

We had to sit on the floor of our cells to study, but when George Peake was released in September, I was allowed to take over his table and stool.

We had been told at the outset that we would be allowed to do only one degree course each. No postgraduate studies would be allowed. This caused some of my comrades to take only a few courses each year, in order to spread their course over the longest possible period, but I decided to complete my undergraduate studies as soon as possible, and take up the fight for further study when the time came.

It was the right choice, and I emerged from prison with a BA in history and criminology, a second bachelor's degree in African politics and library science, and honours in history and African studies.

Our families were allowed to send only enough money to cover our studies and a few personal incidental expenses. The only toiletries we could buy were soap, toothpaste and blades for shaving, and we were allowed to spend R1 a month on such items. It was amazing how much one could buy with R1 then! By the time I was released in 1989, the amount had risen to R80 a month.

Effective communication with our comrades in the rest of the prison was never far from our minds, and we were constantly devising ways to improve our rudimentary methods.

In October, I wrote exams in sociology, history, psychology and criminology. Students from the isolation block and the general section took the exams in the same room, and just before we took our seats, Ebrahim Ismail from the communal cells slipped a little plastic package into my hand. I guessed it must contain a communiqué and news from our ANC comrades.

Unexpectedly, the warder who was acting as examination invigilator decided to search us. I panicked, but Ebrahim quickly whispered that I should pass the package to Dikgang Moseneke, who was unlikely to be searched. Dikgang held a valuable position in the study office. Every now and then he managed to smuggle prohibited books to us.

I did as he suggested, the package escaped detection, and as soon as we had finished writing our papers, Dikgang gave it back to me.

This incident illustrates that well before the communications committee was set up to acquire newspapers and periodicals, we were 'talking' to one another, prison regulations notwithstanding.

While we were allowed to study any of the indigenous languages taught by the Department of Education and Training, foreign languages were not permitted.[26] With willing tutors such as Govan Mbeki and Jackson Fuzile, I had no business not becoming fluent in isiXhosa, but I'm ashamed to admit that though I tried, I never mastered the language.

B Section housed a group of people whose intellectual development ranged from illiterate, as with the Transkei peasants, to doctorate, as with Neville Alexander. Several inmates were qualified teachers and they formed RITA – the Robben Island Teachers' Association – and acted as our tutors in subjects ranging from English and German to history. Even though Neville and I were political opponents, I became indebted to him for his help and guidance in my studies.

Apart from furthering our education, there was little to stimulate or entertain our minds, and we soon risked slumping into mental ennui. All the jokes had been told, all the anecdotes shared, so we requested a selection of board games. Chess and draughts were allowed, but not Scrabble, for no other reason than that on one of his routine inspection tours, the commanding officer had come upon Indres Naidoo and some of the others playing with a handmade set, and noticed the word 'war' on the board. If we were going to build such inflammatory words, there would be no spelling games for us. Some years later, the ban on Scrabble was lifted.

Political debate occupied much of our time, and as early as 1965, some of our comrades were arguing for a party structure to be set up along established ANC lines. As the year drew to a close a High Organ was set up, with Nelson Mandela, Walter Sisulu, Govan Mbeki and Raymond Mhlaba, all members of the ANC's National Executive Committee, as the leaders.

I was a member of the communications committee from inception until my transfer to Pollsmoor. Every so often the authorities would discover something in my handwriting, or I would be caught smuggling a book. On at least three occasions my punishment was the suspension of my study privileges, but the risks were worth taking to ensure that we had access to information.

The authorities went to extraordinary lengths to deprive us of news. Warders had orders to burn their newspapers rather than simply throw them away, but many ignored this instruction, and their carelessly discarded waste became our treasure.

Common-law prisoners who qualified for A-group privileges could buy food and newspapers, and were even allowed to have radios, so they were a prime source of news. Even when we graduated to this highest category of privilege – which took thirteen years in my case – we were not allowed to buy newspapers, so clandestine ways of staying abreast of current events became an enduring challenge.

The established practice was that if someone from whichever section laid hands on a newspaper, they would transcribe the contents for dissemination within our communications network. Once, when this task fell to Madiba, the pages were returned to us with the message that his handwriting was illegible. That put paid to his 'career' as a transcriber!

Such was our need for news that we took serious risks to acquire it. One day, when we had been put to work chopping wood in a fenced enclosure near the refuse dump, Eddie Daniels and Hennie Ferris caught sight of a newspaper lying near the dump. Prison rules stated clearly that anyone found outside the perimeter fence could be shot on sight, but this didn't deter Eddie and Hennie.

While the warders were eating their lunch, they opened a hole in the fence, just big enough for Hennie to slip through, and in no time at all he had recovered the newspaper and rejoined the crew.

No matter how old a newspaper, we always found items of interest to share with our comrades in other sections of the prison.

The refuse dump proved to be a mine of information. We would take the wood camp's slop buckets to rinse in the sea, and, having picked whatever news-papers were available out of the rubbish pile, we stuffed them into the buckets.

They were always filthy, smelt bad and were often wet, but back to the cells they went, to be carefully gutted for any news of value. Of course, I then had to dispose of the contraband by diligently shredding the pages and throwing as many pieces as I dared into my slop bucket. Sometimes, there were just too many pages to get rid of this way, so five or six of us would tear them up and flush them down the toilets in the ablution block when we had the chance.

Handling those newspapers was a truly disgusting job, but the need for information was greater than any qualms about hygiene, so we did it.

Mac Maharaj was an invaluable source of news. Despite the loss of sight in one of his eyes, he could scan text faster than most people with perfect vision, and he had a photographic memory to boot. Whenever he was taken to see a doctor on the mainland, he would flip through as many as ten copies of *Time* magazine and bring back detailed accounts of international news events.

It was Mac, as well, who came up with the ingenious idea of ordering *The Economist*. Masla Pather had moved up into the A group of privileges, and was allowed to order a single magazine. He had to submit a list of six titles and the warders would choose one. Mac suggested that he ask for *The Economist*. We were convinced that this would not be allowed, but amazingly, it was. No one had bothered to look further than the magazine's name, assuming that the content was as innocuous as the title suggests.

When Masla was released, Mac took over the subscription, and for several months we had a steady flow of international news. Unfortunately, one of the brighter warders picked up a copy in one of our cells one day, and after perusing the contents, promptly cancelled the subscription.

In 1980 a friend sent me an Urdu dictionary, but the warders, who obviously could not understand the content, refused to let me have it. I finally received it when I was released, along with my other personal effects.

There was a tiny library, which I ran. A bookstore in Cape Town had donated its stock to the prison when it closed down, and most of the books were romances by Daphne du Maurier or classics by Charles Dickens.

As the fifth anniversary of South Africa becoming a republic approached in 1966, rumours abounded of symbolic gestures, quite possibly including early release for some prisoners. Inmates serving sentences of five years or less were given their civilian clothes to launder, and all of us were questioned about where we would go if released, how many rooms our homes had and who lived there.

Of course we would have been naive to suppose, even for a moment, that any good could come of such contemptible deception. We had served less than two years of our life sentences, and the apartheid regime was not renowned for mercy or magnanimity. Release and remission were limited to common-law prisoners. The republic had no birthday favours for the rest of us.

THE HYPOCRITICAL OATH

Medical doctors came to the island twice a week, but spent most of their time tending to the warders and their families.

Frankly, the professional conduct and standard of care we experienced from these doctors cast serious doubts on their abilities. One of the worst was Dr Edelstein, brother of the infinitely more humane security policeman in Johannesburg with whom I was quite well acquainted.

Edelstein had spent his entire career on the state payroll as a district surgeon, mostly working in prisons, and any humanity he might once have had had been blunted by the time we were exposed to his prejudice and sheer ineptitude.

From the early 1970s a change in policy saw prisoners from the isolation block being transported to the mainland for treatment of serious ailments. Initially we were shackled and handcuffed for the ferry ride, but later the warders were forced to comply with maritime law, which does not allow seaborne voyagers to be restricted in such a manner.

In 1966 I was diagnosed as having haemorrhoids, or 'piles'. The visiting doctor was reluctant to recommend surgery, which would have to be performed in Cape Town, but when the specialist physician paid his annual visit to the island, he confirmed the diagnosis and the need for an operation.

The prison chiefs wanted yet another opinion, and a surgeon was brought to the island to examine me as well. He confirmed that I would need to go to the mainland for proper treatment.

Late one afternoon, I was informed by a hospital orderly that my surgery would take place the next day. I was not to eat or drink anything overnight, and I should take a shower early in the morning.

Naturally, I assumed that I would be taken to a hospital in Cape Town, so I was somewhat surprised when the van that came to fetch me headed for the village rather than the harbour.

We came to a halt outside the sickbay, which was equipped for no more than the primary health care of warders and their families, and to my astonishment, waiting for me were the prison doctor and both the specialists who had previously urged that I be treated on the mainland.

I confronted them about their change of heart, only to realise, from their vague responses, that they, too, had bowed to the dictates of the security police, and instead of taking me to Cape Town they had brought an operating theatre to the island, together with theatre sisters and an anaesthetist.

I was sorely tempted to refuse the treatment on principle, but my physical discomfort forced me to sign the consent form and the procedure went ahead.

I regained consciousness in the prison hospital, lying on a real bed for the first time in years, and the first thing I saw was the entire day's regulation meals

– cold porridge, coffee, soup, mealie rice, dry bread, meat and coffee – covering the top of the bedside locker. I could not bear to look at this unappetising array, much less eat any of it.

That night, I experienced the most excruciating pain, but until the orderlies came on duty early in the morning, there was no one to dispense any form of relief. It was the same every night for the week I spent in hospital. By day I could get painkillers from the orderlies, but when they went off duty, I was alone with my agony.

I was glad to get back to my cell and the warm friendship of my comrades, though Dr Masla Pather soon deflated my hopes of organising a special diet during my recuperation, possibly including jelly and custard. 'These days,' said Masla knowingly, 'we don't pamper patients.'

In August 1966 I did leave the island, for a month. PAC leader Zeph Mothopeng sued the police and the Minister of Justice for injuries sustained when he was tortured in detention. Raymond Mhlaba, Govan Mbeki and I were required to testify on Zeph's behalf during a four-day hearing in Pretoria.

Things had changed dramatically in the two years since our trial, when the courtroom had been packed on a daily basis with supporters. Only six people were in the public gallery for Zeph's case – members of my family, Aminabai Pahad and Ayesha Cajee. The newspapers had publicised the fact that some of the Rivonia Trialists would be in court, but people were just too scared and intimidated to risk public association with struggle leaders. One month before the chief architect of apartheid was assassinated, fear stalked the land.

DIMITRI TSAFENDAS

To those who knew him personally, and I count myself as one of those who had this privilege, his deep sincerity in everything he undertook, his gentleness and his kindness towards all people, his championing of civilised and Christian ideals, and his wise counsel in times of peace and adversity will be greatly missed.
– Ian Smith, prime minister of Rhodesia, September 1966

September 6 began no differently than any other monotonous day on Robben Island. We went to work at the limestone quarry as usual, but that afternoon some of our comrades from the kitchen managed to convey to us the news that the prime minister, Dr Hendrik Verwoerd, had been assassinated. Much as we detested him and opposed his racist policies, there was no jubilation over his death at the hand of a parliamentary messenger, Dimitri Tsafendas.

By December, Tsafendas had joined us on the island to await his trial in the punishment wing of B Section, under twenty-four-hour surveillance. We were strictly forbidden from having any contact with him, but occasionally we watched through our cell windows as he walked slowly up and down in the exercise yard. His request to spend Christmas Day with us was turned down, and a few weeks later, he left.

Tsafendas was declared criminally insane and spent the rest of his life as a prisoner in a mental institution, where he died in October 1999.

If he had a political motive for killing Verwoerd, it was never revealed. Tsafendas claimed he had been instructed by a giant tapeworm living in his abdomen to murder the prime minister. In 1976 the government-funded newspaper, *The Citizen*, published an interview with Tsafendas in which he said he was being well treated in prison, and that in addition to receiving psychiatric counselling, he was regularly given extra helpings of carrots, which helped to keep the tapeworm under control.

Some years later, the journalist who wrote the story, Gordon Winter, revealed in his book, *Inside BOSS*, that he was an undercover agent for the Bureau of State Security, and admitted that the interview with Tsafendas had been specially orchestrated to counter allegations of ill-treatment made by the London *Observer*.[27]

∾ 12 ∾

Islands in Time

God made all things good. Man meddles with them and they become evil.
— Rousseau[1]

Millions of years ago, nature struggled against the might of the oceans to create an eleven-kilometre aperture in the land mass and give birth to an island. About 500 years ago, European navigators found this island to be a convenient halfway station on their voyages to the East, offering penguins, seals and tortoises as food for the hungry sailors.

In the first quarter of the sixteenth century, European explorers dumped a group of convicts there. These men from distant shores had to rely entirely on chance and their own ingenuity to survive. In the ensuing years, Portuguese, English and Dutch colonialists used the island for the same purpose.

In 1652 the Dutch East India Company established itself at the southern tip of Africa, heralding the colonisation of the Cape. Their presence evoked resistance from the indigenous Khoikhoi tribes, who put up a brave fight. In an attempt to end the conflict, the Dutch wooed one of the tribal leaders, Autshumato, but within a year he fell out of favour with the settlers, and was banished to the island by Jan van Riebeeck in 1658.

Also known as Harry the Strandloper, Autshumato escaped within twelve months. Not only was he the first political prisoner on the island, he was also the first to escape, by rowing to the mainland in a tiny boat.

It was under the Dutch that this scrap of dry land in Table Bay, just 4.5 kilometres long and 1.5 kilometres wide, was named Robben Island, derived from *robbe*, the Dutch word for seals.

Under Dutch rule, Muslim political and religious leaders from the East Indies were exiled there. One of them, Sheikh Abdurahman Mantura, died on the island, and a shrine to his memory can be seen to this day.

When the British defeated the Dutch and declared dominion over the Cape, they found it convenient to banish 'troublesome natives' to the island, including the prophet Makana, Chief Siyola and his wife, Chief Maqoma and Chief Langalibalele.

The precedent had been set, and for the next two centuries, Robben Island would be used as an isolated dumping ground for outcasts and undesirables.

From 1842 until 1931 the island was a leper colony. When the last of these particular pariahs was transferred to Westfort, in Pretoria, all the structures on the island were burnt to the ground, with the exception of the Leper Church. Designed by Sir Herbert Baker, who was also the architect of the Union Buildings in Pretoria and the parliament in New Delhi, the building sits on the only piece of the island that belongs not to the Robben Island Museum, but to the Anglican Church.

During the Second World War there was a military base on the island, and in May 1959 the property was transferred to the prisons department, which built a maximum security jail.

Among the first political prisoners sent to the island prison in 1962 was Sedick Levy, who returned as a full-time staff member when the island was declared a national monument in the early 1990s.

DREAMING OF FREEDOM

All dictators know it is safer to kill political opponents than to imprison them. Times change, and new situations open the strongest prison gates.   **– Nicholas Bethell, Gomulka**[2]

One of the questions most frequently asked of Robben Islanders is whether any serious thought was ever given to escape. The answer is yes. During the eighteen years I spent there, at least four plans were made, and one of them reached a fairly advanced stage before it was abandoned.

Jeff Masemola and Sedick Isaacs, with the help of some common-law prisoners, spent hours modifying the door to the wood camp and turning it into a makeshift raft. They worked in stages, so as not to alert the warders, and Sedick went as far as studying the tides and currents in order to determine the most favourable time to launch the bid to reach the mainland.

But they never got the chance, as one of their collaborators alerted warders to the plan, earning Sedick an extended sentence and six lashes.

Mac Maharaj also devised a plan involving the mainland. On a visit to a Cape Town dentist, he noticed an open window in the surgery, which offered just a short drop to the street below.

Mac put the plan to Mandela, who readily agreed that it might work. In due course, they both applied to see the dentist and, as luck would have it, an appointment was also made for Wilton Mkwayi on the same day. With their handcuffs removed, Mac and Madiba were actually standing in front of the open window, looking out at the surprisingly deserted street below, when they suddenly realised it could be a trap and abandoned the plan. If their suspicions were correct, it would have been an ideal opportunity for the authorities to rid themselves of Mandela by shooting him while trying to escape.

The 'Daniels Plan', by far the most ambitious, was to be implemented on New Year's Day 1981, about two years after Eddie's release. Eddie had discussed it with Madiba and Walter, who both agreed, but told Eddie the plan had first to be approved by the ANC's External Mission.

The first day of the year, a public holiday, had been deliberately chosen, as only a skeleton staff would be on duty. While the prisoners were in the exercise yard that morning, a helicopter, with Eddie on board, would hover overhead and lower a basket, covered with the South African flag, to allay suspicion.

Madiba and Sisulu would clamber into the basket and be flown to the roof of the nearest foreign embassy, where they would ask for political asylum.

But the ANC's External Mission would not approve the idea, so it too was shelved.

The last political detainees left the island in 1991, and five years later, approval was given for the prison to become a museum.

STUDIES CONTINUED

Learning makes a man fit company for himself.   — **Thomas Fuller**[3]

I finished my BA in 1968, the first 'islander' to obtain a degree in prison. I was lucky enough to be the first prisoner to attain a second degree as well, and in fact I was well advanced on my third when my studies were suspended as punishment for an infraction.

When we were given permission to study, it was made clear that a single degree per prisoner was allowed. I refused to accept this, on the grounds that too many years of my life sentence lay ahead, and I needed something to fill them. After much argument, I was allowed to enrol for non-degree courses.

But I continued to agitate for permission to do my honours, and eventually was told I could register for a second degree. Once that was under my belt, I reopened the question of honours.

The single advantage of being sent to Robben Island was the education it offered to many of the early inmates in particular. In 1964, a young worker arrived to serve a ten-year sentence. He was barely literate and had no money to pay for tuition, but he devoted his time passionately to acquiring what knowledge he could from his fellow inmates. In 1999, Jacob Zuma was appointed deputy president of South Africa.

Then there was a sixteen-year-old schoolboy from Pretoria, also sentenced to ten years. He started by passing Standard 8, then Standard 10 and a BA degree, and by the time he was released he was enrolled for a law degree. Advocate Dikgang Moseneke went on to become a judge of the Constitutional Court. Prior to that he was chairman of South Africa's largest telecommunications company.

Eddie Daniels had Standard 6 when he began serving a fifteen-year sentence. When he left, he was armed with both a BA and a BCom, and after his release he added a teaching diploma to his portfolio.

Although the lights in our cells burnt all through the night, our jailers decreed that we could study only up to a certain hour. By some arcane logic, they decided that the cut-off point for Standard 8 was 8 p.m., while matriculants had to retire at 10 p.m., and university students an hour later. Some warders would take off their shoes and patrol the corridors in socks after that, trying to catch someone breaking the rules. And offenders were punished.

This ridiculous situation gave rise to some amusing incidents. Dr Masla Pather had not registered for any courses, but he had been allowed to have some of his medical reference books in his cell. One night after the curfew, a warder found him perusing one of the hefty tomes, and naturally challenged him.

The warder could speak no English and Masla's Afrikaans was non-existent, so despite their best efforts it was impossible for Masla to explain that he was not a student, but was merely reading a medical textbook. The warder finally gave up in frustration, having decided that the doctor was a Standard 8 pupil, and should adhere to the 8 p.m. bedtime rule.

Following an argument with a warder – one of many acrimonious exchanges over the years – Don Davids was transferred to our section of the prison while studying for matric. When the officer in charge of our studies came to announce the results of the final exams, no one was more surprised than Don to learn that his credits included Latin, a subject he had not taken.

Don pointed out the error, but the warders were having none of it, insisting that the results were accurate. Don stood his ground. Finally, quite exasperated by this reluctant student, the study officer blurted out in Afrikaans: 'Don Davids, do you want the Latin, or do you not want the Latin?'

Don sheepishly whispered, 'I'll take the Latin,' and walked away.

THE WARDERS

He drew a circle to shut me out –
Heretic, rebel, a thing to flout.
But Love and I had the wit to win:
We drew a circle that took him in.
– **Edwin Markham, 'The Spirit of Magnanimity'**[4]

The warders were hardly the most educated of men, and finding themselves in a position of power over political prisoners, many of them highly qualified in their respective fields, created in some a syndrome of false superiority. When one of them returned after a six week absence, it struck me that he had been on study leave, and, more to pass the time than anything else, I politely inquired what exams he had written.

His smarmy response was, 'Oh, I've just completed two MAs.' The warders did not encourage our studies and, in fact, imposed their petty rules on us – such as a regimented bedtime – to make life as difficult as possible. They also never passed up the chance to belittle our qualifications or efforts to improve them.

There were exceptions, of course. Aubrey du Toit, one of the chief censors of our study material, would later admit: 'I had to censor Andrew Mlangeni's assignments. He was an honours student in political science. Looking back, I think it was a joke for an Afrikaner with Standard 10 to censor these difficult assignments.'[5]

But the general attitude towards our abilities was one of scepticism, even disbelief. When we were locked up during the state of emergency in 1960, Duma Nokwe, one of the first African advocates in South Africa, was with us. The warders simply could not accept that he was a fully qualified legal practitioner and dismissed him as 'just a *tsotsi* advocate', *tsotsis* being the lowest form of street thugs.

African medical doctors, too, came in for more than their share of disparagement, and had to endure constant references to being 'witchdoctors'. Oddly, Indian doctors were treated with somewhat more respect.

Over the years I came to wonder whether many of the prison warders had not been attracted to the authoritarian nature of the job rather than any sense of public service. How it must have boosted their egos to order people around! And the pathetic embellishment of their family backgrounds! For every one who said his father was a farm manager, there were five who claimed their fathers owned vast estates, and that they didn't really need to be working as warders, of course, but were merely doing so in order to escape compulsory military service.

Warders were generally posted to the island for two years, but some refused transfers and stayed much longer. The village was tiny, but there was a primary school, a pub and limited sports facilities, and since there was nothing to spend any money on, many families stayed longer than the norm for economic reasons.

It was a small and closed community, and the chief form of recreation seemed to be heavy drinking. Among the few exceptions I remember were twin brothers who both obtained their BA degrees while stationed on the island. But men of that calibre were rare in the prison service.

The head warder, 'Dup' du Plessis, was in charge of us at the lime quarry during the day, and every afternoon, when we returned to our cellblock, he would go through the same ritual of handing us into the care of the section warder. One day, when I had stayed in my cell due to some or other indisposition, Dup arrived early, and the section warder was nowhere to be seen.

Impatient to be done, Dup shouted at me, twice, '*Waar's die baas?*' ['Where is the master?']. The second time, I answered mildly, 'There is no one here by that name. Perhaps you mean the warder?'

Enraged by my impertinence, Dup stormed off.

Soon after Verwoerd was assassinated, a new warder named Van Rensburg arrived. He had a swastika tattooed on his wrist, and on his first day he lined us up at the quarry and laid down the law. 'I have not lost a war yet. I have come here to fight a war and I'm going to win this war,' he vowed. We did not have it easy under warder Van Rensburg.

We called him 'Suitcase' because, although it was customary for prisoners to carry the warders' lunchboxes, we refused to tote Van Rensburg's 'suitcase' containing a flask of coffee and sandwiches. Much to our mirth, he heard Wilton Mkwayi mention 'Suitcase' one day, and asked whom he was talking about.

'You,' said Wilton. Van Rensburg drew himself up to his full and stocky height and promptly corrected the prisoner. 'You are wrong,' he said. 'My name is not Suitcase, it's *Diknek*' ['thick neck'].

It wasn't only Suitcase's neck that was thick. What little English he knew was spoken with a heavy and guttural Afrikaans accent, and his favourite bellow was: 'You talks too much and works too few.' Another oft-heard order, when we were required to line up, was, 'Stand in a straight stripe!'

As ridiculous as we found most of our jailers, we were at their mercy day in and day out. Suitcase was a brutish man, and during his reign we found ourselves regularly being brought up on charges for offences at the quarry. The most common accusation was that we were malingering, or simply not working hard enough. It was a farce, really, as we would hear Van Rensburg talking to the other warders as we made our way to the quarry in the morning, deciding in advance who would be charged that day.

Mandela, undoubtedly one of the most industrious workers in our group, was a regular target, along with Sisulu, who was responsible for a special brand of pettiness being displayed on one occasion.

Every afternoon, one of us had to empty the toilet bucket before we returned to our cells. On this particular day it was Walter's turn, and after rinsing the bucket and placing it on a wheelbarrow, he decided to rest, for just a moment, in the shade of an old tree at the edge of the quarry. A warder came upon him sitting there, enjoying a moment of peace.

They chopped down the tree the very next day.

CONTACT WITH THE OUTSIDE WORLD

Men can live without justice, and generally must, but they
cannot live without hope. — **Eric Hobsbawm**, *Bandits*[6]

On returning from the quarry one day in 1967, Madiba was moved to a cell at the far end of the passage. We realised immediately that someone was coming to visit the prison, as legend had it that the authorities hoped it would take so long for the visitor to walk the distance that the allotted time would run out before any meaningful conversation could take place. We decided just to greet the visitor and say, 'Mandela is our spokesman.'

Mandela had naturally assumed the role of our leader, and his visitor was none other than Helen Suzman, the Progressive Party's sole member of parliament, who waged a tireless, one-woman battle against the government for years over the conditions under which we were detained.

Madiba raised a number of issues with her and, uncharacteristically, singled out Suitcase for making our lives intolerable. He specifically mentioned the swastika tattoo on the warder's wrist.

A few months later, Suitcase packed his bags and was transferred off the island. Another benefit accruing from Mrs Suzman's visit was the installation of tables and bookshelves in all the single cells.

On May Day that year our comrade Bram Fischer, serving a life sentence in Pretoria, shared the Lenin Peace Prize with Ton Duc Thang and Pastor Niemöller, who is probably best remembered for his moving and immortal reminder that silence and apathy are evil's most intimate friends: *First they came for the communists and I did not speak out because I was not a communist. Then they came for the trade unionists and I did not speak out because I was not a trade unionist. Then they came for the Jews and I did not speak out because I was not a Jew. Finally, they came for me and there was no one left to speak out.*

Towards the end of July we were devastated by the news that Chief Albert Luthuli, Nobel Prize winner and a great leader of the liberation movement, had died, hit by a train on the railway line near Groutville, where he lived. A poem in a book by a young Cape Town poet, Jennifer Davids, which was smuggled onto the island by Mac, poignantly expressed the deep loss that we felt:

For Albert Luthuli

You a fragment of the sun
go turn the world
in the long strength of your fingers

Bounded
you gave me
knowledge of freedom

Silenced
you taught me
how to speak

Somewhere a train
has reached a destination
and tonight
the cold fist of winter
clenches around the world

But beyond it
the endless pulsations of space
grow louder
and stars breaking the dark
grow large

Walk now father
unchecked
from sun to sun[7]

There was another poem, also by a young girl in her matric year, that made a great impact on me when I chanced upon it in a weekly magazine in 1967 or 1968. In translation, it reads:

Build me a land where skin (colour) does not count
Only your understanding
When no goat-face[8] in a parliament can haunt
And keep things permanently verkramp
When I can love you
Lie next to you on the grass without the Church's blessing.
When at night with guitars we can sing together with gifts of flowers.
When I am not willed to feed you with poison
As a strange bird in my nest
When no divorce court

Will blind our children's eyes
When Black and White hand in hand
Can bring peace and love
In my land.

I was greatly moved by this poem and copied it into my secret notebook. It spoke to me of the ability, especially of youth, to transcend their upbringing, to shake off the blinkers of racism and stereotyping that school and society reinforced at every opportunity, every day. It was written by a seventeen-year-old Afrikaans schoolgirl from the Free State town of Kroonstad. Her name was Antjie Krog.[9]

THE UNIVERSITY

To teach is to learn twice. — **Joseph Joubert**[10]

With Suitcase gone, life settled back into a less stressful rhythm. We used our time at the quarry once more to form study and debating groups, and for the most part, the warders let us be.

Walter Sisulu, who probably knew more than any other living person about the ANC's history, resumed his fascinating lessons on the organisation's formation and growth, which were especially useful for the younger cadres. I, in turn, recounted the development and role of the Indian Congress, and it soon became compulsory for all new arrivals from the ANC to absorb the rich verbal history of the liberation movement.

But it wasn't all politics. Some of our liveliest debates at the quarry raged on for years, and had absolutely nothing at all to do with ideology. One, in particular, revolved around the question of whether tigers ever inhabited the wilds of Africa.

Andrew Masondo, an academic from Fort Hare, was adamant that tigers were from India and Asia, cheetahs and leopards from Africa. Mandela made the point that there is a specific word in isiXhosa for tiger, differentiating the animal from other cats, and therefore the logical conclusion was that at some juncture in African history there must have been tigers. Mac retorted that the Indians had a Hindi word for flying machine thousands of years ago, but this in no way indicated that there had been any form of aircraft at the time. The debate raged on – for years, I tell you.

Billy Nair, whose activism spanned more than forty years, from the militant trade unions of the 1950s to the covert Operation Vula headed by Mac in the late 1980s, taking in the Natal Indian Congress, the SACP, MK and the UDF in between, was another fellow who always stood his ground in an argument.

He was on the island in his capacity as a regional MK commander in Natal. He had been found guilty of sabotage and sentenced to twenty years. Originally housed in the general section, he was sent to B Section for a six-month punishment spell, and simply stayed there until his release.

MATTERS OF FAITH

Among the personal details recorded on admission to prison was religious affiliation. Most of my fellow detainees listed a church or faith, but Govan Mbeki and MD Naidoo declared themselves as atheists. I used to tease Govan about this at Christmas, when we were given packets of sweets donated by various churches, suggesting that it was immoral for an atheist to accept Christian charity. He didn't even have a particularly sweet tooth, but he kept the gifts, doling out a few sweets at a time to me as a 'reward' whenever I brought him a particularly interesting news item.

MD Naidoo's atheism was somewhat seasonal. On the eve of Diwali, the Hindu Festival of Light, he learnt that a priest from Pretoria would be visiting Robben Island, bearing special food treats for the Hindu prisoners. MD promptly 'converted', telling the warders he had written 'atheist' on his admission form because it asked for 'church', and Hindus worshipped in a temple.

For the next five years, MD was a devout and occasionally well-fed Hindu.

For the first few years, religious services were led by the official prison chaplain. Later, Christian clergy from outside were allowed to minister to their flocks, and later still, Hindu and Muslim priests were also included.

But even when it came to matters of faith, racist rules applied. One, for example, stipulated: 'Provided that the said leave shall not be granted to such religious worker unless his character has been vouched for by some responsible member of that church denomination: Provided further that a Non-White minister of religion or Non-White religious worker shall not be allowed to minister to the spiritual needs of a White prisoner.'

Some of us, including Mandela, attended all the services, regardless of denomination. I had become familiar with the Bible when I was in ninety-day detention in Pretoria, and during my years in prison I developed a lifelong habit of listening to hymns on a Sunday morning.

Imam Bassier, who was eventually permitted to visit Muslim prisoners on the island, was also a sports administrator and community leader in Cape Town. We knew some of the people he worked with, and consequently he served as a vital link with people with whom we would otherwise not have been in contact. On one occasion I even asked the Imam to convey information to our friends that we were on a hunger strike.

Once Imam Bassier started bringing food parcels on Eid days, his congregation burgeoned, with thirty-five 'new' Muslims, led by Justice Mpanza, turning up for the next prayer service. The jailers saw through this and did not allow the 'new-born' Muslims to attend.

One of our favourite churchmen was Brother September, whose sermons were both down to earth and long. For us, the longer a service, the better. Every minute we spent outside our cells was a welcome bonus, especially on cold winter days.

One Sunday, Hennie Ferris innocently asked Brother September to let him lead the congregation in prayer. He took his time, and was quite insistent that we should all close our eyes and bow our heads. What poor Brother September did not know was that while he was lost in the eloquence of Hennie's entreaties, Eddie Daniels tiptoed up to the pastor's briefcase, opened it, and removed a copy of that day's *Sunday Times*.

On Brother September's next visit, Hennie said a prayer again, a short one this time, in which he begged forgiveness for unspecified transgressions. Brother September never mentioned his missing newspaper, but he didn't bring one to Sunday service again.

It would be both incorrect and unfortunate if these glimpses of our spiritual shenanigans created the impression that we treated religion, or the clergy, flippantly or with irreverence. We had great respect for all faith, and related sincerely to the universal message of peace and brotherhood, and some of the ministers offered us great comfort, both as a group and at a personal level.

Father Hughes, an Anglican priest, was an especially marvellous specimen of humanity. He had been a chaplain in a prisoner-of-war camp during the Second World War, and had tremendous empathy with our loss of freedom. There were times when all of us, including me, succumbed to feelings of despair and self pity, and it was at such low ebbs that I would remind myself of the homily cited by Father Hughes during one of his earliest sermons: *I grumbled and groused because I had no shoes, until I met a man who had no feet.*

VISITS, LETTERS AND BOOKS

By October 1967 I was allowed one thirty-minute visit a month from one person. If no one used the time, it could be added to the next month's visit, provided this was arranged well in advance. The subjects we could talk to visitors about were strictly limited and monitored by warders in close attendance.

When my eldest brother Solly's wife, Ayeshabai, wanted to visit, I resorted to a little subterfuge in order to double the value of the occasion. I told the officials that my sister-in-law spoke only Gujerati, and since conversation had to be in either English or Afrikaans, requested that my niece, Julie, be allowed to accompany her mother and act as interpreter.

After much deliberation, they agreed! But our visit had barely begun when I realised that I had gravely miscalculated. Julie, a teacher, was such a sensitive and soft-hearted soul that she wept for the entire thirty minutes.

Ayeshabai and I, meanwhile, chattered away in a combination of English, Afrikaans and Gujerati, though I was somewhat tense and flustered about the hitch in my plan. Fortunately, the warders monitoring the visit were so intent on making sure that we discussed nothing 'subversive' that it didn't occur to them to question the presence of an 'interpreter' who barely uttered a word.

A few years later I used the same ploy again. This time, my brother Ismail and his wife, Aminabai, came to visit, and once again, it worked … except that, as we were saying goodbye, Ismail, for some inexplicable reason, felt obliged to mention to the warder that his wife spoke only Afrikaans!

Towards the end of 1968 the rigid regulations on reading matter were relaxed slightly, and we were allowed to subscribe to approved magazines such as *Reader's Digest*, *Panorama*, *Farmer's Weekly*, *Lantern* and *Huisgenoot*. We were also given some free publications – *Fiat Lux*, *Alpha*, *Tswelopele* and other deeply boring government-funded journals targeted at specific ethnic groups.

In a major breakthrough, loudspeakers were also installed in our cellblock, and music was broadcast daily between 5 and 8 p.m. For the first time, we were also allowed to play musical instruments.

I had signed up for some of the publications immediately, including *Panorama*, a glossy magazine published by the government's information department. It was an attractive product, filled with colour photographs and quite well-written articles, all designed to portray apartheid South Africa in the best possible light.

As a government publication, it was supposed to be given to us uncensored, but before long I found large chunks missing from my copy, sometimes entire pages. I lodged a complaint with Major Huisamen, the officer in charge of study material, but nothing could have prepared me for his response.

The offending pages had been excised because they featured photographs of young women in bikinis. I was momentarily dumbfounded, but quickly recovered and pointed out that I was studying anthropology, and that my textbooks contained photographs of completely naked women, let alone any in swimsuits.

'Those must be Bantu women,' said the major, and there the matter rested.

In prison, one cannot measure time in days or hours; other landmarks must be found to mark the passage of the years. I used special occasions – family birthdays, wedding anniversaries, graduations. Over a twenty-six-year period there were many of each, and the closest we came to being part of them were photographs. On the occasion of their marriage in December 1988, I wrote to my nephew Nazir and his young bride Yasmin as follows:

The most common form of measuring one's time in prison is by calculating the number of years; in our case in terms of cold statistics this amounts to 25 years, 5 months and some days. Looked at from such a restricted angle, one simply gets a picture of fragmented units of time – monotonous, drab, unchanging, unexciting and tedious. It does not cover the essentially vibrant community that inhabits a world within a world – its spectrum of experiences, its collective and individual emotions, thrills and responses, its fears, its joys and sorrows, its hopes, its confidence, its loves and hates, the unbreakable spirit, the fellowship, the hardships, the morale. These and much more make up the prison community. Naturally these generalised feelings find expression in a myriad specific forms in every hour of every day of every year.

One may choose any one (or more) of the specific forms and use them to measure his period of incarceration. In this letter I propose to use births and marriages (of my nieces and nephews) to measure my time. At the time of my arrest there were 16 nephews and nieces – all unmarried. Two joined the clan later. Fourteen of them got married while I've been in jail, thus adding to the number of nieces and nephews. Then followed their offspring – 21 of them ...

Each one of the marriages meant a lot to me, and I celebrated them in my own way. And the arrival of each baby provided its own special kind of thrill. (You know, of course, that until a few years ago, we had not seen or touched a child.)

Your coming marriage marks another milestone in my incarceration, and I want to join with all the family members and friends in extending my heartiest congratulations to you. Though I will not be with you physically, my thoughts and good wishes will be with you on the big day and always.

As on previous occasions, I should like to point out some similarities between marriage and the prison situation! Difficult to believe when the institution of marriage represents beauty, grace, nobility, elegance, love while the general picture of the prison institution is one replete with vulgarity, harshness, violence, filth, corruption, inhumanity and much else. Admittedly, these elements are not absent in prisons, but they are not relevant to the aspect which I am dealing with today. I want to talk about aspects such as a break from past lifestyles and the entry into new environments, about new friends and new relationships, about the need to curb one's individualistic streaks in order to fit into the greater whole, about new responsibilities and new priorities, about a situation where the pronoun 'I' will be used less and less while 'we' will come into more general usage. Yes, they are both situations which call for sacrifices and compromises — and radical adjustments.

One enters into marriage voluntarily, while one has no control over one's imprisonment. By its nature, a marriage is virtually synonymous with happiness and the fulfilment of dreams. A prison situation, on the other hand, is tailor-made for everything that is negative; it can be an ordeal and a period of unmitigated hardship and unhappiness and the destruction of dreams. But it does not have to be this way — and indeed, I would like to think that our quarter of a century in jail has been anything but negative or wasted. At the very outset we realised that there was no magic or secret formula to meet the challenge that lay ahead. What was needed was determination, a positive approach and above all to doggedly maintain the basic values with which we have grown up. I believe that these requirements are equally valid for a successful marriage.

More than anything else, books helped to keep our minds occupied. By February 1969 I had completed my first degree, and had registered for non-degree courses in anthropology, archaeology, ancient history and English. Both for academic and recreational purposes, I read everything I could lay my hands on: Tolstoy's *War and Peace*, Zola, Balzac, Stendhal, Thomas Mann, Byron, Schreiner and Dickens. Modern authors that I enjoyed included Paul Gallico, Antoine de Saint Exupéry, Howard Fast, Pearl Buck, Hemingway, Steinbeck and Nadine Gordimer.

I also kept secret notebooks, filling about seven over the years with favourite quotations and extracts that struck a chord in me. Anyone who has ever been imprisoned will understand that something quite insignificant can spark a reverie of nostalgia. One evening, I was in my cell reading heart surgeon Chris Barnard's biography, engrossed in accounts of his childhood at Beaufort West — the boyish pranks, the games, the fights, the rivalries, the ambitions — when a medley of traditional Afrikaans songs began playing through the loudspeakers: 'Suikerbossie', 'Daar Kom Die Wa', 'Sarie Marais' — songs of my childhood. I was transported back in time, memories of Schweizer-Reneke flooding my mind until I drifted into sleep, a deep and carefree sleep, the sleep of the innocent. For those few, restful hours, my mind, at least, roamed free outside the prison walls.

THE END OF THE 1960S

In 1969, PAC leader Robert Sobukwe was released from detention on Robben Island, where he had been held in a house since 1963, but his exit was merely a prelude to further restriction, as he was banished to Kimberley.

As the new decade dawned, we had come to a point where relations with the warders were generally more cordial, and some of our conditions had been improved. At the quarry, when some of the prisoners set traps for birds or rabbits, the warders would turn a blind eye, though they expected their share of the booty. They had also stopped driving us as hard during our work shifts as previously, though we were constantly reminded that if we saw a vehicle approaching, we should double our efforts lest an officer be making an unscheduled inspection.

We had slowly managed to break down some of the ingrained antagonism towards us and were generally being treated with more respect and fewer punitive measures. But that was about to change.

The prison got a new commanding officer, a cruel and heartless man who made no secret of his contempt for us. The young warders we had begun to befriend were replaced at short notice by older, harder men, who cared for nothing but the rigid enforcement of discipline.

On 9 January 1971, I wrote to Sylvia, trying to capture every facet of my life in a single smuggled letter – the trivia and tragedy, the pettiness and prejudice, the boredom and bad food:

I want to try to give you a picture of some aspects of our life here. I can only speak authoritatively of life in the single cell section. There are over 80 single cells but our permanent population remains about 30. Except for the occasional new arrival, we live with the same persons all the years. In this way they have effectively isolated us from the rest of the population which totals ± 800. I believe, of these, under 400 are politicals. Since their arrival 3 years ago we've only managed to have one accidental glimpse of the Namibians. The ANC guerrillas are confined to their yard, even for work, so we don't see them at all. We are taken to and from work in a closed lorry, are taken separately to visits, have separate church services, write exams separately – film shows, games, everything is separate. A conscientious warder would even clear the road when our lorry approaches. So you see the extent of our isolation. My cell is about 8 × 8 ft - the only items of furniture are a table and a bench. We sleep on two mats on the cement floor. It can be terribly cold. Living with the same faces day in and day out must be having adverse psychological effects on us. We do get on one another's nerves & we have long exhausted all conversation relating to our experiences outside. All the jokes have been told, even gossip has become repetitive. There are inevitable tensions arising from such a situation. But on the whole we have coped remarkably well. The studies are a great help. Wish they'd allow us newspapers. We sometimes look forward to new arrivals, especially if they are lively & talkative, like our mutual friends, the 'Capies'.

Our (single cells) relationship with warders has been quite cordial & with some decidedly warm. There is considerable exchange of small talk, which is not without benefit. Most warders are very young, some barely 17. Generally they are decent and if they spend their impressionable years working with political prisoners I am sure it will have a healthy impact on their outlook. Unfortunately they stay a very short time with us, and are once again exposed to the unwholesome and brutalising influences of prison life. Then I suppose they become the ordinary white South Africans with all their prejudices, hates, fears and irrationality. Isn't it tragic? Because, ironically, it is in jail that we have closest fraternisation between the opponents and supporters of apartheid; we have eaten of their food, and they ours; they have blown the same musical instruments that have been 'soiled' by black lips; they have discussed most intimate matters and sought advice; a blind man listening in to a tête-à-tête will find it hard to believe it is between prisoner and warder. One of them once related to me an argument among them which centred on the visit to SA of a black dignitary and the lavish entertainments meted out. His stand was that if Vorster could eat & drink with a neighbouring African, why couldn't he do so with Mandela, and for this he received much support.

But of course there are the *verkramptes* and rabid racialists as well. What a job we will have to rehabilitate them. To get back to jail life. Work. Our official work still remains the lime quarry & pick & shovels. But for the past few years we have not really worked. We have demanded creative work. They say they are unable to. So we just go to the quarry & do nothing. We are not on strike, only bored & frustrated with this type of work. They of course don't like our not working. But there is a stalemate. I don't know how long this farce will last. Incidentally the Congress chaps addressed a letter to the Minister of Justice last year, demanding that we be treated as political prisoners, which inter alia means we do only the essential work. Food. They've been promising improvements. But there has been little change. On 14 Nov they surprised us by giving chicken instead of beef. Since then we've been getting chicken every Saturday. Since then we are also being given one egg three times a week. But there had to be a catch somewhere. The timing of this innovation coincided with the visit to the island of members of the International Red Cross. Secondly they've made it clear that chicken and eggs will be given as long as the glut continues. Finally, in their cockeyed way of reasoning, they believe that non-white prisoners do not need as much protein as whites. Therefore when they introduced chicken and eggs, they officially cut down the already meagre ration of beef, pork and fish. The meat ration is as little as 5 cubes of ¾" each. Censorship. In our studies and general reading we suffer from narrow *verkrampte* censorship. Then, from next year we will no longer be allowed to do politics, history, economic history, and any other subject which necessitates books considered objectionable. So much for the *verligte* winds of change. Visits. For me 1970 has been a bad year for visits. My brother Solly continued his efforts to see me, but has been unsuccessful. They are refusing to grant him a visiting permit for the Cape so that rules out Robben Island. The local Nat. MP even took up the matter with the minister, but it was in vain. In July Fatima Meer from Durban applied to see me but was refused. No reasons given. Moms, who had visited me in previous years, was told by the Special Branch that she will not get a passport if she continues. So that put paid to her visits. Poor woman. She feels terrible about it. This story naturally got around, with the result that a number of CT friends are now afraid. Helen Suzman promised to do something about the visits. But I haven't heard. I wish a row is kicked up. The SB has also interfered with people with whom I correspond. Assaults. Here again there is differential treatment. In our section there have been virtually no assaults ever since our arrival. And among the rest of the political prisoners assaults have almost ceased, tho there are occasional incidents. But this cannot be said for our non-political fellows. For them jail is still what it has always been for non-whites – a veritable hell. On 14, 15 and 16 November, for instance, a series of organised brutal assaults were conducted on them which resulted in broken arms, heads and huge weals all over the body. The matter was reported to the Red Cross chaps, but they said they could do nothing about it as their mission was restricted to political prisoners. Suddenly there are political prisoners in SA. General. They've started installing a warm water system. This will be most welcome, tho over the years I became quite used to cold water on the coldest of days. There are all sorts of rumours of other improvements. Now that the 10th anniversary of the Republic is approaching there are fresh rumours of remissions. What does remission on a life sentence mean? There is nothing I'd like more than being with Yasmin as soon as possible. I shall let you know if something tangible arises. Until then we'll sit and wait – or pray! Have just heard there is a departmental committee presently reviewing all long sentences especially of 1963, 1964 period. But then this is the time for all sorts of rumours.

I am writing this on 9 January. Beginning from about Christmas time there have been vast changes in our way of life. A new officer commanding has been installed and a host of new head warders have been brought over. We are told they have come to 'clean up' this jail and to impose discipline, which they maintain has completely broken down. In pursuance of this aim they have launched a sort of reign of terror, short of physical violence, although we know of at least one prisoner who was actually beaten up. It is clear that the whole onslaught has been well planned, with the fullest connivance of Pretoria. The kick-off was about three weeks ago. When the chaps arrived at work at the big quarry they found that all their improvised seats (for which they had received permission from the previous administration) had been taken and burnt. The chaps sought an immediate interview with the higher ups. In the meantime they stopped working. To the best of knowledge they are still not working, tho they are taken out to work daily. The 5-man delegation appointed to see the authorities were summarily taken and locked up in our section, which is the isolation section. Of course, tho in our section they are in their own wing and are isolated from us as well. When the authorities refused to see them they, together with 5 others who had already been previously isolated, went on a hunger strike, which lasted for 4½ days. The authorities just did not budge. When they eventually resumed eating each of them was seen by the Colonel, who arbitrarily downgraded them one group, and five of the ten were sent back to the big section. This more or less ended this episode.

In the big section, tension continued to rise as the prisoners faced one provocation after another. On Monday while on their way to work the authorities felt they were walking too slowly and they set the dogs upon them. 4 prisoners were bitten, one of whom I believe has been hospitalised. This naturally incensed the population, and since Wednesday all the prisoners in the big section have been on hunger strike. Today is Saturday and I believe they are still on. For various reasons our section has not joined in yet. But by the looks of things we will not be able to keep out of action much longer.

It seems we have entered a period of intensive provocation and repression, which will require tremendous patience, careful planning, and bold action. They have brought the most backward group of officials to 'discipline' us, men of the old school who have not the slightest ideas of their own reputedly 'progressive' thought on penology. The younger lot just graduating from warders' training college at least talk of rehabilitation and many of them seem sincere. But as for this lot they only know one thing, and that is revenge and constant punishment. Every moment the prisoner must be made to feel that he is in jail. For this they use all sorts of pinpricks. Such petty little things. The Colonel also turned up to our quarry and finding no work going on, demoted the chaps one group. Luckily I was not at work that day, so I am still 'C'. He has made known that he does not believe in charging us. He will use other methods, like taking away our privileges. For instance we are no longer allowed to play games during lunch at work. They have also taken away the long trousers and jerseys from the chaps in the big section, even from the old and sickly. This is terrible, especially the last winter has been severe. In fact we still have cold days.

So you see we have a tremendous task ahead of us. It has been relatively easy to educate and even rehabilitate the younger warders. But it is not going to be so smooth with this lot. However, we are in good spirits and prepared for the attacks. We've been through worse days and I am confident we will weather the storm.

∾ 13 ∾

The Bad Years

He who has a why *to live for can bear almost any* how.
— **Friedrich Nietzsche**[1]

From the moment we were confronted with Piet Badenhorst just before Christmas in 1970, we knew that tough times lay ahead. No longer would we benefit from the comparative decency of the amiable Colonel van Aarde. The new commanding officer was a vicious man, almost sadistic in fact, and he brought with him a crew of brutal warders. We nicknamed Badenhorst 'Kid Ruction'.

At this time, Africa was gripped by independence fever, as one country after another shrugged off the onerous yoke of colonialism or faced the onslaught of those prepared to fight for freedom.

The vast land known as South West Africa had been governed by South Africa since 1920 in terms of a mandate from the League of Nations. By the end of the 1960s, a number of members of the South West African People's

Organisation had been detained, including secretary general Andimba Toivo ya Toivo.

They were incarcerated in an old corrugated iron structure, quite separate from the rest of the buildings on Robben Island. But soon after Badenhorst arrived, the SWAPO prisoners were moved to our cellblock in B Section.

Fraternisation was strictly forbidden and strict measures were enforced to ensure that our paths never crossed, even accidentally. But as soon as I heard that Comrade Toivo was being housed in the next wing, I wrote him a letter of welcome, on toilet paper.

Govan Mbeki, who was considerably older than most of us, had been exempted from hard labour, and his duties now included accompanying the medical orderly on his daily cell rounds, with Govan carrying the medicine chest. This meant he had access to the punishment wing in B Section, so I asked him to smuggle my letter to Toivo.

But before he could deliver the message, a warder approached Govan and, fearing he was about to be searched, he dropped the letter on the floor. Of course the warders picked it up and recognised my handwriting. We were both punished, and that wasn't the last time the two of us got into trouble.

THE HUNGER STRIKE OF MAY 1971

Whenever I hear a man express hatred for any race, I wonder just what it is in themselves they hate so much. You can always be sure of this: You cannot express hatred for anything or anybody unless you make use of the supply of hatred within yourself. The only hatred you can express is your own personal possession. To hate is to be enslaved by evil.

– Thomas Dreier[2]

When a dispute erupted between Toivo and the warders, he was moved to an empty cell away from his colleagues. They immediately went on a hunger strike in protest, and as soon as we heard about this, we joined them in solidarity. There were strong bonds between SWAPO and MK, with members training side by side in military camps, and both organisations had the same allies: Frelimo, the MPLA and ZAPU.

On Friday 28 May 1971, two or three days into the hunger strike, the warders, many of them drunk, raided our cells. They had been to the common-law prison first, where several prisoners were so severely beaten with fists and truncheons that some had to be hospitalised.

All our cells were unlocked, and we were made to strip and stand facing the wall. It was a bitterly cold night, we had not eaten for a few days and the search of our cells seemed to take forever.

Govan Mbeki collapsed, and the warders, suddenly scared that he might have had a heart attack, ordered us to get dressed immediately and moved to the next wing, where Toivo ya Toivo and some other prisoners were held.

One of the warders, a huge brute of a man named Carstens, taunted Toivo, deliberately provoking him, and Andimba hit back, knocking the warder to the floor. Not only was he thoroughly assaulted, but several of the other prisoners in that wing were beaten too.

The retribution exacted by the warders for Andimba's humiliation of one of their own was nothing short of inhumane. He had been fairly isolated before, but was still allowed to shower and exercise at the same time as the other SWAPO prisoners. After the raid, all the SWAPO detainees were transferred to the main section of the prison and Andimba was placed in one of the cells in an otherwise deserted wing.

Apart from two thirty-minute exercise periods a day, alone, Andimba was kept in that cell, deprived of any company, for more than nine months. Every time a visitor or high-ranking prison official came to the island, Madiba would demand that Toivo be moved back to our wing and released from conditions that were enough to drive a man out of his mind.

When a general from head office came to the island, Madiba reiterated his demands. One of the highest ranking officers in the prison service responded by going to Andimba's cell and suggesting that he submit a request to be moved to a wing with other prisoners. Andimba refused, telling the general: 'You put me here without asking my permission, so you don't need my permission to take me out.'

When the Red Cross came, Toivo talked to them, and not long afterwards he was finally taken out of solitary confinement.

QUEST FOR NEWS

In the Nazi concentration camp, the basic message of fairy stories stayed with me: that in life you encounter terrible events, but if you can hold on to your values, you might survive to be the better for it.

— **Professor Bruno Bettelheim**[3]

We were powerless against Badenhorst and his thugs. We tried to send messages to lawyers about his reign of terror, but failed. When Eddie Daniels attempted to convey the situation to his brother, the warders cut short their visit.

We resisted as best we could, but there was really nothing we could do. From 1 April 1971, after seven years, my privileges had been upgraded to the B category, which meant I could see two visitors at a time, and write and receive two letters a month. But my pleasure was short-lived.

In June I was suddenly demoted back to the D group, the lowest and least privileged of all. From the beginning of that year, D prisoners had been barred from studying, for example, and I still believe I was downgraded to prevent me from pursuing my studies.

When we were imprisoned, our first challenge was to assert our right to be treated as human beings and not to allow the enemy to impinge on our dignity in any way. The next and equally important priority was to keep ourselves informed.

Although it was a fairly lengthy and uphill battle, I think we can rightly claim that we succeeded in humanising many of our jailers and inculcated in a fair number of the common-law prisoners, some of whom really were the dregs of the underworld, a sense that even they were entitled to certain basic human rights.

Common-law prisoners were our main source of news. They could get newspapers and could even lay their hands on radios. A radio was smuggled into the prison for us at one point, which was wonderful, but when the batteries ran out we had no way of replacing them. We had no safe place to hide the radio, and in the end we dismantled and buried it at the quarry.

We never handled the money sent by our families to pay for study material and toiletries, so we bartered items such as soap, toothpaste and cigarettes in exchange for newspapers. As soon as the common-law prisoners realised how desperate for news we were, they turned the arrangement to their greater advantage, trading single pages rather than entire publications at a time.

One surprisingly astute warder brought in by Badenhorst summed up the difference between common-law and political prisoners as follows: if he left food, money and a newspaper on his desk, the common-law prisoner would steal the food and money, while the political detainee would take only the newspaper.

The ban on certain news defied all logic. For example, when the Americans put a man on the moon, it took some time before we were allowed to know about this achievement, though what possible political capital we might have made of it, no one could ever fathom.

Govan Mbeki would later say that our communications committee was top of his shortlist of positive memories about prison life. Laloo Chiba and Mac Maharaj were particularly innovative in coming up with ways to access news, smuggle material off the island and share information with prisoners in other sections. Both were also skilled at writing in tiny but legible script and identifying secret hiding places for contraband.

In addition to our early use of empty matchboxes to convey messages, we used shoes. Laloo had worked as a tailor and was skilled at producing minute stitches. We would hide a message in the back of a shoe, stitch over the opening and send the shoe for repair to the shoe shop in the general section, manned predominantly by ANC supporters.

Mac experimented with another innovative method of communication, invisible messages. Milk could be used for the purpose, but it had to be undiluted. Once an 'invisible' letter reached its destination, all the comrades had to do was a hot electric iron over it. Because fresh milk was not easy to come by, Mac experimented with a substance he somehow managed to obtain from the prison hospital. I think it was called Eusol.

During Badenhorst's tenure, news and communication became more important than ever, and helped us retain our sanity in the face of relentless persecution.

Raids and searches were conducted regularly, sometimes twice a day. Letters, banned reading material disguised as textbooks, notes and various other items were confiscated. While the prison was being repainted in the colour known as 'olive drab' and beloved of the military, Mac Maharaj, Laloo Chiba, Samson Fadana and Lionel Davis were drafted into the paint squad.

While the rest of us were at the quarry, they observed that the warders placed all the confiscated items in the library near our cells. They also realised that when the warders took their lunch break, the contraband was left unattended.

Samson contrived to attach a wire hook to the end of a broom handle, and by poking it through the bars of the library door, the painters managed to retrieve a fair amount of the confiscated material, which they then wrapped in plastic and immersed in the drums of paint they were using.

The increased vigilance of Badenhorst's men forced us to find new hiding places. Jafta 'Jeff' Masemola proved to be both a creative genius and excellent handyman in this respect. He made false bottoms and secret compartments for some of the stools in our cells. These hidey-holes were so well crafted that they escaped detection during raids so thorough that the warders would even unroll our toilet paper, just in case we had written messages on some sheets.

When a radio was smuggled to us, it was hidden in a secret compartment of someone's stool. Discovery would have resulted in dire punishment, but the warders never found the radio. However, it was such a high-risk item that eventually the High Organ ordered its destruction. By that time we had no batteries to power the radio in any event, but it had been of so much value that we carried out the order with great reluctance.

Masemola also made a master key from a piece of metal that Mac had picked up at the quarry some years before. We never intended to use the key to escape from the prison, but it came in extremely handy, as it could be used to open every cell in B Section.

How and when Jeff gained access to the original key in order to make a copy I cannot recall, but Mac and Laloo were involved. There were eighty cells in our section, of which only about thirty were occupied at any given time. Once we could unlock the empty cells, we were able to hide all kinds of contraband in them, knowing that the warders seldom, if ever, searched cells that were not in use. Much, much later, our trusty key was buried somewhere on the island.

One of the few enriching experiences of prison life was the opportunity to meet and come to know people from all over the country, with diverse backgrounds, religious beliefs, languages and education. Prison, by its very nature, is a trying experience. It gives rise to a twisted interpretation of reality on a day-to-day basis, while at the same time forcing the individual to distil the chaff from the essence of life itself. How one deals with the challenges and deprivations is an intensely personal experience.

JAMES APRIL

James April began serving his fifteen-year sentence in mid-1971. Selfishly, every new arrival was welcomed as a source of recent news from the outside world.

Although relatively young, James was a veteran activist and well informed. Having received his military training in East Germany, he was familiar with developments in the international socialist movement and the tensions between the Soviet Union and China. He had also played a heroic role in the clash between MK's Luthuli Detachment and Rhodesian security forces at Wankie, and was able to give us a first-hand account of this confrontation.

Sadly his closest friend, Basil February, had been killed in a skirmish – and Basil's brother-in-law, Leslie van der Heiden, had been one of our fellow prisoners.

More importantly, James could bring us up to date on developments within the ANC in exile, most notably the historic Morogoro Conference, which he had attended.

> It was at Morogoro, Tanzania, that the ANC was able to hold its first conference outside South Africa, in 1969. It was Tambo's constructive response to criticism by cadres who were itching to return home to wage the armed struggle inside.
>
> The outcome of the Morogoro Conference was a significant step forward. Conference agreed that in future political interest was to take precedence over the military, and that a Revolutionary Council (RC) be formed to give direction. The non-racial composition of the RC, though, proved to be a problem with a small, Africanist group of middle level membership. After many discussions with OR, they were unable to come to terms with the inclusion of 'non-Africans' in the structures.[4]

According to the Report of the Truth and Reconciliation Commission,

> the Revolutionary Council [was] tasked with concentrating on the home
> front, developing internal structures, creating publicity for the ANC, and
> waging armed struggle. The RC expanded over the years by co-opting new
> members and developing structures or portfolios, including communica-
> tions, ordnance, intelligence and security.[5]

A debate had been raging for years on Robben Island about the movement's
approach to racially exclusive organisations, which were, after all, a pillar of
apartheid. Decisions taken by the ANC at its 1969 conference helped us resolve
differences in this regard, as in addition to reports by James, we were able to
lay our hands on a post-Morogoro article written by Joe Matthews about the
strategy and tactics that had been adopted.

It was at Morogoro that the ANC decided for the first time to open its
membership to all. For me, and many other non-Africans, this was special
reason for celebration, even though office-bearers would still be drawn only
from within African ranks.

Terms such as 'non-racist' or 'multiracial' could not be found in ANC
resolutions or documents, and the 1943 constitution, drafted by Bram Fischer,
limited membership to Africans. Despite this, the organisation was implicitly
non-racist, as illustrated by the Freedom Charter, the ANC's refusal to bow to
the PAC's demands of exclusivity and the bold decision of the leadership to
expel the 'Gang of Eight' for opposing the Morogoro decisions.

I had found the membership restriction both contradictory and humiliating.
I was serving life imprisonment for participating in ANC activities, yet I was not
allowed to become a member until 1969. It was only at the Kabwe Conference
in 1985 that a further policy amendment opened the door for office-bearers of
all races.

In addition to his political acumen, James April was well read and quite
knowledgeable about music and the arts. Soon after he joined us, he was
punished with six days of spare rations for some or other offence. Billy Nair
decided to try to alleviate his plight by persuading the night warder to smuggle
some food to James in the punishment wing.

Risky though this was, Billy succeeded in securing the warder's cooperation,
and a small package containing a few slices of bread, some meat, biscuits and
chocolates was put together for James.

If caught assisting us, the young warder would have suffered serious consequences, but, as agreed, he duly took the package to James's cell. A few
minutes later he returned, the package intact.

Billy was flummoxed. Had James been asleep? Unwell? Was the warder
certain he had gone to the right cell?

The answer was as amusing as it was perplexing. James had refused to accept the package, though he sent his thanks to Billy and the others for their kindness, but he would not have been able to eat the food, as he had already brushed his teeth!

My mother

Don't be too impressed by long words. They stand for small things. All the big things, on the other hand, have short names: life, death, hunger, thirst, fear, joy, day, night, hope, love.
– Marcel Aymé's advice to a young writer[6]

Letters at six-monthly intervals and two thirty-minute visits a year were wholly inadequate as far as my need to maintain contact with my family was concerned. My mother, a sensitive woman with strong maternal instincts, was for some time not even aware that I was serving a life sentence, with no end in sight. The family had made up some story about how long I would be away, and because my mother could neither speak nor read English, she never learnt otherwise from news reports. We would never see one another again, and on 26 March 1972, I wrote the following letter to my siblings:

My Dear Folks,
On Friday 24 March at about 4.30 pm I was called to the office and informed that Ma had passed away. Unfortunately the telegram has not yet arrived so I do not know any details, but I assume she never recovered from the illness with which she was afflicted earlier this year. Thanks to Zohra, the shock of the news was not so great.

Nevertheless, it is not possible to condition oneself fully for death. Deep in the recesses of the mind there always flickers a hope that somehow this spectre will be kept away from one's near and dear ones. One has reasoned and convinced oneself that one day it has to come; yet when the blow strikes the faculties are numbed and one reacts with all the emotion that is normal to human beings.

Of all our family, I have spent the least time with Ma. I'm sure each of these [trials and prison terms] must have caused Ma tremendous anxiety and sorrow. I'll never forget how she collapsed that day in June 1961, when I was brought home under escort on my way to Christiana jail. How happy she was for the few months in 1962 when I was free from bans and came home a good few times. But alas, the respite was too short. I last saw her about 10 years ago. In jail, I have often reflected over the fact that I have been a constant source of worry and trouble to Ma, and to all of you. I have lived with a slight feeling of guilt, and have thought of ways and means of making good. But now Ma has been removed from us and I've been deprived of the opportunity. I do, however, find some consolation from the fact that all of you, more particularly her many grandchildren, and now the great-grandchildren, more than made up for my absence.

We have always been a close-knit family, and our attachment to one another, and to Ma, has therefore been greater. Consequently we will all feel her loss a lot more. Yet we realise that the procession of life moves on. While we honour, remember and always commemorate the dead, we have to think of the present and the future – of the living, especially the young ones. We must continue to behave to one another, and to remain as a whole in a manner which would have made Ma happy. That would be the best way of honouring her memory.

All my colleagues here, especially Mr Mandela and Mr Sisulu, have asked to convey their deepest sympathy.

Love to all of you, from AMK

SOLITARY, AGAIN

We can forgive cruelty – to wound a person means that one still has faith in [him] – but not indifference! Indifference is like ice at the poles, it deadens everything. – **Balzac, Lost Illusions**[7]

When Govan Mbeki was caught trying to smuggle a note from me to Toivo ya Toivo, he was punished with three months in solitary confinement. I got six months. All I was allowed to take with me were my toiletries and the Bible.

While conditions could not be compared with the harshness and trauma of my ninety-day detention, this stint of solitary confinement was not without hardship. But thanks to colleagues such as Chiba, Eddie, Billy and others, the loneliness and boredom were somewhat mitigated when someone managed to smuggle me a book or some news.

As before, I whiled away the time by trying to recall and recite every bit of poetry, prose and song that I had learnt since childhood. The only diversion was the thirty minutes of exercise each morning and afternoon when we were allowed to walk around the yard, but very often the warders cheated us out of several minutes.

One particularly cold Sunday morning, we really wished we could linger outside in the sun for more than half an hour. But the rigid prison regulations did not lend themselves to being bent and the warders were not inclined towards kindness. Govan's ingenuity was our salvation.

I was momentarily taken aback when he suggested I ask the warder to arrange that we attend the church service in the sunny courtyard later that morning. I teased Govan, 'I'm a Muslim and you're an Anglican, and now an atheist. How can I ask for a Christian service?'

I made the request and surprisingly, it was granted. After that, we became regular 'sun' worshippers, regardless of what religious denomination was holding an outdoor service.

For good or for bad, the one thing solitary confinement offers is time to think, and naturally, much of that time is devoted to thoughts about oneself, and one's situation. This was the scenario when Thomas Mann made an entry into my life.

The one book that I wish Laloo had never smuggled to me is Mann's *The Magic Mountain*. I could only read in short bursts, surreptitiously at night when the cellblock was silent and I could hear the night warder's footsteps as he did his rounds.

I should have abandoned the book at an early stage, but the more I read about the illnesses of the characters, the more I was drawn to them, until not only did they have my total sympathy, but I found myself experiencing the very symptoms Mann described. My persistent requests to see a doctor must have prompted an entry in my prison file, which I came across years afterwards: 'Ahmed Kathrada is just a frustrated man who has lost his objectivity and is lodging all kinds of petty complaints instead of accepting his position and trying to make the best out of it.'[8]

To try to fill the hours, I ordered a German Bible. Not only could I read the psalms in another language, but by comparing the German version with the English, I could improve my German. Surprisingly, the authorities granted my request.

When Brigadier Aucamp, head of security in the prisons department and an old acquaintance, visited the island, I told him that I wanted a Koran. He either misunderstood or misheard me, and was astonished that I would ask for a *koerant*, which is Afrikaans for a newspaper. But, because it was in Arabic, I did not get a Koran then, though several years later, one was allowed.

Towards the end of 1972, three judges – Steyn, Theron and Corbett – came to the island. When they spoke to Madiba in the presence of Badenhorst and the commissioner of prisons, he relayed all our complaints, especially about Badenhorst's harsh treatment.

In front of his superior, Badenhorst intervened, warning Mandela: 'Be careful what you say, because you are going back to jail after this.' Mandela turned to the judges and said: 'Well, there you have it, that's what I am talking about.'

Badenhorst was removed soon afterwards and under his successor, Colonel Willemse, conditions began to improve. Just before Christmas, I was taken out of solitary confinement and life, such as it was, returned to normal.

Many people have asked me about life in prison. I would like to quote from a letter I wrote (after twenty-five years in jail) to a young couple on the verge of marriage:

> The stereotype image of a prison is one of forbidding high walls; a grim, cold atmosphere, prosaic, harsh, vulgar, violent; an atmosphere of desperate, unsmiling faces; angry, bitter and frustrated beings. Admittedly, a prison situation was tailor-made for the projection of such an image. It is easy to succumb when faced with prospects of a lengthy and nightmarish existence; and consequently dwell on one's miseries, hardships, the manifold deprivations and negative experiences. Someone has written about two prisoners looking out of their cell window – one saw iron bars, while the other saw stars. How true! Naturally one does not uncomplainingly accept all the wrongs and hope for the best. No; but one has to accept that there are certain realities over which one has no control. For example, the very fact of being in prison means that one has to endure certain deprivations, the chief of which is the loss of one's freedom. Secondly, one is thrust into a community in which you have no say as to who your fellow inmates should be. Having come to terms with these and similar unchangeables, you immediately set about the task of adapting yourself to the unending task of changing the environment in order to make the stay less intolerable. In the process, brick by brick, you are building up the other – and certainly in the case of 'security prisoners', the real – picture of prison life. It is a picture of great warmth, fellowship, friendship, humour and laughter; of strong convictions, of a generosity of spirit, of compassion, solidarity and care. It is a picture of continuous learning, of getting to know and live with your fellow beings, their strengths as well as their idiosyncrasies; but more important, where one comes to know one self, one's weaknesses, inadequacies and one's potentials. Unbelievably, it is a very positive, confident, determined – yes, even a happy community.
>
> To move away from a self-centred lifestyle to one where the individual personality is largely submerged in a wider social unit is a profoundly humbling, but enormously rewarding experience.[9]

～ 14 ～

By Stealth and Subterfuge

We talk of killing time as if, alas, it weren't time that kills us.
— Reader's Digest[1]

Shrugging off the yoke of colonial oppression cut deeply into Africa's shoulders, drawing blood and sweat and tears. On 20 January 1973, Amílcar Cabral, the cultural, intellectual and revolutionary leader of Cape Verde, was assassinated outside his home in Conakry. Despite the loss of this dynamic man, Guinea-Bissau would gain its rocky independence a year later. For us, the struggle continued.

The 1974 coup in Portugal, the 'revolution of the flowers', led to the overthrow of a dictatorship introduced by Antonio de Oliviera Salazar and continued by his successor, Marcello Caetano, and brought into power the former military commander in Guinea. General António Ribeiro de Spínola argued that 'the wars in Africa could not be settled by force of arms and advocated negotiated autonomy for the colonies and an alternative to Caetano's leadership'.[2]

Although government by a military junta could by no means be described as enlightened democratic rule, it was substantially better than the previous regime, especially with regard to policies on the Portuguese colonies.

I was enrolled as a history student at the time and had submitted an assignment that dealt, coincidentally, with Portugal's African colonies. The advanced paranoia of our jailers led them to suspect that there was some contact between us and the Portuguese coup leaders! I was closely questioned about the contents of my academic paper before it was given back to me.

TOILET PAPER, DANGEROUS POLITICAL WEAPON

In the chronicles of South Africa's liberation struggle, the humble toilet roll deserves a special place. This essential component of personal hygiene played a major role in all the prisons in which I was detained, either because it was simply not available, or was issued to us under strict conditions of use.

For common-law prisoners, toilet tissue was not a problem, simply because it was a non-existent 'luxury'. They were obliged to make do with anything that was available, usually newsprint. But that was not an option for political detainees, since access to newspapers was totally out of bounds.

When we were granted permission to study, we had to sign an undertaking acknowledging that 'to study while I am in prison is a privilege granted to me personally. Should I misuse this privilege by using my study material, stationery, books and time for any other purposes except for my studies, or allow that it be used by any other person for any purpose, I shall forfeit the privilege to continue with my studies for the full duration of my incarceration.'

So, when it came to news items, letters and political messages for circulation throughout the prison, we frequently had to write them on toilet paper.

One of my missives was to Salim Essop, a medical student arrested with Ahmed Timol, who was thrown to his death from the tenth floor of police headquarters in Johannesburg.

Soon after Essop arrived to serve a five-year sentence, I wrote to him as follows:

Dear Comrade,
First of all, welcome to Robben Island. We have all been pleased to see you and the comrades looking so well and in such good spirits. It makes us also feel good, for we are certain your demeanour is but a reflection of the spirit of our people outside.

At present things are not so bad on the island, tho 1971–72 have been relatively bad, we did not reach the repression of 1963. The pendulum is swinging in our favour - gradually but surely. There has seemingly been a planned removal of the bad types of warders and their replacement by more civil and civilised ones. But don't be surprised if things don't remain consistent. We move in cycles – and in a way it does help to lessen the boredom.

Just a tip or two from an old-timer:

- Keep yourself warm, especially in the cells; use your mats and blankets freely.
- Try to get used to the food – unpalatable as it often is. After all, we get just enough to survive.

As you can imagine, we are so much in the dark about many happenings outside. I am going to pose a number of questions. Please answer only those that are safe or ones that the enemy already knows about. Do you need smokes, toiletries etc or anything else? I mean all of you. [There were also a number of political questions.]

We are all well – just getting old. Finishing 10 years soon. But confident as ever.

I will refer to you in future as Alex. Pahads = Gool; ANC = Stars; PAC = Pat; APDUSA = Solly; CP = Leo; Ind Cong = Monty.

Best wishes to you and everyone else, from all of us. Zik

The letter was intercepted by the warders, who charged me with illegally communicating with another prisoner. I was acquitted on a technicality, namely that since the letter had been confiscated prior to delivery, communication had not actually taken place.

After so many years of the farcical rules applied in apartheid's prisons we thought we had seen it all, until Govan Mbeki was assigned to a new task. He had to measure off eight squares of toilet paper in the morning and another eight at night for each prisoner in our section. Not a single additional square was to be given to anyone, Mbeki was warned.

We knew that like so many other petty restrictions this one would soon fall away, and we were right.

CHANGES

Ten years into our arrest, news sources indicated that a social revolution was sweeping the world. We kept hearing about youth problems, youth unrest, youth movements, youth rebelling against tradition and rejecting their roots. There were reports of hippies and flower children, of a generation gap defined, at least in part, by the length of men's hair and the shortness of women's skirts. Cut off as we were, these strange events emphasised that we were growing older.

Colonel Willemse, who was stationed on the island for two or three years, was the first officer who invited us to sit down when we were called to his office. More intelligent than most of the senior warders, Willemse always treated us with courtesy, but he never lost sight of his duty.

I was studying what was then called Native Administration, later African Politics, and according to the regulations, we were entitled to receive all the prescribed textbooks but not the additional 'recommended reading' material.

Willemse withheld some of my prescribed books. I wrote a letter of complaint to the university, seeking support for my argument that I required all the text-books to which I was entitled, and was disgusted to receive a letter from my Unisa professor suggesting that since I was doing 'very well' in my assignments with the literature I had, I should 'carry on without the prescribed texts'.

After toiling at the limestone quarry for a decade, we were given a new job: collecting kelp that washed up on the shoreline. It was a dreadful task to gather the slimy fronds that act as a natural magnet for swarms of insects and clouds of flies, but working at the ocean's edge gave us an opportunity to supplement our meagre diet with mussels, limpets and abalone pulled off the rocks. Sometimes we even caught crayfish.

Once, a seal beached itself, and it was clubbed to death so that we could eat it. Skinning it presented a problem, but eventually we found some bottles on the beach, broke them and used the shards of glass to get to this unexpected supply of red meat.

The warders were quite happy to collude with us when it came to collecting shellfish, partridge and guinea fowl. They would have paid a fortune on the mainland for such delicacies, so as long as we shared the loot, they allowed us to cook whatever we foraged over an open fire.

We found all manner of things washed up by the tide, including articles of clothing. Madiba once picked up a jersey, in fairly good condition, and I expect he still has it – nothing would induce him to part with that souvenir! But the most sought-after item was driftwood, which we took back to our colleague, Jeff Masemola, a genius with his hands. Over the years he crafted musical instruments, carpenter's tools, ornaments and various other articles in the little workshop he had been allowed to set up in a storeroom.

Jeff also made bookshelves for our cells, including a special one for me, to my own design. Because of my position on the communications committee, I needed more hiding places than most, so my bookshelf had a secret compartment in which I could stash news clippings and other material. It was so well made that it survived every single raid by the warders.

Jeff varnished the bookcase, but my cell was still too grey and drab, so I ordered some bright gift wrap and covered the little metal locker with it. The difference was amazing, and when a party of journalists visited the island, my colourful cell was photographed, along with Mandela's.

Willemse's successor, Colonel Roelofse, was an innately suspicious man, who refused, for example, to give the Muslim prisoners Eid greeting cards, because they contained printed texts in Arabic, and he had no idea what these messages meant. He would also visit our section of the prison at night, and if he saw us reading, would insist on being shown the book. So sure was he that the political prisoners were conspiring night and day that he would even sift through the dustbins after dark, just in case we had hidden or thrown any contraband away.

Shortly after marrying my brother Solly's son Enver in 1971, my niece Zohra came to the island to introduce herself and let me know that she was going to assume responsibility on behalf of the family to maintain contact with me. It was a task she performed superbly, hardly ever missing a letter, keeping me fully informed about all family matters and taking care of my financial needs.

In 1973, via information smuggled out of the prison, the wives of two new-comers to the island, Mrs Kader Hashim and Therisa Vankatratnam, learnt that their husbands had been placed in solitary confinement for petitioning the authorities about the awful conditions under which they were held. The two women brought an urgent application before the Supreme Court, and won a major victory when the judge ruled that 'warders had no right to arbitrarily deprive prisoners of meals or to put them in solitary confinement without a hearing'.[3] It was a decision from which we would all benefit.

ANTIGONE

> Creon: No other touchstone can test the heart of man,
> The temper of his mind and spirit, till he be tried
> In the practice of authority and rule.
> A king whose lips are sealed
> By fear, unwilling to seek advice, is damned.
> And no less damned is he who puts a friend
> Above his country.   — Sophocles, *Oedipus at Colonus*[4]

One of the best Christmases we spent in prison was in 1974. As part of the festivities, our section staged a respectable production of Jean Anouilh's play, *Antigone*, in which the main characters reject any tampering with their ideals. Madiba played Creon, and his performance more than compensated for his dethronement as the dominos champion a year before.

He followed his stage debut with another triumph in the year-end sports tournament. Madiba was selected to play chess against Salim Essop and, as in politics, his every move was carefully considered, slow and deliberate. The game went on for three days, the board being locked away in an empty cell overnight by the warders, until Salim was so exhausted that he conceded defeat and abandoned the challenge. It was a war of attrition.

In March 1975 I was awarded my B Bibl degree. Tired of writing exams, I enrolled for only one more course, ancient history. Frankly, I hated the actual study, and often wished there was some way of acquiring the knowledge without the drudgery! I was always much happier reading a novel than preparing for exams.

THE GARDEN

The next big event was that we were given permission to establish a small garden in our exercise courtyard. The area we cultivated was only 20 metres long and about 1.2 metres wide, but my letters overflowed with enthusiasm for the project. In one, I wrote:

> Let me tell you about our little garden. It is about a year old. Come into the yard any morning and you're sure to witness the daily inspection, mostly by our Indian community (they're the chief gardeners). They walk along the patch, give a glance in the direction of the dozen or so flowers, make a few appropriate remarks about the effect of the south-easter on tomatoes, then the next time you look, they'll be gathered around a modest little plant and engaged in animated discussion. Out come the crepe bandage, string, sticks, label and ballpoint. The innocent onlooker surveying the scene and the actors would easily conclude that it's just Chiba and his economics class. But you go nearer and find no economics or any other class. It is the Orientals gauging the maturation (or otherwise) of the chilli plant. This explains the un-gardenlike tools. For they measure every millimetre of its growth, and make some record on a yellow label suspended from the neck of the chilli. Some weeks ago it reached the size of a marble, then it just stopped growing. After numerous confabs, our friends announced that it's a variety that does not grow any bigger. So they plucked half a dozen and cut them up into the salad. The community sighed with relief that only half a dozen were available, otherwise the only consumers of the salad would have been the half a dozen Indians. The chillies were mighty powerful.

As time passed, it was not only the plants and produce that provided us with entertainment, but also the visitors, as described in a letter I wrote to Tom Vassen in November:

> We've got a little garden patch here, which has yielded, according to Isu's statistics, about 2 000 chillies, close to 1 000 tomatoes, a few radishes, onions, sweet melons (about 6), and 2 watermelons. One day he even got me to count tomato seeds, if you please! Nowadays the garden is Nelson's baby, and he is fanatical about it. As expected, he has read everything he could lay his hands on pertaining to the garden. But one little event of the pastmonth has flummoxed all the gardeners, and indeed the whole community. Early in the year, our community of 32 found itself suddenly increased by the arrival,

out of the blue, of one chameleon. It caused some excitement, speculation and talk. Now this lady moved from chilli plant to tomato and from radish to lettuce – and in vain tried to display her propensity to colour her pigment accordingly. To my mind, Lady Chameleon was a singular failure, and I virtually dismissed her from my mind. But about 3 weeks ago, this lady did something that forcibly drew attention to herself once more. She suddenly gave birth to 6 little babies and promptly abandoned them. This excited all our parental feelings, and our concern for the orphan, the lowly, the helpless. Each morning, and throughout the day, you'd find a cluster of chaps around one little baby, engaged in animated discussion. The weather took a bad turn suddenly, and the concern for the babies increased in proportion. But the question that hit us the first day and still remains unsolved is: where is Papa chameleon? If indeed there was one. Some say the lady is bisexual, others say she arrived here pregnant. Yours truly has agreed with both sides. Some enlightenment from you will not be out of place. The debate continues. Lady has reappeared. But, incredibly, she's never with her offspring. Some are fed up with her, and may have already passed sentence banishing her. Overt excuse: shortage of insects for her to feed on! But in fact I think everybody is fed up because she abandoned her infants at so tender an age.[5]

People are often surprised at how relatively small things assume major proportions for prisoners. It's almost unavoidable, and cannot be otherwise. Ours was a very small world, and it was mostly small talk, minor events and insignificant interests that helped to fill our days. The chameleon was a good example of this. She evoked a variety of reactions, and aroused emotions ranging from pity to love to an intense dislike. Few were indifferent to her. Encyclopaedias were consulted for information about the particular species and its reproduction, while grown men, headed by a seventy-year-old, spent hours swatting flies to ensure that she was fed, and vigorously debated her fate.

Some felt she should be removed from the confines of the courtyard and released in the veld. Others opposed this suggestion on the grounds that she would surely fall prey to a butcher bird. One caregiver wanted to keep the chameleon in his cell at night so that she might catch the flies that troubled him.

Quite apart from the chameleon, our tiny garden brought much pleasure. In moments of despondency it was a reminder of renewal, of new life and fresh hope. Because so much of our incoming mail was withheld, and requests for visits turned down, it was easy to feel abandoned by those on the outside, and that was probably just what the authorities wanted.

CORRESPONDENCE

All contact with Sylvia was prohibited, though with the aid of code names and friends we did manage some communication, but there were others, friends and family members alike, from whom we were deliberately isolated. More than once I learnt that someone had died only months – sometimes years – afterwards.

When I was released and finally gained access to my confiscated mail, I was genuinely perplexed about the possible reasons for certain correspondence being withheld. Among the letters never posted was this one to my grand niece, which I wrote in October 1977:

> To my dearest Leila Natasha Refentse,
> All my love and good wishes for 30th Nov. Two years old – and already rich in names, embracing far-off Asia and Europe and Africa, the continent of your birth. Two years old – and millennia behind you. Yet with no burdens of the past, and no anxiety for the future. Two years. No language to confuse; no riches to excite envy; no boundaries to contain the vision; no laws to confound; no religion to dispute. No strife; no war; no hatred, no cruelty, no jealousy, no anger, no sorrow, no hunger, no hardship. Only bright eyes and laughter and limitless love. Blue skies without clouds, green trees and the singing of birds. Happy, happy citizeness of the world. Refentse! Resolute conqueror of all evil. Refentse! Bringer of joy. May your tomorrows always be as your todays are – at the age of two.
> Lots and lots of love to you, and to your little brother, and to Mummy and Daddy, from your godfather, AMK.

Leila was only a toddler, so if my message to her was judged objectionable, one can only imagine the trouble we had corresponding with adults! Sadly, a year or two later I received the shocking news that she and her little cousin had been killed in a car accident.

The prison censors kept back literally thousands of letters over the years, including any that expressed political support or solidarity. For the duration of my sentence, not a single letter from Sylvia reached me, apart from one or two early ones signed Yasmin.

My letters to Sukthi, a child of ten, were withheld as readily as those to Wolfie Kodesh, a known communist. Letters were also used, at times, to make mischief. Some of the prisoners had both a wife and a girlfriend, and the censors were not averse to sending mail to the wrong address – all in error, naturally.

The Gujerati word 'Behn' means sister, and it is commonly used as a nickname or to denote affection and respect. To everyone in our family, my only sister, Amina, was 'Behn'. As it happened, Fatima Meer was known to many people by the same name, and the use of the term in my correspondence with the two women caused so much confusion among the censors that they tried to stop me from writing to either. A similar situation arose regarding the name Yasmin, one of the codes I used when referring to Sylvia. Because I also had a niece by that name, I was asked at one point to produce proof that a birthday card was, indeed, being sent to my sister's daughter and not to Sylvia.

In prison, as in life, it is the little things that mean the most – a good meal shared with loved ones, a relaxing day at the beach, a hot bath before going to bed at night. It was thus with much appreciation that from April 1975, a water heater was installed and, for the first time in twelve years, we were able to take hot showers. We were even more grateful for the introduction of fresh water in place of the brackish brew that we had been forced to drink since arriving on the island.

Having music piped into our cells for a few hours each evening was another huge improvement. We were enchanted by the voice and popularity of Margaret Singana, and surprised by the enthusiasm the white warders showed for her hit songs. In February 1975 I wrote to a friend:

> We started off this afternoon with Nat King Cole, who is still quite a hit with many of us. Then a few minutes ago we had Miriam Makeba and Harry Belafonte. Just now he is singing 'There's a hole in my bucket'. In a while he will be singing Havanagila (I hope the spelling's right) and then Silvie, who brought him 'a little coffee and a little tea. She brought me nearly every damned thing, but she didn't bring the jailhouse key'. What a treat. And Miriam still sends us. We had been cut off from music for some years. And when it started we were met with a barrage of pop stuff, and for some time we didn't know what hit us. It all sounded like one hell of a big noise, and I was imprudent enough to say so. But alas, I had to retract, for after a little while this noise – or at least some of it – managed to insinuate itself into my system. And I quite unashamedly started looking forward to Mardi Gras, Johnny and others, much to the annoyance of our 'culture vultures'.

Unfortunately, the sound system broke down later that year and remained out of order for months.

BRAM FISCHER'S DEATH

Bram Fischer's death was a great blow to us. Decades later, when I read Hugh Lewin's account of how badly Bram was treated in prison, it made me very heartsore. On 11 May 1975 I wrote to his daughters:

> My dear Ruth and Ilse,
> For the third time in the last decade, death has struck and removed a beloved member of your family. We had only been on the island about a fortnight in 1964 when we received the shocking news of your mother's

death. A few years ago Paul breathed his last. And now your dad. You have been cruelly singled out for tragedy to strike its harsh and relentless blows – almost as if to test your power of endurance. I am well aware that words can do little to lessen the impact of such irreparable loss. But I'm writing, nevertheless, in the hope that knowledge of shared grief will perhaps help to bring a little bit of comfort at this dark hour.

For you Bram was father, the kindliest and very best that any child could wish for. But he also meant so much for so many people throughout our country and, indeed, all over the world. Literally millions will therefore grieve at his passing.

South Africa could ill afford to lose him; for he was a great patriot and statesman, rich in wisdom, selfless, fearless and determined in leadership. To the legal fraternity he brought brilliance, lustre and distinction. To his political colleagues he showed the path of courage, clarity, and undying hope. To the prisoner he re-enacted the well-established maxim that the path to light and progress traverses through the darkness of prison walls. To humanity at large he gave of his abundant love, his charm, his unequalled modesty, quiet dignity and disinterestedness. Bram possessed in profusion all the elements that go to make a perfect human being.

In all these capacities I lovingly remember and honour him – my fellow countryman, my mentor, my comrade, my lawyer, my co-prisoner, my friend. It is above all as a human being that he will forever stand out in my memory. His stature and eminence in all other fields stem essentially from his greatness as a human being. For this he enjoyed the love and respect, devotion and admiration of everyone.

Innumerable are the incidents and events that spring to mind relating to Molly and Bram since I first met them, way back, I think in 1944. I was only 15 and enthusiastic, with almost four years of 'political involvement' behind me. It was at an age when one sought and attached oneself to one's own brand of heroes.

Already looming large on my horizon was Yusuf Dadoo. He was soon joined, among others, by Bram and Molly! They made a big impression on my little mind, and my childish heart responded with a love that only children know how to give. I went with Bram to Pietersburg, and in 1949 I went with Molly to Potchefstroom. Every minute that I was in their company, I was bursting with pride. This was the beginning of a personal relationship, which grew, with the passage of years. And with it grew my love and respect and admiration. How I looked forward to being with them again after this incarceration is over. But alas, death has snatched them both away. It has caused me deep hurt and left a huge void in my life.

Yet I dare not allow myself to give way to despair, dejection or disillusionment. That would be disobedient to the wishes of Bram and Molly. Sorrow

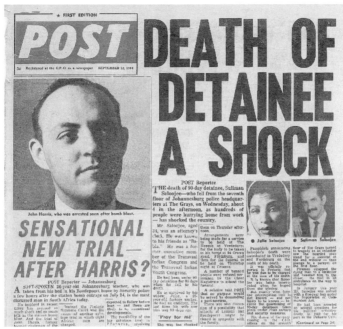

Newspaper reports of Babla Saloojee's death

Nelson Mandela and Walter Sisulu, secretly photographed on Robben Island in 1965

With Walter Sisulu on 16 October 1989,
the day after their release

At Ahmed Kathrada's seventieth birthday.
From left to right, Mac Maharaj, Herbie Pillay,
Ahmed Kathrada and Laloo Chiba

Laloo Chiba and Amien Cajee

Ahmed Kathrada, Eddie Daniels, Barbara Hogan and Laloo Chiba

Barbara Hogan   Dullah Omar and his wife Farieda

Greeting Andimba Toivo ya Toivo, with Frene Ginwala and Sydney Mufamadi

With Nelson Mandela and Walter Sisulu

On the Robben Island ferry with Fidel Castro and Ronnie Kasrils (left)

With Yasser Arafat on Robben Island

With the Clintons and Nelson Mandela in the courtyard on Robben Island

With Thabo Mbeki and Al Gore in front of Mandela's cell

I cannot help, but mingled with it is the overpowering feeling of richness, pride and gratitude at having been privileged to be so closely associated with them. If I could but emulate to the slightest degree their exemplary lives, their goodness, warmth and love of humanity, their generosity, their confidence and tireless contribution towards the attainment of our common ideals, I shall have paid my tribute to two of the most wonderful people I have known.

Lots of love and good wishes to you, Ruth and Ilse, and to all relatives and friends, from AM Kathrada.

THE MEMOIRS

Our little garden, developed to provide us with pleasure and fresh produce to supplement our frugal diet, became a vital component of a far greater project: Mandela's autobiography, of which he wrote:

> One day, Kathy, Walter and I were talking in the courtyard when they suggested that I ought to write my memoirs. Kathy noted that the perfect time for such a book to be published would be on my sixtieth birthday. Walter said that such a story, if told truly and fairly, would serve to remind people of what we had fought and were still fighting for. He added that it could become a source of inspiration for young freedom fighters. The idea appealed to me, and during a subsequent discussion, I agreed to go ahead.[6]

Chronicling Mandela's life was illegal and dangerous. Discovery would result in harsh collective punishment, and given Walter's view of his story's historical and political significance, the decision to proceed would have to be a political one. The High Organ decided that the secret project should go ahead, but knowledge of it was to be limited to those directly involved.

Because most of the writing would have to be done at night, Mandela feigned illness and was excused from the daily work schedule. He slept for a few hours while the cellblock was deserted and wrote deep into the night. As a registered student of Afrikaans, Madiba was allowed to subscribe to the popular weekly magazine *Huisgenoot*, and he made a deal with the night-duty warders. They were not allowed to bring any reading matter to work to pass the time, and were only too glad to borrow Mandela's magazines in exchange for allowing him to pursue his 'studies' beyond the 11 p.m. curfew.

Early every morning he would give Walter and me the written pages for comment. The final draft was then transferred to sheets of rice paper by Mac Maharaj and Laloo Chiba in miniscule script. By this time, some of us were allowed to buy a few extra groceries, and Madiba's originals were rolled up inside empty Cadbury's Bourneville Cocoa canisters and buried in our garden.

The transcripts on rice paper were hidden in a secret compartment fashioned by Jeff Masemola in one of the benches in our cells, and within the thick cardboard covers of an album made by Laloo Chiba. Mac came up with the idea of filling the album with statistical maps that he had obtained, as part of his studies, from the Bureau of Statistics.

The album also served to conceal the fruit of a second project that Mac launched. He asked eight of the imprisoned leaders, including John Pokela, who would later serve as chairman of the PAC, and SWAPO's Andimba Toivo ya Toivo, to each write an essay on the issues confronting champions of freedom. In this way, Mac believed, the 'hidden' struggle leaders would be given a voice beyond the prison walls. My contribution was 'Indian South Africans – A Future Bound with the Cause of the African Majority'.[7]

Mac was due for release in December 1976, and he would smuggle the album containing the precious secret writings off the island. He made no attempt to hide the album, and it was doubtless scrutinised by the authorities before he left, but it was so expertly made that the jailers let it through without hesitation.

No sooner was he home at his brother's flat in Durban, than Mac was placed under house arrest. Despite this restriction, the exceptionally wily Mr Maharaj ensured that the manuscript reached London. By prior arrangement he sent me a perfectly innocuous greeting card as the signal that his mission had been accomplished.

Once we knew the manuscript was in safe hands, we could destroy the originals, but somehow we never got around to it. For almost a year, the canisters had lain undisturbed in the garden, and we had probably been lulled into a sense of complacency.

The rude awakening came when a construction crew moved into the court-yard without warning and started building a wall that would run straight through our patch of garden.

The loss of the garden paled into insignificance in the face of the imminent danger of the canisters being unearthed. Not only would we be severely punished, but the authorities would be alerted to the existence of Mandela's strictly unauthorised autobiography.

As early as possible the next day, we went to retrieve the buried treasure, but only managed to save a couple of canisters. We couldn't reach the rest.

A few months later, Mandela, Sisulu and I were summoned to a meeting with General Jannie Roux, one of the most senior prison officers in the country. He officially informed us that part of the manuscript had been retrieved from its hiding place. As punishment for our transgression, our study privileges would be withdrawn for the duration of our sentences.

We were relieved that the entire section was not being punished, only the three of us whose handwriting was on the manuscript. And, as it happened, our study privileges were restored four years later.

Mandela's memoirs were not published to coincide with his sixtieth birthday in July 1978, but following his release from prison in 1990. The smuggled manuscript served as the basis of his autobiography, *Long Walk to Freedom*, which was translated into thirty foreign languages.

In recent years, I have often joked that Mac, who for some strange reason had done a course in transport economics on the island, was appointed Mandela's first Minister of Transport in recognition of his successful transportation of the secret manuscript from Robben Island to Durban, and then to London.

GENERAL JANNIE ROUX

Playing the 'speculation game' was one of our favourite pastimes, so when Jeff Masemola was called to the prison commander's office 'urgently' just after breakfast one morning, we wondered why.

As one prisoner after another was summoned in succession, and none of them came back, our imaginations ran riot. A whispered exchange with our comrades from the communal cells when they delivered our lunch drums failed to shed any light on the mystery, and by late afternoon, when Mandela was called, the remaining handful of us were convinced that people were being spirited off the island.

Eventually it was my turn, and as I waited in the corridor outside the office, I could hear familiar voices coming from a nearby room, but not Madiba's. On entering the office, I was confronted by an array of senior prison officers from Pretoria, led by General Roux.

Armed with a doctorate in psychology, Roux had risen swiftly through the ranks, and lower-ranking warders were in awe of him. They never lost an opportunity to sing his praises to our well-qualified group of 'terrorists'.

The pleasantries of greeting disposed of, Roux asked me if I had any complaints or requests. I said I had many complaints, but did not wish to discuss them with him and his colleagues. They were visibly surprised. It was extremely unusual for any prisoner to be brought before a panel of such high-ranking officers; refusing to talk to them was probably unheard of.

Roux indicated that I was to be escorted from the office, but instead of being taken to the room where my colleagues were, I was taken to an office in the prison hospital. My guard was young, bored and talkative. He was also very much in love, and asked me to draft a special 'love letter' for him that would touch his girlfriend's heart. I agreed, and as a quid pro quo, he informed me that Madiba had also refused to talk to Roux, and had been isolated in another section of the hospital.

It was about midnight when all of us were returned to our cells and exchanged information about the day's events. Only Mandela and I had declined the offer to lodge requests or complaints. He had protested about being 'ambushed' and refused to say anything further.

We heard no more of this decidedly peculiar day, but a few weeks later, I was told to see the prison doctor. He wanted to know what ailed me, and when I said nothing, he ushered me to another office. Behind the desk was a psychiatrist from Valkenberg, the mental hospital near Cape Town.

Naturally, he asked why I wanted to talk to him. I said I hadn't asked to see him, and the prison doctor then admitted that the appointment had been made at the request of General Roux. My refusal to talk to Roux had evidently persuaded the psychologist in him that there was something seriously wrong with me.

The psychiatrist was not happy at this turn of events and I was allowed to leave, since there was clearly no need for a consultation.

On the few occasions that I saw Roux after that I treated him with indifference, but really, I pitied him. He was the quintessential small man in a big pond, whose academic qualifications had secured him a position of authority, but could never win him respect.

Some time after my encounter with the psychiatrist, Roux resigned from the prisons department and became PW Botha's private secretary. In one of the most supreme ironies of the new political dispensation, one of the first executive orders signed by President Mandela was the appointment of Jannie Roux as South Africa's ambassador to Austria.

MANDELA

To change Mandela's mind about a friend is virtually impossible. In the absence of incontrovertible proof to the contrary, he will continue to believe in someone's goodness and show extraordinary loyalty. So it was with Chief Kaiser Matanzima when he intimated that he wanted to visit Madiba.

Matanzima, head of the Transkei Bantustan, was a blood relative – Madiba's nephew – and had presided over the burial of his mother. Mandela was keen to hear first-hand details of this family occasion, but because he and Matanzima were at opposite ends of the political spectrum, he thought it prudent to seek the views of his ANC colleagues. In an unprecedented concession, the authorities allowed a meeting of ANC members from different sections of the prison.

Madiba offered the High Organ in B Section a forceful argument in favour of the visit. Govan Mbeki, Raymond Mhlaba and I were opposed to the meeting, while Walter kept his own counsel. The majority vote went against Mandela, and though he must have been disappointed, he accepted the decision.

Madiba was a dedicated student of Afrikaans on the island. He knows and speaks the language well, though his pronunciation is atrocious. Somewhere around 1976 or 1977, the Minister of Prisons, Jimmy Kruger, visited the island, and during talks with Mandela, realised that he was quite fluent in Afrikaans. Soon afterwards, Kruger sent Madiba a parcel of Afrikaans books as a gift.

The purpose of his visit, however, was insidious. The Transkei had been granted its sham independence in 1976, but the only country in the world that recognised its government was South Africa.

The liberation movement roundly rejected this next phase in the Bantustan plan, which stripped all Xhosa-speakers of their South African citizenship and made them citizens of the Transkei. The Organisation of African Unity, backed by the United Nations, had urged the international community to shun this parody of independence, and the puppet masters in Pretoria were desperate to find some way of giving the Transkei legitimacy.

Kruger offered to release Mandela – on condition that he agreed to live in the Transkei. Needless to say, Madiba refused.

Mandela's stubborn streak came to the fore in the mid-1970s when he suddenly proposed a defiance campaign against the prison rules. The plan was rejected by the members in B Section, and later by those in the general section as well. But Madiba would not give up, and began to seek a broader support base among the other political organisations on the island.

Predictably, he got support from Eddie Daniels, a die-hard Mandela loyalist, and Toivo ya Toivo, who was always ready for a fight against the authorities. As opposition to the plan continued to mount, Toivo was persuaded to withdraw his support, and after several weeks of feverish debate, Madiba finally accepted the majority view. Decades later I tried to prod Madiba's memory on why he had finally backed down, but all I got from him was a sheepish grin and a claim that he could not remember.

VISITS AND ACTIVITIES

Visits to Robben Island were never easy, but from 1975, they became impossible for some. Every application was thoroughly vetted to establish the exact relationship between the prisoner and the proposed visitor, and the rules were tightened to allow visits by only 'first-degree' family members – one's wife, children, parents and siblings. This hit me hard. My parents were both dead, I was not married, and my brothers and sister lived at the opposite end of the country, and hardly ever travelled. My most regular visitors had been my nieces and nephews, and when they were excluded, there was a period of an entire year when I had not a single visitor.

But, harsh and hateful as this was, there was always someone in an even worse position. One member of our group was not visited by anyone at all during the fifteen years he spent on the island, and he received only a handful of letters.

He came from a poor family, who simply could not afford to travel to Cape Town, and because they were also illiterate, they had to rely on others to both write to him occasionally and read his letters at home.

And he was only able to communicate with them after some years. He had also never learnt to read or write, and spoke no English before he was imprisoned. Thanks to Dr Neville Alexander and his group of dedicated teachers, my neighbour left the island literate.

In order to correspond with, send messages to or even write about some of my acquaintances, we used agreed code names. Wolfie Kodesh was Walied; Ruth Slovo became Rabia; Moses Kotane was Moosabhai, Oliver Tambo was Ortam and Essop Pahad was Stretch. The ANC was Baji (which means 'father' in Gujerati) and the PAC was Magan.

But every so often we had to improvise and change codes without notice, which gave rise to some frustrating, albeit amusing, situations. After Mac Maharaj was released, we needed to get a message to him in London, but he had no code name. After much deliberation, we decided that since Mac had only one eye, the most appropriate pointer to his identity would be the one-eyed giant in Greek mythology, the Cyclops. The message reached Mac as intended.

Amien Cajee was banned and thus not allowed to correspond with me. So he would type his letters and his wife Ayesha would sign them in her name. Amien and I had a splendid code system worked out, and the arrangement went well for a considerable time.

But, inevitably, at some point the security police confronted Ayesha with some of the letters, and quizzed her relentlessly about the names they contained. Of course she had no idea who the real people were, much less who these fictional characters were supposed to be. The incident put a stop to my communication with the Cajees for several years.

In January 1976, I woke up one Sunday morning with excruciating back pain. The prison doctor, Dr Edelstein, recommended traction, and a hospital bed was moved into an empty cell in B Section.

For two weeks, I wallowed in the luxury of being in a bed, with crisp white sheets, pillows and 'room service'. All the time I was tied down, and weights were suspended from my feet in order to stretch the back. When the iron weights proved to be insufficient, they put half a brick in the bag and later topped it up with gravel. My food was brought to me, and my comrades took turns to shave and wash me. Eddie Daniels and Laloo Chiba did bedpan duty, and Madiba spent a great deal of time at my bedside, talking and sharing meals.

The best part about my backache was that even after the treatment ended, I was allowed to keep the bed, in my own cell, on doctor's orders, and was also given a chair with a backrest.

My attempts to develop latent talents in the fields of sport and music were short-lived. An unfortunate collision between a volleyball and one of my little fingers put paid to athletic ambition in February 1976. Eddie Daniels thought the injury that caused my premature retirement as a budding star was a blessing in disguise, but I think he was secretly relieved that some of the competition had been removed!

At one of the variety concerts organised from time to time, I gave my very best rendition, in German, of *Freiheit*. The compere had alluded to my 'hidden talents' in his introduction, but the applause was not exactly tumultuous. I ascribed the lack of demand for an encore to the full programme ... until my friend Mr Daniels, in a stage whisper loud enough for the entire audience to hear, commented dryly: 'May your talent remain hidden far away and forever!'

Eddie was one of the true 'characters' in B Section. He was serving a fifteen-year sentence for carrying out a number of acts of sabotage as a member of the African Resistance Movement, an offshoot of the Liberal Party. Midway through his sentence, two judges, Grosskopf and Steyn, visited the island and took a liking to Eddie.

Without consulting him, Steyn made representations for Eddie's release, was given a sympathetic hearing, and returned to the island to tell Eddie that he could be a free man, provided he agreed not to involve himself in politics again.

Eddie refused. 'If I did that, I would be sentencing my own children to slavery in the land of their birth,' he said.[8] He served his full sentence, and when he was released, joined the ANC, and we remained close friends.

With the passage of years, there were small improvements in conditions that all helped to make our lives a little easier. It didn't matter that what for us were milestones would have been minutiae under normal circumstances. These were the benchmarks of a 'good' or 'bad' year in prison.

When we took stock at the end of 1975, it turned out to have been a good year. We had been given hot water for ablutions, we had eaten guavas twice, Isu had been promoted to the A group and was entitled to buy small quantities of chocolates, coffee, sugar and cocoa each month, and at Christmas the prison authorities gave each of us a small packet of sugar in addition to the traditional mug of black coffee.

HEALTH AND NEWS

Medical treatment on the island was, at best, erratic. I was treated for TB for a year, though subsequent tests showed that, in all likelihood, I had never had it in the first place. From the time of our arrival we found that medical treatment would largely be dependent on the particular doctor on duty. Generally there was much to be desired. By the late 1970s, there were sweeping changes to our medical care, with access to top Cape Town specialists almost on demand.

They came to us, or we were taken across the bay to see them on the mainland. No matter what medication was prescribed, or how much it cost, we got it. A mobile X-ray unit was even brought to the island, and all of us were X-rayed.

Some of the improvements might have been sparked by an epidemic of virulent flu in 1974, which hit almost all of the prisoners in our section and several hundred in the rest of the prison simultaneously. In B Section, the only people who were not sick were Madiba and two recent arrivals. Between the three of them, they nursed and cared for the rest of us, removing our slop buckets every morning, washing them and leaving them in the sun outside to dry while they patiently went from cell to cell to fill our water jugs or bring us our food.

Fortunately, a sympathetic hospital orderly put his foot down and insisted that all the flu patients be given hot, nutritious soup instead of the normal prison fare.

My health was generally good on the island, but this didn't stop the government's 'dirty tricks' squad from terrorising families with false reports of deaths in detention. More than once I would have to write to someone in my family, or a friend, with reassurances that the condolences they had received on my reported death had been entirely premature.

The one thing I did need, though, was a pair of dark glasses. Working in the harsh glare of the lime quarry, combined with the wind and dust, had taken a toll on my eyes. I was sent to an eye specialist, Dr Neethling, who prescribed darker lenses than the ones I had been wearing, which he said would limit any further damage and might even improve my vision over time.

But the authorities resisted, and it was only when I went through my prison file after my release that I found out why. An internal prison memo said I considered myself a member of the 'intelligentzia' [sic] and simply wanted to emulate communists outside, who wore dark glasses and carried umbrellas and briefcases to show that they were members of the 'intelligentsia'. Dr Neethling insisted that I needed the prescribed lenses, which were eventually given to me.

It was as preposterous as another memo, dated May 1976, from the Commanding Officer on Robben Island to the Commissioner of Prisons, was laughable. Translated from the original Afrikaans, it reads:

> This prisoner is one of the most hardened communists and will do everything in his power to promote his objectives, and therefore, this has nothing to do with humane considerations, but is principally in the interests of security. In closing, I should mention that this prisoner lives only for the ideology and political aims that led to his conviction and all his contact, whether by post or personal visit, is calculated, and he is regarded as one of the most dangerous types. No reasons will be given to him when correspondence is not released or visits not approved.

The first time I went to Cape Town for medical reasons was in the early 1970s. It was the first time in more than a decade that I had been in a city, and I was bewildered by the bustling throngs. A dentist's appointment in September 1974 marked the third time in eleven years that I had seen the city, which is a mere thirteen nautical miles from Robben Island.

I had lived in the heart of South Africa's largest city, Johannesburg, since my early teens, but years of isolation on a bucolic little island had rendered me metrophobic. I was too scared to cross the street, quite intimidated by the volume of traffic and how fast it was moving.

As for the fashion fads, nothing I had seen in magazines and movies had prepared me for the bright colours and high heels the long-haired men were wearing, and there seemed to be as many women in miniskirts as in dresses down to their ankles. It felt as though I had landed on a different planet, and I wanted to return to the island as quickly as possible.

As if the strange sights and unfamiliar sounds of the city weren't unsettling enough, I had a rather distressing encounter with someone I was convinced was Sylvia. At a distance, the blonde hair, the walk, even the figure, looked so much like her that my heart skipped several beats.

Imagine my devastation when this vision from my past came into focus and I realised that it wasn't Sylvia, or even a woman! The cruel truth and reality of the seventies that confronted me on a Cape Town pavement was, in fact, a young man wearing a unisex outfit. The moustache, only visible as we came face to face, was the final giveaway.

The warders took their habitual paranoia with them on trips to the mainland. Drivers were instructed to take secondary roads, so that we would not be able to see the posters on the lamp posts, blaring out the news headlines of the day.

Private patients in doctors' waiting rooms were asked not to read their newspapers in our presence and once, when a man refused, four warders stood shoulder to shoulder in front of him to block my view, totally oblivious to how silly they looked. Fortunately, their instructions extended only to newspapers, and I was more than happy to page through the copies of *Time* and *Newsweek* stacked on the table next to me.

For all the tumult and tragedy that made up the second half of 1976, when we did our annual 'stocktaking', two things stood out in our memories. One was the bunch of fat and succulent grapes each of us had been given in February, while the other was an abundance of ripe yellow peaches – more than two dozen each over a two-day period! – that had come our way one weekend.

That fruit was so delicious, and such a departure from our usual stodgy prison food that it was almost worth waiting twelve years for.

～ 15 ～

Changing Times

Encore une victoire comme celle – lá et je suis perdu.
– Pyrrhus, after the victory at Ausculum, 279 BC[1]

By 1976 there were nineteen of us working as unskilled labourers, two as gardeners, nine as cleaners and one, Jeff Masemola, as a maintenance man. For no apparent reason, we were simply told in June that we would no longer be going out to work.

We were truly perplexed. Such a sudden change in prison routine was almost unheard of, but we were in the middle of a periodic news blackout and had no way of finding out what was happening outside. We turned to our favourite pastime, speculation.

It was not until August when Eric Molobi arrived that we learnt of the student uprising in Soweto on 16 June and subsequent events. Actually, we were lucky to hear about the spreading unrest as soon as we did – at times it took up to six months before we knew what was going on in South Africa.

Our first detailed account of the Soweto uprising came from Eric Molobi. His cell was in another wing, but I managed to have a brief exchange with him before the warders realised what I was doing.

Of course we were shocked at the brutality unleashed against the children by the security forces, but strangely heartened, too, by their courage in the face of bullets and batons. Confused and inaccurate as those early accounts were, we realised almost at once that a new chapter in the struggle had been opened, and that the younger generation was sending an unequivocal message to the country and the world. The fear that had taken hold in the post-Rivonia decade had been overcome, and freedom in our lifetime was within reach.

Ironically, the prison walls that had been erected to punish and remove us from the political arena had become the very bastion that protected us from the horrendous fate that befell the martyrs of Soweto and so many of our comrades. Our nemesis, Rooi Rus Swanepoel, had not changed one iota, and publicly boasted that he could have crushed the uprising with a handful of men armed with machine guns. No doubt he would have been more than happy, had circumstances allowed, to train those barrels on us.

Some fifteen years later, on the day that white South Africans went to the polls in a referendum that would decide the course of all our futures, I paid homage to the younger generation in one of my early speeches as a free man: 'After Soweto, everything changed. That fear is gone now.'[2]

WALTER'S PAIN

From the welter of painful incidents that belonged to a particular web,
he would pull out a strand that would help you hold together.
                                                    – Mac Maharaj[3]

Serving on the communications committee had its downside, most notably when we had to convey bad news about friends or family members to our fellow prisoners. In the second half of 1976, such a news item caught Mac Maharaj's eye. Walter and Albertina Sisulu's daughter had been arrested three days before the 16 June uprising. Since then, she had been held in solitary confinement and was being severely tortured.

I was deeply affected by this news. I had been with Walter on the night Lindi was born, and had always felt somewhat paternal towards her. Walter, of course, loved her deeply, and it was humbling to witness the dignity and integrity with which he received the tiding of his daughter's predicament.

Mac broke the news. 'Lindiwe has been tortured severely; here's the news report,' he said.

Walter was quiet for several moments while he digested the devastating news, and then he said: 'At least I know my children are socially aware and committed to the struggle.' It was an extraordinary example of his strength and courage.

As soon as possible, he wrote a carefully worded but forceful letter to the Minister of Justice, Jimmy Kruger, protesting the injustice of waging political battle against his children. It had little or no effect. Lindi remained in solitary confinement for eleven months and underwent horrendous torture. She later said: 'I was subjected to all kinds of physical assault, and they were interrogating me all the time. The cells were like dungeons.'⁴ She was abused with electric shocks, isolated and psychologically tormented by being told, *inter alia*, that her mother and other family members had been detained, were ill or had died. On her release in 1977, Lindiwe went into exile abroad.

While South Africa was seething with the new surge of energy from a generation of increasingly politicised youth, life on the island continued at the same dreary pace, except that we no longer left our cells to go to work. Our routine settled into a pattern of study, eat, read, write and receiving letters, a fortnightly film show, daily musical programme, sports and reminiscing. Weekends lost all meaning, and each day flowed into the next with nothing to distinguish one from another. What a colossal waste of time it was!

Only later did we realise that during this tumultuous period the authorities were shutting down all our channels of communication with the outside world. One of my letters from that time bemoaned the lack of correspondence: '1976 has not been such a good year for letters. I can't remember when last I received so few letters as I did this year. And you know something? This is the first time that I did not get a single birthday message. I suppose there is a point in not being reminded that one is getting on in years. So one should really be glad about the omission. But unfortunately, one's mind does not function this way in jail …'

RELATIONS WITH THE YOUNG LIONS

I spent a lot of time talking to the young prisoners who flooded into our midst and, more importantly, learning from them. It was painful to see so many bright and capable people being locked up for years when they should have been at school or university, carving out a future for themselves and for their people.

But I understood only too well the reasons and circumstances that had influenced their lives and led to their imprisonment. It was not for me to criticise or condemn — I had been removed from the reality of the situation outside for too long.

A number of the youngsters rejected study as a waste of time. Their first priority was to achieve liberation, and everything else was of secondary importance. This was one area in which we could guide them, and we spent many hours persuading them that they should use their time in prison to equip themselves for the future. By and large we were successful and many of them did extremely well, and were grateful for our advice.

The young lions brought fresh spirit to our debates, but we all shared a common political objective. In the words of WH Auden: 'I don't go along with talk of a generation gap. We are all contemporaries. There's only a difference of memories. That is all.' Of course there were differences in our approach, but we shared enough common ground for age not to be an insurmountable barrier to the fruitful exchange of ideas.

A friend once told me that when he expressed surprise that IB Tabata had made a speech at a ceremony marking the anniversary of JB Marks's death, Tabata reproached him by observing: 'The trouble with you young chaps is that you have enemies, whereas we have opponents.' I wonder what Tabata would have said had he known that a few of the 'young chaps' on the island refused to attend commemorations because a 'liberal' was going to speak, or because we were going to sing 'Nkosi Sikelel'iAfrika'! The 'liberal' they objected to was Eddie Daniels. But the ANC decided to carry on without the objectors.

Some overenthusiastic MK cadres came to prison with assertions that during our long years of isolation we had lost touch with ANC policy. We were told that the organisation's goal was to achieve 'people's democracy and socialism', and it was at times such as these that the wisdom, cool head, realism and foresight of leaders such as Madiba became indispensable. He invariably brought the endless polemics down to earth, reminding us that it had never been envisaged that MK could achieve a military victory over the South African security forces, and that MK's primary aim was to wage an armed struggle in tandem with the political battle and mass mobilisation. No single component would force the enemy to the negotiating table, but the combined power of all these efforts would win our freedom.

By 1977 the authorities had put a stop to our purchase from outside of records, sports equipment, musical instruments, anything that made our lives more bearable. The news drought continued, and we knew nothing of Steve Biko's contribution to the struggle until September, when we heard of his death. I don't recall his name being singled out in any communication from our comrades in the Black Consciousness Movement before that time.

Later, as details filtered through to us of his political life and his horrific murder, we became increasingly aware of his role in the rise of Black Consciousness; of his broad view of South African politics; of his efforts at promoting unity among the liberation forces; of his courage and charisma. There is no doubt that he had the necessary qualities, foresight and potential to make a meaningful contribution towards the building of the new South Africa, and it is a terrible tragedy that his young life was cut short.

SOME IMPROVEMENTS

One cannot prevent the birds of sadness from flying over your head, but you can prevent them from building nests in your hair.
– Chinese proverb[5]

By 1978, Captain JW Harding was the officer in charge of security prisoners on Robben Island.

He was an enlightened man, apolitical, a decent human being and never petty, but, more importantly, he introduced some radical changes that improved our lot immeasurably.

It began with something as simple as permission, after fifteen years of sleeping with our cell lights on, to turn them off when we pleased. By the time Harding left the island, he had been promoted to the rank of major, every prisoner in B Section had a bed and two SABC radio news bulletins were being relayed to our cells each day. Harding also lifted the small-minded restriction on the number of photographs we could have.

There was talk that the prisons department had finally agreed to a single dietary scale for all race groups, and our tiny library was greatly augmented by the provincial library service in Cape Town.

But our hunger for news remained insatiable, and despite now having access to the SABC bulletins and *Time* magazine, the communications committee continued to scour every possible source for news of politics, sport, drama, anthropology, book reviews and anything else that helped connect us to the outside world, the world in which our families lived.

This was how it came to our attention that a South African musical, *Ipi Tombi*, was a smash hit in London, and had broken box office records in Johannesburg. We searched in vain, of course, for reports about the show's reception in Umlazi or Fordsburg or Soweto, because although the stars of the show were Africans, and the entire storyline had an African theme, African audiences were not allowed access to the theatres in which it was staged in South Africa.

My niece Zohra continued to be the bedrock of my contact with the outside world. She wrote regularly, showed a deep concern for my needs and circumstances, and was innovative in decoding some of the hidden material in my letters and ensuring that messages reached the people they were intended for. It was not until I had been out of prison for some years that I discovered how much harassment by the Special Branch Zohra and Enver had endured due to their unflagging support of me.

As apartheid once more tightened its grip on those outside, the many tentacles of repression penetrated our small world as well. The position on 'first-degree' visitors remained the same, so Zohra and all my other nieces and nephews were excluded. This often made me regret not getting married. At least I would have had a 'first-degree' loved one to visit me. My siblings were getting older and less inclined to make the long trip to Cape Town, while the younger family members were refused permission to visit.

When my nephew Nazir was just a toddler, his parents had sent me a photograph and written on the back: 'Uncle, I shall be coming to see you one of these days.' I chuckled at the time, perhaps because my mind could not comprehend still being in jail when he turned sixteen, the minimum age for prison visitors. By late 1977 he was almost old enough to make that promised visit, but, as my only sister's son, he would not be eligible to do so.

In the absence of meaningful contact with the outside world and curtailment of our interaction with family members, the relationships we formed with our fellow prisoners became as strong as any family bond. My closest friends were Laloo Chiba, Eddie Daniels and Walter Sisulu. I regarded Walter as a father figure and Laloo as a brother.

Walter was strong, but he suffered continually from the flu on Robben Island. He could not stand the cold, but in spite of that, his gregarious nature made him prefer going out to work with us rather than staying in his cell alone all day.

His physical condition was such that he really should not still have been doing manual labour, but he felt happier in company. Walter had a deep love for his fellow human beings, the nature of which I have rarely seen. We all loved him too, of course. In jail, one learns the personal habits, likes and dislikes of many human beings. Some prefer to be alone, while others crave social interaction. In the late 1970s, when things were relaxed, and when we had stopped working altogether, our cell doors were left open all day. Those who wanted to take a nap at lunchtime could do so, but Walter never did. Instead, he would gather a group together and play Scrabble.

Govan Mbeki, on the other hand, was quite content to spend time alone with his thoughts. He was one of the oldest prisoners in our section, and his health was not good. In August 1975, his blood pressure escalated and caused concern, but then he recovered and was up and about again before long. He even wrote and passed his exams.

Govan was an intellectual, and perhaps it was this that drew him to spending time alone, ruminating on the struggle and on his life. I spent many afternoons walking around the courtyard and in the passage with Govan. We used to joke about the habits of some of our fellow prisoners, and I always teased Govan that if the revolution ever broke out between noon and 2 p.m., he, Billy Nair and Mike Dingake would miss it, as they religiously took a nap during that time.

Entertainment had improved tremendously, and by the mid-1970s we were seeing some rather good films every now and then: *Marooned*, *Genghis Khan*, *iLollipop, The Godfather, The Party* (I loved Peter Sellers' impersonation of Indians) and, believe it or not, *The Great Escape*. Some fleeting ideas evoked by the latter were swiftly dispelled by the forbidding roar of the chilly Atlantic.

Wilton Mkwayi, Mike Dingake and I had set up a daily tea club. Every morning at ten, Mkwayi would make a flask of tea or coffee, we would go to his cell, and just sit down and talk. Wilton and I continued to take tea together after Mike was released, and Walter, in his inimitable manner, would frequently arrive, smile disarmingly, and demand a cup. We would jokingly dismiss him, reminding him that he was not a member, but Walter would just continue smiling and take a chair until he got his tea. Later, Theophilus Cholo joined our club.

Mike Dingake was born in Botswana, but joined the ANC long before it was banned, and then went underground. He was on his way back to South Africa from Dar es Salaam when he was picked up by the police in Rhodesia and handed over to the security police. He was severely tortured before being given a thirteen-year sentence.

Raymond Mhlaba was nothing if not a gentleman. The product of a mission school, he was so well bred that not even the most insidious goading by the warders could provoke him into being rude or uncouth.

During possibly one of his worst verbal clashes with a warder, we watched with anxiety, fear and interest to see how long Raymond's self-restraint would last. His anger and frustration were clearly mounting, but even when he erupted, he was incapable of going against form. 'You ... you ... you ...' he stuttered, and we felt for sure his next words would make a trooper blanch. 'You fascist!' he blurted out. Those were probably the strongest words that Raymond ever uttered.

The aversion to foul language extended to Mandela, Sisulu and Mbeki as well. The worst I ever heard from Govan was 'you swine'.

They set an admirable example, and one I tried to emulate, but, being a lot younger and having grown up in Johannesburg, I must admit that my vocabulary included words they never would have used. One could not even tell them a blue joke, as they would almost certainly have taken offence!

As my fiftieth birthday approached, my thoughts turned to people with whom I had shared some of the best years of my life. The Vassen family had never wavered in their support, and I still regarded Tommy, who was in exile in London, and Bobby, who had gone to the USA, as my brothers. On 17 June 1978, I wrote to Tommy:

My Dear Tom,
I'm sure you must be thinking jail has made me a bit of a sadist: tormenting your conscience as I do. I suppose I'll just have to risk that appellation, especially if it eventually leads to some sort of a response from you.
Let me tell you of my night out from Robben Island. It was in May, a

bit on the cool and windy side, not an ideal day for a sea trip. I went out with Susan. Having been out with her once before, I wasn't very apprehensive about the weather. She was well togged, elegant, almost luxurious. Well, believe it or not, yours truly sat behind the bar counter, the powers that be having first ensured that all the consumables were safely out of reach. Anyway, thanks to her gentle care I did not really need artificial supplements in order to brave the heavy seas, and within 45 minutes we docked at Cape Town. I hardly left Susan, and almost my very next step was to plunge myself into a world dominated by the fair sex. My bedroom at the slopes of Table Mountain, a soft rain and mist, warm beverages and delicious food much enhanced by the beautiful ladies serving it. Add to this the kindly interest and care, the tender caresses, the coaxing, the whispers and charming smiles. What's more, I was taken by young ladies to the theatre! Yes, there only to be thrust in the company of yet more young ladies, albeit this time they being in purdah, I could only derive comfort and satisfaction from watching the smiles in their eyes. Call it a harem, Arabian nights or what you will. But it was very heaven, I tell you. And in those brief – alas too brief – hours I was king. No longer a prisoner. I shed the anxieties, the responsibilities and worries which to a greater or lesser degree are concomitants of jail life.

Daydreaming? A little touched? Escaped? No, nothing as dramatic as all that. Let me set your mind at ease. The 'lady' Susan I talked about is no female acquaintance of mine, but the name of the new Robben Island boat – the Susan Kruger. And all the other ladies I referred to were the nurses, staff and theatre sisters of the Woodstock Hospital. You see, I had to go there for an examination that could only be done under anaesthetic. They didn't find anything that warranted an operation, so they sent me packing back to the island.

We had a tea party on my birthday, though I must say I felt no older than when I first arrived on the island. I also hired a film, *J'Accuse*, based on the book by Emile Zola. After thirteen years, I was finally promoted into the A group of privileges – the last of the Rivonia Trialists to reach this milestone. Finally, I could have two visitors at a time, twice a month, though physical contact was strictly taboo and we were separated by a pane of glass, with warders monitoring our every word.

TRADITIONS AND INNOVATIONS

Among certain ethnic groups in South Africa, notably the Xhosa, age is not the only criterion for a young man's graduation to adulthood. He has to undergo certain customary rituals in order to command respect and status, in the absence of which he is still regarded as a boy (or *kwedini*).

His rite of passage is barred until he has been circumcised. Manhood is equated with bravery, and no matter how painful the procedure, the initiate is expected to remain silent until the ritual has been completed, at which point he proudly proclaims: '*Ndiyandoda!*' ['I am a man!']

We had become aware that Comrade Mkabela was running an illegal circumcision school from the prison hospital. He had no medical training, but had somehow acquired the skill to perform circumcisions, and we knew that several of the prisoners from the general section had gone through the ritual.

For a long time, we avoided talking about this initiation school, partly for security reasons, partly because no one from our section was affected, but mainly, perhaps, because we did not want to become embroiled in a potentially controversial debate. But in a closed community such as a prison, it's impossible to remain neutral forever.

Wilton Mkwayi told me that Kwedi Mkalipi had asked us to organise a tea party to celebrate the coming-to-manhood of two young men from our section. I had just passed them in the passage, wrapped in blankets, but it did not dawn on me, until Wilton spoke, that they had recently been circumcised.

We duly laid on what refreshments we could, and welcomed the pair into adulthood. News of their circumcision was routinely passed on to comrades in the rest of the prison.

Reaction from the young lions in A Section was both swift and scathing. Harry Gwala led the charge, peppering his criticism with such epithets as 'reactionaries', 'tribalists', 'counter-revolutionaries', 'unhygienic'. And Harry's views on just about anything were regarded as gospel by his army of youthful loyalists – mostly trained MK soldiers and passionate communists.

A fierce debate ensued, with some of the most radical missives – some were really vicious, quite derogatory – being fired off by one of the gentlest and most respectful comrades. Few people except political detainees would have had the time, energy or ability to turn a purely cultural issue such as circumcision into a heated political polemic, but that is precisely what happened, and all because of a well-intentioned effort to bring a semblance of normal society into an abnormal situation.

By the end of July 1980 the ban on further degree studies was lifted, and in September we received some of the best news we had ever had. A-group prisoners would be allowed to subscribe to any South African newspaper! Our sixteen-year drought was broken, and we immediately ordered the *Cape Times*, the *Rand Daily Mail*, the *Post*, the *Sunday Times*, the *Argus* and others. People cannot imagine how thrilling it was for us to be able to read a daily newspaper without fear of being punished. It was as though we had been granted permits to re-enter the world after being shut out for years.

In addition to reports about political colleagues and friends, I relished stories about the 'Fordsburg Fox', Ismail Pahad, and his Dynamos Football Club, and wallowed in the antics of Andy Capp, Jiggs, Blondie and a host of other cartoon characters. Soccer fans devoured accounts of the fortunes of Liverpool and Manchester United, Hamburg and Real Madrid; there were crossword puzzles to solve and advertisements to bring us up to date about the cost of living.

The Sunday papers were thicker than we remembered, but still the same old rags. I mourned the absence of Stanley Uys in the *Sunday Times*. It had been worth buying the newspaper just to read his column, but since moving abroad, he seemed to be out of his depth. Nevertheless, after our long years of deprivation, we devoured even the Sunday papers from cover to cover, trashy though some of the content was.

FORCED REMOVALS

In early 1981, I had to face the reality of my family being forced to move from my childhood home. Under the Group Areas Act, the part of Schweizer-Reneke where our shop and the house where I was born stood, was declared 'white'. My brothers received a mere pittance in compensation, and were removed to an undeveloped Indian suburb on the outskirts of the town.

My brother Ismail put on a brave face, but I knew instinctively that he was going through a traumatic experience. So many memories, good and bad, were rooted in that property, yet the buildings were simply razed to the ground.

Rumours of forced removal had first reached me in early 1964, and in a letter to Sylvia during the Rivonia Trial I had written:

> The house where I was born and where my father settled in 1919 has to be moved. Not because of any road or town development project, not for hygienic reasons or slum clearance, but simply because we are Indians and because our house happens to be next to the Dutch Reformed Church. The fact that my father and other Indians settled there before the church was built, indeed when the town was almost barren, seems to be of no consequence. The apartheid juggernaut must move on, trampling mercilessly on life and livelihood, oblivious to any injury to human feelings and desires. And on more or less the same day, the so-called Minister of Indian Affairs, with cruel callousness, can say that the Indian people are happy under the Group Areas Act and speak of its so-called advantages. What is worse is white South Africa believes him, and those who don't are acquiescing by their silence. Can it be that they feel so snug and secure within the laager that they can comfortably close their eyes to all this and not expect to be disturbed in their way of life? Altogether it presents a frightening picture. Not that the march to freedom can be stopped by this apathy. But just think of the colossal problems of adjustment after freedom.

My brother Ismail had died of a heart attack a few years after the eviction, and I have little doubt that his health problems started when he was forced to surrender the only home he had ever known.

Many, many others suffered the same fate. When JN Singh's family had to move from their house in Mansfield Road, Durban, where I had stayed so often, a friend wrote me a touching letter, in which she made the poignant point that no one can successfully transplant old trees. I am not sure it is possible to ever forget, or forgive, the indescribable hardships caused by the removals.

Es'kia Mphahlele wrote nostalgically and so powerfully about 'the tyranny of place and time'. I had never thought of the invisible umbilical cord that bound me to Schweizer-Reneke and our family home as a 'tyranny', but looking back, to my hometown, to Sophiatown and Newlands, to District Six, the bond of memory is as strong as ever, the mental images barely dimmed by the passing of the years.

Letters from outside about the effects of the infamous Group Areas Act filled me with sadness and that ineffable sense of loss and emptiness that irrevocable change brings. The only thing that countered my gloom was the prospect, thanks to relaxations in the visiting regulations, that my nieces and nephews could come and see me at last.

Leading Questions

The great advantage we have over common-law prisoners is that all of us share certain basic ideals and we are all sentenced for similar offences. There is a harmony and sense of oneness among security prisoners which transcends parochial differences; a relationship which is unfortunately absent outside.[1]

The Congress component of prisoners on Robben Island was in many respects a microcosm of the ANC outside. We came from different parts of the country and were Africans, Coloureds and Indians. We were atheists, believers and agnostics, communists, non-communists, perhaps a couple of anti-communists, some who would later become significant capitalists, trade unionists, lawyers, doctors, teachers, semi-literate or totally illiterate comrades, industrial workers, skilled and unskilled labourers, peasants, shop owners, young and old, MK cadres, leaders and rank and file members.

Our ideas converged on the fundamental policy and goal of the Congress movement – to eradicate white domination and replace it with a non-racial, democratic, non-sexist system. Our situation lent itself ideally to endless discussion, analysis, debate and polemics. The exchange of ideas helped us all to gain a better understanding, not only of policy and goals, but of the diversity of thinking in our constituency, especially regarding interpretation of policy documents, chief among them being the Freedom Charter.

Of no less importance in a prison situation was the fact that, rather than succumb to self-pity, boredom, cynicism or dejection, comrades spent their time profitably. Madiba's consistent advice to all newcomers was not to waste the years spent behind bars, but use them to equip themselves so as to serve the people and the country better.

The majority of debates were of short duration, but there was one topic that came up soon after the first ANC prisoners arrived on the island and resumed intermittently until virtually the last political prisoners were released. The subject was 'Marxism and the ANC'.

When Harry Gwala arrived in 1964,[2] he wasted little time in starting Marxist classes, apparently with a view to establishing cells of the Communist Party. Not surprisingly, he had a ready-made class of enthusiastic students. But this created unhappiness among some comrades, especially those who felt excluded from these groups that met privately. The matter was referred to the High Organ.

The leadership informed Harry that there was no objection to his classes, and suggested that he could include them in the ANC's political education syllabus. However, the formation of Communist Party cells would not be advisable, as this would merely duplicate the ANC's functions within the closed community, and might even prove divisive.

Security considerations also had to be taken into account. It was difficult enough to maintain contact between the different sections of the prison, and any additional organisation would place undue strain on the tenuous communication channels. The High Organ's views were accepted, albeit reluctantly by some, especially Comrade Gwala.

The discussions on Marxism were cordial, healthy and non-controversial. Socialism was favoured by many as the ideology of the future, and received a boost when MK cadres such as Theo Cholo and his colleagues arrived in the early 1970s, filled with enthusiasm. They had come from Somalia, which at the time was regarded as part of the socialist world, and were quite enamoured with what they saw as a budding paradise of socialism.

I was a great admirer of the socialist system, and in particular of the Soviet Union, the People's Democracies, Cuba and – unconventionally – the People's Democratic Republic of China, but after the invasions of Hungary in 1956 and Czechoslovakia in 1968, I had matured enough not to accept everything about the socialist world without question. As a younger man, I had joined enthusiastically, while in the German Democratic Republic, in the singing of:

Zie had uns alles gegeben, sonne und wind, und zie geitste nicht
Die partei, die partei die had immer richt.

[You have given us all; the sun and the wind, and
The Party, the Party, it is always right, and comrades so it will remain.]

And I continued to sing with pride the songs that I had grown up with since joining the Young Communist League in my teens, such as 'Soviet Land':

Soviet land so dear to every toiler,
Peace and progress build their hopes on thee,
There's no other land the whole world over,
Where man walks the earth so proud and free.

But I was no longer so blinded by ideology that I was prepared to overlook human rights abuses taking place before my eyes.

On a cold Saturday night in Budapest in 1952, I was with a group of friends who had gone across the Danube to a party. Walking back over the bridge at about two in the morning, we came across men in civilian clothes clearing the snow under the watchful eyes of warmly clad and armed police or soldiers. One of my friends, who spoke some Hungarian, asked what was going on, and was told that these were political prisoners. My reaction was, 'Oh well, they are counter-revolutionary enemies of socialism and deserve what they get.'

After the violent crushing of the revolt in 1956 with the aid of invading Soviet troops, I was haunted by that picture, and it never really left me. My guilt was compounded by the fact that even after I awakened to the gross human rights abuses, I did not speak out. At public meetings and in private conversations, I continued to glowingly praise socialist Hungary.

I should have conveyed my misgivings to my young comrades who, though they had received their military training in socialist countries, were shielded from such abuse. They would have been largely confined to training camps, and without having been exposed to the day-to-day experiences of ordinary people, they could not have been prepared for the sudden collapse of the Soviet Union and Eastern Europe.

I at least had the advantage of seeing the cracks appear over a period, and as a result, I was able to acknowledge the violations and abuses, yet agree with analysts who held the view that the wrongs were not an indictment of socialism as such, but rather of the manner in which the system had been implemented. Even with all the major setbacks and reverses, my faith in socialism remained unshaken.

Most of the young MK comrades who came to Robben Island after 1976 were trained in the Soviet Union or satellite states. They had acquitted themselves with distinction in the 'trenches', and included Tokyo Sexwale, Naledi Tsiki, Andrew Mapetho, Mandla Mthethwa, Vusyisile Mbundu and Felix Ali Lumkwana. We were immensely proud of them.

The young freedom fighters were housed in A Section, which had been specially prepared for the post-1976 detainees and the activists from the South African Students' Organisation, who became known as the SASO 9. Their militancy towards the prison officials and their socialist ardour caught us unawares.

In the constant flux of prison conditions, we had been enjoying a brief respite, with confrontations between prisoners and our jailers at an all-time minimum. Against the defiance and aggression of the post-Soweto generation, we probably seemed tame. Indeed, Comrade Harry Gwala's powerful socialist rhetoric might have given a stranger the impression that the rest of us were liberals, or even anti-communists.

We learnt soon enough that if Cholo and his comrades were blind in their loyalty to 'socialist' Somalia, they were slavish in their support of the Soviet Union. Dr Nchaupe Mokoape of the Black Consciousness Movement listened patiently, day after day, to their endless, and often provocative singing, their slogans, their enthusing, their exaggerated claims, until one day his tolerance was exhausted. He confronted the young activists with a single, stinging question: 'Comrades, please tell me. Do the people in the Soviet Union ever catch a cold?'

The injection of fresh rhetoric fuelled the ongoing debate about the ANC and Marxism, of course, which rested broadly on two fundamental issues:

• The struggle was no longer for 'national' or 'bourgeois' democracy, but against capitalism and for 'people's democracy', which was really just a euphemism for socialism. Those of us who held the opposing view were accused of being in prison for too long and therefore being out of touch with ANC policy shifts.

• The ANC and the Communist Party were one organisation. This took my thoughts back to Rivonia, where I did a fair amount of administrative work for the ANC, the party and MK. When I asked Govan Mbeki why all correspondence to the three organisations went to the same postal address in Port Elizabeth, his answer left no doubt that while the Communist Party functioned as a separate entity in Johannesburg and at Rivonia, in the Eastern Cape, at least, the three were one.

Another debate concerned the role of the Bantustans and separate institutions for different races.

Harry Gwala remained the central figure around whom the 'communists' rallied, and through the years, the most senior ANC leader who came to be identified with his views was Govan Mbeki, or 'Geezer', as I affectionately called him. In time to come, two schools of thought emerged – the 'communists' under Gwala and Govan, and the 'nationalists' under Mandela.

These terms are used loosely used, and should not give the impression that the Congress organisation was split into two distinct or antagonistic camps. Moreover, there was never a clear-cut division of support. There were communists who disagreed with Gwala and felt more comfortable in the nationalist camp. Walter, of course, was in the nationalist camp all along, and no one would have dared single him out for criticism or attack. One does not readily turn against a father.

The debate certainly became tense and heated many times, but contrary to claims by outsiders, it never came anywhere close to causing a split in the ranks. It is also entirely untrue – perhaps even mischievous – to allege that tensions between Madiba and Mbeki reached a point where they did not even greet one another for more than a year.

What is undeniably true, however, is that the policy debate ultimately came down to a clash of two strong personalities. There was never a leadership battle between the two, but at the same time, the Mbeki supporters opposed all moves aimed at Mandela being regarded as 'the' leader.

But leader he was, and not by virtue only of the positions to which he had been elected in the ANC and the Youth League before he was banned. From childhood, when he was brought up as a chief, Mandela was groomed to be a leader. Added to that were his political experience, foresight, courage and dynamism. Throughout the period that he operated underground, and during the Rivonia Trial, he displayed the undeniable qualities of leadership, culminating with his address from the dock. Our lawyers, the media, the outside world and all the accused, including Govan, accepted him as the leader, and from the moment we set foot on Robben Island, every prison officer, from the rookies to the generals, treated him as such.

So did the International Red Cross and visiting judges, parliamentarians and foreign dignitaries. It was not as though we ever held a meeting and elected him our leader, it was just that the mantle of leadership fell naturally upon his shoulders.

However, the nationalist–communist controversy inevitably spilt over into a leadership debate, and the ANC, especially in B Section, entered the most unfortunate and embarrassing period of our entire sojourn on Robben Island. It was perhaps the only time in my political life that I felt uncomfortable with a couple of my comrades, and for a while I spent more time with my friend, Comrade Kwedi Mkaliphi of the PAC, than with them.

No candidate was ever put forward to contest Madiba's leadership. From the 'communist' camp, Govan would have been the logical choice, but the objective seemed not so much to challenge Mandela as to do away entirely with the appellation of 'leader', thus automatically and unrealistically neutralising Madiba.

As the debate rose to a crescendo, everything pointed towards an election. The 'communist bloc' realised that in order to have a fighting chance, they needed to reduce the number of potential Mandela supporters, and in desperation employed a tactic that, in my opinion, was unprecedented in an underground organisation: they turned to the ANC constitution!

And that was where things became nasty and painful. I would never have imagined that a handful of cadres with experience in the ANC's culture and ethos would resort to methods that were both unethical and opportunistic.

They argued that because the ANC constitution limited membership to Africans, Indian and Coloured comrades would not be allowed to vote. In their eagerness to achieve their aims, they conveniently ignored the fact that not even the enemy courts had recognised the niceties of constitutions, and had sentenced Coloureds, Indians and Africans alike to lengthy terms of imprisonment for MK and ANC activities.

In any event, James April had briefed us fully on the decision taken by the ANC at the Morogoro Conference, which opened membership to all.

Matters came to a head at a meeting of members in B Section. Walter Sisulu moved that Nelson Mandela was the leader of the ANC on Robben Island. I seconded the motion, describing his position as *primus inter pares*, first among equals, which in my view was an accurate reflection of his status. Even without the non-African vote, the motion would have been carried, and it was interesting that the communist–nationalist debate was not even raised at the meeting.

Bantustan opposition politics covered a broad spectrum of issues, all rooted in the arid soil of apartheid: the separation of people based on race. Discussion thus centred on the so-called independent homelands of Transkei, Ciskei, Bophuthatswana and Venda, as well as apartheid institutions such as the Labour Party and the South African Indian Council.

The question of separate institutions dated back to 1936 when the Native Representative Council was established. Leaders such as Dr Xuma, Dr Moroka, Chief Luthuli and Professor Matthews had served on the council, but in 1949, when the government's Programme of Action was introduced, the ANC decided to boycott the NRC. It was later abolished and replaced by so-called Bantu Authorities.

The concept of 'homelands' for different ethnic groups was first raised during the 1960s, and was opposed by the ANC from the start.

In the early 1970s, with Hennie Ferris facing imminent release, the issue of apartheid institutions sparked a new debate. In the absence of any significant opposition organisation, ought he to work for change from within the Labour Party? The nationalist camp accepted that the party was a reality, and offered scope for exploitation. If ANC supporters infiltrated the party, we reasoned, they could surreptitiously further the policy of the Congress movement.

The communist camp, on the other hand, vigorously punted a boycott of all apartheid surrogates, as agreed at the ANC's 1962 conference at Lobatse. Both groups agreed that there should be no participation in Bantustan governments.

No formal decision was taken, but Hennie left the island believing that by joining the Labour Party he would have the blessing of High Organ members like Madiba and Walter. He soon rose to a leadership position, propagating ANC policy, but whether or not Hennie was acting in accordance with the High Organ's instructions continued to be the subject of informal accusations, denials, clarifications and arguments. However, the Ferris issue was soon overshadowed by the broader and more urgent theoretical debate.

A document drafted in the late 1970s by the High Organ and unanimously approved by the members in B Section was smuggled to the ANC structures throughout the prison. The idea was to formally place the debate on a proper footing as part of the political education programme, and the document identified various points for comment and discussion. Concurrent with this was the debate on the Bantustans and separate institutions.

There were a number of proactive attempts to resolve the disputes between the communist and nationalist camps. ANC units from the different sections of the prison submitted consensus views as well as those of dissenting individuals. I was asked by the High Organ to summarise the various responses and con-solidate them in a single document that would include the unanimous view of the High Organ and all the members in B Section.

This document was headed 'Marxism and Inqindi'. It consisted of twenty-one pages in my tiny writing and a covering letter from Madiba, inviting further comment from the recipients. I cannot recall the outcome, quite possibly because my sudden transfer to Pollsmoor intervened, but I heard much later from Tokyo Sexwale that the controversy continued.

All this, of course, took place before the collapse of the Soviet Union and the Berlin Wall, and the domino effect these events had on the People's Democracies of Europe, but the document may still be of some value to historians, and there are portions of it that remain relevant to the ANC and its allies. A summary of the main points is given below, in the order in which they appear in the document:

> The two basic aims of 'Marxism and Inqindi' are to encourage comrades to study M and to remind them of the distinction between a national struggle and a class struggle.

M&I welcomes the deep interest shown by comrades in M. But speaking purely as Congressites, we expect all our members to specialise first and foremost in the history of the Congresses and to be able to speak authoritatively on our policy.

M&I warns that the growing interest in the study of M and the 57-year-old heritage of the joint campaign by the Congress movement and the CP should not be allowed to obscure the basic differences between the policies of the two organisations. ANC and the other Congresses are neither M organisations nor CP fronts. They are national organisations that lead the struggle against racial oppression and not against capitalism. The Freedom Charter (FC), not Marxism (M) is the policy of the Congress Movement (CM).

M&I adds that the democratic changes envisaged will create the ideal conditions for the CP to pursue the struggle for a socialist SA.

M&I says the FC is not the programme of the CP for socialism but of the national liberation movement (NLM) for a National Democracy (ND).

M&I dismisses the argument that the CM is presently fighting against capitalism in order to establish a proletarian dictatorship as unrealistic. It ascribes this incorrect approach to failure to distinguish between a political party and a broad NLM like Inq (ANC).

The oppressed people of South Africa face the dual problem of class and national oppression. In striving to solve this twin problem, the CP and CM have each worked out a definite strategy which they have consistently followed. Although the long-term objectives of the Congresses coincide with the short-term aims of the CP, the CM leads the national struggle and the CP leads the class struggle.

The FC, a product of the peculiar conditions of our country, was drafted against the background of the realities of our struggle, and must be viewed accordingly. A short review of some of the policy declarations of the Congresses clearly shows that the idea of private property has played an important role in their demands.

Comrade Michael Harmel prepared a memorandum for the defence team in the Treason Trial in which he emphasised that the FC was not the programme of the CP but of the national movement (NM) embracing several classes and social groups.

The same point was made in the address (of Madiba) from the dock in the Rivonia Trial. It may well be that comrades may not be aware that the Rivonia address represented not only the views of those who were on trial, but of the entire leadership of the organisation. Before it was read in court, it was shown and approved both by the National President, Chief Luthuli, and by the External Mission.

In the two-pronged nature of our struggle against national oppression and class oppression, the two prongs overlap, and the CM and CP cooperate in the execution of their respective tasks. But both have always acknowledged the independent roles of the two prongs.

Closely connected with the question of national oppression is that of the content of our revolution. Both CM and CP have consistently advocated the principle that the liberation of the African people is the main content of the struggle against white domination.

The ANC has always stood for a progressive nationalism. After opening its doors to all, that nationalism will become even more tempered and broad. But it would be a mistake to overemphasise the importance of African nationalism. Unlike M, which guides the CP before and after the taking of power, the role of African nationalism is limited to the pre-liberation phase of the struggle. It cannot be used to reshape society after liberation, nor for the purpose of developing a new mode of production different from capitalism or socialism, as some political organisations claim.

But the broadness of the CM is also its weakness. At the best of times it is never easy to keep together people with contrasting social backgrounds and conflicting interests. A compromise programme, such as the FC, correct as it is in the light of our concrete situation, does not allow us to gain maximum speed in the struggle, because by doing so, the rate of march may be too fast for certain sections of the membership. They may fall by the wayside before the journey is completed. That danger becomes even more real as class divisions among the people become sharper. As the working class organisations in the country intensify their campaign to organise the workers, and as the unity and level of political consciousness of workers rises, the working class inside the CM will press increasingly for more radical interpretation of the FC. They will even press for its repeal if they feel it has become a fetter to further progress.

There is a complex interdependence between the class and national struggle. The promotion of the interests of the one struggle involves the promotion of the interests of the other. It is this cardinal truth that has made cooperation between the Inq, the CM and the CP inevitable. But this interdependence does not blur the distinction between the basic objectives of the CM and CP. The CM cannot take the revolution to socialism. The effective transfer of power to the working class means that the working class must have its own political party, the CP, and the working class party must have its own philosophy – dialectical materialism.

In the early 1990s, I was part of an ANC delegation that met with cabinet minister Adriaan Vlok and senior officials of the prisons department. At the end of the meeting, I asked the prisons commissioner to return all the letters and books that had been withheld from me. He immediately responded that there were none, but a few weeks later I had a telephone call, telling me I could collect my belongings from headquarters in Pretoria.

To my surprise, I was handed a single file, so slim that I was in no hurry to open it. When I did, however, I was shocked to find, among a few letters and telegrams, a copy of 'Marxism and Inqindi'!

When I became a member of parliament in 1994, I again raised the question of my prison files, and it turned out that there were almost thirty of them. Among the contents was a five-page summary, in Afrikaans, of 'Marxism and Inqindi', with a note stating: 'Unauthorised document confiscated from Mr Kathrada's cell'.

Two things struck me immediately. First, this was the only prison document in which I was ever referred to as 'Mr', and, secondly, the document was not found in my cell, but in A Section. Tokyo Sexwale confirmed this.

So much water has flowed under the bridge in the three decades since Rivonia, Operation Mayibuye and 'Marxism and Inqindi'. Harry Gwala, Govan Mbeki, Elias Motsoaledi (Mkoni), Joe Gqabi and Walter Sisulu are all dead.

I knew Mkoni from the late 1940s or early 1950s. We served together on the MK Regional Command and worked closely on various Congress campaigns. I met Joe in the late 1950s, but the first time we worked together was on the communications committee in B Section. I had not met Harry before he was sent to the island, but Govan Mbeki and I were introduced at Walter Sisulu's home in Orlando West in 1960. In a letter to Sylvia during the Rivonia Trial, I conveyed my impressions of him. They never changed.

> We have had another good day in court. The tall, dignified figure and intellect of Mbeki still dominates the court. It is in many ways a tragedy that a man of this calibre has been forced into politics, when he should be giving his all to fields where he would make an undoubted mark. Yet I suppose I shouldn't be complaining. It must be precisely the frustrations that the non-white intellectual comes up against which forced him into politics. And, his life and achievements so effectively mirror the lives of hundreds and thousands of thinking non-whites.[3]

At the Communist Party's last conference before our arrest, he was elected to the Central Committee. A considerable amount of time was devoted to debate on the question of participation in apartheid institutions, and I remember clearly the eloquent contribution of Chris Hani, supported by Govan, in support of a boycott.

Govan was a teacher, not only in his choice of profession, but in essence and in soul. It was only his commitment to the struggle that took him away from teaching, which was his first love. Most of his political work had to be carried on underground, but in the end the security police caught up with him, and he lost his job.

Whereas almost all the senior political leaders were banned from 1952 onwards, Govan only received his first banning orders in 1962. He was not among those charged in the three trials of leaders of the 1952 Defiance Campaign in Port Elizabeth, Kimberley and Johannesburg, and he also managed to escape the countrywide arrests in 1956, which led to the Treason Trial of 156 accused. After his dismissal from the teaching profession, he moved to Port Elizabeth in 1955 or 1956. The Eastern Cape had already become an ANC stronghold, thanks to the efforts of powerful leaders such as Raymond Mhlaba, Gladstone Tshume, Dr Jimmy Njongwe and Wilton Mkwayi. What was lacking, though, was a systematic programme of political education, and Govan filled that vacuum, bringing to the organisation all the skills he had honed in the classroom.

But he could not expect to lead a charmed life forever. Comrade Mkoni was fond of quoting a Sepedi proverb: *Mulato gao bole, go bole nama*, which means, 'The long arm of the law will catch up with you, some time.' Towards the end of 1962, while visiting Johannesburg, Govan was spotted by the security police while he was a passenger on the pillion of Joe Gqabi's scooter. How things have changed! I cannot imagine the politicians of today, let alone a leader, riding on a scooter, much less the horse and cart we occasionally used when organising for the COP!

In fact, as recently as November 2003, a comrade was most upset when a car rental agency issued me with a VW Polo instead of 'something more suitable for a leader'. It's all a matter of values, in the end.

Thoughts About Jail

If we can find the courage, and love is the greatest source of that, the knowledge that our years are limited can illuminate our every day and help us enrich what surrounds us.
– Barney Simon on the death of his friend Joe Slovo[1]

Letters both to and from friends and family are the lifeblood of a prisoner's existence. Because of the restrictions on subject matter and length, great thought and care go into a letter, and there is little as disheartening as having it returned to you with instruction to delete words, sentences or entire passages. This letter of mine, penned on 17 November 1979, is a case in point. It was written a day after my dear friend, Eddie Daniels, was released after having spent fifteen years with us. The compulsory cuts ordered by the censors on 24 November have a line drawn through them.

My Dear Daso,

I'm writing this in the early hours of the morning. It is so quiet, except for the rhythmic sound of the waves breaking against the shore, as if they are keeping time with the equally rhythmic whistling of the wind. The birds and the crickets and the mosquitoes are all silent. There is not even a stir or a snore from my neighbours. It's as if I am alone on the island. One feels almost driven towards 'sessions of sweet silent thoughts and remembrance of things past'. It seems so incongruous to be concerning oneself with mundane things instead of just lying in bed and enjoying the silence and just thinking. If only one were endowed with the talent of a musician, a poet, a writer – any creative artist – then surely this would be the ideal atmosphere.

A door has just banged. A vehicle has come to a screeching stop. And with that we come back to reality. A solitary bird has begun to sing. Soon it will be joined by others, and it will be dawn. That means I better hurry in order to get this away. I've been wondering why I had to choose this moment to write about the wind and the sea and the birds. Is it some form of escapism? Yes. I think it is. Yesterday a very dear friend was released from jail – after 15 years! I suppose I wanted to avoid thinking about the vacuum this has created. He came in just a few months after us. We soon became friends. Over the years we shared many experiences together, exchanged confidences, read, played, ate, discussed, worked, differed, argued. We came from two completely different backgrounds and in many respects held differing ideas and outlooks. We were thrown together in the same confined environment, to face common problems, and more important, to gear ourselves for the years that lay ahead. In the process, a close bond developed between us. And this week we had to part, perhaps never to see each other again. We were in the original foursome who started playing bridge – surreptitiously at first and with hand made cards. We played a number of other games together. Just a few hours before the boat took him away we played a couple of rubbers of bridge, we drank tea, ate biscuits, sang a few songs, teased each other – and said goodbye. It was a very difficult moment, and we let it pass as quickly as possible. I'm sorry that you had to be the victim of my present state of mind.

I'm glad that Rookie has been able to visit you all. How long is she staying? It must have been wonderful to see her. She must have told you of her visit to Robben Island some years ago. Nice to hear of Sakina as well. Is she still studying or lecturing? Pass my love to her. Only recently I was reading something that covered similar ground as her thesis. Was it ever published? – AMK

PASSING TIME

Memory is the joy and sorrow of mankind.
– Howard Fast, *Spartacus*[2]

I once read somewhere that the years roll by very quickly in jail – it's the minutes and the hours that go slowly. There is much truth in this statement. Reckoned in terms of the thousands of minutes, and hour upon hour of monotonous, dull routine that go to make up prison life, what a colossal age a year can seem! From a distance, the mere thought of such a life seems prohibitive. But once in it, one finds that adaptation, both physical and mental, comes quite easily.

The prison situation is tailor-made for both the good and the negative in human nature to come to the fore. The numerous deprivations give rise to temptations and concomitant unwholesome manifestations of greed and selfishness. Fortunately, while political prisoners by and large did not succumb to this sort of negative behaviour, it would be overly idealistic to assume that we were entirely exempt. The one deprivation that – perhaps understandably – lends itself more readily to abuse, is food. For years, while the shady common-law elements were in charge of the kitchen, the entire prison population suffered as a result of widespread smuggling. They often worked hand in hand with prison warders. At length the prison authorities caved in and allowed political prisoners to staff the kitchen. This led to immediate improvement, but, alas, did not succeed in wiping out smuggling altogether. There were isolated instances of abuse, including at least one of very serious assault leading to permanent disability. However, thanks to the ANC and PAC uniting to combat this curse, there was a radical and welcome change in the kitchen.

But then it must also be recorded that some political prisoners – thankfully not many – either did not support actions such as hunger strikes, or publicly agreed but ate on the sly. Madiba recalls one young man coming to him and saying: 'Madiba, I want my food, I don't see why I should go without. I have served the struggle for many years.'

Comrades would sometimes eat on the sly. We knew this for a simple reason: by the second day of a hunger strike, no one needed to use the toilet. Yet one morning you would see a fellow going to the toilet. We had our own internal intelligence service, because we knew that certain men were weak in this regard.[3]

For me, the test came when towards the end of our imprisonment we were allowed to receive civilian clothing from outside. Members of my family, especially, and friends from Cape Town sent me more clothes than I needed. I was placed in a quandary. The easiest part was not to have to share with my comrades, because of the significant difference in size. So the surplus remained, and I wrestled with the problem. What should I do with it? Should I simply keep it, or send it back? After much agonising, I kept mainly the clothes that I received from my family members, and gave the surplus to my friend Dullah to return to the senders.

I must confess it wasn't an easy decision at the time, but I felt relieved once I'd taken the step. Alas, the matter did not end there. A few months after my release, I visited Cape Town for work reasons, and stayed at the home of Dullah and Farieda. And there, neatly packed away and waiting for me was the clothing that I had returned! Dullah explained that my friends had refused to accept the clothes, and insisted that all of it be given back to me.

While the craving for food and nourishment is normal, I could never explain our gnawing hunger for photographs, except that frozen images were the nearest we could come to actually being with our dear ones, or even seeing them in the flesh.

Music and films both had the power to transport us back in time or to another place. When Miriam Makeba sang the hits from *King Kong*, we were reminded of so many people we knew, so many happy hours that we had shared with them. When we saw the movie *Holocaust*, I was jolted back to 1951, when I went to Europe. Berlin, Prague, Warsaw: it was all there.

Unlikely as it may sound, I met young people on Robben Island who had no idea of the atrocities committed by the Nazis, and who found it difficult to believe that millions of people were murdered or simply disappeared.

SEPARATION

At the end of March 1982, the Rivonia 7 were separated from one another for the first time. It was after lock-up one night, while we waited for the radio news, that a group of warders appeared, carrying empty cartons, and the commander unlocked four cells.

After eighteen years on the island, Nelson Mandela, Walter Sisulu, Raymond Mhlaba and Andrew Mlangeni were given thirty minutes to pack their belongings before being moved to Pollsmoor Prison, on the mainland.

I sorely missed my colleagues. As May approached I realised that for the first time in years, I would not be spending Walter's birthday with him, and it was a special anniversary, too, his seventieth.

On 18 May, in response to a call by the United Nations Centre Against Apartheid, freedom-loving people around the world sent messages to Walter at Pollsmoor and to Mama Albertina Sisulu in Orlando West.[4] They bombarded 'the racist prime minister of South Africa' with letters of protest, and organised events highlighting the struggle of the people of South Africa, 'especially the plight of political prisoners and detainees'.[5]

In her tribute, Ruth First said of Walter:

He has committed all his life to the struggle for liberation – in the legal days, in the days of the underground and now in prison on Robben Island and in Pollsmoor. And in his person, he is committed to the practice of liberation because he is committed to the liberation of his people, of our people, but he is a liberated man in himself. He uses no devices to overwhelm others. He has pride, but no false pride. He has no arrogance, he has no malice. He is a plain and a straightforward man, he is a soft-spoken man, but he is a committed man, a man who makes no concessions when questions of principle are at stake. He is a decisive man but he is not an authoritarian leader. Politics is his life and he believes in people.

Just a few months later, we would be devastated by the news that Ruth had been killed when a letter bomb exploded in her office in Maputo.

As though I somehow divined that it would be important, I took a special interest, in 1982, in the arrest, trial and sentence of Barbara Hogan. As a bachelor, I generally tended to pay a little more than average attention to reports about our female comrades, but in Barbara's case, my interest went even further, for reasons I could not explain. I managed to obtain a transcript of her court application dealing with prison conditions, but this only increased my latent curiosity about a woman who was serving a ten-year sentence for high treason. It would be a while before I found the answers. It was as if our future as partners was already being shaped. Barbara and I met a few days after her release from prison in February 1990, four months after my release, and we rapidly gravitated towards a romantic relationship, which still continues.

RELIGION

The world is my country; mankind are my brethren;
to do good is my religion. **– Thomas Paine**[6]

While having a deep respect for religious beliefs, I am not a religious person. However, I was born and grew up as a Muslim, and I remain a Muslim. I have read the Koran, I have read the Bible, and in prison I attended as many religious services as possible. The clergymen and spiritual leaders who came to Robben Island all endeavoured to enrich our lives and feed our souls. There were some wonderful human beings among them, and I have both a great regard for their sincerity and an abiding gratitude for the interest and sympathy they unfailingly showed us.

I support the freedom of people to worship as they see fit, but believe in a secular state.

In an age of globalisation, it is inevitable that as knowledge spreads and

enlightenment permeates existing cultures, age-old myths, beliefs and ideas –
and ultimately prejudices – must be shed, but for any life to be truly enriched,
it must embrace and venerate the diversity of many customs.

By 1982, Tokyo Sexwale was my neighbour in B Section. I shall never forget
his enthusiastic reaction to a book on traditional Indian dress, *Nanima's Chest*.[7]
He was simply ecstatic about the book, which was circulated throughout the
prison, an environment in which I would not have thought there would be any
interest in women's clothing, Indian or not! My own views on multiculturalism
are best summed up in a passage by Gandhi: 'I want the culture of all lands to
be blown about my house as freely as possible. But I refuse to be blown off my
feet by any.'

REFLECTIONS IN PRISON

Since time immemorial, ants have been the prisoner's constant companions.
They are so industrious, systematic and well organised that it is fascinating to
watch them at work, and we can learn much from them. When Albert Schweitzer
formulated his philosophy on the reverence of life, he must surely have been
influenced by the humble ant.

Normally, I would let ants be, but when an army of them invaded my cell,
I diligently followed their trail, found and blocked their hole, and killed all the
survivors. I felt bad about this afterwards, and my mind went back to an article
I had read in the *Courier* and copied into one of my notebooks:

> Ants practice many of the arts – and have many of the vices – of man. Each
> colony has a highly organised social system. Ant slaves (prisoners of war) do
> the most irksome jobs. Some slave-owning ants have become so lazy that
> when the colony moves house they have to be carried by slaves. The job
> each ant will do is determined from the time of its birth. Ants are the result
> of Nature's first great experiment in designing social animals. Man came
> only 150 million years later. Has man, as a social animal, progressed much
> further than the ant?[8]

Ours was a small world in prison, and I suppose in some ways our concerns,
interests and anxieties were proportionate. We may have tended to worry
about what really were small things, and we may have exaggerated our fears
and imaginings to some extent.

Before the Rivonia raid, it had been suggested that I should leave the
country. I stubbornly refused, and ended up serving life imprisonment instead.
But I never regretted my decision to stay. Certainly prison was unpleasant, and
especially for the length of time I spent there, but when I chose not to go into
exile, I knew that it was only a matter of time before I was caught.

From what I have read and heard of life in exile, it was fraught with its own difficulties and problems. In some ways, we might have been better off in prison, but in any event, I have always thought our incarceration to be a perfect example of what the poet Milton meant when he wrote: 'They also serve who [only] stand and wait.'

As for those who might have compromised themselves politically, my personal philosophy has always been: We must try to retain old friendships and constantly aspire to win new ones; we should avoid increasing the circle of enemies.

By setting one's expectations too high, people are increasingly and automatically excluded from one's circle, until very few remain. In the process, a lot of bitterness, anger, gossip, disappointment, strife and jealousy are engendered. Perhaps one has to be deprived of normal relationships and interaction in order to appreciate fully the value of human contact, because if asked what the greatest single hardship of imprisonment was, I would have to say the separation from family and friends.

And within that category, the worst sacrifice of all was not being able to see or hear a child for months or years at a stretch.

Children have such faith in miracles. My little niece Aziza wrote and told me how she had prayed for me over Ramadan. I don't think the prison authorities heard her pleas for my release. My grand-nephew Yusuf gave R20 to another niece, Zohra, and told her to send it to me so that I could pay the police to let me go home. She dutifully sent the money, but it wasn't until years later that I went home. And yet, hope kept my soul alive and fed my faith that I would see them all one day, even if I had to miss their childhood.

So often in prison I called up a memory of two little girls, Munira and Farida, going about hand in hand in Schweizer-Reneke. I used to tease them endlessly, and they would always respond with giggles and shy glances. Once, those two little imps went with us to the zoo, and in my mournful reverie, I felt like one of the caged birds and animals we saw, while the two little girls ran forever free.

First offer of release

Only put off until tomorrow what you are willing to die having left undone. — **Pablo Picasso**[9]

On a Saturday afternoon in May 1982, I had unexpected visitors. As soon as the warders led me to the conference room, where we went only to consult with our lawyers, I realised this was no ordinary visit. Normally, we would sit on one side of a Perspex partition, our visitor on the other, in a tiny cubicle monitored by warders.

All kinds of thoughts and fears raced through my mind as I sat at the table alone, wondering what — and who — to expect.

Two or three senior prison officers, including at least one from Pretoria, entered the room, followed by the Robben Island top brass, and my brother Ismail. I was delighted to see my brother, but shocked almost speechless by what he told me.

He had come to convey an offer from the government. I would be released, on condition that I took no part in political activity of any kind.

There was no explanation, no indication of why, after eighteen years, freedom was available not to the Rivonia 7 as a group, not to the sickly and elderly members, but to me, the youngest. Why me? And why now?

I had instinctively already decided to reject the offer, but I told my brother and the waiting prison officers that I could not possibly give them an answer at once. Such an important undertaking on my part should at least be carefully considered, I replied.

When I went back to my cell, I conveyed the offer to my colleagues, and consulted with them on my response. Mandela and Sisulu had gone, of course, but there were others whose opinions I respected, and I had little doubt that they would support my refusal to renounce politics.

But there was no reason we should not exploit this extraordinary set of circumstances to our benefit. Dullah Omar, a long-standing activist and member of the Unity Movement at the time, had been trying for some time to meet with me on the island. Because there were no legal grounds for a visit, he had been turned down repeatedly.

The next morning, I told the prison officers that I could not make an informed decision without discussing the legal implications with my nominated lawyer, and a visit from Dullah was arranged with uncommon speed.

Of course, we spent no time at all debating the merits of the offer. There were none – freedom could not be bought at the cost of my principles and everything I believed in. Dullah agreed to write a letter rejecting the offer, and we spent the rest of our 'consultation' laying the ground for future contact.

The prison officials thought I was a fool and my brother was obviously disappointed, but he made no attempt to influence or pressurise me. Members of my family did not always agree with my political views or support my activities, but they never interfered, and I was grateful for their understanding.

But I remained puzzled about what lay behind the offer. It had come without warning, and either Ismail had been told not to divulge any details of how it came about, or perhaps he did not know. My family had strict instructions from me never to approach the authorities and ask for special treatment of any kind for me, so the initiative must have come from within the government. But who? And why?

By the time I was released unconditionally, Ismail had died, and no one else in the family seemed to know the answers. When I went to parliament, I put the question to Kobie Coetsee, Minister of Justice and Prisons during the 1980s and a member of the Government of National Unity after the 1994 elections. I was also keen to establish why I was transferred to Pollsmoor a few months after the release offer was made.

He told me to make an appointment to see him in his office, and he would satisfy my curiosity. I fully intended doing so, but between the heady atmosphere and sheer hard work that marked the ANC's first few months in government, I never got around to it, and alas, he died before I could.

Official documents to which I have had access have not helped shed light on the matter. On 23 October 1987 an official from the Department of Foreign Affairs, JCH Landman, noted in a secret memorandum that it would not be 'in the national interest' for one of the Rivonia group to die in detention, yet as late as May 1989, the chairman of the Central Release Board was still advising the government that we should not be released unconditionally, and not before July 1990.

My research assistant has suggested that the 1982 offer made to me was part of the divide and rule strategy that preceded the launch of the nefarious House of Delegates and House of Representatives. This makes good sense, and would also explain why I remained on Robben Island when other members of the Rivonia 7 went to Pollsmoor. I was, after all, the only Indian among the trialists, and the House of Delegates was formed just one year later. Had I accepted the offer, it might well have been used to try to drive a wedge between Africans and Indians, and to garner support for the House of Delegates.

Whatever the reason for the release offer, I remained on the island, and a few months later was transferred to Pollsmoor. However much I pined to be outside and to be united with the people I loved, I never experienced a moment's regret for turning down the offer to release me.

While I was at Pollsmoor, I was told that a member of one of the parties in the House of Delegates, Mr Pat Poovalingam, had applied to see me; the authorities wanted to know if I would agree to the visit. Had Pat not joined the House of Delegates, I would gladly have accepted the visit. He and I were in Durban Central Prison together during the 1946 Passive Resistance Campaign, and maintained contact for some time afterwards. But later he distanced himself from the Congress, and to my disappointment joined the Liberal Party. For me this was bad enough, but when he joined the House of Delegates, he had lowered himself to the pits. I regarded the tricameral system and the Bantustans as aberrations.

It was around this time, too, that I began to experience momentary feelings of sadness and regret over the fact that I had not married and raised a family of my own.

∽ 18 ∽

Pollsmoor

If I were to transport myself back to 1963 and look at the future from that point I'd find it difficult to believe that the time would come when I would actually long for the smell of the soil after rain; or simply to feel sand and soil with my hands.[1]

Around 10 a.m. on Thursday 21 October 1982, I was called to the prison commander's office. 'Pack up,' he told me, 'you are leaving this afternoon.'

No one would tell me where I was going, and after eighteen years on Robben Island, I had less than four hours to pack my belongings and say goodbye to my friends. Amid the excitement of being moved and the trauma of leaving my colleagues, there was barely time to reflect on the supreme irony of some warders making me an unwitting accomplice to their illegal activities!

I had a number of cartons containing books and other effects, and the warders, unbeknown to me, had stuffed parcels of frozen crayfish – caught without the requisite permits – into boxes, which they placed among mine, telling me hastily that their counterparts on the mainland would take delivery of the cartons at the Cape Town harbour.

As the 2 p.m. deadline neared, there was time for no more than a quick handshake with my colleagues, and then it was through the main gate and onto the ferryboat.

Despite the fact that I was aiding and abetting, albeit unconsciously, their crayfish smuggling operation, none of my escorts would reveal my destination, but they couldn't resist a few last jibes. 'You'll never see Mandela again,' said one.

But, around 6.30 p.m., I *was* reunited with Mandela – as well as with Walter Sisulu, Raymond Mhlaba and Andrew Mlangeni, at Pollsmoor Prison. It was wonderful to see them again, but none of us had any idea why I had suddenly been transferred.

When opposition leader Frederik Van Zyl Slabbert asked the commissioner of prisons why I had been moved to Pollsmoor, he was evidently told: 'That coolie tried to be too big, he tried to take Mandela's place on the island, so we transferred him.'

On the day of my transfer I was given the very first letter written to me on Robben Island in November 1964. It was from my brother Solly, and had been withheld because of an 'offending' reference to the outcome of the British election, which said: 'Harold Wilson and the Labour Party are now in power.'

Not only was the letter held back, but the security police made it impossible for Solly to visit me on the island by ensuring that he was not issued with the permit needed by Indians to travel from one province to another.

When I arrived at Pollsmoor I was also given an Eid card and a photograph of a baby, captioned: 'The day I was exactly one year old. With lots of love to my Daddy'. It was from Djamilla Cajee, whom I had named some sixteen years before.

The move to Pollsmoor came in the middle of preparations for my final examinations for a BA Hons degree in history, so it was not until January that I really settled in.

For the first time since our arrests, five of us were sharing a communal cell. We were all early risers, but Mandela was up before anyone else to do his exercises – running on the spot and a few laps around the cell.

Living in such close proximity, we learnt a few other things about Madiba as well. One very cold night, we were all kept from our sleep by the loud chirping of a cricket. Eventually, Mandela left his bed and captured the noisy insect by throwing a towel over it. He went into the bathroom, and we naturally assumed he was going to flush the insect down the toilet, but instead he opened the window and released it into the dark.

Of course the cricket continued chirping throughout the night, thanks to Madiba's concern for the preservation of all life. We should have expected it – he wouldn't kill invading ants or hovering bees, either.

VISITS AND ROUTINES

In 1983 I instructed Advocate Dullah Omar to institute legal proceedings against the government on two fronts: refusing to allow Zohra to visit me for fourteen years, and refusing to allow me to enrol for my MA degree.

Over the next six years I had dozens of 'legal' visits from Dullah Omar, but a warder, due to a mixture of kindness and negligence, recorded only a small number. At his first or second visit, Dullah brought two packages of samoosas; he gave the warder one package, and immediately asked if he could give the other to me. Thereafter, on almost every visit, his wife Farieda ensured that his bulky briefcase had more food and fruit than law books.

By 1985 Dullah was spending so much time in 'consultations' with me that I jokingly suggested that we should prepare a cell for him. It was not long afterwards that he was detained under the state of emergency, and incarcerated in Pollsmoor Prison. Our 'consultations' resumed after his release, and continued until the day before we were transferred to Johannesburg prison.

Dullah was a senior official in the United Democratic Front, and many of his colleagues were also held. My thoughts went out to Farieda and their children, as well as the families of all the other detainees.

Dullah and I became good friends, and I was privileged to share some of his last moments before he died of leukaemia in March 2004. Just hours before he passed away, I visited him in hospital and whispered a few words in his ear, to which he responded. Like many others, I was honoured to have known and called Dullah Omar a friend and comrade.

I did not much care for Pollsmoor. Strange as it may seem, I missed the island – not the prison or the pettiness of the warders, but the 'family' we had formed in B Section, and the setting.

As a descendant of peasants, I always was a rustic man at heart, and I longed to see the grass and trees and flowers, the ostriches, tortoises and buck that roamed the island.

Pollsmoor was a concrete edifice, cold and mean. One day, I saw a rainbow, and was quite overwhelmed by its beauty. I must have seen hundreds of rainbows in my life, but that is the one I remember.

On the credit side, our relatives no longer had to make the trip by ferryboat – often over rough and choppy seas – and since all the water at Pollsmoor was fresh, there were no more salty showers or stiff laundry!

The food at Pollsmoor was far superior in both quality and quantity to any other prison of our collective experience, but the diet still became monotonous. We were permitted to purchase a few additional groceries with our toiletries every month, and to receive food from outside at Eid.

On our first festival at Pollsmoor, Fatima Meer organised a veritable feast, flown to Cape Town from Durban. There were only five of us, but she sent enough food for fifty, hoping that the other prisoners might share our bounty. Other well-wishers followed suit, and eventually we had to appeal to them to cut back on the quantities, as no other prisoner was allowed anywhere near us.

Mindful of the pleasure our tiny patch of garden on the island had brought, Madiba decided to establish another one at Pollsmoor. In the absence of a suitable piece of ground, Madiba persuaded our jailers to provide a dozen or so oil drums, cut in half lengthwise, and fill them with soil. It was really his garden and he nurtured it almost obsessively, spending an inordinate amount of time and energy on his plants. Our contribution was largely confined to enjoying the end products.

When Mandela went to hospital, he left me in charge of the garden after writing out two pages of detailed instructions. Now, I knew absolutely nothing about gardening, but luck and nature combined to yield a first-class harvest of onions and a profusion of spinach. We also had a fair crop of leeks, a handful of beans and a few dozen berries. The beetroot and maize looked promising, but the tomatoes and cucumbers produced specimens that no self-respecting salad would publicly acknowledge as kin. Fortunately, my colleagues were not exactly gourmets, so my offerings were generally received with praise and appreciation.

Madiba paid almost as much attention to his physical appearance as to his plants, and his insistence on a certain brand of hair oil sparked what became known as 'The Pantene Crisis'. No substitute would do, and Christo Brand was instructed by the prison chiefs to scour the pharmacies of Cape Town on Mandela's behalf. I think he even took the matter up with Helen Suzman on one of her visits.

Brand finally managed to locate the last remaining stock of Pantene – possibly in the whole of South Africa! – and bought the few he managed to find. No one wanted to go through that particular 'mass action' again.

A few years later, some of us conspired to give Madiba a surprise birthday gift. I managed to acquire two bottles of Pantene from a friend in the US. Walter and I, together with Brand, went off to Pretoria, and in the presence of a media contingent, surprised him with the two bottles, which were presented to him by Brand from behind a huge cardboard cut-out in the shape of a Pantene bottle. He thoroughly enjoyed the surprise.

One of the people who brought us food on Eid was Ramesh Vassen, a lawyer who was tremendously good to us while we were at Pollsmoor. On 24 July 1983 his little daughter Priya accompanied him to the prison. She was too small and too scared to wait alone for him in the car, so the warders relented and allowed her to come in with her father.

For the first time in twenty years, I was able to hug and kiss a child. Ours was a world devoid of the laughter and chatter of children, and when I returned to my cell after meeting Priya, my colleagues could see how excited I was. It would be several more years before I would know such joy again.

On 31 May 1985, I wrote to Dullah: 'Priya remains the only child whom I was able to touch, cuddle and kiss. Since then I've had a number of visits with children, but I had to see them all through the glass. Because of the antediluvian "first degree" rule I may not get contact visits from my nieces and nephews and their kids.'

The year before, Zohra's sister Shireen had brought her two-year-old daughter, Shameez, to see me. She was a lively little girl, and as I watched through the glass partition, she danced and sang and played. She had only been in the visiting room a few minutes when she pointed to a warder and said 'police'. Almost immediately, she followed up with: 'I don't like police.'

'Well,' I thought to myself with amusement, '*there's* a left-wing radical in the making!' Alas, the next words from Shameez, looking straight at me, were, 'I don't like you!'

Another special visitor during 1984 was Rookie Saloojee, my dear friend Babla's widow. She had refused to be cowed by his terrible death, and had stepped into the breach with courage and enthusiasm.

I never really got over Babla's loss. The years have taken a heavy toll on my near and dear ones – at last count, there were around eighty names on the mournful list – but if anyone ever asked who I missed the most, I would reply, without hesitation, in addition to my mother and family members, it would be Babla and Aminabai Pahad. The one was more than a brother to me, the other a second mother.

EVENTS OUTSIDE

The experience of the war, like the experience of every crisis in human history, of every great disaster and every sudden turn in human life, stuns and shatters some, but it enlightens and hardens others.
                                        – Vladimir Ilyich Lenin, 1915[2]

The early eighties witnessed the revival of the trade union movement and the rise of the powerful United Democratic Front. Although we had finally been granted access to newspapers, our hunger now was for information about the movement – we needed to know what was happening within the movement and what political developments were taking place, not just what the media reported. Apartheid's fortress was no longer impregnable and the march to freedom was unstoppable, but we wanted reliable reports on every step.

The UDF was formed in 1983 in direct response to the government's introduction of a tricameral parliament and various other 'reforms'. Along with Helen Joseph, Walter Sisulu, Nelson Mandela, Govan Mbeki and other Rivonia colleagues, I was also named a patron of the organisation.

The government's restructured parliament was designed to accommodate the Coloured and Indian communities by offering them sham representation in the House of Representatives and the House of Delegates respectively. Members were almost generally those who had been discredited by their own people as puppets of apartheid, and the whole system was a device to shore up the apartheid regime as it came increasingly under siege.

There were no black warders on Robben Island, and at Pollsmoor the black warders were not allowed anywhere near us, lest we win them over to our cause. But we did run into Suitcase van Rensburg, of swastika tattoo fame, at Pollsmoor. Oddly enough, he denied ever having had anything to do with us.

During a single week in September 1983, three of the important people in my life died: the Reverend Michael Scott, Advocate Vernon Berrangé and my hero, Dr Yusuf Dadoo. It had never entered my mind that we would never see Dadoo again. He was a man of courage and devotion, a patriot and champion of the underdog, a brilliant, generous, modest and hospitable humanitarian with a keen sense of humour and a powerful oratory. His death was a source of great pain to me.

ANOTHER OFFER OF RELEASE

Life sentences in South Africa can actually last a lifetime, but the State President reviews all cases after 21 years and can commute the sentence.[3]

What had become perennial rumours of our release were crushed in 1984 by the president, PW Botha. The media reported him saying that Mandela had been sentenced after a fair trial, and as a political leader, Botha would not interfere with the courts.

His attitude was no doubt influenced by a top secret report from the Special Branch to a meeting on 28 November of the intelligence community, which read as follows in translation:

The advanced age of some of the Rivonia prisoners does not, unfortunately, make them any less dangerous as propagandists or messengers of the ANC. In fact, their age heightens the danger and evokes sympathy that makes it even more difficult to implement counter-measures. The best example to illustrate this situation is that of Oscar Mpeta, who was treated with unwarranted sympathy by the court and as a result, despite his age and poor health, continues to be at the forefront of attacks on the state and resistance to the new dispensation.

Within three months the government had revised its hard-line policy on our release. On the morning of 8 February 1985, Mandela was summoned by the head of the prison. He returned with the news that Botha had offered to release all political prisoners, provided we undertook not to fuel the flames of the violence that was sweeping the country.

Our response, dated 13 February and signed by Mandela, Sisulu, Mlangeni, Mhlaba and me, emphatically rejected this condition. This is an abbreviated version of the letter we sent to President PW Botha:

Sir

Copies of the Hansard Parliamentary record of 25th January to 1st February 1985 were delivered to us on 8th February.

We note that during the debate in the House of Assembly you indicated that you were prepared to release prisoners in our particular category provided that we unconditionally renounce violence as a means of furthering our political objectives.

We have given earnest consideration to your offer, but we regret to inform you that it is not acceptable in its present form. We hesitate to associate you with a move which, on a proper analysis, appears to be no more than a shrewd and calculated attempt to mislead the world into the belief that you have magnanimously offered us release from prison which we ourselves have rejected. Coming in the face of such unprecedented and widespread demands for our release your remarks can only be seen as the height of cynical politicking.

We refuse to be party to anything which is really intended to create division, confusion and uncertainty within the African National Congress at a time when the unity of the organisation has become a matter of crucial importance to the whole country. The refusal by the Department of Prisons to allow us to consult fellow prisoners in other prisons has confirmed our view.

Just as some of us refused the humiliating condition that we should be released to the Transkei, we also reject your offer on the same ground. No self-respecting human being will demean and humiliate himself by making a commitment of the nature you demand. You ought not to perpetuate our imprisonment by the simple expedient of setting conditions which, to your own knowledge, we will never under any circumstances accept.

Our political beliefs are largely influenced by the Freedom Charter, a programme of principles whose basic premise is the equality of all human beings. It is not only the clearest repudiation of all forms of racial discrimination, but also the country's most advanced statement of political principles. It calls for universal franchise in a united South Africa and for the equitable distribution of the wealth of the country.

Apartheid, which is condemned not only by blacks, but also by a substantial section of the whites, is the greatest single source of violence against our people. As leader of the National Party, which seeks to uphold apartheid through force and violence, we expect you to be the first to renounce violence.

Again on pages 318–319 you state that you cannot talk with people who do not want to cooperate, that you hold talks with every possible leader who is prepared to renounce violence.

It is clear from this statement that you would prefer to talk only to people who accept apartheid, even though they are emphatically repudiated by the very community on whom you want to impose it, through violence if necessary.

If your government seriously wants to halt the escalating violence, the only method open is to declare your commitment to end the evil of apartheid and show your willingness to negotiate with the true leaders at local and national levels. At no time have the oppressed people, especially the youth, displayed such unity in action, such resistance to racial oppression, and such prolonged demonstrations in the face of brutal military and political action. Those who 'cooperate' with you, who have served you so loyally throughout these troubled years, have not at all helped you to stem the rapidly rising tide. The coming confrontation will only be averted if the following steps are taken without delay.

1. The government must renounce violence first.
2. It must dismantle apartheid.
3. It must unban the ANC.
4. It must free all who have been imprisoned, banished or exiled for their opposition to apartheid.
5. It must guarantee free political activity.

A private letter to Paul Joseph captured my personal feelings on the matter:

To many, it may have seemed as if we were a hair's breadth away from 'freedom'. But in fact, from the very moment that the announcement was made, it was already a non-starter. Now I don't want to indulge in any false modesty when I say that I haven't got the stuff that heroes are made of; but really I didn't have to go through any sleepless nights to arrive at the decision. It was so patently designed to humiliate us that there just could be no other decision for me but to reject it. But please understand that I'm not for a moment holding it against anybody who has accepted the offer.

In matters such as these it is unwise to ignore individual cases; for one may find that there may in fact be differing circumstances which may lead individuals to take another approach. So it is not advisable to point fingers and condemn without taking into account all the factors involved.

Every so often, the media would speculate that our release was imminent. Expectant crowds would gather at the prison gates and media crews would camp out there for hours, but it was just an annual charade that sold newspapers and appeased the government's few remaining allies in the international community.

It was as well that we had long since seen through the ploys, otherwise each new bout of 'release fever' would have caused me to suffer from hypertension, ulcers or worse. In the event, I treated the government's games with what former Robben Islander Mandla Masondo would call 'philosophic detachment'.

REPRESSION AND REFORM

Things fall apart: the centre cannot hold;
Mere anarchy is loosed upon the world,
The blood-dimmed tide is loosed, and everywhere
The ceremony of innocence is drowned.
                    – WB Yeats, 'The Second Coming'

South Africa was on a downward spiral to destruction. Violence and callousness marked the actions of the security forces, which had moved into townships around the country in great numbers.

Thousands of activists were detained without trial and there were running battles in the dusty township streets on a daily basis. But no matter what the state threw at them, the masses fought back with resolution and courage. On 20 July 1985, for only the second time in twenty-five years, a state of emergency was declared.

Ironically, even as the government unleashed its iron fist against apartheid's opponents, it repealed one of its most discriminatory laws, the Mixed Marriages Act.

July 11 had marked the twenty-first anniversary of the Rivonia raid, but there was no symbolic key for us. I submitted an application to subscribe to *Hansard*, the official public record of parliamentary proceedings. It was turned down, and years later I found a note in my prison file explaining why: 'Taking into account that the prisoner is not studying, he does not have a valid reason to subscribe to *Hansard*. It appears that the prisoner wants to obtain it only out of curiosity and to keep abreast of current political decisions. His application is refused.'

After Raymond Mhlaba married Dideka at Pollsmoor in 1986, I held a double distinction among the Rivonia 7. Not only was I the youngest, but I was now also the only bachelor. The ceremony was small but meaningful, with Walter and Nelson acting as witnesses.

During 1986, there was an avalanche of improvements in prison conditions. We were allowed to watch television, even videos, and to wear personal jewellery, such as rings and wristwatches. We could have thirty visits a year, each lasting forty minutes, and as A category prisoners, we were entitled to 'contact' visits, which meant we were no longer separated by partitions, but could meet our visitors face to face. Our correspondence quota was pushed up to forty incoming and forty outgoing letters a year, and we were allowed to write essays or poetry, but not biographies or books.

And, although none of us took up the offer, prisoners in the highest category of privilege were also allowed to keep birds or fish as pets. The reforms were quite radical, and made a huge difference to our lives. In August, Djamilla Cajee visited me for the first time. I was thrilled to finally meet the teenager whose name I had chosen, and we bonded almost instantly. Djamilla awakened deep-seated fatherly feelings in me that I had not even realised were there, and our visit left me feeling warm and happy.

On 15 November we were given our own TV set, and delighted in the weekly escapades of the Huxtable family in *The Cosby Show*. Little Rudi was my favourite, though I also enjoyed *Cagney and Lacey* and the regular *boeremusiek* contests, which took me back to my childhood in rural Schweizer-Reneke.

WITH WALTER SISULU

He who wishes to secure the good of others has
already secured his own. — Confucius[4]

When Madiba was discharged from hospital after his prostate surgery in 1985, he did not come back to our communal cell, but was moved to a different part of the prison, alone. We were unhappy about the separation, but Mandela advised: 'Look chaps, I don't think we should oppose this thing. Perhaps something good will come of this. I'm now in a position where the government can make an approach to us.'[5]

We saw him only occasionally after that, and before long, we, too, were moved to quite roomy and self-contained cells. Raymond and Andrew shared one, while Walter and I were next door. They were the most comfortable cells any of us had ever seen, with proper beds – and crisp white sheets – cupboards, chairs and tables. We also had our own bathrooms.

The most memorable years of my incarceration were those when I was privileged to have Walter as my cellmate. At the risk of overdoing the adjectives, he was humane, caring, courageous, foresighted, knowledgeable, sober, balanced, objective – and so many other things as well.

Walter was the acknowledged authority on the liberation movement's history. It had been captured, on the island, by Laloo Chiba and Mike Dingake, and smuggled out for safekeeping, but Walter knew it all by heart. I should have kept a detailed record of our many conversations on the subject, but to my shame the relaxation of the rules offered too many diversions. Apart from our nightly sessions in front of the TV set, we spent many hours listening to pop music, thanks to audio tapes that chief warder Christo Brand brought us. Walter actually loved classical music, but he took to pop quite readily, and Whitney Houston became a firm favourite.

The UDF comrades also kept us supplied with excellent videos, and we watched banned films like *Cry Freedom*, in which Denzel Washington played Steve Biko, and the entire series of Alex Haley's *Roots* before it was flighted by the SABC. We also thoroughly enjoyed the many hours of the concert at London's Wembley Stadium in honour of Madiba's seventieth birthday.

While Walter made good use of the exercise bicycle at our disposal, he was also a great drinker of tea, and especially coffee. For months he hungered for the particular brand of coffee that used to be served on board trains in South Africa, and we finally established that it was Ellis Brown. We laid in a supply, and every Friday and Saturday night before going to bed, I prepared a flask of coffee for Walter to enjoy first thing in the morning.

His worst enemy was winter, when arthritis plagued him and he seemed to have a chronic cold or flu. As Andimba Toivo ya Toivo had done on the island, Walter would take off his shoes and socks, find a warm spot in the exercise yard and sit there quietly, reading.

My most haunting and painful memory of Walter was formed one Saturday night. We had both turned in, and I read for a while. Walter was so silent that at some point I glanced over at his bed, to make sure he was all right.

He was sitting up, carefully studying his photograph album. For what must have been the best part of an hour, he slowly paged through his collection of family photographs, occasionally lifting the album up close to his eyes and peering intently at a page. Then he would put the album down on his legs and lean back against the pillows, deeply immersed in thought.

The expression on his face was the saddest I had ever seen. Once or twice, I thought I saw the shadow of a smile as he turned a page, but the overwhelming feeling emanating from his side of the cell was sadness.

This was a Walter whom our colleagues would never see. By day, he wore a constant smile and his concern was always for the welfare of others. But on Saturday nights he paged through his photo album in silent communion with Mama Albertina, Max, Lungi, Lindi, Zwelakhe and Nkuli, and with Gerald and Beryl and Jongumzi.

Our leaders were so consumed by and inextricably linked to the struggle that it was all too easy to see them as one-dimensional politicians. But that wasn't who they were at all, and that Saturday night at Pollsmoor, I was privy to Walter Sisulu the family man – a devoted husband and loving father, deprived of a normal home life by an abiding need to serve his people.

In half a century of knowing Nelson Mandela and Walter Sisulu, I came to know one sure thing: it is impossible to speak of the one without mentioning the other.

Two distinct and unique individuals, these two struggle leaders were inextricably bound by their foresight, courage, wisdom and shared experiences.

We loved Walter like a father, revered Nelson as a hero. Two more selfless men would be hard to find, but Madiba was the born leader, Sisulu the elder statesman.

Mike Dingake once observed that Laloo Chiba was the most generous person he had ever met; he gave away almost everything he possessed. This was certainly true, but there was one other person who outdid even Laloo when it came to sharing, and that was Walter. In all the time I knew him, he never imbibed the concept of 'private' property, and when he had nothing more of his own to share, he would simply expropriate the belongings of his comrades! At one time or another, we were all victims of Walter's extremely giving nature. It was just one of the many traits that endeared him to all of us.

Walter and I trudged the path to freedom in tandem. We were together on campaigns, at conferences and in court cases. We shared the joy of his daughter Lindiwe's birth and the hardship of several prisons. We were issued with banning orders on the same day and went underground at approximately the same juncture. We were arrested together at Liliesleaf Farm and released from prison simultaneously, twenty-six years later.

He was the man on whom I relied most heavily for political guidance and counsel, and one of only two mentors with whom I felt comfortable enough to discuss my delicate personal situation, the other being Ismail Meer.

When I became romantically involved with Sylvia in 1961, I was fully conscious that if our relationship was exposed, there would be adverse consequences, not only for the two of us, but for our political organisations.

My political involvement implicitly required that I conduct myself in a manner that would not reflect negatively on the liberation movement. Walter was seventeen years my senior, but I knew he would not regard my forbidden romance as a youthful indiscretion.

When I approached him, he carefully considered both the long-term implications and the immediate danger of possible arrest and imprisonment. His view, in the end, was that the Immorality Act and the Mixed Marriages Act were no less unjust than the six laws targeted by the ANC and the South African Indian Congress through the Defiance Campaign. On that basis, he gave us his blessing, along with an earnest warning that we should be both discreet and vigilant. It was a great relief.

TALKS BEGIN

How tired he (the general Crassus) was of killing and death and torture! Yet where did one go to escape it? More and more they were creating a society where life rested on death. Never before in the whole history of the world had slaughter been elevated to such a place of precision and quantity and where did it end and where would it end?

— Howard Fast, *Spartacus*[6]

Mandela's new accommodation at Pollsmoor consisted of three cells on the ground floor – the prison equivalent of a private apartment! He was completely isolated, and our initial efforts to see him were in vain.

Not too long after he was moved, Christo Brand, the chief warder, came to see us. We had got to know one another well, and I sensed that he had something on his mind, but was not sure that he should tell me, lest I shared it with Walter, Raymond and Andrew. Eventually, I reassured him that I did not expect him to disclose anything that made him feel uncomfortable, and he just came right out and said it: 'We took Mandela to Kobie Coetsee's house last night.'

It didn't take a political analyst to understand the implications of this startling news. Unbeknown to Mandela, Christo kept me informed of events after that. Naturally, he had no idea what direction discussions were taking, but my cellmates and I concluded that, after serious deliberation, Madiba had decided to engage the enemy in talks, aimed at initiating dialogue with the ANC.

In his autobiography, he later confirmed that he had decided to take the first step without consulting us, or the leadership in Lusaka: 'I knew that my colleagues upstairs would condemn my proposal. There are times when a leader must move out ahead of the flock ...'[7]

He was wrong about our reactions. Two of us supported his action whole-heartedly and the other two accepted the situation with some reservations, but none of us condemned his decision. In due course, he briefed each of us individually about his initiative. Walter, according to Madiba, was 'uncomfortable and at best lukewarm'. He did not oppose the talks in principle, but would have preferred the first move to come from the government. Raymond Mhlaba and Andrew Mlangeni felt that Madiba should have launched negotiations years before.

As for me, Mandela later wrote: 'His response was negative; he was as resolutely against what I was suggesting as Raymond and Andrew were in favour. Even more strongly than Walter, he felt that by initiating talks it would appear that we were capitulating. Kathy was adamant; he felt I was going down the wrong path. But, despite his misgivings, he said he would not stand in my way.'[8]

As the secret talks progressed, I came to realise that my initial judgment had been flawed, but I was never really reconciled to this course of action.

The last time we met with Madiba at Pollsmoor was on 14 August 1988. It was not a satisfactory encounter, because he was clearly unwell and drank one glass of water after another. Either later that day or the next, we learnt that he had been admitted to hospital, suffering from tuberculosis. He did not return to Pollsmoor.

∽ 19 ∽

Last Steps to Freedom

People said that time was an enemy. It wasn't true. Time wore away the husk; the insincere sorrows and artificial passions disappeared, but the genuine sentiments remained. – **Ilya Ehrenburg,** ***The Fall of Paris***[1]

In the second half of 1988, at the age of seventy, Nelson Mandela was moved to Victor Verster Prison at Paarl, the last of the numerous jails in which he spent so many years of his life.

Although we were housed in different sections of Pollsmoor, a special concession on his birthday in July had allowed us to order food from outside and eat it together.

It was hard to believe, but I was almost fifty-nine, seven years older than Walter had been when we were arrested in 1963. The Rivonia 7 were ageing gracefully. Prison life might not have arrested the process, but it certainly seemed to slow the march of time.

THE ISITHWALANDWE AWARD

Towards the end of 1988, I felt compelled to smuggle the following letter to Oliver Tambo:

My Dear Brother,

My main purpose is to put right certain perceptions about myself. I am concerned that an image is being fostered, both locally and abroad, which is not strictly in keeping with my real status and contribution in the political field.

The recent conferment of the Isithwalandwe Award [the ANC's highest honour] upon me, and other proposed plans, have aggravated the position; and induced me to write this.

Before proceeding further I wish to very clearly state that I feel most grateful and proud of the honour that the movement has seen fit to bestow upon me, and I sincerely hope that my action will not be taken amiss. I do, however, feel that I should state my feelings. I do so, not out of modesty, but because I believe that it is in the general interest of the movement to promote an accurate record of events and personalities in the struggle.

I believe that my role in the struggle, and my status in the organisations, did not warrant my inclusion among the recipients of Isithwalandwe. I do not for a moment minimise the significance of my 25 years in prison, but if it is felt that this achievement should be recognised, consideration should perhaps have been given to either a separate award for prisoners, or even Isithwalandwe Class 1, 2, 3.

Placing my name in the same league as Luthuli, Dadoo, Huddleston, Sisulu, Mandela, Kotane, etc, does not only not reflect the correct historical and political position, but carries the danger of reducing the prestige of the award.

It has been my understanding that Isithwalandwe is intended to honour outstanding national leaders for their exceptional qualities and leadership roles, for initiating innovative thought and direction, and for their pivotal contribution to the struggle.

I am not attempting to play down my long involvement in the movement, but I do not think that fact alone qualifies me for elevation to the 'first team'.

I understand that there are tentative plans outside to celebrate my 60th birthday in 1989. There is a suggestion of some sort of publication to coincide with the occasion.

The sentiments I have expressed above apply here as well. For basically the same reasons, I think that whatever is done should be commensurate with the information I have provided about myself, as well as my views.

But, more important than that, I think the following should be borne in mind:

There had been plans to publish a biography of Walter on the occasion of his 70th birthday in 1982. This did not materialise. In 1987 he turned 75; for all intents and purposes, the birthday passed virtually unobserved by the movement. No one will dispute the fact that he is among the most senior leaders of the liberation movement, and if any birthday deserved to be widely observed, it was his.

No doubt there must have been reasons for the omission, and I am not for a moment expressing any criticisms. At the same time, it should be expected that at some stage the omission will invite questions. Any 'high profile' celebration of my 60th birthday will serve to focus more strongly on the non-observance of Walter's.

LITTLE ONES

Children do not belong in prison. None of us ever thought otherwise, but we nonetheless relished the rare occasions when our visitors included little ones. Every child was a breath of fresh air, a reminder of our responsibilities, an alluring glimpse of the solid foundation on which tomorrows would be built, a reassurance that we remained part of the world outside.

After Priya's unforgettable visit in 1983, it would be five long years before I cuddled another child. In August 1988, with great joy and trepidation, I held a baby, little Khatija, for the first time. I was so worried that I would not do it right – she was so small and delicate – that I handed her back to her mother almost immediately, but it was a wonderful experience.

For more than twenty-three years we had lived in a closed, regimented world of adult males in uniform. Cut off from normality, one almost became enslaved to routine. Weaknesses and strengths became accentuated; prejudice, virtue, aptitude, the full gamut of emotion and attitude, lurked just below the surface. The situation essentially demanded that one adopt a child's approach to life: guileless, generous, unselfish, unburdened by property, oblivious to red tape, unfamiliar with unrighteousness and injustice, wholly carefree. Our group included some truly remarkable men, whose humanity, patience and empathy greatly eased the burden of incarceration, but could not help us escape the shackles, encumbrances and inhibitions of the adult world.

Fatima and Ismail Meer's daughter Shehnaz had applied repeatedly to visit me and been turned down. A young warder with whom we had developed a good relationship suggested she should pretend to be my niece, Rabia, and come to the prison on a specific day.

The plan worked, and Shehnaz arrived with her white husband, Joel, and two daughters. The older girl, Nadia, was a sweet child, who lost little time recounting a recent adventure.

'Uncle, last week we went to the beach, and PW Botha's police came, and the helicopters came, and the dogs, and they chased us, and we had to run.'

This was at the time when activists were waging a defiance campaign against the government's policy of reserving beaches, and the waves that lapped them, for whites only. Nadia's story made an unexpected impact on the warder monitoring our visit, and afterwards he told me: 'This is madness. Why can't they [the government] allow these people to swim? I don't see anything wrong with that.'

It was most likely the first time he had been exposed to people who were directly affected by government policies that he had read about or heard about, and realised that far from being threatening ogres, they were just two attractive young people with a couple of sweet daughters, who had been chased off a beach.

The irony was that the warder had not even realised that my visitors were a mixed race couple! On the way back to the cells, he made the comment: 'You know, your niece's husband looks just like a white man.'

On another visit, little Nadia walked through the prison with the confidence of a regular caller, ignoring both convention and prison regulations, and climbed up into my lap, from where she chattered happily. For that brief, precious time, I was as free as any man beyond the cold, grey walls.

After being prevented from visiting me for fourteen years, my niece Zohra was finally granted permission to do so after I had taken legal action against the government.

MADIBA MOVED TO VICTOR VERSTER

In December 1988 Nelson Mandela was transferred from the clinic in Cape Town to Victor Verster Prison in Paarl. Two days before the move, Walter was allowed to visit him. They had lunch together, but although the private hospital was in the five-star category, Walter came away unimpressed by the food, and not unduly enthusiastic about the medical facility either. Throughout his life, Walter remained a man of humble tastes and simple needs.

During the lunch he was introduced to Appletiser, but Walter was a tee-totaller, and when he saw the tiny bubbles in the golden liquid, he concluded it was some or other alcoholic drink. When Madiba added ice cubes to his glass, Walter was sure he was correct. Eventually, he was persuaded that it was nothing more than pure apple juice, and took a few sips, though he swore he felt groggy immediately.

Still, something about the beverage must have pleased him, as he later suggested we should order Appletiser for our Christmas meal. I teased him that he was an inveterate alcoholic, but he just laughed.

Madiba's new surroundings were vastly different from the tiny Cell No. 7

on Robben Island or the larger accommodation he had at Pollsmoor. He was settled in a house that had been recently vacated by a senior prison officer, which was equipped with all the accoutrements that form part of a modern household – a TV, radio, microwave and refrigerator. The fully furnished house had a kitchen, bedrooms, dining room, lounge, exercise room, bathroom and toilet, and a specially equipped doctor's consulting room.

For Mandela, gone were the green uniform, the metal dish and spoon. No more would he wield a pick or shovel in a lime quarry, or be forced out of bed at 5.30 every morning by a piercing bell. He could bid farewell to the obligatory 'lights-out' of 11 p.m., and, best of all, he could eat all the bread he wanted.

He had a full-time chef, who prepared meals in accordance with Madiba's wishes, and a well-stocked liquor cabinet for guests, though he, like Walter, did not imbibe.

There were no bars on his windows, no cold stone floor beneath his feet. He could bath in steaming hot water at any time of the day or night, and watch TV from the comfort of an armchair.

But he could still not leave the prison precinct.

Justice minister Kobie Coetsee described Mandela's status during this time as somewhere between prison and freedom, and not everyone was pleased that his life had taken such a dramatic turn. The rumour that Madiba had 'sold out' reached even the ANC leadership in exile.

Walter Sisulu moved

On 15 March 1989 – the infamous Ides of March – Walter, too, was moved – to a cell in a different section of the prison, suddenly and alone. Two days later, I wrote to the head of the prison:

Sir,
I am writing this letter in my personal capacity, and not on behalf of my colleagues.

I was very surprised and disappointed at the manner in which Mr Sisulu was removed from our section. He is old and not in the best of health, and it was painful to see him being treated the way he was. In my view, the high degree of secrecy, the over-dramatisation and the haste were unwarranted, and I fear that the day's happenings could have adversely affected his blood pressure.

For the record, this is what happened on 15 March:
(i) At about 9.30 a.m. Mr Sisulu was informed that the Officer Commanding wished to see him. He was given 10 minutes to get ready. No reasons were given and the first thought that came to his mind was that there may be unwelcome news about a member of his family.

(ii) At about 2.30 p.m. my two colleagues and I were told that the Head of the Prison wished to see us at Maximum Prison.

(iii) While we were waiting to see you, Mr Sisulu was brought to this section and hurriedly told to pack all his belongings.

(iv) As a result of his insistence, and our request to you, we were eventually allowed to meet Mr Sisulu and spend about 45 minutes with him. He seemed upset by the day's events. I could detect signs of tension in him.

Sir, with due respect, I cannot believe that the good order, discipline and security of the Prison could have in any way been threatened

(i)   if Mr Sisulu, and we, were informed beforehand that he was to visit Mr Mandela, as was done when he visited Mr Mandela at the Clinic, and when we visited him at Victor Verster;

(ii) if Mr Sisulu was informed beforehand that he was going to be removed from us and accommodated in the cells previously occupied by Mr Mandela; as you are probably aware, right up to the time that he was taken to those cells he was left with the impression that he was going to be taken to the Constantia Clinic;

(iii) if, instead of us being taken to Maximum, we had been allowed to be with him and help him pack his belongings in a calm and relaxed atmosphere.

I am anxious about the fact that he is being kept alone. The authorities are well aware of the fears that I have expressed about those cells, and I can only hope that his stay there will be very short. Having stayed together for such a long time, I am particularly concerned about the effects of the oncoming cold days upon Mr Sisulu's health. The lack of company is also likely to have adverse effects.

There are a number of practical disadvantages he is likely to suffer as a result of his staying alone: the primary one being that at his age and state of health he should not be made to stay by himself, and should always have someone staying with him.

(i) There are a number of things for which he needs assistance. For instance, he has to be given eye drops regularly, including at night. From time to time, especially in colder weather, he may need to be massaged for his arthritic pains.

(ii) From time to time I had to translate for him from Afrikaans.

I am mentioning just a few of [the] deprivations he must be suffering. I cannot overemphasise the fact that his greatest need is to have company, and assistance at all times.

I wish to make it clear once more that I am not writing this letter in order to make allegations against the Prisons Department. I am seriously concerned about the well being of my colleague, and I appeal to you to do everything in your power to ensure that serious and urgent consideration is given to the contents of this letter.

On 18 May, Walter's seventy-seventh birthday, we were allowed to have a special lunch and spend about three hours with him. The following month, I was pleasantly surprised at being able to spend an hour with him. He was a constant source of encouragement and inspiration.

I missed him a great deal, but it was a joy to have Wilton Mkwayi as my new cellmate. Raymond Mhlaba, or Baca, as we called him, and Andrew Mlangeni were our neighbours.

FREEDOM BECKONS

On 14 July we paid our second visit to Madiba, the first having been on 23 December. He had made a complete recovery and we celebrated his birthday, although it was still four days away. Elias Motsoaledi, or Mr Pres, was brought from the island for the occasion.

A month later, I requested that the five of us, Wilton, Raymond, Andrew, Walter and I, be allowed to spend my sixtieth birthday with Mandela at Victor Verster as well. The authorities refused, but about two weeks later, I was taken to Paarl to spend a few hours alone with him. Madiba had written a couple of memorandums to the government and a report to the ANC leadership in exile. During one of our visits, he asked me to read to our colleagues a lengthy draft memorandum that he intended sending to the president, PW Botha.

Assuming that electronic bugs had been secreted all through the house in which Madiba was living, we sat outside, under a tree, where I read the memorandum. We learnt much later that the garden furniture had been bugged!

By this juncture we had been instructed to wear civilian clothing when we received visitors or were taken out of the prison. After so many years of living in the drab uniforms provided, many of us had to make arrangements with friends and family in a hurry to acquire other clothes.

For twenty-six years, a spoon had been my safe, reliable and all-purpose eating utensil – a prisoner goes nowhere without his spoon – so when people outside began sending me dinner invitations in anticipation of my release, I wrote to warn them that they would have to excuse me from using anything in the line of 'posh' cutlery, crockery and table linen. One evening, my letter writing was interrupted by a most unexpected guest, a parrot. An escapee from a cage, somewhere, the bird had found its way to our exercise courtyard, and stayed a while. We had no idea what to feed it, and all our offerings were rejected, but the bird was tame and friendly.

When he made his way into my cell, I put him on my bed, but he was not happy, so I tried the desk where I was working, but that wasn't good enough either. He was satisfied only when perched on my shoulder, or strutting down the length of my arm and back again. I had been too long behind bars myself to foster any thoughts of keeping a caged bird, and after a while we gave it to one of the warders.

On Tuesday 3 October, I wrote my last letter from prison, to Paul Joseph. On 10 October, a public holiday set aside in honour of the Afrikaner hero, Paul Kruger, we visited Mandela again.

Govan Mbeki had been released two years earlier, and there had been persistent rumours of further releases since, but despite his obvious excitement, we didn't really believe Madiba when he told us: 'Chaps, this is a goodbye visit.' He had met with two cabinet ministers that very morning, and although he did not know the exact date, he was sure our release was imminent. We remained unconvinced.

However, when we took our leave of Mandela, we were not taken straight back to Pollsmoor as usual. The warders told us there was a large media contingent at the prison gates, and they wanted to avoid any publicity, so we were to enjoy the refreshments on offer in the officers' mess until a little later.

Evening found us still at Victor Verster, and we were told we would leave after dinner. An observer would have found the scene at the table incongruous at least, incredible at best. There we were, men vilified as terrorists, saboteurs and dangerous criminals of a different type, wearing suits and ties and dining with high-ranking prison officers in full uniform, being served a fine meal, accompanied by drinks of our choice.

Just before 8 p.m. someone wheeled a television set into the dining room, and the face of FW de Klerk, who had replaced PW Botha as president a month before, filled the screen, and the room, with a dramatic announcement. Eight political prisoners were to be given their freedom – Walter Sisulu, Raymond Mhlaba, Wilton Mkwayi, Andrew Mlangeni, Elias Motsoaledi, Japhta Masemola, Oscar Mphetha and me!

De Klerk did not say when, but as we returned to Pollsmoor that night, we knew Madiba had been right, and that freedom was in sight.

The very next day the chief warder, Christo Brand, had a number of cardboard cartons brought to our cells and told us to pack all our belongings, as we were being transferred to another prison. He advised us to tie the boxes securely, and twenty-four hours later they were taken from our cells to be sent to an undisclosed destination. At lock-up time on Thursday we were told to be ready on Friday morning, when we would be transferred to another prison.

On Friday morning, before dawn, we dressed in our suits and ties and were taken to the Cape Town airport. The vehicles drove right up to a waiting aircraft and we went aboard before any of the regular passengers arrived. None of us had ever flown in a jet before, and our escorts had to show us what to do with our seatbelts and refreshment trays.

If the government had hoped to keep our presence on the aircraft quiet, they were defeated by that morning's edition of the *Cape Times*, which carried banner headlines about our 'imminent' release, and photographs which, although taken before 1963, were close enough to our present appearance for the majority of passengers to recognise and wish us well.

As the aircraft soared above the city that still slept in its cradle between the mountain and the sea, I looked down on the shimmering lights and drank in the beauty of my last view of Cape Town as Prisoner No. 468/64.

On arrival in Johannesburg, we were driven directly to the new prison at Diepkloof, dubbed 'Sun City' by inmates after the glitzy casino and resort near Rustenburg, which had become the favourite playground of the rich and some-times famous. The commanding officer told us he had no idea what we were doing at his institution, but offered us his hospitality and asked for our help.

Jeff Masemola, whom we had not seen since Robben Island, was on a hunger strike, and the prison chief wanted us to persuade him to call it off, as Mandela wanted Jeff flown to Cape Town for a meeting.

It was good to be reunited with Jeff. We told him that Madiba had been meeting with groups of prisoners from Robben Island, representatives of COSATU and officials from the United Democratic Front, and he agreed to call off his hunger strike. He was taken to Cape Town the next morning, and returned again that night.

Of course, we were not yet free, and still had to be locked into cells overnight. On the Friday, I spent a few hours writing a detailed report on events for a group of ANC prisoners who had sent a message, via a sympathetic black warder, that they wanted to know what was going on. Included in the group was Patrick Maqubela, who had spent a short time with us at Pollsmoor.

Saturday passed uneventfully, but that night the commanding officer sought us out and informed us that he had just received a fax from headquarters in Pretoria. We were to be released in the morning.

If ever there was life-changing news, this was it. But what was our first question?

'What is a fax?'

We had read and heard about this strange new contraption, but none of us had ever seen a fax machine or message, and we simply could not grasp the concept of a sheet of paper being transmitted by telephone, and an exact replica arriving within minutes thousands of kilometres or several continents away. Not too many years before, it had taken days for me to painstakingly copy news reports by hand and send them to an adjoining cellblock!

On the morning of Sunday 15 October, we had to go through the formalities required to get the paperwork in order and undergo a medical examination, and then it was over.

15 OCTOBER 1989

Time is too slow for those who wait, too swift for those who fear, too long for those who grieve, too short for those who rejoice. But for those who love, time is not.   **– Henry van Dyke**[2]

A convoy of vehicles waited to transport us to our homes. Three cars were allocated to each of us – one for the prison warders and security policemen escorting us, one for our cartons from Pollsmoor, and one for us. As we left the prison, we were assured that our families had been told to expect us. Even as they were setting us free, the authorities were incapable of telling the truth.

My brother and his family had been awake until 4 a.m., when the last of the journalists and photographers finally gave up waiting, but when I knocked on the door of their home in Willow Street, Lenasia, shortly after six, they were up and about within minutes.

No one had told them I was coming that morning, but it took less than fifteen minutes for the news to be all over Lenasia, and for the first well-wishers to arrive. My dear friend and old comrade Laloo Chiba was the first. Within a few hours there were hundreds of people in and outside the house, and someone had draped a huge ANC flag over the balcony.

There must have been a hundred friends and family members for lunch. Media representatives vied with the children for my attention, the atmosphere was electric, the noise level many decibels higher than anything I had heard in years.

Except for a few indelible memories, most of that first day has always been a blank. My most precious recollections are of my little grand-nieces and nephews, clambering all over me, clasping their little arms around my neck, holding my hands, hugging and kissing this strange man they had never seen, but had learnt to love in absentia. After twenty-six years on my own, no other welcome could have meant as much as this spontaneous display of unconditional love and immediate acceptance.

Of course, there were also official delegations. A large contingent of ANC Women's League members, resplendent in their black, green and gold outfits, danced and sang old freedom songs. This was another emotional moment that took me back to the 1950s, to the historic anti-pass march on the Union Buildings, to the Congress of the People and to scores of meetings and demonstrations. It was most inspiring to see stalwarts of the movement still soldiering on, full of confidence, courage and determination.

Teachers, trade unionists, church and community leaders, and schoolchildren were followed by a group representing the Islamic Medical Association. I was filled with pride and admiration for the high qualifications of each member of the group and their generosity in setting up a mobile clinic at our 'welcome rally' at the FNB Stadium. That evening there was a hastily arranged reception for me at a park near our house in Lenasia, which the media claimed drew 6 000 people.

All day long, individuals and groups of friends just kept on coming. From Durban, there were my mentors, Ismail Meer and JN Singh, along with leaders such as Dr Chota Motala and Mewa Ramgobin. From Johannesburg came Cyril Ramaphosa, delegations from COSATU and the Mass Democratic Movement, and the indefatigable and much-loved 'Oom Bey' – Beyers Naudé, the Dutch Reformed Church minister defrocked for his political beliefs.

Although we had been watching television at Pollsmoor since 1985, I had never been in front of the cameras before, and I was quite dumbfounded when confronted with a cylindrical, black, hairy object that was pushed into my face. I learnt very quickly, that day, that this was a 'boom', and that I was expected to speak into it.

First the fax, now the boom. Clearly, I was going to have a lot to learn about technology, and I still do! I have yet to master the new-fangled public telephones, ATM machines, parking meters and a few more electronic marvels.

Fortunately, the entire day of celebration was captured on video, because it was only when I watched the tapes a week or two later that I remembered having gone to Soweto twice that Sunday, and remembered some of the hundreds of people I had spoken to.

But I needed no video to remind me of the sea of ANC flags that appeared, as if by magic, on vehicles, on fences and garden walls, on poles and in shop windows. It would be another four months before the ANC was unbanned on 2 February 1990, but the people of Lenasia – indeed, the entire country – claimed their right to political expression on the day we came home from prison.

In the weeks leading up to our release, a series of newspaper reports had appeared claiming that there were 'two' ANCs – the ANC of the terrorists based in the Zambian capital of Lusaka under Tambo, and the 'moderate' ANC led by Mandela. Of course, not a single released prisoner spoke of anything but a united ANC, of which the president was OR Tambo.

The London *Observer* of 14 June 1964 had been over-optimistic, by a decade or so, when we were spared the death sentence and they wrote: 'The saving of these lives may, in ten years or so, prove immensely valuable to the safety of the Republic. When white South Africans eventually have to treat with the African opposition, the need for intermediaries will be urgent.'[3]

It had taken sixteen years longer than the newspaper anticipated, but the time to treat had come.

A Crime Against Humanity

Generosity does honour to great revolutions.   **– André Malraux**[1]

R acial discrimination did not suddenly blight the southern tip of Africa when the National Party won the 1948 election. It went by many different names, but *apartheid* had its roots in the wild almond hedge planted by Jan van Riebeeck, in today's Kirstenbosch, to keep the Khoikhoi out of the first Dutch settlement.

It was, after all, Van Riebeeck who referred in his diary to the indigenous people of the Cape as '*die schwartze stinkende hunde*' ['the black, stinking dogs'].

Three centuries later, the teachings of John Calvin had been so distorted by the Dutch Reformed Church that Daniel François Malan's disciples believed that they were God's chosen people, divinely ordained to rule forever over the hewers of wood and bearers of water.

Freed within living memory from the yoke of British domination, the oppressed became the oppressors, turning an iniquitous tradition of segregation into a crime against humanity.

In *Apartheid: The Closing Phase*, CG Veeramantry captures the essence of Calvinism's effect on development of the nascent Afrikaner nation's character: 'Calvinism resulted in a symbiotic alliance between the rulers and the Church. Each supported the other, often in such close relationship as to be practically indistinguishable. Those who came under Afrikaner dominion owed a complete duty of obedience to their rulers, for their station in life, like their state, was preordained, and had the sanction of God.'

Conflict between the British and the Afrikaners amplified the latter's feelings of persecution and drove them inland. The threat of subjugation forged a bond of unity and fed the fire of determination to create a self-sufficient Afrikaner state, based on religious principles. The British administration in South Africa, as in other countries around the world, was distinguished by cultural arrogance and opportunism. Thus, from 1652 until the first democratic elections in 1994, successive white ruling parties embraced and perpetrated the policies of racial segregation and apartheid. Even the supposedly enlightened so-called international statesman, General Jan Smuts, was culpable.

'It is dishonourable,' he said, 'to mix white and black blood. It is useless to try and govern black and white in the same system. They are different not only in colour, but in mind and in political capacity.'

Erstwhile professor of psychology and architect of apartheid, Dr HF Verwoerd, was blatantly patronising: 'There is no place [for the black person] in the European community above the level of certain forms of labour. Until now, he has been subjected to a school system which drew him away from his community and misled him, by showing him the green pastures of European society in which he was not allowed to graze.'

When Chief Albert Luthuli, president of the African National Congress, received the Nobel Peace Prize in 1960, however, he decried South Africa as a place 'where the brotherhood of man is an illegal doctrine, outlawed, banned, censured, proscribed and prohibited; where to work, talk and campaign for the realisation in fact and deed of the brotherhood of man is hazardous, punished with banishment or confinement without trial, or imprisonment; where effective democratic channels to peaceful settlement of the race problem have never existed these 300 years. Here the cult of race superiority and of white supremacy is worshipped like a god.'

The most effective barometer by which to measure individual freedom is the Universal Declaration of Human Rights. South Africa's racial policies and practices essentially violated each and every one of the thirty clauses of this noble document. For millions of South Africans, the hallmarks of daily life were inequality, injustice, indignity and inhumanity.

From the moment I became involved in politics as a schoolboy, I realised that, unacceptable as my own circumstances were, the lot of my African colleagues and leaders – Mandela, Tutu, Sisulu, Tambo, Mbeki – who would become household names, was infinitely worse.

Within the plethora of legislation that dictated the daily life of anyone who was not white, the most vicious and demeaning law was the perversion that assigned to every person an identity based on nothing else but random genetics: white, black, Coloured, Indian. The entire system of apartheid was constructed on the foundation of the Population Registration Act.

At the whim of an untrained, often semi-literate but always white public servant, wielding something as scientifically crude as a pencil, the fate of millions was decided.

What it came down to, was this. The bureaucrat would push a pencil into the hair of a 'non-white' applicant. If the pencil stayed in place, regardless of skin colour or any other distinguishing features, the applicant was declared 'black'. The seriously flawed reasoning was that full-blooded Africans had tight and tiny curls, while those of mixed parentage tended to have sleek rather than frizzy hair, and were thus designated 'Coloured'.

The sheer arbitrariness of the 'test' saw families torn apart. Couples who had been married for years became lawbreakers overnight as one spouse was classified 'white' and the other 'black' or 'Coloured'. Parents suddenly found themselves in a different racial category than their children, siblings were forced to attend different schools because, regardless of what their birth certificates said, a cheap pencil and a nasty bigot had sealed their fate.

Race was the single factor that determined where people could live and work, what hospital or university they could go to, which church or cinema they could attend, what bus or train they could use to get there. I was twenty-two years old, and in Europe, when I saw the inside of a theatre, library, restaurant or hotel for the first time. My sixtieth birthday had passed before I knew what a ballot paper or a voting booth looked like, and that was in Europe. The first time I was allowed to take part in an election in the country of my birth was in 1994.

The true legacy of apartheid lies in graveyards and court archives throughout South Africa. Many chose suicide over the devastating consequences of 'reclassification', or were murdered by the state, while hundreds of thousands were turned into criminals because they were in the wrong place at the wrong time, or fell in love with the wrong person.

While still a law student, Nelson Mandela and two friends, Ismail Meer and JN Singh, one afternoon inadvertently boarded a 'whites only' tram – which offered half a dozen seats for Indians, but none for Africans – and were prosecuted for their transgression. Although a qualified legal practitioner, Mandela was not allowed to be in an urban area for more than seventy-two hours at a time, and all Africans had to be off the city streets by 11 p.m.

Under the Group Areas Act, more than three million people were forcibly uprooted from homes they had occupied for years, sometimes generations, and dumped in barren ghettoes without electricity or running water and very often, without shelter of any kind.

As the African National Congress and its allies in the liberation movement tried to redress egregious wrongs by peaceful means and passive resistance, the government systematically set about crushing every semblance of political activism, until the last remaining avenues of legitimate protest were shut down by the Sharpeville massacre in March 1960, and the state of emergency that followed. On 8 April 1960 the ANC and PAC were declared illegal. In the face of increased repression and no further possibility of peaceful protest, the ANC switched to an armed struggle.

The initial phase of the banned ANC's armed struggle was specifically aimed at sabotaging state installations. Those charged with blowing up power pylons, government buildings, telephone exchanges and electrical sub-stations had strict instructions to avoid injury to people.

The government's response included house arrest and draconian laws allowing detention without trial. The most conservative estimate puts at 100 the number of political activists who died in custody as the result of torture and vicious assault by the security police. The methods used to extract information ranged from sustained psychological torture to brutal physical attack, and not even those who were sent to prison by the courts were spared.

On Robben Island, punishment for even the most minor of infractions reached levels of depravity that defy normal comprehension. While serving a twenty-year sentence, Johnson Mlambo paid for a verbal altercation with a prison warder by being ordered into a hole in the ground and buried up to his neck. It was a blistering midsummer day, and when he pleaded for water after several hours, the warders laughed, and urinated on his face and head.

Sometimes, punishment was consequential rather than prescribed. Nelson Mandela's daughters, Zindzi and Zenani, were toddlers when he went to prison, and he did not see them again until they were sixteen years old. On Robben Island, some of the cruellest deprivations were the ban on news access, the fact that we were not allowed to keep diaries and suspension of our studies. As if being locked up for life was not enough, the authorities did everything in their power to stifle our intellects. If apartheid's enemies could not be murdered or sent to the gallows, their ideas, at least, must be put to death, it seemed.

TRUTH AND RECONCILIATION

Let justice roll down like waters
And righteousness like an everlasting stream. **– The Bible**[2]

When the Truth and Reconciliation Commission convened in 1996, victims of apartheid lined up in their hundreds to bear witness to atrocities perpetrated against them or members of their families.

The worst culprits by far were the omnipotent security police. Immune for decades to any accountability for their heinous deeds, apartheid's enforcers were exposed to the world when they had to confess what they had done in order to gain amnesty from prosecution. The revelations were shocking and reminiscent of some of the evidence at the Nuremberg Trials, yet some of the most heartrending appeals came from relatives who wanted only to know where their loved ones were buried.

Some were denied even that simple need as the killers confessed that bodies had been burnt or thrown into rivers.

Former police hit squad leader Dirk Coetzee told the commission how Durban lawyer and prominent ANC activist Griffiths Mxenge was stabbed, how the knife was plunged between his ribs and twisted, how his throat was slit and how, some months later, his wife Victoria was murdered as well.

Jeffrey Benzien graphically described how he had applied electric shocks to the noses, genitals, ears and rectum of detainees, and demonstrated how he would straddle a detainee lying on the floor, cover his head with a wet sack and pull it tight, thus suffocating the victim repeatedly.

Chris Ribeiro, son of a prominent medical doctor, recounted the harrowing experience of coming upon his parents, Fabian and Florence, just moments after they were gunned down in their own home in the Pretoria township of Mamelodi by covert military agents: 'I found my father sprawled at the drain in our courtyard with twenty-five bullets in his head. My mother was spread-eagled further away with one shot only. I held her in my arms and she sighed – that was her last breath.'

A woman activist told the TRC: 'I have bullets in my body, some are still in my leg, some of the bullets are in my vagina. These were the first bullets that were shot at me. He shot directly there ...'

Thenjiwe Mthintso testified that, in detention, 'you had to strip in front of a whole range of policemen making remarks about your body. Women had to do star-jumps naked, breasts flying. Fallopian tubes were flooded with water until they burst, rats were pushed into vaginas ...'

The commission heard that prisoner Sicelo was tortured to death. One of his hands was severed from his arm by the security police and placed in a bottle. The bottled hand was then shown to other detainees in order to frighten them into giving information. One former detainee testified that he was shown this bottle and told that it was the hand of a communist or a baboon. Sicelo's widow appeared before the commission to make a simple, human plea: 'Please show me where my husband was buried, so that we can exhume the body and give him a dignified burial.'

The most well-known political leader who was tortured to death while in detention was Steve Biko.

Those of us who were old enough to witness the end of the Second World War in 1945 must be forgiven our naivety for believing the rhetoric of Allied leaders who proclaimed that the world had emerged from 'the war to end all wars', ushering in a time of peace, liberty and freedom from all forms of oppression. I ask myself how I could possibly have believed those empty promises after the American forces had dropped horrendous nuclear bombs on Hiroshima and Nagasaki, killing hundreds of thousands of innocent women, children and men.

In the promised 'peaceful decades', we witnessed Korea and Vietnam, and the napalm bomb. And the invasion of weaker countries by superpowers. And now we have Afghanistan and Iraq and the unbelievable atrocities of Guatanamo Bay and Abu Ghraib. We couldn't believe our ears when a few years ago a senior American diplomat unashamedly responded to Barbara Hogan's concern about Guatanamo Bay by saying: 'We cannot bring those prisoners to America because then the Bill of Rights would apply!' And in our own country we had Sharpeville in 1960, and Soweto in 1976.

Not even those who had fled into exile were safe. Ruth Slovo died when a parcel bomb sent by the security police exploded in her office in neighbouring Mozambique. Jeanette Schoon and her daughter Katryn, aged twelve, suffered a similar fate in Angola, while Dulcie September was assassinated outside the ANC's office in Paris. My former Robben Island neighbour, Joe Gqabi, was killed by South African agents in Zimbabwe, and Zola Nqini was among the victims of a cross-border raid into Lesotho. No one has ever been prosecuted for these and dozens of other political murders.

It is beyond the scope of this book to detail the support of many countries in Africa for our struggle; nor can I begin to describe the atrocities perpetrated by the South African regime in what were known as the Frontline States. I would, however, be remiss if I were not at least to mention these important issues.

Among my personal friends and acquaintances who were tortured to death in detention were Babla Saloojee, Caleb Mayekiso and Alpheus Madiba. Flag Boshielo and Mobbs Gqirana simply vanished off the face of the earth.

And the security forces killed hundreds of schoolchildren in the violence that erupted when the youth of Soweto rose up against their oppressors in June 1976.

The Soweto uprising, which quickly spread throughout the country, was the turning point in the liberation struggle. From 1976, no amount of violence, repression or brutality could stem the tide of freedom. Mass mobilisation and defiance, strikes and consumer boycotts, international embargoes and economic sanctions combined to force apartheid to its knees.

Against this background, Mandela, in pursuance of the ANC's policy to force the enemy to the negotiating table, embarked on a process of dialogue with FW de Klerk's government that culminated in what has come to be known as a miracle: a democracy based on a Constitution that many envy, and a Bill of Rights designed to ensure that never again will any South African be oppressed or persecuted on the grounds of race or creed or colour.

But the true miracle is the reservoir of forgiveness that has nurtured a society in embryo. Where bitterness, hatred and revenge might so easily have found fertile soil, the ANC and Nelson Mandela planted the seeds of tolerance, reconciliation and goodwill. Remarkably, some of those who suffered most have been the least vocal advocates of retribution.

On the morning of 7 April 1988, lawyer Albie Sachs, living in exile in Maputo, unlocked his car door to go to work. The massive explosion triggered by this everyday act was meant to kill, but he survived the blast, albeit with the loss of an arm and an eye, and became one of the first judges appointed to South Africa's Constitutional Court.

'I am not a victim seeking revenge or compensation or sympathy,' Sachs has said, 'but someone who voluntarily engaged himself in the freedom struggle, aware that risks at some stage or the other were involved, delighted that I have survived and determined to establish an active and happy relationship with the world.'

As Archbishop Desmond Tutu, chairman of the Truth and Reconciliation Commission, pointed out, Sachs 'should by rights have been consumed by a burning desire to get even with those who had planned this dastardly deed. Instead, Albie fights for the inclusion of strong human rights provisions in the new Constitution – provisions that will guarantee his opponents rights that were denied to him and so many others who had fought for a free and democratic South Africa.'

Father Michael Lapsley lost both hands and one eye when he opened a parcel bomb, sent by South African agents, in his office in Harare. A friend who visited him in hospital soon afterwards recalled: 'It was terrible to witness. His face was charred and black ... his beard had melted into his face, which had swollen to twice its normal size. Both his hands were amputated, he lost an eye, his eardrums were burst.'

And yet, says Lapsley: 'I am someone without hands and I had never ... never met someone before without hands. I do not see myself as a victim, but as a survivor of apartheid. This is part of my triumph of returning to South Africa and living my life as meaningfully and joyfully as possible. I am not captured by hatred, because then they would not only have destroyed my body, but also my soul. Ironically, even without hands and an eye, I am much more free than the person who did this to me. I say to everyone who supported apartheid, your freedom is waiting for you.'

↢ Part III ↣

The End

of the

Long Walk

While we will not forget the brutality of apartheid, we will not want Robben Island to be a monument to our hardship and suffering. We would want it to be a triumph of the human spirit against the forces of evil. A triumph of wisdom and largeness of spirit against small minds and pettiness; a triumph of courage and determination over human frailty and weakness; a triumph of the new South Africa over the old.

— **Ahmed Kathrada, speech at the opening of the Robben Island Exhibition in Cape Town, 1993**

Going Home

God had infinite time to give us; but how did he give it? In one immense
tract of lazy millenniums? No, He cut it up into a neat succession of new
mornings. — **Ralph Waldo Emerson**[1]

The first day of freedom passed quickly. Before going to a media conference
in Soweto that evening, I attended a hastily organised 'Welcome Home' rally
in the park near my brother's house. An estimated 6 000 people turned out for
what I was told was the biggest gathering of its kind that Lenasia had seen.

The ANC would not be unbanned for another four months, but for the
people of Lenasia and environs, 15 October 1989 was emancipation day. Everywhere you looked there were ANC flags and banners, and that night in Soweto,
what was supposed to be a media conference turned into an impromptu ANC
rally. The hall was packed with supporters, and a large contingent of local and
international media fired questions at me and my colleagues.

We took the opportunity to dispel government propaganda about a split in the organisation, and stated unequivocally that there was only one ANC, headed by Oliver Tambo, and temporarily headquartered in the Zambian capital of Lusaka. That night, I slept deep and peacefully in the bosom of my family for the first time in more than a quarter-century.

My friends Amien and Ayesha Cajee and their children, Djamilla and Iqbal, had lived in and looked after my flat at No. 13 Kholvad House throughout my absence. Even the telephone was still registered in my name.

When I came home, they moved to their own house. In a spectacular gesture of love and friendship, my godchild, Djamilla, redecorated the flat for me, and it looked quite wonderful. But my closest family had settled in Lenasia and I felt the need to be near them. Some years before, my brother had built a compact little flat over the garage of their house in Willow Street, and that became my main base, though it was convenient to have the flat in town as well.

When I went to prison, Lenasia had consisted of no more than a few scattered houses on a large tract of open veld. People resisted the forced removal from the bustling inner city suburbs for as long as they could, but eventually Lenasia became the hub of Johannesburg's large Indian community.

A few nights after I arrived home, someone came to my flat and wanted me to accept the keys to a Volkswagen Beetle. He had heard, he said, that all the time that I was in prison, I had told people that when I was finally released I would want another Beetle, just like the car I had in the early 1960s. I already had a car, provided by my friend Yunus Ravat, and of course there were also the family cars, but it was generosity and goodwill like this that helped me adjust to a world that had changed almost beyond recognition.

PEOPLE AND PLACES

The type of future a society has doesn't depend on how close its organisation comes to perfection, but on the amount of idealism its individual members have.   **– Albert Schweitzer**[2]

Being reunited with old friends and seeing familiar places again was thrilling, but a little intimidating. People had aged and the city had changed, but the love and the memories were no different. Among the unforgettable experiences was my meeting with the indefatigable Helen Joseph a day or two after my release.

There was no such thing as easing back into the real world or taking time to adjust. From the word go people took control of our lives, drawing up agendas and arranging programmes of appearance morning, noon and night. My life was no less regulated, my movements no less restricted, than when I was in prison!

Choice is a vital element of freedom, and thus one of the first sacrifices made in captivity. Prison regulations dictating when to get up in the morning, when to shower, what to eat, who may visit, how many words to write in a letter, what time to go to sleep, are as much about discipline as deprivation. The rules are sacrosanct and leave no room for personal preference; the rigid and regimented routine takes no account of individual preference, which prisoners surrender on admission along with their street clothes.

It might sound unreasonable, even ungrateful, but I harboured a deep desire to be allowed the freedom of choice in what I wore and where I went. Family members and friends had provided me with a whole new wardrobe, but I had no say in the selection of the garments. After a few months of being shuttled from meeting to rally to interview, I thought it was about time to let the marshalls and bodyguards get back to their own lives. I believe that they, too, must have felt relieved.

More than anything else, I wanted to fill my life with colour and variety.

On my first visit to Schweizer-Reneke, I paused at the vacant lots where our shop and houses had been razed to the ground in 1981, and let the memories flood over me. My father had died when I was fourteen, but I was in prison when my mother, my brother Ismail and his wife Amina passed away. Relatives told me that Ismail lost all zest for life and was never the same after our family home was destroyed by the government, and as I gazed at the weeds growing where we had played as children, it was cold comfort to remember that ours was one of three million families that suffered the same – and often much worse – fate under the Group Areas Act.

NEW IMPRESSIONS

For some years after my release I could not count money. I went to prison soon after South Africa converted to a decimal currency system, and of course I had not handled cash at all for twenty-six years. For a long time, something as simple as buying a newspaper was inhibiting, and I would just give the street vendors a handful of coins or a note and trust them to give me the correct change. I almost never went into a shop during the first few years.

And everywhere I turned, there were gadgets and electronic devices and other strange items I had never seen before, each with a name that wasn't in my vocabulary: Walkman and beeper and steering-lock and laser printer and so many, many more. I started keeping a list of all the new terminology I came across, and it became a very long list indeed.

The first time I found a non-slip rubber mat in a bath, I took it out and placed it on the floor, assuming one was supposed to step onto it, dripping wet. Freezers in private homes and a microwave oven on every kitchen counter were also new to me.

In the late 1950s, we had been awestruck when the OK Bazaars placed the most advanced scientific invention of the twentieth century on display – the computer. It was a huge, ugly piece of equipment, the size of a smallish room. Imagine my astonishment when I was introduced to the personal computer and learnt that a mouse is not necessarily a rodent, or a virus always a disease!

Of course I have succumbed to the inevitable, and I unashamedly confess that this manuscript has been written on my laptop.

Other innovations that took some getting used to included access cards instead of keys, credit cards, coffee-makers in hotel bedrooms, hot air dispensers in public washrooms, salt and pepper grinders, tinfoil food containers and plastic freezer bags, security tags on merchandise and electronic scanners at super-market tills.

The food revolution has brought us papaya, kiwi fruit and pizza, to say nothing of ready-to-eat gourmet meals. Before going to prison, I don't think I ever saw a mushroom in an Indian kitchen, or baby vegetables ranging from miniature ears of corn to tiny little squash.

As for language usage, efficiency aids and jargon, I recall how activists in the 1940s and 1950s managed to organise the Passive Resistance Campaign and the Defiance Campaign, the boycotts of potatoes, tobacco and buses, and the Congress of the People without the benefit of consultants, events organisers, brainstorming sessions, strategic workshops, think tanks, keynote addresses, organograms, and so on. I still have not fully adjusted to these, and I suspect my comrades are exasperated whenever I question the necessity for these so-called aids.

As for the alphabet soup of acronyms in everyday parlance, I sometimes wonder if anyone remembers how to speak in anything but abbreviations!

I also find it fascinating that some perfectly useful words have acquired wholly different connotations, the most obvious example being 'gay'.

An early edition of The King's English Dictionary offers the following definition: 'merry, cheerful, sportive, showy, bright, loose, dissipated'. The 1998 edition of the Shorter Oxford Dictionary says the word means 'light-hearted, cheerful, showy, homosexual'.

The latter is assuredly not what Helen Joseph had in mind when she wrote in her autobiography: 'We chose a home for "Kathy", Ahmed Kathrada, the young Indian bachelor, so gay, who often travelled with us.'[3]

Something else that took a little getting used to is the custom of naming residential areas, especially informal settlements or squatter camps, after people. Now towns have been named for founding fathers since time immemorial, but were generally distinguished by the addition of something like 'park' or 'heights' or, especially in South Africa, 'burg'. The modern trend, however, is to identify an area by name alone, as in Chris Hani, Joe Slovo and Winnie Mandela.

This tendency caused me great confusion and concern at a meeting where delegates kept talking about 'Kathrada'. It was Kathrada this, Kathrada that, Kathrada has an inadequate water supply – on and on, until so many complaints had been lodged about Kathrada that I was reminded of something I had read in a biography of General Jan Smuts. A group of newly converted Khoikhoi tribesmen were praying to the Lord to deliver them from a difficult situation.

'Oh Lord,' they prayed, 'our troubles are very big, so please don't send your Son, but come along Yourself.'

I was spared from a similar supplication when someone enlightened me to the fact that a township outside Klerksdorp had been named after me!

Prior to the Rivonia raid, I was passionately fond of driving. On 13 April 1990, six months after leaving Pollsmoor, I got behind a steering wheel for the first time since my release.

I had managed to develop a working relationship with seatbelts, hazard and indicator lights, child locks, five-gear stick shifts, battery boosters, power steering, immobilisers and car alarms. But when I took to the road to travel the short distance from Lenasia to the centre of Johannesburg, my love of driving was conquered by the ubiquitous minibus taxi.

The first challenge was negotiating the multiple-lane highways, complete with double-decker sections, off-ramps and confusing signs marked 'M1 South' or 'N24', with no hint whatsoever of where you would end up if you followed them.

Switching lanes was hopelessly beyond my driving skills, and I had been advised before setting out to stay in the 'slow' lane. That was a direction I followed religiously, but neither my 'driving instructors' nor I had factored in the new phenomenon that had invaded our motorways and become a virtual occupation force. The 'weapons' unleashed on the driving public come in various sizes, shapes, guises and colours, but the common denominator that binds them are four wheels.

Ostensibly safe in the slow lane, I was assailed by minibus taxis hooting incessantly, speeding past, swearing, shouting, cajoling and intimidating me. Unlike the struggle against apartheid, this was a war we could not win. I cut short my journey, conceded defeat and have yet to pluck up the courage to brave the tarmac battlefield again.

I still prefer motor cars to any other mode of transport, but I'm happy to leave the driving to someone else.

In December 1989 I went back to Cape Town with Shaan Bolton to speak at the South African Student Congress conference. While we were there, Shaan received a phone call informing him of the death of two people who had been killed while placing a bomb. I had been in daily contact with both men since my release – they were in my team of minders and bodyguards – and had no inkling that they were trained MK cadres or that Shaan was their unit leader. Yusuf Akhalwaya and Prakash Napier were wonderful, courageous and dedicated comrades. Their death left a void in our lives.

In those first few months, much of what was happening was shrouded in great secrecy. I was a member of the ANC delegation at the Groote Schuur talks, the first formal interaction with the government, and before that at a small exploratory meeting between the ANC and government officials. Penuell Maduna and Mathews Phosa were allowed to come to South Africa from Lusaka, and Curnick Ndlovu and I joined them to meet with Niel Barnard, head of the National Intelligence Service, and high-ranking security force officers.

The presence of our comrades from Lusaka had to be kept absolutely secret from everyone except the leaders on both sides, but Maduna asked me to take his suitcase, containing everything he had brought with him from exile, to his family in Soweto. It probably wasn't the best idea. They were convinced that he was dead and that I was hiding the awful truth from them. It was a difficult situation, highly emotional, but I was sworn to secrecy and could not ease their minds with the news that I had seen Penuell shortly before. Later, another one of my missions was to go back to Robben Island with Phosa to persuade the remaining ANC members who had refused to be released that they should accept the changing circumstances and embrace their freedom.

MADIBA RELEASED

I shall never believe that God plays dice with the world.
– Albert Einstein[4]

On 2 February 1990, when FW de Klerk announced the unbanning of the ANC and various other political organisations, as well as the release of Mandela, I was in Gaberone, Botswana.

Nine days later, when Madiba walked through the gates of Victor Verster Prison, I was stuck in Johannesburg with a BBC television crew filming at the Old Fort.

I accompanied Madiba to Sweden when he went to visit Oliver Tambo, who was recovering from a stroke, and to Norway when he was presented with the Nobel Peace Prize. At the first legal ANC conference in Durban in 1991, I was among those honoured by being elected to the National Executive Committee, and spent the next few years as head of the ANC's public relations department. My wonderful colleagues – Feroza Adams, Thandi Shongwe, Audrey Mothlamme, Dorcas Raditsela, Lilian, Dumisane and others – inspired me with their enthusiasm and commitment. Feroza was tragically killed in a car accident in 1994, soon after she was elected as an MP, thus ending a promising future. She was in her early thirties.

I gave so many media interviews that they soon became routine events, but some were memorable for specific reasons.

Conservative Party member of parliament Koos van der Merwe, for instance, refused to appear with Walter and me in interviews by the BBC or CNN, because he would not consort with 'terrorists'. After the first democratic elections of 1994, I had the pleasure of meeting Koos, now as an equal, fellow parliamentarian, representing the predominantly Zulu-speaking Inkatha Freedom Party, and benefiting from his experience and wit. Welcome to the new South Africa, Koos.

A young French filmmaker, Paskal Chelet, wanted me to take part in a TV documentary called *24 Hours*. She and a camera crew would shadow me for a full day and night, filming everything I did, from my morning ablutions to my last sigh before going to sleep.

My natural shyness and years of isolation could not permit such an intimate intrusion. We compromised, and they filmed me from breakfast until just before bedtime.

Paskal also asked me to take part in another documentary, about Robben Island. The last of the political detainees had been released in 1991, but a number of common-law offenders were still housed in the fully functioning prison. The Department of Correctional Services agreed that we could film there, on condition that none of the inmates featured in the programme.

I could hardly believe how eager and impatient I was to go back to the island and revisit the familiar settings: the lime quarry, the shoreline where we had collected the stinking kelp, the dump where we had scavenged for newspapers.

When I stood in the doorway of Cell 14, B Section, however, I was momentarily speechless. Had it always been so small? How could I have forgotten so quickly that for eighteen of my twenty-six years in prison, I lived in a tiny compartment no more than 4.5 metres square?

Since then I have been to Robben Island hundreds of times, usually with visitors from abroad or local delegations. Someone always asks me how it feels to be back there, and my answer is always the same: it's become routine.

But once in a while, the island still throws up surprises, such as when I accompanied Hollywood film stars Danny Glover and Angela Bassett. Someone in their group mentioned that he was born on 12 June 1964, and I remarked: 'That's interesting, because that was the date on which we were sentenced to life imprisonment.' We continued down the passage to my cell, and the next thing, this man collapsed on the ground, quite overcome by his emotions. We had to help him up and comfort him, but that was one occasion when I had a hard time hiding my emotions.

BABLA SALOOJEE

It is harder to disintegrate prejudice than an atom. – **Albert Einstein**[5]

As soon as I was able, I had visited my friend Babla Saloojee's grave, but it was not until the Truth Commission hearings began in 1996 that I finally learnt the heartbreaking truth about his last hours on earth. The relevant extracts from the TRC Report are reprinted here:

51 Abdullay [*sic*] Jassat's description of his torture[6] provides a clue as to what may have happened to 32-year-old Suliman Saloojee, who died in detention in September 1964, two months after being detained under the 90-day detention law. Suliman Saloojee, the fourth person to die while held under security legislation, allegedly jumped from the seventh floor of the Special Branch offices in Gray's Building, Johannesburg.

52 In a submission to the Commission, Saloojee's widow, Rokaya, said she struggled to be allowed access to her husband, whom she suspected was ill. Ms Saloojee had become suspicious about her husband's condition when neither the clothes nor the dishes for the food she had been bringing for him at the Rosebank police station were returned to her. She was eventually allowed a five-minute visit with him several weeks after his detention and found that he had a wound at the side of his forehead.

When they opened the cell door, I saw my husband had a patch on his head. When I asked him – I didn't even greet, I just asked what happened to you and this one policeman said that he bumped his head in the cell. So I said that's funny, he must have been drunk, because there is nothing that's in the cell that you can bump your head on. They closed the door on me and told me to go away, which I did. I had no alternative. I didn't even speak to my husband. All he said to me in Gujarati is that I should keep quiet.

53 Some time later, Ms Saloojee was preparing to take her husband food when she was visited by police who told her that her husband was in the Johannesburg hospital. She failed to trace him at the Johannesburg hospital or at any of the local hospitals. She heard of his death when a journalist approached her for a statement. After her husband's death, Rokaya Saloojee continued to be harassed by security police. She tried to leave the country but was refused a passport five times.

54 At Saloojee's inquest, Captain 'Rooi Rus' Swanepoel, Major Brits from the railway police, Sergeant CJ van Zyl, Constable Van den Heever and Lieutenant HC Muller were identified as his interrogators. Swanepoel said that he had questioned Saloojee on 9 September but that he had been out of the room at the time of the fall. He denied that any violence had been used in the interrogation. The magistrate, Mr AJ Kotze, found that no one was to blame and that nothing in the evidence suggested that the methods used in interrogating him had been irregular.[7]

In the 1987 general election, the brutal Swanepoel stood unsuccessfully for the Conservative Party against the incumbent foreign minister, Pik Botha. Until the day he died in the 1990s, Swanepoel never expressed any remorse for the sadistic cruelty he had inflicted on hundreds of political detainees, including Sylvia.

SYLVIA

I had consciously avoided forming a relationship with a white woman throughout my twenties, because I certainly had no wish to become embroiled in criminal charges under the Immorality Act, and the consequent repercussions. I had a lot of white friends and political colleagues, but I avoided intimacy with the young women.

But then came a period of tension, increased surveillance and less association, and it was almost impossible to avoid Sylvia. Nor, to be frank, did I really want to, though in retrospect I fully acknowledge that this was one of my most irresponsible actions.

While I was under house arrest, the security police raided my flat regularly, hoping to catch me breaking the terms of my order. Yet when December came in 1962, I convinced myself that with so many people away on holiday, the raids would almost certainly diminish, perhaps not take place at all.

So, over the extended holiday weekend, Sylvia stayed at the flat. And sure enough, there was a raid.

I told her to go into one of the bedrooms and lock the door, having decided that the best, perhaps only, form of defence this time would be to go on the offensive. I opened the door and let them have it, both barrels blazing. How dare they disturb me on the holiday? I had been taking a nap, and they had no right to harass me at all hours.

Warming to my indignant attack, I told them I would not allow them to enter the flat unless they produced a warrant. A crowd of neighbours had gathered by this time, and banking somehow on there being safety in numbers, I threatened to just walk out, upbraiding them that if I found anything missing when I returned, I would charge them with theft.

No one was more surprised than I, but it worked. They turned around and went away, and from then until I went underground in April, they never came back.

But I had gambled everything, and it was sheer luck that it worked. If they had set so much as a foot inside the flat, one of the first things they would have seen were Sylvia's shoes, lying on the sitting-room floor.

My behaviour during our relationship was contrary to everything I had learnt during my political training. We grew ever closer, which made the enforced separation when I was arrested so much harder, and took a sad toll on Sylvia, too, when she was detained a few months afterwards. She really had a torrid time of it in detention, and then spent two years in prison, not for breaking the Immorality Act, but for her political activities.

In April 1986, I wrote to Paul Joseph: 'It's lovely to hear that you have been in touch with Sakina; do pass my love when next you write. One of these days I should like you to tell me about Sylvia. These days, particularly in view of the abolition of the two Acts [the immorality and mixed marriages legislation] I don't think the Prisons Dept will have any objections to information about her. I have heard that she is married and is lecturing at a university. Tell me something about her thesis, whether it was published, etc.'

I had accepted that Sylvia was happily married and settled in her new life in Europe. When I travelled to Germany in September 1990, I went to see her, but on subsequent visits to Europe, I went nowhere near Berlin.

I had just had my sixtieth birthday when I was released, and friends and family never let pass a chance of introducing me to potential companions, but I met no one I wanted to see on a permanent basis.

Towards the end of my prison term, I had jokingly written to Eddie Daniels: 'I'm still single and eligible. Now don't let the young ladies rush to end my bachelorhood! Who knows, just as Genghis [his treasured dog] has acquired the looks and characteristics of his companion/master (and vice versa) I, too, may not have remained free of such mutations. After all, for two decades plus, I have lived among a variety of fauna – ostriches, rabbits, buck, Alsatians, Dobermans – and yourself! At this stage I don't know resemblance to which of these species is least preferable.'

BARBARA

Having served some nine years of her sentence, Barbara Hogan was released two days before Mandela. Not long afterwards, our paths crossed for the first time in a television studio at the SABC's headquarters in Auckland Park, Johannesburg. Walter and I were taking part in a BBC panel discussion and Barbara was in the audience.

While on the island, I had taken a keen interest in her case, and when we were introduced, I was definitely impressed. When Barbara came to work at the ANC's head office in Shell House, Johannesburg, our offices were in close proximity and we chatted often.

When Madiba flew to London for the second Wembley concert, Barbara and I were both in his party, and spent the long flight getting to know one another better. We discovered much in common besides our political affiliations and prison sentences. Most importantly, we were both single and there was a definite chemistry between us, even though she had been all of twelve when I was sentenced in 1964.

Barbara has many endearing and admirable traits and few faults. She is loyal, committed, brave, frank, disciplined, adventurous, impulsive, reticent and difficult; passionate about nature, enjoys travel and loves animals, especially cats and dogs.

When the violence that consumed South Africa in the early 1990s was at its worst in the Pretoria-Witwatersrand-Vereeniging (PWV) region, she served as the ANC's regional secretary. Almost daily, working men's hostels were raided, commuters thrown off moving trains, minibus taxis shot at, ANC supporters attacked and killed, all at the instigation, as we would learn later, of a covert element of the security forces. No one was safe from the so-called Third Force. An armed man was apprehended outside Barbara's office, and the security police mistakenly planted a bomb intended for her car under a vehicle owned by another woman living at the same address.

Barbara refused to be intimidated and carried on with her sterling work, both at head office and in various troubled townships.

One of the many groups that I accompanied on a guided tour of Robben Island included a former prison wardress. She asked me if I knew Barbara Hogan, and when I said yes, her comment was: 'She's a difficult person!'

As Ma Sisulu told her daughter-in-law, Elinor: 'The prison staff told me that Barbara was giving them a hard time. She would demand to know whether I was being kept under the same conditions. She would say: "Is Ma Sisulu being given this food? If she is not, then I don't want it. Take it away."'[8]

No one is immune from Barbara's candour. While she was secretary of the PWV region, Mandela summoned a number of officials to Shell House in order to reprimand them over some alleged misdemeanour. All the national leaders were present when he spelled out his reasons for calling the meeting.

As he finished, Barbara asked if this was a disciplinary hearing. Madiba said it might well turn into one, at which she shot back: 'You are behaving like a prison warder,' and left the room banging the door behind her.

The next time they met, Madiba called her 'the Irish devil', and consistently referred to her thereafter, with affection, as 'the wardress'.

When President Thabo Mbeki appointed her to the chair of the parliamentary finance committee, a *Sunday Times* columnist described Barbara as 'feisty', and I certainly would not argue with that description.

However, she is not 'house-trained', and in our fourteen years together I have had no success at all in converting her to my favourite foods, especially curry. My only real problem with Barbara is her continued reticence to write and share with a broad audience the trials, triumphs and tribulations of her political activism.

So little has been documented about conditions anywhere except on Robben Island that people are constantly surprised to learn that political detainees were held in numerous other prisons around South Africa. And apart from a book by Jean Middleton and Elinor Sisulu's biography of Walter and Albertina, there is nothing by or about the women who were jailed for their political activity.

It took almost ten years before Barbara casually mentioned to me that she had attempted a rather dramatic escape from prison, which ended with her being stopped by a medical doctor who hailed from Ian Smith's Rhodesia!

I shall continue to encourage Barbara, and colleagues such as Thandi Modise, to record their experiences as underground ANC operatives and unsung heroines of the struggle.

TRAVELS AND HAJ

Der sieger schreibt die Geschichte.[9]

Given my communist background and my sentiments on the Vietnam War and the Latin American brutalities, most notably the atrocities carried out by the CIA's puppet dictators in Guatamala, Panama, Chile and elsewhere, I had no particularly warm feelings towards America. In fact, in one of my letters from prison, I wrote: 'I have never been to America, tho given a chance, I don't think I'd want to visit that place. Somehow I've never been attracted by it. Of course if I had to visit friends settled there, it's a different matter.'

But reality is often very different from one's expectations, and it turned out that I developed firm friendships with a number of Americans and received my first honorary doctorate from the University of Massachusetts, and a second one from the University of Missouri.

Among my friends and family, it is well known that I have a special fondness for ice cream. Whenever I visit Bobby and Ursula Vassen in the US, they stock up on 'Death by Chocolate' and 'Moose Tracks' to feed my craving. It was thus with much amusement, while preparing this manuscript, that my researcher found the following extract among Warrant Officer Dirker's testimony during the Rivonia Trial: 'In the kitchen [of the house at Liliesleaf Farm] I met two of the employees, Solomon and Thomas. Solomon was busy with an electric ice-cream machine and said he was preparing it for Pedro.'[10] I refuted this in my evidence, pointing out that a midwinter's day was hardly conducive to eating ice cream. What is true, however, is that old habits die hard, and some not at all. More than forty years later, I still love ice cream.

Throughout my prison term I received letters from friends who had travelled to India. Without exception, they had been profoundly impressed and excited by what they found there. I could not understand what they found so pleasant. Born and educated in South Africa, they had all grown up, as I did, with a mental picture of a vast country besieged by famine, malnutrition, disease, indescribable poverty, communal strife, lawlessness, corruption and filth.

It was only when I went to India myself, after my release, that I understood the enchantment, and realised that the picture sketched by the media in the West was grievously distorted, with so much emphasis on the negative aspects of the country that we were ignorant of the hospitality, warmth, simplicity, cultural richness and beautiful architecture of the subcontinent.

Unfortunately, Third World countries all too frequently fall victim to slanted reporting that relies on sensationalism and unfavourable news at the expense of the positive.

Although born and raised as a Muslim, I have never been deeply religious, but in May 1992, I went on Haj, the pilgrimage to the holy cities of Mecca and Medina. I travelled with my brother Solly, his wife Ayesha, their daughters Zuleikha and Farieda, and their sons-in-law, Samad and Ahmed. I knew that Dr Dadoo had made the same journey in his later years, and my primary motivation was to fulfil one of my late mother's dying wishes, but nothing had prepared me for the spiritual experience I had.

From the moment I landed in Jeddah, I was deeply moved by the multitudes from around the world, speaking different languages, wearing different garments, displaying different mannerisms, but united in their singular worship of Allah. The spirit of non-racialism and multiculturalism in Islam was all-pervasive.

The spiritual rites were complex. The movement of two million people from Mecca to Mina, to Arafat, to Muzdallifah, and back to Mina and Mecca, was taxing. But it sparked something within me, an unexpected sense of enhanced spirituality. Unfortunately, two events marred the experience. One was the sudden death of my brother at the Jeddah airport after I had boarded my flight home, and the fact that I could not be involved in his funeral rites.

The other was the crass consumerism of some of my fellow Hajis, and their attempts to bribe customs officials at Johannesburg International Airport when they returned with loads of electronic goods and jewellery. Somehow, I felt that the entire essence of Haj was lost on these pilgrims.

CODESA

We must be prudent, for he that is slow to anger is stronger than the mighty, and he who controls his temper is more powerful than he who rules a city. — **James Michener,** *The Source*[11]

Madiba has a well-deserved reputation for being level-headed, cool and un-flappable. It is virtually impossible to gauge his inner emotions; by and large he remains inscrutable. He felt deep hurt and sorrow at the deaths of his mother and his son while he was in prison, and must have been greatly affected and angered by the harassment that his family experienced at the hands of the police, but he never allowed his inner turmoil to overshadow his responsibilities towards his fellow prisoners.

Mandela is also slow to anger, but on the rare occasions that I have witnessed his cold wrath, it verged on the uncontrollable and dangerous.

By his own admission, he once came close to physically assaulting a prison officer who had made some highly offensive remarks. Eddie Daniels and I happened to be outside the office at the time, but as Mandela stormed out, cursing and mumbling to himself, he did not even notice us.

In 1993 the whole of South Africa, and much of the world, witnessed a public display of his anger against FW de Klerk, courtesy of television.

The occasion was a joint media conference to mark the opening of talks between the government and the ANC. Unbeknown to Mandela, De Klerk had arranged that he be given the last word, and used the opportunity to launch a scathing attack on the ANC.

Madiba was furious, and the cameras continued to roll as he sought special permission to address the gathering for a second time. He then made it abundantly clear that the ANC had not taken its place at the negotiating table as a defeated or spent force, but as a proud and triumphant participant. His forceful response put paid to any residual doubt about the wisdom of the ANC entering into talks with the enemy, and brought thousands of supporters in townships around the country onto the streets, singing and dancing in celebration.

It would take a few more years for all the documents to be signed and all the agreements to be made, but that was really the night when the 'new' South Africa was born.

❧ 22 ❧

Our Brave New World

Take note what men of old concluded:
That what there is shall go to those that are good for it,
Children to the motherly, that they prosper,
Carts to good drivers, that they be driven well,
The valley to the waterers, that it yield fruit.   **– Bertolt Brecht[1]**

Casting my ballot in the country of my birth was a thrilling experience. In Lenasia, the sight of thousands of people queuing in a patient and orderly manner brought tears to my eyes. Not even a bomb scare could deter the throng of determined first-time voters.

Images of the peaceful crowds waiting patiently to exercise the right to choose their government were relayed around the world. It was as though a dark shroud of paranoia, fear and desperation had been drawn aside, to reveal a shining beacon of optimism, love and pride.

There was never any doubt that the ANC would be victorious, but none of us anticipated such a significant majority, and the affirmation of support was thrilling.

The run-up to the 1994 elections witnessed the beginnings of speculation around ANC policies on a wide variety of issues, including the composition of an ANC cabinet. The ANC's National List Conference Assembly voted my name in the seventh position among members of the Constituent Assembly. This in turn led to media forecasts, which included me as a member of the cabinet. Not in my wildest dreams did I expect this to happen.

Before the announcement of the cabinet I attempted to convey, via comrades Walter Sisulu and Thabo Mbeki, that if my name came up for consideration, they should convey to Madiba to exclude me. I took this position, not out of modesty, but primarily because I believed I did not have the aptitude to serve on such as august body.

Unfortunately, when Madiba announced the first cabinet, I was surprised to see that he had made me Minister of Correctional Services! Obviously my message had never reached him. In the meantime I received reports of celebrations in several prisons, because the prisoners believed that 'one of their own' was now to occupy the position.

As matters transpired, in response to demands by the IFP to be given one of the 'security' positions, the problem was solved by giving them the Correctional Services post. This suited me.

I was appointed parliamentary counsellor in the Office of the President, and spent five years in a multifaceted, demanding, inspiring and fascinating position. We were part of a unique process, as we built a young democracy in what had been a country riddled with oppression, and social and economic fragmentation. We met hundreds of wonderful people and travelled widely, both in South Africa and abroad.

At the ANC's Mafikeng Conference in 1997, I stepped down from the National Executive Committee, and relinquished my parliamentary seat in 1999.

Madiba's intense loyalty and sense of gratitude sometimes border on naivety. He doesn't easily forget a good turn done to him or to his family, no matter how small. His attitude is based on the premise that individuals are inherently good, unless proven otherwise. If cautioned about a dubious or questionable character, the lawyer in him immediately comes to the fore. 'Where is your evidence?' he will ask.

Opportunists seldom leave a trail of clues, but somewhere deep in the recesses of his mind, Madiba must surely recognise the venal nature of those who trade on his signature or personalised photograph, a solitary letter written by him from prison, a superficial acquaintance of decades past suddenly elevated to 'close friendship'. As guileless as he is, he must, at the very least, be aware of the machinations of those who ingratiate themselves in order to promote their dubious and even fraudulent agendas.

Informally, he and I call one another Madala [old man], but even those who know him best, acknowledge that Mandela is no ordinary man. Charming and charismatic, he has both a magnetic personality and a commanding presence. An uncommon amalgam of peasant and aristocrat, he is a living paradox: a democrat par excellence, with just a touch of the autocrat; at once proud but simple; soft yet tenacious; obstinate and flexible; vain one moment and humble the next; infinitely tolerant but also impatient. For all the public exposure and media attention, Madiba remains an enigma to all but his most intimate circle.

THE ISLAND

Soon after the first democratic elections, President Mandela set in train a process that led to Robben Island being declared a National Monument and Heritage Site. Since then, it has also become a World Heritage Site. In 1995, the island played host to former political prisoners – black and white, male and female – who had been incarcerated in various jails throughout the country. It was a joyous and exciting reunion of some 1 200 former prisoners.

On 24 September 1997, the president opened the Robben Island Museum, developed and managed by a council of which I was elected chairman. Transformation, said Mandela, had turned 'a place of pain and banishment for centuries' into a monument to triumph, with its 'pre-eminent character as a symbol of the victory of the human spirit over political oppression; and of reconciliation over enforced division'.[2]

I have visited Robben Island many times since then, often escorting high-profile individuals and groups from across the political spectrum and all walks of life on tours of the facilities. Of all my visits, one holds a special place in my heart.

I was hosting Nadine Gordimer and Verna Hunt, when a little girl named Michelle Brits asked if she could have my autograph, or be photographed with me. Amid much light-hearted banter (I asked her if she had money to pay me), I happily posed with her for the camera, and we moved on.

Shortly afterwards, I learnt with shock that Michelle was terminally ill with leukaemia, and that her trip to Robben Island had fulfilled half of her dearest wish, thanks to the wonderful organisation Reach for a Dream.

The other thing the little girl wanted was to meet President Mandela.

At the earliest opportunity, I conveyed this gravely ill child's wish to Madiba, and asked if I could arrange for her to visit him either at home or in his office. His response was pure and vintage Mandela.

'I don't think we should give this young girl the trouble of coming all the way to me. Let's rather go to her,' he suggested.

The president of South Africa, a universally respected statesman with one of the busiest schedules on earth, flew to the Mpumalanga town of Secunda by helicopter, bearing gifts for a sick child. It seemed the entire population of the town turned out to welcome him, and to pray for Michelle's recovery. The emotional meeting between Madiba and Michelle was shown on national television, and as she clasped her little arms around his neck and kissed him, the eyes of millions must have filled with tears, just as mine did.

Michelle was an Afrikaner child, born and raised in a right-wing environment, but her dying wish was to meet the first black president of South Africa, and to see his prison. By her simple and spontaneous gesture of affection, she brought home, more powerfully than all the complex documents and carefully crafted speeches that are the lifeblood of the politicians, that our children truly are the future.

Thank you, Michelle. In your last days, you enriched more lives than you could ever have imagined, and to the end of my own, I will cherish the memory of our chance encounter on Robben Island.

On my seventieth birthday, I was surprised and honoured by a wonderful party organised by filmmaker Anant Singh, with the secret collaboration of many of my friends. The occasion was made more special still by publication of my correspondence, written and secretly stored on both the island and at Pollsmoor. *Letters From Robben Island* was launched by President Thabo Mbeki in Cape Town and by Cyril Ramaphosa in Lenasia. The book was first published by Michigan State University, and my friend Bob Vassen was given the task of selecting the letters and editing the book.

DEATH

Varinia said to Gracchus: 'Spartacus wanted a world where there were no slaves and no masters, only people living together in peace and brotherhood. He said that we would take from Rome what was good and beautiful. We would build cities without walls, and all men would live in peace and brotherhood and there would be no more war and no more misery and no more suffering.'

'So that was the dream of Spartacus,' he said, 'to make a world with no whips and none to be whipped – with no palaces and no mud huts. How do you know that Spartacus was pure and gentle?'

'It is hard for some people to know. Do you know what I will tell my son? I think you will understand me. I will tell him a very simple thing. I will explain to him that Spartacus was pure and gentle because he set his face against evil and opposed evil and fought evil – and never in all his life did he make his peace with what was wrong.'

'And how did Spartacus know what was right and what was wrong?'
Gracchus asked. 'What was good for his people was right. What hurt
them was wrong.'   **– Howard Fast, Spartacus³**

Sadly, though inevitably, I have had to come to terms with the loss of many friends and family members over time. The passing of Ismail Meer on 1 May 2000 not only left a vacuum in my life but, as I wrote to his widow Fatima and their family, 'left South Africa poorer. May the example of his life serve to nourish the ideas and practices for which he devoted so much of his time and energy.'

On 5 May 2003, 'in the arms of his wife, friend and comrade, Albertina, my father and most gentle hero, Walter Sisulu, a lifelong servant of the people of South Africa, left us'.⁴

'Xhamela is no more. May he live forever! His absence has carved a void. A part of me is gone,' lamented Nelson Mandela.

I was informed of the tragedy a few minutes after he passed away. I was devastated. For years I had lived with the recurring thought: 'What will my world be like if I have the misfortune of being alive when he passes on?'

Now the crushing news had come, and fate had been especially unkind. Barbara, who loved Walter and Mama Albertina as much as I did, was in Johannesburg. I desperately needed her to be with me, not only to share my grief, but also to offer whatever comfort I could get.

I sat at my computer, trying to get to grips with this great tragedy. Kim, my research assistance and close friend, happened to be with me when the phone call brought this most unwelcome news. Just a few weeks before she had accompanied me on a visit to Walter and Mama and, not surprisingly, fell instantly in love with both of them.

Over the months that we had been working together, she came to know how much I loved them too, and was able to empathise with me. Sensing my state of mind, she suggested that we inform friends and comrades both in South Africa and abroad. She switched on the computer and got down to work. By well past midnight, scores of e-mails and faxes had gone out. Kim rested for a while near the computer, and persuaded me to try to get some sleep. The responses started coming in almost immediately, and Kim relayed them to Elinor Sisulu and ANC headquarters.

My rest was fitful. I tried to comprehend the magnitude of the loss for our people, but my thoughts kept returning to my personal grief. Ever since my father died, when I was fourteen, I must subconsciously have searched for a surrogate, and it was in Walter Sisulu that I found him.

That night, while Kim manned the computer, I remembered Walter's generosity and his pure understanding that we all share what this earth has to offer, and that private ownership is a strange concept. I remembered how in prison, whenever someone was missing an item of clothing from the washing line, the entire passage would lovingly sing out, 'Tshopo Lo', knowing instinctively that Walter had invariably removed the first clothes he found, with absolutely no regard for this 'yours and mine' business!

By the time of our release, Walter and I had grown so close that I knew I could take for granted his reaction, and Mama Albertina's, to my personal affairs, and I was right. They accepted my relationship with Barbara without question or hesitation. Barbara and Mama had, in fact, briefly been imprisoned in the same jail, though in separate sections, of course. Nonetheless, Mama had come to know that Barbara refused to eat her 'white' food unless the warders gave Mama Albertina the same.

After our release, it was an honour and a privilege for me to be invited to speak at Walter's eightieth birthday, Mama's birthday and their fiftieth wedding anniversary.

While we were still in prison, I learnt that I had been welcomed into the fold as a member of the extended Sisulu family, so for me the ultimate honour was being asked by the family to read Walter's obituary, with my long-time comrade, Bertha Xowa, at the funeral.

Thank you, Mama, and all the members of the family, for affording me the great honour of bidding farewell to our father in the presence of tens of thousands of mourners at the ceremony, and the millions more who watched and listened on television and radio.

Tributes poured in from everywhere. 'We shall equally remember him for his warmth and personal simplicity,' said Prime Minister Vajpayee of India. 'He was a rare political personality who had a stature that did not depend on status.'

Deputy President Jacob Zuma's words rang especially true: 'He was always sober and was one of the living examples of how a disciplined ANC cadre should be. I am not certain if we are still able to produce this kind of leadership.'

COSATU's statement captured his role in the struggle perfectly:

Comrade Walter occupied a special place in the history of our liberation movement and the hearts of millions of South Africans and peace loving people across the world. Throughout his life in the struggle, comrade Walter was the unassuming, humble, gentle giant of the revolution. He was generally known as an intellectual tower that mentored and groomed many comrades, not least of all comrade Nelson Mandela. For this he will be sorely missed by all who were close to him and those that he inspired over the years.

Comrade Walter symbolised unflagging commitment to the cause of the oppressed people. He was indeed a man of honour, dignity, magnanimity and integrity and selflessness. We shall miss his non-sectarian approach to the liberation struggle and his wisdom. Above all, he leaves a rich legacy of building a strong organisation and a firm commitment to principles even under adverse circumstances.

There was massive press coverage of Walter's passing, acknowledging his pivotal role. During the 1950s, he was 'repeatedly described by colleagues as the organisational and tactical dynamo who transformed the ANC from a genteel lobby group into a vehicle of mass resistance. He was clearly an influential personality who made a deep impression on his fellow activists and on political prisoners on Robben Island, where he and other elder statesmen of the "struggle" administered political education to succeeding generations of prisoners. The fact that we avoided the abyss, and continue to do so nine years after the end of apartheid, owes much to Walter Sisulu and those who worked with him.'[5]

Fittingly, Walter was laid to rest among the ordinary people at Croesus Cemetery.

~ (~

Epilogue

I have fought against white domination, and I have fought against black domination. I have cherished the ideal of a democratic and free society in which all persons live together in harmony and with equal opportunities. It is an ideal which I hope to live for and to achieve. But if needs be, it is an ideal for which I am prepared to die. — **Nelson Mandela**[1]

Throughout my twenty-six years in prison, this courageous and historic peroration of Madiba's statement from the dock during the Rivonia Trial kept alive the vision of the society we were striving to achieve. With a possible death sentence looming, he had boldly and clearly reaffirmed ANC policy, and its commitment to the Freedom Charter, embracing its political, economic and cultural clauses.

At home and in exile, in the face of great danger, the ANC leadership stuck rigidly to this policy and acted firmly against any deviation from it.

Hence I emerged from prison full of confidence, albeit with somewhat idealistic – even utopian – ideas about the practical implementation of this policy.

It did not take long for me to wake up to the realities of the South Africa to which we had returned. More than three centuries of apartheid had left a legacy of massive poverty, hunger, illiteracy, unemployment, homelessness and – above all – racial polarisation and state-orchestrated violence.

There was an atmosphere of understandable frustration and impatience among our people. While the unbanned ANC was engaged in re-establishing itself in branches and regions, the UDF and COSATU continued to lead the oppressed to new heights of disciplined non-violent struggle and political consciousness. On the other hand, the continuing Third Force violence led to the CODESA process facing collapse on more than one occasion.

That was the situation twelve months before the 1994 elections. Then came the dastardly assassination of Comrade Chris Hani, the widely revered and charismatic ANC and Communist Party leader. This single act propelled South Africa to the brink of a bloodbath, the like of which had never been seen before. The situation called for utmost calm, courage, statesmanship and foresight. President FW de Klerk's government found itself in a state of panic, confusion, helplessness and impotence. In this atmosphere of unprecedented tension, ANC president Nelson Mandela rushed to Johannesburg from the Transkei and was asked to appear on television. His simple, forceful words saved the country from imminent disaster:

> Tonight I am reaching out to every single South African, black and white, from the very depths of my being. A white man, full of prejudice and hate, came to our country and committed a deed so foul that our whole nation now teeters on the brink of disaster. A white woman, of Afrikaner origin, risked her life so that we may know, and bring to justice, this assassin. Now is the time for all South Africans to stand together against those who, from any quarter, wish to destroy what Chris Hani gave his life for – the freedom of all of us.[2]

The country responded positively to his appeal for peace, and that night, a full year before his official inauguration, Mandela effectively became the new president of South Africa. Not a single individual in government ranks, nor even among the other leaders of the liberation movement, had the stature of Madiba, and no one else could have commanded the respect needed to avert disaster.

We had hardly buried Chris Hani when the ANC suffered another irreparable loss with the death of Oliver Tambo. As the organisation's president, he and the leaders in exile had worked day and night to direct the course of the struggle and mobilised international support for the isolation of apartheid South Africa.

OR's death was an enormous personal loss for Madiba. Their political involvement and personal friendship stretched across half a century, during which they developed close bonds of comradeship. Using Plato's allegory, Madiba wrote:

> Oliver was pure gold; there was gold in his intellectual brilliance, gold in his warmth and humanity, gold in his tolerance and generosity, gold in his unfailing loyalty and self-sacrifice. As much as I respected him as a leader, that is how much I loved him as a man. When I looked at him in his coffin, it was as if a part of myself had died.[3]

I had always regarded Madiba, OR and Walter Sisulu as the Triumvirate, bound to one another by unshakeable loyalty and selfless admiration. But ten years after OR's death, Walter, too, was gone. Madiba was devastated:

'In a sense I feel cheated by Walter. If there be another life beyond this physical world, I would have loved to be there first so that I could welcome him.'[4]

During the five years of his presidency, Madiba concentrated on spreading and consolidating a message of forgiveness, reconciliation, unity, peace and nation-building. Among his earliest gestures was to invite the wives and widows of former prime ministers and presidents to tea, and to take a special trip to the white Afrikaner enclave of Orania to pay a courtesy call on Betsie Verwoerd, the ailing widow of the assassinated architect of apartheid, Hendrik Frensch Verwoerd.

In its first decade of democracy under an ANC government under presidents Mandela and Mbeki, South Africa has made gigantic strides, maintaining a sophisticated financial sector and a strengthening economy, and providing basic services to the previously disadvantaged. In every sphere – education, culture, commerce, sport, politics – there is visible evidence of progress.

Such achievements, as well as the presence in Zurich of President Mbeki, Archbishop Tutu and Madiba, must have been of crucial importance in the decision taken on 15 May 2004 by the international football fraternity to award the 2010 FIFA World Cup – the first on the African continent – to South Africa.

The explosion of joy, the mass celebrations that greeted this exciting announcement across the length and breadth of the country were ample confirmation that democratic South Africa had arrived, and that the world acknowledged our place in it.

I feel sure that all the former Robben Island prisoners noted with pride that the final presentation in Zurich was made against a backdrop that included clips of island soccer games between the inmates. Soccer was undoubtedly the most popular game on the island, and did much to promote unity and friendship among prisoners from diverse cultural and political groups.

In 2003, the Robben Island Museum was included in the itinerary of the visiting FIFA delegation, and it will almost certainly play host to thousands of visiting soccer players, officials and fans in 2010 as well.

As proud as all South Africans are entitled to be over the first decade of democracy, euphoria should not be allowed to lull us into complacency. Huge tasks and responsibilities of great magnitude lie ahead. We need to continue reaching out to the masses of our people to explain our policies. We need to continue guarding against the temptations of careerism, self-interest and corruption. Uppermost in our minds should be the strengthening of our non-racial, non-sexist democracy, and the priority of uplifting the lives of the poorest of the poor. We have to face the challenges of unemployment, hunger, education, homelessness, crime and HIV/AIDS.

It is a pity that occasional incidents, sometimes innocent, are blown out of proportion and described as 'racism'. Some media practitioners seem to thrive on sensational reporting, ignoring one of the basic tenets of media freedom, namely objective and balanced reporting. How much more rewarding it would be if the media paid as much attention to the peaceful and incident-free reconciliation taking place between millions of South Africans across the board on a daily basis, as to the occasional ugly incidents.

It is to be fervently hoped that the media will make a point of rooting out the tendency towards sensationalism, especially when this is at the cost of truth. While genuine examples of racism need to be exposed, the media should guard against labelling as 'racist' every incident that happens to take place across the colour line. To do so, especially where race is not the root cause of the problem, is to diminish the numerous, but mostly untold, stories of successful integration.

South Africa in 2004, with its positive achievements since 1994 and its universally acclaimed Constitution, continues to be identified as a role model for people in conflict areas striving to bring about peaceful transformation. Among the tens of thousands of foreign visitors who flock to our country in growing numbers are many individuals and groups who make a point of visiting Robben Island. As chairperson of the Robben Island Museum Council, I have had the privilege of hosting many of these visitors.

We have hosted leaders and groups from countries that in one way or another are experiencing conflicts. Thus, on different occasions, we have had President Clinton and President Castro; Chairman Arafat and a dozen retired Israeli generals, some of whom had previously occupied ministerial positions; Dame Margaret Thatcher and Gerry Adams of Sinn Fein; and many more. We have had former IRA prisoners, as well as former Unionist prisoners.

I am frequently asked to explain the so-called 'miracle' of our peaceful transformation. In keeping with what I believe is our government's policy, my response has been that it would be presumptuous of us to prescribe to other countries how they should solve their problems. We recall that, with only a handful of exceptions, virtually all wars and conflicts end at the negotiation table. All we can do is to relate our experiences – how in the face of seemingly insurmountable odds, with a background of over three centuries of white rule and a great deal of violence and bloodshed, the ANC and the incumbent government had agreed to enter into discussions; how these talks had led to the formal CODESA Conference, at which the basis of the Interim Constitution was agreed upon. This in turn had led to the first democratic elections of 1994.

On her visit to Robben Island in 1996, Prime Minister Gro Harlem of Norway suggested the establishment of a conflict resolution centre on the Island. Former Prime Minister Gujral of India echoed this idea. Sadly we haven't made much progress. In my view, with its recent history and the universal interest it attracts, Robben Island would be the ideal venue for such a centre.

I conclude this Epilogue with these ubiquitous pictures in my mind; FIFA, and Zurich; of President Mbeki and Archbishop Tutu and Madiba; of Danny Jordaan and Irvin Khoza; and, most inspiring of all, the pictures and reports of a united South Africa joining hands and hearts in celebration. To some extent this outburst of euphoria surpassed 1994. Ten years ago our democracy was ushered in amidst unprecedented ecstasy and joy. But it was overwhelmingly a celebration of African, Coloured and Indian South Africans, while our white compatriots were by and large reserved, subdued, even hostile.

After a decade of democracy, and with our eyes and ears turned to Zurich in our millions, we walked tall. We were unwaveringly proudly South African. With such confidence we can look forward to 2010 and beyond – to the decades and more that lie in the distant future. United we can and will march forward to the brighter dawn that awaits our people, our nation and our country.

The scenes of jubilation, the spontaneous outpouring of celebration following FIFA's decision, the solidarity of pride and unity evoked by a sporting event should serve as a shining example to black and white alike.

Those images, indelibly imprinted on my mind, bode well for the future of our people, our nation, and our country.

Appendix A
Brief Biographical Overview

21 AUGUST 1929	Born in Western Transvaal town of Schweizer-Reneke
1938	Sent to 'Indian' school in Johannesburg
1940S	Meets Yusuf Dadoo, IC Meer, Yusuf and Molvi Cachalia, JN Singh
1941	Joins Young Communist League (with Ruth First, Harold Wolpe and others)
JUNE 1946	Leaves school in matric year to join Passive Resistance Campaign under the mentorship of IC Meer; serves a month in Durban jail in December
1945–1946	Helps form the Transvaal Indian Youth Congress and is later elected as its chair
1947	Moves into IC Meer's flat, No. 13 Kholvad House

1947	Elected to attend the first World Youth Festival, in Prague. A hit-and-run accident prevents him from going
1949	Makes two trips to Botswana with Reverend Michael Scott
1950	In Commissioner Street, Johannesburg, has first and only real argument with Nelson Mandela
1950	Communist Party dissolved following the passing of the Suppression of Communism Act
1951	Enrols as student at Wits University; elected to go to Berlin Festival and abandons studies
1951	Leaves South Africa to work at the headquarters of the World Federation of Democratic Youth in Budapest
AUGUST 1951	Heads the sixty-strong South African delegation to the World Festival of Youth and Students in Berlin
MAY 1952	Returns to South Africa
28 FEBRUARY 1952	Barbara Hogan born
1952	Accused in trial of twenty leaders of Defiance Campaign; receives nine months' suspended sentence
1953	Becomes secretary of Youth Action Committee of ANC Youth League and Indian Youth Congress. Elected to executive of World Federation of Democratic Youth
1953	Joins reconstituted Communist Party, operating from underground
1954	Banned from gatherings and ordered to resign from thirty-nine organisations – first banning order
1954–1956	Active in organising Congress of the People, secretary of Central Indian High School Parents' Association – a private school established to combat the Group Areas Act
OCTOBER 1956	First ban expires
5 AND 12 DECEMBER 1956	Treason Trial arrests of 156 Congress leaders and activists
16 JANUARY 1957	Issued with a five-year banning order
1960	Law practice of Mandela & Tambo closed – Mandela practises from Flat 13
29 MARCH 1961	Treason Trial ends with 'not guilty' verdict for remaining thirty accused
5 AUGUST 1962	Mandela arrested; AMK secretary of the Free Mandela Committee
1962	Placed under house arrest
24 MAY 1963	Goes underground; moves to Liliesleaf Farm, Rivonia
2 JULY 1963	Moves out of Rivonia to cottage in Mountain View

11 JULY 1963	Arrested at Liliesleaf Farm and held in solitary confinement
9 OCTOBER 1963	Rivonia Trial begins; co-accused are Nelson Mandela, Walter Sisulu, Elias Motsoeledi, Andrew Mlangeni, Dennis Goldberg, Raymond Mhlaba, Govan Mbeki, Rusty Bernstein and Jimmy Kantor. Bernstein and Kantor are later acquitted
12 JUNE 1964	Sentenced to life imprisonment with hard labour at end of Rivonia Trial
13 JUNE 1964	Arrives to serve sentence at Robben Island Prison
1965–1982	BA – History and Criminology (1965-68) B Bibliography – Library Science and African Politics BA Honours – History (1981-82)
21 OCTOBER 1982	Moved from Robben Island Prison to Pollsmoor Prison
1983	Made a patron (with other Rivonia men) of the newly launched United Democratic Front
1980s	BA Honours – African Politics
1986	Honoured by the University of Guelph, Canada, with an honourary community degree
1988	Awarded the ANC's highest possible award, the Isitwalandwe Award
8 FEBRUARY 1986	Honoured by Central London Polytechnic
15 OCTOBER 1989	Released from prison
1991	Elected to NEC of ANC. Head of ANC public relations
1991	Appointed Fellow of the Mayibuye Centre, University of the Western Cape
1992	Goes on Haj pilgrimage to Mecca
1994	Elected Member of Parliament
1994	Appointed parliamentary counsellor in the office of the president, Nelson Mandela
1997	Elected chairperson, Robben Island Council
1997	Steps down from the National Executive Committee at the ANC's Mafikeng conference
1999	Does not stand for re-election in 1999 elections
10 JUNE 1999	Presidential Award of the Order for Meritorious Service Class 1 from President Nelson Mandela
2002	Awarded honorary doctorate by the University of Massachusetts
	Awarded honorary doctorate by the University of Durban-Westville

4 OCTOBER 2003	Awarded the Mahatma Gandhi Award by the Congress of Business and Economics, presented by President Thabo Mbeki
2004	Awarded a doctorate of Humane Letters by the University of Missouri
CURRENT	Serves as patron of the Trauma Centre, chair of Robben Island Council, on the executive of the Nelson Mandela Foundation board, on the board of Freedom Park, on the Presidential Advisory Council for Awards board

Appendix B

Senior Officers at Robben Island Jail and Pollsmoor Prison

ROBBEN ISLAND

Year	Commanding Officer	Officer in Charge of Political Section (Head of Prison)
1965	'Beloftes' Wessels	Daantjie Theron
1966	Kellerman	Daantjie Theron
1967	Prinsloo ('Staalbaard')	Daantjie Theron
1968	Prinsloo ('Staalbaard')	Daantjie Theron
1969	Prinsloo ('Staalbaard')	Daantjie Theron
1970	Col. JJ van Aarde	Chief Warder PJ Fourie
1971	Col. Piet Badenhorst ('Kid Ruction')	Chief Warder PJ Fourie

Year	Commanding Officer	Officer in Charge of Political Section (Head of Prison)
1972	Col. P. Badenhorst	Chief Warder PJ Fourie
1973	Col. WH Willemse	Lt. R Terblanche
1974	Col. WH Willemse	Lt. R Terblanche
1975	Lt. Col. HJ Roelofse	Lt. R Terblanche
1976	Lt. Col. HJ Roelofse	WO PJ Prins
1977	Col. TW Richards	Lt. PJ Prins
1978	Col. TW Richards	Capt. JW Harding
1979	Brig. Hennie J Botha	Capt. JW Harding
1980	Brigadier MD Bosman	Maj. JW Harding
1981	Brig. M Bosman	Maj. W Badenhorst
1982	Brig. FC Munro	

POLLSMOOR

Year	Commanding Officer	Officer in Charge of Political Section (Head of Prison)
1982	Brig. CL de Fortier	Van Sittert
1983	Col. AKJ Ritter	Lt. H Bester
1984	Brig. FC Munro	Maj. FP van Sittert
1985	Col. AKJ Ritter	Maj. AE Smit
1986	Brig. FC Munro	Maj. FP van Sittert
1987	Brig. Booysen	
1988	Brig. Booysen	
1989	Brig. Booysen	

Notes

PREFACE

1   Ahmed Kathrada, Private notebooks kept secretly on Robben Island, No. 4.
2   Ahmed Kathrada, *Letters from Robben Island*, Cape Town: Zebra Press, 1999, p. 270.

PROLOGUE

1   Cited by Mario Puzo in *The Fortunate Pilgrim*. AM Kathrada, secret prison notebooks, No. 6.
2   Elinor Sisulu, *Walter and Albertina Sisulu, In Our Lifetime*. Cape Town: David Philip, 2003, p. 156.
3   Kathrada, secret prison notebooks, No. 4.
4   *Ibid.*
5   *Ibid.*
6   'Our Beloved Czech Song' from *To Sing with the Angels*, dedicated to the students of Charles University massacred by the Gestapo on the night of 17 November 1939. AM Kathrada, secret prison notebooks, No. 2.
7   South Africa oh land of my birth / South Africa I love you so / Most beautiful are your lovely open grass-lands / Most precious are your dear blue skies / South Africa / This is why you are simply the best country for me.
8   I like a man who can stand his man / I like an arm that can strike a blow / An eye that doesn't waver, a gaze that doesn't flinch / And a will that stands as steadfast as a rock.

CHAPTER 2

1   Kathrada, secret prison notebooks, No. 6.
2   In my last year at school in Johannesburg (1946) there were only two girls in our class. Today the ratio would be about 50-50.
3   PS Joshi, *The Tyranny of Colour/Crusade Against Racism*, p. 238.
4   Tagore was born in 1861 and died in 1941. He was awarded the Nobel Prize for Literature in 1913.
5   T Karis and GM Carter, *From Protest to Challenge*, Vol. 2, *Hope and Challenge 1935–1952*, Stanford: Hoover Institution Press, 1979, p. 98.
6   Kathrada, secret prison notebooks, No. 4.
7   Cf Karis and Carter, Vol. 2, p. 124, note 51: 'The ANC Youth League was born', Raboroko has claimed, 'at a meeting held at the Domestic and Cultural Workers Club Hall in Diagonal Street, Johannesburg, in October 1943; a meeting convened and presided over by the present writer'. *Africa South*, April–June 1960, p. 29.

CHAPTER 3

1   Kathrada, secret prison notebooks, No. 3.
2   S Bhana and B Pachai, *A Documentary History of Indian South Africans*, Cape Town: David Philip, 1989, p. 200.
3   Gool and the first batch of Cape Resisters were sentenced in Durban on 13 August 1946.
4   Karis and Carter, *From Protest to Challenge*, Vol. 2, p. 114.

5 Kathrada, secret prison notebooks, No. 4.

6 See Rusty Bernstein, *Memory Against Forgetting*, Sandton: Viking Press, 1999, p. 105.

7 Mary Benson, *A Far Cry: The Making of a South African*, Randburg: Ravan Press, 1996.

8 ES Reddy, *India, Britain and the Struggle Against Apartheid*. Lecture at a meeting of the Nehru Centre, London, 13 August 1992.

9 http://www.afribeat.com/ archiveafrica.html

10 Kathrada, secret prison notebooks, No. 4.

11 Karis and Carter, *From Protest to Challenge*, Vol. 2, testimony of ZK Matthews, Treason Trial Record, Vol. 9, p. 891.

12 Bhana and Pachai, p. 189.

13 Kathrada, secret prison notebooks, No. 4.

14 Joshi, *Crusade Against Racism*.

15 'In 1946, 75 000 African mineworkers in 21 mines on the Witwatersrand came out on strike for higher wages. As in 1920, troops were called in to drive the miners back to the mines at bayonet point.' African National Congress, *Unity in Action – A Photographic History of the African National Congress 1912–1982*, Kent: AG Bishop & Sons, 1982.

16 Kathrada, secret prison notebooks, No. 6.

17 Karis and Gerhart, *From Protest to Challenge*, Vol. 4, *Political Profiles 1882–1964*, p. 56.

18 Elinor Sisulu, *In Our Lifetime*, pp. 77–78.

19 *The Passive Resister*, Thursday 12 June 1947, p. 7.

20 *The Passive Resister*, Thursday 3 July 1947.

21 Kathrada, secret prison notebooks, No. 4.

22 GM Houser and H Shore, *I Will Go Singing*, Robben Island Museum.

23 Kathrada, secret prison notebooks, No. 4.

24 Albert Luthuli, *Let My People Go*, London: Collins, 1962.

CHAPTER 4

1 South African Police, secret memorandum WD.10/3/34/58 from Inspector Botha to the Commissioner of Police: Communist Party Meeting, Corner Gerty Street and Victoria Road, Sophiatown, Johannesburg, Sunday 26 February 1950, p. 3.

2 Ismail Meer, *A Fortunate Man*, Cape Town: Zebra Press, 2002, p. 113.

3 South African Police, secret memorandum, 25 April 1950: Defend Free Speech Convention Meeting, Indian Sports Grounds, Benoni, 16 April 1950.

4 SA Police, secret memorandum from Inspector Botha to Commissioner of Police, pp. 2–3.

5 *Letters from Robben Island*.

6 The Indian tradition of adding 'bhai' (brother) or 'bai' (sister) to a first name is a sign of respect and affection

7 Nelson Mandela, *Long Walk to Freedom*, London: Abacus, 1994, p. 98.

8 An alcoholic beverage.

9 Kathrada, secret prison notebooks, No. 4.

10 Can Themba, 'Sophiatown Magic' in J Schadeberg, *Sof'town Blues: Images from the Black 50s*, Jürgen Schadeberg, Pinegowrie, 1994, p. 136.

11 Literally, 'little brother of the kaffir' a highly derogatory term used in apartheid South Africa to describe whites who had non-white friends, including but not limited to, political activists. The term 'kaffir' from an Arabic word for non-believer or infidel was widely used by racists to describe blacks. Since 1994 it has been officially declared hate speech.

12 Justice Rumpff also presided over the lengthy Treason Trial in which the author was one of the accused.

13 I read of Howard Lawrence's death in a newspaper report on 26 September 1981.

14 Kathrada, secret prison notebooks, No. 4.

CHAPTER 5

1   Primo Levi, 'The Reawakening' in
J Miller (ed.), *On Suicide*, San Francisco,
Chronicle, 1992, p. 184.
2   Pablo Neruda, *Memoirs*, New York:
Farrar, Straus and Giroux, 1977,
p. 359.
3   Kathrada, secret prison notebooks, No. 4.
4   *Ibid.*
5   South African Communist Party website.
6   Nelson Mandela, *Long Walk to Freedom*,
pp. 96–98, 107.
7   Kathrada, secret prison notebooks, No. 4.
8   *Star*, 6 May 2003.

CHAPTER 6

1   ES Reddy, *Education Against
Apartheid: Some observations.* Paper
presented to international seminar on
education against apartheid, organised
by the Non-governmental
Organisations Sub-Committee
on Racism, Racial Discrimination,
Apartheid and Decolonisation in
cooperation with the United Nations
Special Committee against Apartheid,
Palais des Nations, Geneva,
September 4–6, 1989
2   Nelson Mandela, *Long Walk to Freedom*,
p. 115.
3   Elinor Sisulu, *In Our Lifetime*, p. 97.
4   *Ibid*, p. 99.
5   Karis and Carter, Vol. 2, pp. 476–477.
6   *Ibid.*
7   *Ibid*, p. 433.
8   Eddie Roux, *Time Longer Than Rope*,
p. 391.
9   Elinor Sisulu, p. 102.
10 Karis and Carter, Vol. 2, p. 484.
11 Nelson Mandela, *Long Walk to Freedom*,
pp. 127–128.
12 Karis and Carter, Vol. 2, p. 422.
13 *Ibid.*
14 *Ibid*, p. 421.

15 Nelson Mandela, *Long Walk to Freedom*,
pp. 129–130.

CHAPTER 7

1   SA History Online website:
*Independence of African Colonies
Chronology.*
2   Kathrada, secret prison notebooks, No. 4.
3   Xhosa and Afrikaans words respectively
for elephant.
4   Weinber, E, *Portrait of a People: A
Personal Photographic Record of the South
African Liberation Struggle*, International
Defence and Aid Fund for Southern
Africa, London, 1981, p. 121.
5   *Ibid.*
6   ANC, *Unity in Action*, p. 66.
7   *New Age*, Vol. 1, No. 33, 9 June 1955,
'Freedom Awards to People's Leaders'.
8   ANC, *Unity in Action*, p. 79.
9   http://www.anc.org.za/ancdocs/
history/campaigns/cop/
10 ANC, *Unity in Action*, p. 63.
11 Kathrada, AM, personal notebook kept
during Rivonia Trial.
12 *Ibid.*
13 http://www.anc.org.za/ancdocs/
history/lutuli/jordan.html
14 AM Kathrada quoted in secret memorandum from Inspector Botha to Commissioner of Police, 25 April 1950, p. 1.
15 http://www.anc.org.za/ancdocs/
history/women/petition560809.html

CHAPTER 8

1   Helen Joseph, *If this Be Treason*, Contra
Press, Johannesburg, 1998, p. 29.
2   *Ibid*, p. 273.
3   See also Professor Thomas Karis, 'Guide
to the Microfilm Record of the Trial'.
4   Joseph, Helen, *If this Be Treason*, p. 277.
5   Kathrada, secret prison notebooks, No. 4.
6   *Ibid*, No. 6.
7   Helen Joseph, *Side by Side*, p. 68.

8 See *A Trumpet from the Housetops*, p. 221.
9 Kathrada, secret prison notebooks, No. 4.
10 Reader's Digest, *Illustrated History of South Africa – The Real Story*, p. 402.
11 Kathrada, secret prison notebooks, No. 4.
12 Traditional remedies, magic potions.
13 Nelson Mandela, *Long Walk to Freedom*, p. 288.
14 *Ibid*, p. 289.
15 Helen Joseph, *If This Be Treason*, p. 101.
16 Elinor Sisulu, *In Our Lifetime*, p. 142.
17 Helen Joseph, *If This Be Treason*, p. 106.
18 Mac Maharaj's complaints to the court of torture by the police during the so-called 'Little Rivonia' trial were ignored and he was returned night after night to barbaric and obscene abuse. See Hilda Bernstein, *The Terrorism of Torture*.
19 Helen Joseph, *If This Be Treason*, p. 109.
20 Nelson Mandela, *Long Walk to Freedom*, p. 134.
21 http://www.africacrime-mystery.co.za/ books/fsac/chp14.htm
22 Chris Nthite, 'Joburg, bloody Joburg', *Sunday Times*, 15 February 2004
23 Karis and Carter, p. 676.

CHAPTER 9

1 Kathrada, secret prison notebooks, No. 4.
2 Edgar Allan Poe's story, 'The Purloined Letter' illustrates the cleverness of choosing the most obvious place to hide an object that is being looked for.
3 Patrick O'Donovan, 'The Serene African Fighter', *Observer*, 14 June 1964.
4 Kathrada, secret prison notebooks, No. 4.
5 Heidi Holland, *The Struggle: A History of the ANC*, Grafton Books, London, 1989, p. 138.
6 Helen Joseph, *Side by Side*, p. 74.
7 Kathrada, secret prison notebooks, No. 4.
8 *Ibid*, No. 6.
9 *Ibid*, No. 4.
10 Karis and Carter, Vol. 3, p. 661.

11 TRC Report, Vol. 3, Chapter 6: *Regional Profile Transvaal, 1960–1975*.
12 Kathrada, secret prison notebooks, No. 7.
13 *State vs Nelson Mandela and others*.
14 Rusty Bernstein, *Memory Against Forgetting*, London: Viking Books, 1999, p. 249.
15 Nelson Mandela, *Long Walk to Freedom*, p. 343.
16 Elinor Sisulu, *In Our Lifetime*, p. 169.
17 Rusty Bernstein, *Memory Against Forgetting*, pp. 250–252.
18 Karis and Carter, pp. 676–677.
19 I have relied on Karis and Carter, pp. 760–767 to refresh my memory.
20 Kathrada, personal notebook kept during trial.
21 Heidi Holland, *The Struggle*, pp. 149–151.
22 Bernstein, Rusty, *Memory Against Forgetting*, pp. 237–238.
23 Joel Joffe, *The Rivonia Trial*, Cape Town: Mayibuye Books, p. 1.
24 *Ibid*, p. 4.
25 Harold had been arrested earlier while trying to cross the Bechuanaland border in disguise.
26 Greef was a youth of eighteen. The authorities took revenge by deeply humiliating him and sentencing him to the maximum punishment, six years in prison.

CHAPTER 10

1 Kathrada, secret prison notebooks, No. 4.
2 *Ibid*.
3 'UN Call To Prevent African Executions', *The Times*, 1 June 1964.
4 'Call for Sanctions made in UN', *The Times*, Saturday 13 June 1964.
5 LB Fleming, 'Sentences for Treason draw Criticism in UN', *Los Angeles Times*, 13 June 1964.
6 Kathrada, secret prison notebooks, No. 4.

7 Joel Joffe, *The Rivonia Trial*, pp. 37–38.
8 *Ibid.*
9 *Ibid*, pp. 42–43.
10 *Ibid*, p. 192.
11 Kathrada, personal notebook kept during the trial.
12 *Ibid.*
13 Cassandra, 'The People's Courts', *Daily Mirror*, Monday 15 June 1964.
14 'Eight Convicted in South Africa Treason Trial', *Los Angeles Times*, Friday 12 June 1964.
15 *Guardian*, 13 June 1964.
16 Hilda Bernstein, *South Africa: The Terrorism of Torture*, London: Christian Action Publications, 1972, p. 24.
17 *State vs Nelson Mandela and others*, South African National Archives.
18 Letter smuggled to Sylvia during the trial.
19 http://www.anc.org.za/un/undocs1b.html
20 Kathrada, secret prison notebooks, No. 4.
21 Joel Joffe, *The Rivonia Trial*, p. 142.
22 *Ibid*, p. 151.
23 Joel Joffe, Talent Consortium interview.
24 SA History website: Sisulu biography.
25 Joel Joffe, *The Rivonia Trial*, p. 151.
26 Kathrada, secret prison notebooks, No. 4.
27 Joel Joffe, *The Rivonia Trial*, pp. 111, 151–153.
28 Rivonia Trial court record, pp. 154–156.
29 Kathrada, private notebook kept during trial, p. 8.
30 *Ibid*, p. 119.
31 *Ibid*, pp. 80–81.
32 Kathrada, secret prison notebooks, No. 4.
33 'Judge on Possibility of Evidence Concocted after Detention', *The Times*, 12 June 1964.
34 A Klaaste, 'I'll Never Forget … Rivonia', *Drum*, July 1964, p. 54.
35 'MPs Join London Protest March', *The Times*, Friday 12 June 1964.
36 'South Africa Sentences 8 to Life Terms', *Washington Post*, 13 June 1964.
37 'Dr Luther King Arrested', *The Times*, 12 June 1964.
38 A Klaaste, *Drum*, July 1964, p. 56.
39 Stephen Clingman, *Bram Fischer: Afrikaner Revolutionary*, Cape Town: David Philip, 1998, p. 322.
40 'Plea for Clemency at Trial', *The Times*, Saturday 13 June 1964.
41 Leslie Beilby, 'Mandela Life Sentence', *Daily Telegraph*, Saturday 13 June 1964.
42 'Plea for Clemency at Trial', *The Times*, Saturday 13 June 1964.
43 'Smiles, but no cheers', *Drum*, July 1964, p. 55.
44 A Klaaste, *Drum*, July 1964, p. 54.
45 Mary Benson, *A Far Cry*, p. 157.
46 Stanley Uys, 'An Uncertain Silence After Rivonia Trial', *Observer*, 14 June 1964.
47 Carmel Rickard, 'Rivonia: The Trial of the Century', *Sunday Times* supplement, 2000, pp. 10–11, 23.

CHAPTER 11

1 Kathrada, secret prison notebooks, No. 4.
2 *Ibid.*
3 Stephen Clingman, *Bram Fischer*, p. 327.
4 After a bloody war, Algeria received independence from the French in 1962. Developments in South Africa were influenced by a number of factors relating to the Algerian situation. Some of the primary evidence against me in the Rivonia Trial was a pamphlet expressing solidarity with the Algerian struggle for freedom. At a more sinister level, although no official record of this remains extant, a group of Security Branch officers, including Viktor and Erasmus, was sent by the South African government to be schooled by the French in Algeria in methods of torture. Torture in Algeria under the

French had gained world notoriety as some of the worst ever perpetrated.

5 Stephen Clingman, *Bram Fischer*, p. 328.
6 Joel Joffe, *The Rivonia Trial*, p. 214.
7 Stephen Clingman, *Bram Fischer*, p. 330.
8 'Prison Visitor to Mandela', *The Times*, 14 August 1964.
9 Nelson Mandela, *Long Walk to Freedom*, p. 459.
10 *Ibid*, p. 458.
11 'South Africa on Trial', *Daily Telegraph*, Friday 12 June 1964.
12 *Ibid*.
13 In later years, inquest after inquest – in the cases of Imam Haron, Ahmed Timol, Neil Aggett, to name but a few – returned verdicts of suicide. I cannot recall a single case among the scores of deaths under 90-day detention in which an inquest magistrate held the security police responsible.
14 Hilda Bernstein, *The Terrorism of Torture*, pp. 32–33; pamphlet published by the Inter-national Defence and Aid Fund, 1972.
15 Mary Benson, *A Far Cry*, p. 160.
16 Kathrada, secret prison notebooks, No. 4.
17 Hilda Bernstein, *The Terrorism of Torture*, p. 43.
18 Kathrada, secret prison notebooks, No. 4.
19 'Bar Council Action on Fischer', *The Times*, Saturday 30 January 1965.
20 Kathrada, secret prison notebooks, No. 4.
21 TRC Report, Vol. 3, Chapter 6.
22 *Ibid*.
23 Secret Memo 24652 of 29 January 1970 from PJB van Wyk to Commissioner of Prisons.
24 Hugh Lewin, *Bandiet: Out of Jail*, Johannesburg: Random House, 1992, p. 186.
25 Kathrada, secret prison notebooks, No. 4.
26 *Conditions for Prisoners' Studies*, Annexure A.

27 http://www.africacrime-mystery.co.za/books/fsac/chp14.htm

CHAPTER 12

1 Kathrada, secret prison notebooks, No. 4.
2 *Ibid*.
3 *Ibid*, No. 6.
4 *Ibid*, No. 4.
5 Aubrey du Toit quoted in Jurgen Schadeberg, *Voices from Robben Island*, Randburg: Ravan Press, 1994.
6 Kathrada, secret prison notebooks, No. 4.
7 *Ibid*. From Jennifer Davids, *Searching for Words*, Cape Town: David Philip, 1974.
8 A reference to Dr Albert Hertzog.
9 Antjie Krog went on to become a major literary force for change and self-examination for all South Africans. Her work with the Truth and Reconciliation Commission in the 1990s was documented in the award-winning *Country of my Skull*. She was also entrusted with translating Mandela's autobiography, *Long Walk to Freedom*, into Afrikaans.
10 Kathrada, secret prison notebooks, No. 4.

CHAPTER 13

1 Kathrada, secret prison notebooks, No. 6.
2 *Ibid*, No. 4.
3 *Ibid*.
4 http://www.sahistory.org.za/pages/people/tambo,o.htm: Luli Callinicos, *Oliver Tambo: His Life and Legacy 1917–1993*.
5 TRC Report, Appendix 1: 'ANC Structures and Personnel, 1960–1994'.
6 Kathrada, secret prison notebooks, No. 4.
7 *Ibid*.
8 This was a later incident, but is typical of the notes made in our prison files.
9 Letter to Fati and Kader, 14 January 1989, *Letters from Robben Island*, p. 269.

CHAPTER 14

1 Kathrada, secret prison notebooks, No. 4.
2 *Encyclopaedia Britannica*, Deluxe Edition, CD-Rom, 2004.
3 Elinor Sisulu, *In Our Lifetime*, p. 240.
4 Kathrada, secret prison notebooks, No. 2.
5 *Letters from Robben Island*, pp. 77–78.
6 Nelson Mandela, *Long Walk to Freedom*, p. 463.
7 All eight essays were published in Mac Maharaj (ed.), *Reflections in Prison*, Cape Town: Zebra Press and Robben Island Museum, 2001.
8 Eddie Daniels, *There and Back*, Cape Town: Mayibuye Books, p. 172.

CHAPTER 15

1 Kathrada, secret prison notebooks, No. 4. 'One more victory like that and I am ruined.'
2 AM Kathrada, 18 March 1992.
3 Mac Maharaj, Talent Consortium Interview, 1993.
4 'The Torture of Lindiwe Sisulu', *Sechaba*, Second Quarter, 1978, pp. 26–29.
5 Kathrada, secret prison notebooks, No. 4.

CHAPTER 16

1 Letter to Zuleikhabehn, 25 March 1989.
2 Harry Gwala was imprisoned on Robben Island twice – from 1964 to 1971 and again from 1977, when he was given a life sentence.
3 *Letters from Robben Island*, p. 18

CHAPTER 17

1 Mary Benson, *A Far Cry*, p. 263.
2 Kathrada, secret prison notebooks, No. 4.
3 Nelson Mandela, *Long Walk to Freedom*, p. 409.
4 Until 1981, Ma Sisulu was under successive banning orders for seventeen years.
5 J Jele, *Seventieth Birthday of Walter Sisulu*, United Nations Centre Against Apartheid: Department of Political and Security Council Affairs, May 1982.
6 Kathrada, secret prison notebooks, No. 4.
7 Z Mayat's second published work. The first was *Indian Delights*.
8 Kathrada, secret prison notebooks, No. 4.
9 *Ibid.*

CHAPTER 18

1 Letter to Ben Shek, 10 June 1989.
2 Kathrada, secret prison notebooks, No. 4.
3 'Plea for Clemency at Trial', *The Times*, Saturday 13 June 1964.
4 Nelson Mandela, *Long Walk to Freedom*, p. 514.
5 Kathrada, secret prison notebooks, No. 4.
6 *Ibid.*
7 Nelson Mandela, *Long Walk to Freedom*.
8 *Ibid*, pp. 523–524.

CHAPTER 19

1 Kathrada, secret prison notebooks, No. 1.
2 *Ibid*, No. 6. Henry van Dyke, quoted in *Reader's Digest*.
3 'Mandela's Future', *Observer*, 14 June 1964.

CHAPTER 20

1 Kathrada, secret prison notebooks, No. 4.
2 *Ibid.*

CHAPTER 21

1 Kathrada, secret prison notebooks, No. 4.
2 *Ibid*, No. 6.
3 Helen Joseph, *Side by Side*, p. 68.
4 Kathrada, secret prison notebooks, No. 4.
5 *Ibid.*
6 TRC Report, Vol. 3, Chapter 6. The activists described severe torture, involving the use of electric shocks, suffocation and severe beating leading to concussion and broken bones. Abdullay (*sic*) Jassat described

how the security police dangled him from a window: *They then pushed me into a louvre-fitting window and [I was] made to lie on it. I was held by both my feet by the police whilst they were simulating me trying to commit suicide. This was a known method of killing people in detention and they were well co-ordinated in their actions whilst the one was holding my foot and the other making as if to let me fall down from the window. I was then fearing that I was going to die.*

7　*Ibid*, 'Regional Profile Transvaal, 1960–1975'.

8　Elinor Sisulu, *In Our Lifetime*, p. 297.

9　Kathrada, secret prison notebooks, No. 4.

10　Kathrada, personal notebook kept during Rivonia Trial, p. 18.

11　Kathrada, secret prison notebooks, No. 4.

CHAPTER 22

1　Kathrada, secret prison notebooks, No. 3. Bertoldt Brecht, *The Caucasian Chalk Circle*.

2　Fran Buntman, *Politics and Secrets of Political Prisoner History*, paper presented at South African Historical Biennial Conference, University of the Western Cape, 11–14 July 1999.

3　Kathrada, secret prison notebooks, No. 4.

4　Media statement issued by Max Sisulu on the night of his father's death.

5　Steven Friedman, *Business Day*.

EPILOGUE

1　CD-Rom: *Nelson Mandela – The Symbol of a Nation*.

2　Nelson Mandela, *Long Walk to Freedom*, p. 354.

3　*Ibid*, p. 600.

4　*Ibid*, p. 601.

Select Bibliography

African National Congress. *Unity in Action – A photographic history of the African National Congress South Africa 1912–1982*. Kent: AG Bishop & Sons Ltd, 1982

Alexander, Neville. *Robben Island Dossier 1964–1974*. Cape Town: UCT Press, 1994

Benson, Mary. *A Far Cry: The Making of a South African*. London: Viking, 1989

Bernstein, Hilda. *South Africa: The Terrorism of Torture: An analysis of political trials and the use of torture in South Africa today*. London: An International Defence and Aid Fund pamphlet, Christian Action Publications Ltd, 1972
———. *The World that was Ours: The Story of the Rivonia Trial*. London: SA Writers, 1989

Bernstein, Rusty. *Memory Against Forgetting*. London: Viking, 1999

Bhana, S, and B Pachai (eds.). *A documentary history of Indian South Africans*. Cape Town and Stanford: David Philip and Hoover Institution Press, 1984

Bunting, Brian. *Moses Kotane*. London: Inkululeko Publications, 1975
——— (ed.). *South African Communists Speak 1915–1980*. London: Inkululeko Publications, 1981

Buntman, Fran L. *The Politics of Conviction: Political Prisoner Resistance on Robben Island, 1962–1991*. Unpublished PhD thesis

Clingman, Stephen. *Bram Fischer, Afrikaner Revolutionary*. Cape Town: David Philip Publishers and Mayibuye Books, 1998

Daniels, Eddie. *There and Back*. Bellville: Mayibuye Books, 1998

De Beer, Leon. *A Political Analysis of the ANC as an Extra-Parliamentary Movement*. MA thesis, University of the Orange Free State

De Villiers, H. *Operation Mayibuye: A Review of the Rivonia Trial*. Johannesburg: Afrikaanse Pers-Boekhandel, 1964

De Villiers, Simon A. *Robben Island: Out of Reach, Out of Mind: A History of Robben Island*. Cape Town: Struik, 1971

Deacon, Harriet, Nigel Penn, André Odendaal and Patricia Davidson. *The Robben Island Exhibition EsiQithini*. Bellville: Mayibuye Books, 1996

Desai, Barney. *The Killing of the Imam*. London and New York: Quartet Books, 1978

Dingake, Michael. *My fight against apartheid*. London: Kliptown Books, 1987

Dlamini, Moses. *Robben Island Hell-hole*. Nottingham: Spokesman, 1984

Dutta, K, and A Robinson. *Rabindranath Tagore: The Myriad-minded Man.*
London: Bloomsbury, 1995

First, Ruth. *117 Days.* London: Bloomsbury, 1965

Forman, Lionel, and ES Sachs. *The Treason Cage.* London: John Calder, 1957

Forman, Sadie, and André Odendaal (eds.). *Lionel Forman: A Trumpet from the Housetops.* London: Zed Books, 1992

Gordimer, Nadine. *The House Gun.* London: Bloomsbury, 1999

Holland, Heidi. *The Struggle: A History of the ANC.* London: Grafton Books, 1989

Houser, George, and Herb Shore. *I will go singing: Walter Sisulu speaks of his life and the struggle for freedom in South Africa.* Cape Town: Robben Island Museum, 2000

Joffe, Joel. *The Rivonia Story.* Cape Town: Mayibuye Books, 1995

Joseph, Helen. *If this Be Treason.* London: Andre Deutsch, 1963

————. *Side by Side.* London: Zed books, 1986

Joshi, PS. *The Tyranny of Colour.* Durban: EP & Commercial Printing Co., 1942

Kantor, James. *A Healthy Grave.* London: Hamish Hamilton Ltd, 1967

Karis, Thomas, and GM Carter (eds.). *From Protest to Challenge,* Volumes 1-5. Stanford: Hoover Institution Press, 1977-1997

Kathrada, Ahmed. *Letters from Robben Island: A selection of Ahmed Kathrada's prison correspondence 1964–1989* (ed. Robert D Vassen). Rivonia: Zebra Press, 1999

Lewin, Hugh. *Bandiet.* London: Heinemann, 1974

Lodge, Tom. *Black Politics in South Africa since 1945.* Cape Town: Ravan Press, 1983

Ludi, Gerard, and B Grobbelaar. *The Amazing Mr Fischer.* Johannesburg: Nasionale Boekhandel, 1966

Luthuli, Albert. *Let my People Go.* London: Collins, 1962

Maharaj, Mac (ed.). *Reflections in Prison.* Cape Town: Zebra Press and Robben Island Museum, 2001

Mandela, Nelson Rolihlahla. *Long Walk to Freedom.* Abacus: London, 1994

Mandela, Winnie. *Part of my Soul.* London: Penguin, 1985

Mayibuye Centre, University of the Western Cape, Ahmed Kathrada and Various Collections; photographic collection (including work of Eli Weinberg)

Meer, Fatima. *Higher than Hope.* London: Hamish Hamilton, 1990

Meer, Fatima, and Enuga Reddy (eds.). *Passive Resistance 1946.* Durban: Madiba Publishers & Institute for Black Research, 1996

Meer, Ismail. *A Fortunate Man.* Cape Town: Zebra Press, 2002

Meli, Francis. *South Africa belongs to us: a history of the ANC.* Zimbabwe: Zimbabwe Publishing House, 1988

Miller, J (ed.). *On Suicide.* San Francisco: Chronicle Books, 1992

Naidoo, Indres. *Island in Chains.* London: Penguin, 1982

Oakes, D (ed.). *Reader's Digest Illustrated History of South Africa: The Real Story.* Cape Town: The Reader's Digest Association of South Africa (Pty) Ltd, 1995

Roux, Eddie. *Time Longer than Rope.* Madison: University of Wisconsin Press, 1964

Sampson, Anthony. *Mandela: The Authorised Biography.* London: Harper Collins Publishers, 1999

————. *The Treason Cage.* London: Heinemann, 1958

Schadeberg, J. *Voices from Robben Island.* Johannesburg: Ravan Press, 1994

Scott, Michael. *A Time to Speak.* New York: Doubleday & Company, 1958

Sisulu, Elinor. *Walter and Albertina Sisulu: In our lifetime.* Cape Town: David Philip Publishers, 2002

Sisulu, Walter. *I will go singing.* Cape Town: Robben Island Museum, 2001

South African Institute of Race Relations, *Annual Survey.* SAIRR: Braamfontein

Strydom, Lauritz. *Rivonia Unmasked.* Johannesburg: Voortrekker Pers, 1965

Truth and Reconciliation Commission. *Truth and Reconciliation Commission of South Africa Report, Volumes 1–5.* Cape Town: TRC, 1998

Vadi, Ismail. *The Congress of the People and the Freedom Charter Campaign.* New Delhi: Sterling Publishers Limited, 1995

Van Zyl Slabbert, Frederik. *The Last White Parliament.* London: Sidgwick & Jackson, 1985

Waldmeir, Patty. *Anatomy of a miracle: The end of Apartheid and the birth of the New South Africa.* London: Viking Press, 1997

DOCUMENTS

Full court records of the Case of the State vs Faried Adams and others (Member evidence – Treason Trial of 1956–61)

Full court records of the Case of the State vs Nelson Mandela and others (Member evidence – Rivonia Trial)

International Defence and Aid Fund Papers

Kathrada, AM. Books of Quotations compiled in prison

————. Unisa assignments and other academic work completed during incarceration

————. Unpublished personal correspondence and prison writings

Prison Authorities Memo: from Brigadier Munro to Lt Col Strydom, 82/08/23 (Prison memo between censors and 'Die Majoor', 8 – 10/01/73); many other memoranda between prisons and other authorities

South African Department of Justice: Files on Ahmed Kathrada

South African Prisons Service: Prison Files on Ahmed Kathrada

United Nations Centre Against Apartheid: Notes and documents

William Curren Library, University of the Witwatersrand: Record of the 1956-1961 Treason Trial; other documentation including the 1956 NAM Summit, Indian Congress and other; photographic collection

SPEECHES
Kathrada, Ahmed. Various speeches
Mandela, Nelson. Various speeches
Verwoerd, HF. Various speeches
Vorster, BJ. Various speeches

NEWSPAPERS
New Age, 'Freedom Awards to People's Leaders'. Volume 1, No. 33, 9 June 1955
Posthumous memoirs of AC Meer in *The Leader*
Supplement published by the Independent Group on the occasion of Nelson
    Mandela's 80th birthday, written by Ahmed Kathrada
Guardian
New Age
Observer
The Passive Resister, 1946 and 1947
Rand Daily Mail
Star
Sunday Times
The Times of London
The Treason Trial Bulletin
Vaderland

FILMS
Interviews with AMK – Robben Island Heritage Department
Talent Consortium interviews, produced by Miriam Patsanza and directed by
    John Matshikiza, 1993

CD-ROM
Britannica 2001 Standard Edition CD-ROM. Copyright © 1994–2000
    Britannica.com Inc.
Mandela, Nelson Rolihlahla; CD-ROM *Nelson Mandela – The Symbol of
a Nation*. Q-Data Consulting (Pty) Ltd; Mayibuye Centre and Robben
Island Museum, 1997

WEBSITES
http://www.anc.org.za
http://www.gov.za
http://www.sahistory.org.za
http://www.truth.org.za

Index